REGIONS OF SORROW

MERIDIAN

Crossing Aesthetics

Werner Hamacher

Editor

Stanford
University
Press

———

Stanford
California
2003

REGIONS OF SORROW

Anxiety and Messianism in
Hannah Arendt and W. H. Auden

Susannah Young-ah Gottlieb

Published with assistance from the Northwestern University
Research Grants Committee.

Stanford University Press
Stanford, California

Printed in the United States of America
on acid-free, archival-quality paper.

Library of Congress Cataloging-in-Publication Data

Gottlieb, Susannah Young-ah.
   Regions of sorrow : anxiety and messianism in Hannah
Arendt and W. H. Auden / Susannah Young-ah Gottlieb.
      p.   cm.—(Meridian)
   Includes bibliographical references and index.
   ISBN 0-8047-4510-2 (cloth : alk. paper)—ISBN
   0-8047-4511-0 (pbk. : alk. paper)
      1. Arendt, Hannah.   2. Anxiety—History—20th century.
3. Messianism—History—20th century.   4. Totalitarianism
—History—20th century   5. Auden, W. H. (Wystan
Hugh), 1907–1973.   6. Anxiety in literature.   7. Messianism
in literature.   8. Totalitarianism and literature.   I. Title.
II. Meridian (Stanford, Calif.)
B945.A694 G68 2003
179'.9—dc21   2002005861

Original Printing 2003

Last figure below indicates year of this printing:
12   11   10   09   08   07   06   05   04   03

Typeset by Alan Noyes in 10.9 / 13 Adobe Garamond

For my parents,
for Peter,
and for Inbo

Contents

Acknowledgments

Many people and institutions have supported this project, and it is my pleasure to acknowledge them. The Hannah-Arendt-Forschungszentrum at the Universität Oldenburg, under the directorship of Stefan Ahrens, helped me secure important documents for my research; Edward Mendelson, Auden's literary executor, generously responded to a number of queries; the Mrs. Giles Whiting Foundation and the University of Chicago provided me with a fellowship during the year in which I completed this book; and the Northwestern University Research Grants Committee provided additional support. I would also like to thank Peter Jaros for his excellent work preparing the index.

An earlier version of Chapter 4 appeared in Comparative Literature 53, 2 (spring 2001): 131–50. This chapter was first presented as a talk at Northwestern University's Department of English and again at the University of Chicago's Committee on Social Thought. I also had the opportunity to present an earlier version of Chapter 3 at a colloquium on Hannah Arendt sponsored by the Department of Rhetoric at the University of California, Berkeley. I am grateful to these audiences, and particularly to Frederick M. Dolan, for their helpful questions and remarks.

Timothy Bahti, Werner Hamacher, Don Levine, Lawrence Lipking, and Helen Tartar carefully read and reviewed the manuscript at various stages. Without their astute critical comments, expert counsel, and generous support, I would never have been able to complete this book.

Wendy Doniger, W. R. Johnson, and Herman Sinaiko served as models of integrity, acuity, wit, and elegance during the writing of an earlier draft of this project. They follow four earlier teachers who first helped me explore the literary and philosophical works that would remain so important throughout my life: Peter Gibbon, Karsten Harries, Arthur Naething, and Maurice Natanson.

Saad Ahmed, Richard O. Block, Pheng Cheah, Robert Ellis, Daniel Heller-Roazen, Bruce M. King, Mary Kinzie, Maureen McLane, Anke Pinkert, Géza von Molnár, Myung-Soon Choe Tam, and Sarah Young have helped me think about, improve, and survive this book—in diverse, if sometimes oblique, ways: with steadfast support, iconoclastic hilarity, critical intelligence, and deep affection. As Hannah Arendt once put it, "Nothing in the world counts like friends."

Except, of course, for family. It is my privilege to acknowledge those people whose abiding love, richness of feeling, and unflagging encouragement have shaped my world in immeasurable ways: my godparents, Bruce and Joan Grynbaum, my grandfather, Sam Friedman, my brothers, Peter and Richard Gottlieb, their wives, Jeri Riggs and Leslie Gottlieb, and their children, Degen, Michael, Robert, and Samantha Gottlieb.

Now I turn to those acknowledgments that are most personal and therefore hardest to articulate. More than any other people I know, my parents, Bernice and Ferdinand Gottlieb, and my husband, Peter Fenves, possess the rare gift of knowing how to live. They are deeply passionate but always clear-sighted in their convictions and endlessly generous in their love. I am filled with admiration at the manifold of experiences they have endured, embraced, railed against, and sometimes loved, and at the manner in which they have remained open to life's richness—with gratitude, strength, delicacy, sometimes with outrage, and often with contagious exuberance and very great joy. Finally, my son, Inbo Gottlieb Fenves, has given me an entirely new sense of what it means to appreciate the gift of life. Whatever part of this project does not already belong to these four people, I dedicate to them with all my heart.

REGIONS OF SORROW

Introduction

"The Common Life"

The twentieth century has put to test the central tenets of the European Enlightenment that culminated in the Kantian self-critique of reason: human beings could come to understand themselves, carry out the duties they assign themselves, and arrive at a rational ordering of the world in the course of historical development. By bringing together the general ideas of responsibility and history, the Enlightenment gave strength to its particular projects of illuminating what was hitherto unknown. Humanity could be seen as on the march toward this universal condition of self-fulfillment; history, in turn, could be understood as the product of human ingenuity as a whole. Becoming responsible for oneself and taking charge of the world in which one lives—overcoming, in Kant's words, the innate tendency toward "immaturity"[1]—doubtless takes a great deal of time and may even be an "endless task," but each step toward greater responsibility is a step closer to the goal of history: the establishment of the universal Rights of Man and the creation of a world in which each person's talents can develop unhindered. The catastrophic events of the twentieth century, however, made these convictions untenable, for they showed how thoroughly the connection between responsibility and history could be severed. Word and deed could proceed in entirely different directions: as the Rights of Man were being more widely proclaimed, they were being more egregiously violated. W. H. Auden and Hannah Arendt belong to the generation of European and American intellectuals who experienced these catastrophic events, and they both undertook the task of developing novel—and one might say, responsible—responses to the enormity of the novel phenomena they witnessed: "homelessness on an unprecedented scale, rootlessness to an unprecedented depth . . . [and] forces that look like sheer insanity."[2]

Both Auden and Arendt experienced these forces firsthand. For eighteen years Hannah Arendt lived as a "stateless person." As Elisabeth Young-Bruehl recounts in her fine biography, this tumultuous period began when Arendt was arrested in Berlin for work she was doing with Kurt Blumenfeld's Zionist organization. Although jailed for only eight days, she immediately recognized that she had to leave Germany. She fled without travel documents through Karlsbad, Prague, and Geneva and eventually made her way to Paris, where she worked first with "Agriculture et Artisanat," an organization designed to prepare young Jewish émigrés for life in Palestine, and later with Youth Aliyah, where she became the secretary general of the Paris office and traveled briefly in that capacity to Palestine. By 1939, the French government began interning refugees, and Arendt's soon-to-be husband, Heinrich Blücher, spent three months from September to December at a camp in Villemalard. Only a few months after his release, both Arendt and Blücher were called as "enemy aliens" to report for transport to internment camps. Arendt was interned at Gurs but escaped after a few weeks to Montaubon, where by a stroke of luck she met her husband, whose camp had been evacuated when German troops reached Paris. Narrowly escaping the French police, Arendt and Blücher fled France via Spain and Portugal, landing in New York in 1941, where she resided for ten years before receiving American citizenship. In 1949, Arendt returned to Europe for six months as executive director of the Commission on European Jewish Cultural Reconstruction, during which time she saw the devastation of the war and guided "an operation that eventually recovered 1.5 million volumes of Hebraica and Judaica, thousands of ceremonial and artistic objects, and over a thousand scrolls of law."[3] Despite the admirable efforts of Young-Bruehl to document Arendt's life, little is known of her experience of statelessness. Many of her private letters are lost, most significantly, perhaps, those she sent to Blücher during his internment at Villemalard. And Arendt is in any case reluctant to introduce her own experiences into her many broader discussions of the conditions and times through which she lived. Although she writes extensively throughout her career about the insanity of the "mad world" and "mad changes"[4] she survived, Arendt writes very little, either in her published works or in her private letters, about her own experiences during her eighteen years as a "displaced person." An index of this reticence is one of the few public remarks she makes about her internment: "At the camp of Gurs, for instance, where I had the opportunity of spending some time, I heard only once about suicide."[5] The bitter sarcasm of the central clause—"where I had the opportunity of spending some time"—clearly registers what remains unspoken: an unwillingness or inability to articulate her own experiences of mad times.

Auden's experiences of the "forces that look like sheer insanity" are less closely associated with his public image than Arendt's—and for good reason: he was never imprisoned or interned. Nevertheless, he was intimately familiar with the events of what he famously called the "low dishonest decade" of the 1930s.[6] Having traveled to Spain in 1937, he worked as an ambulance driver and propaganda broadcaster on the Republican side. After realizing that he could successfully make a "fighting demagogic speech and have the audience roaring," he said that he "felt just covered with dirt afterwards" and promised himself never to speak again at a political gathering.[7] In 1938 he traveled to China with Christopher Isherwood, where they saw, photographed, and recounted in verse and prose certain events of the Sino-Japanese War. One of the last lines of their *Journey to a War* summarizes its direction: "And mingling with the distant mutter of guerrilla fighting, / The voice of Man: 'O teach me to outgrow my madness.'"[8] Significantly less familiar than these episodes to readers of Auden's poetry and prose is his service with the American military as a Bombing Research Analyst in the Morale Division of the U.S. Strategic Bombing Survey. His job was to interview German civilians about the effects of Allied bombing on their morale. About this morbid job Auden said little and wrote nothing. Nicolas Nabokov, who also served with this Division, preserves a few of his comments:

> "I know that they had asked for it," [Auden] would say, "but still, this kind of total destruction is beyond reasoning. . . . It seems like madness! . . . It is absolutely ghastly. . . . [I]s it justified to reply to *their* mass-murder by *our* mass-murder? It seems terrifying to me . . . And I cannot help ask myself, 'Was there no other way?'"[9]

In the course of his "inspection tours" of bombed-out cities Auden also came into contact with survivors of Nazi extermination camps: "'None of us could have imagined that [the Germans] could go that far. . . . They applied to it the same pedantic organizational skills a piano-tuner does when he tunes a virtuoso's concert piano grand,' and Auden would stare in front of him shaking his head."[10] Auden had an informal agreement with his friend James Stern, another member of the Strategic Bombing Survey, that the two of them would write a book about their experiences in Germany, but on his return to the States Auden simply declined to do so.[11] That "none of us could have imagined" what took place also meant, for Auden at least, that the hitherto unimaginable should not be made into the subject matter of an aesthetic image.

Auden's silence about the catastrophes he "surveyed" is, in sum, the sign of another and intimately related catastrophe: that language—which is the source of all human talents and capabilities, especially those of the poet— can nevertheless be rendered incapable of doing what it is supposed to do, namely, communicate. Or if it does communicate, it soon becomes mendacious, regardless of what anyone tries to say. Arendt's silence may be even more acute than Auden's. And one suspects that even if we were in possession of her lost letters, Arendt's silence would not be fundamentally broken. The brutality of the events makes those who experience them into "brutes": bereft of language at the very moment it may be needed most. As the etymological relation between *brutality* and *brute* already suggests, the conviction that brutality is not simply, or even primarily, a physical phenomenon but, above all, a linguistic event is ancient: Thucydides' bitter account of the revolution in Corcyra and Sallust's savagely insightful exposition of the corruption to which Roman moral language had succumbed communicate this conviction with incomparable vividness.[12] Auden and Arendt revive, and revise the terms of, Thucydides' and Sallust's ancient conviction. And so, too, in other ways, do the more astute members of their generation: Orwell, Camus, and Benjamin—to name only three very different writers from different traditions—all seek to come to terms with the loss of language from which brutality arises and into which it issues. Wherever language and action no longer correspond with each other; wherever the relationship between language and action is misunderstood, misrepresented, or obscured, there emerge the conditions for brutality. Propaganda, ideology, mass indoctrination, the technique of the "big lie"—everything that Walter Benjamin summarized under the term "objective mendacity"[13]—falsify reality to such an extent that descriptions of the world cannot be distinguished from prescriptions for wide-scale murder. As Arendt notes with her usual acumen, "a 'dying class' consisted of people condemned to death; races that are 'unfit to live' were to be exterminated."[14]

Auden and Arendt seek to develop articulate responses to the cata-strophic events of the twentieth century that are at every moment respon-sive to the incapacity of language in the presence of outrageous brutality. Whereas the thinkers of the eighteenth-century Enlightenment tended to conceive of responsibility in terms of duties toward oneself and others, Auden and Arendt think of it, as the etymology suggests, in terms of lan-guage: they both understand that once language is threatened, no appeal to "duties" is of any service, and any such appeal may be nothing other than a mendacious mode of irresponsibility. Auden expresses the convic-tion under which both of them conceive of their obligation as writers in a particularly succinct manner: "The duties of a writer as a writer and a cit-izen are not the same. The only duty a writer has as a citizen is to defend language. And this is a *political* duty. Because, if language is corrupted, thought is corrupted."[15] If thought is corrupted—the suggestion runs—not only is there no possibility of "enlightenment," but a finely tuned bru-tality can soon take its place.

I. Making Distinctions, Becoming Friends

The duty to defend language against those forces that would corrupt it enters into the very texture of both Arendt's and Auden's work. One of the indispensable dimensions of their defense of language consists in making distinctions among ethical and juridical terms that are often used inter-changeably. As an inconspicuous example of this tendency, Auden inter-rupts a wide-ranging reflection on the character of Falstaff he publishes in the journal *Encounter* to distinguish between forgiveness and pardon.[16] Because drama cannot display this distinction with sufficient clarity, for-giveness, according to Auden, cannot be unambiguously made into a dramatic act. For this reason, the parable of forgiveness from which Shakespeare's *Measure for Measure* can be seen to develop, as Auden pro-ceeds to explain, "does not quite work."[17] However one understands his evaluation of the play and its parable—which he compares unfavorably with the Hasidic parable of "the ten principles of service"[18]—his insis-tence that forgiveness be distinguished from pardon implicitly responds to Hannah Arendt's *Human Condition*, which he had elaborately praised in *Encounter* five months before.[19] Apparently, Auden mentioned to Arendt that his Falstaff essay touches on issues with which she, too, is con-cerned.[20] After obtaining a copy of this essay, Arendt writes a tightly argued, conceptually dense letter to Auden, in which she concedes that she had failed to distinguish between forgiveness and judicial pardon.[21] This concession generates a whole series of further distinctions—all of which serve to defend language against the threat of corruption that, as Auden subtly suggests in his essay, appears in the almost diabolical figure of Angelo, who is both pardoned and forgiven at the end of *Measure for Measure*.

Arendt's letter to Auden brings into view the deeply serious and at the same time lightly comic relationship between these two equally imposing figures of twentieth-century literature and thought. Auden's interlude on *Measure for Measure* can be distilled into a single insight: even Shakespeare could not produce a drama of forgiveness equal to the absolute claims of Christian charity. Arendt, while recognizing her failure to distinguish forgiveness from judicial pardon in *The Human Condition*, nevertheless insists on what she modestly calls her "prejudice": "Of course I am prejudiced, namely against charity. But let me make a stand for my prejudices. . . . Charity indeed forgives *ueberhaupt*, it forgives betrayal in the person who betrayed—on the ground, to be sure, of human sinfulness and its solidarity with the sinner. I would admit that there is a great temptation to forgive in the spirit of Who am I to judge?, but I'd rather resist it."[22] Auden's Falstaff essay and, in even more expansive form, *The Dyer's Hand* as a whole, is committed to the kind of charity against which Arendt takes her stand:

> Temporal Justice demands the use of force to quell the unjust; it demands prudence, a practical reckoning with time and place; and it demands publicity for its laws and its penalties. But Charity forbids all three—we are not to resist evil, if a man demand our coat we are to give him our cloak also, we are to take no thought for the morrow and, while secretly fasting and giving alms, we are to appear in public as persons who do neither.[23]

To which Arendt replies in her letter: "I do not know what is more difficult: to demand a coat or to give the cloak also, but I am quite sure that it is more difficult to ask than to give forgiveness."[24]

The fundamentally different attitudes that Arendt and Auden held with respect to Christian charity did not hinder their intellectual exchange; on the contrary, this disagreement gives meaning and direction to their friendship. Arendt recognizes Auden's exceptional critical intelligence. Not only does she concede in her letter that forgiveness must be sharply distinguished from judicial pardon; she also acknowledges two other inadequacies in her account of forgiveness: "I was wrong when I said that we forgive what was done for the sake of who did it" and "You are entirely right (and I was entirely wrong) in that punishment is a necessary alternative only to judicial pardon." Auden, for his part, calls Arendt "one of the most intelligent persons now living,"[25] and much of *The Dyer's Hand* closely parallels the direction of thought Arendt takes in her *Human Condition*—so much so that an irate reader once wrote an indignant letter to Auden, accusing him of plagiarism. Auden obviously forwarded this ludicrous letter to Arendt, who lovingly preserved it among her papers.[26] Its author had failed to note that much of the book was written before the publication of Arendt's volume and that, in any case, Auden acknowledges the similarity between their lines of thought. The epigraph to the essay devoted to Shakespeare's *Merchant of Venice*, for example, derives from Arendt's discussion of plurality in *The Human Condition* and is in particular concerned with what she calls "the faculty of forgiving."[27]

Arendt's letter to Auden, which begins in a mood of serious intellectual debate, ends as an RSVP: "Thanks ever so much for birthday invitation. I accept with pleasure. I'll be a bit late (have a dinner engagement before) but long before 'carriage time.'" Of the remaining handful of extent letters, none is as long, detailed, or philosophically substantial as this one; but all of them share the bantering tone with which the initial letter ends: "Carriage time" refers to Auden's habit, from 1955 onward, of closing his annual birthday party invitations with "carriages at one A.M."[28] Although they had crossed paths earlier, Auden and Arendt became acquainted only in late 1958, the same year that *The Human Condition* was first published. Auden was so taken by the book that he telephoned Arendt to thank her for having written it and then wrote a review for *Encounter*, which was published in June of 1959.[29] His review was so laudatory that the editors of the University of Chicago Press decided to quote a passage from it for promotional purposes, and this passage continues to be reprinted on the back of every volume today: "Every now and then, I come across a book which gives me the impression of having been especially written for me. . . . *The Human Condition* belongs to this small and select class."[30] Although Arendt was rather embarrassed by the effusive tone of Auden's review, they nevertheless developed a close friendship that lasted until Auden's death in 1973.[31] Both living in New York City, the two saw each other fairly regularly, although it was Auden who was more frequently hosted by Arendt and her husband at their home on Riverside Drive. Auden would often arrive at Arendt's apartment in the afternoon, and their conversations would last so long that he would be invited to stay for dinner.[32] Arendt, who worried over Auden and his "slum apartment,"[33] describes her friend's habits with a mixture of deep affection and unmistakable dismay. She was particularly exasperated by the fact that Auden had only one suit, which meant that he could never get it cleaned.[34] Despite her dismay, Arendt tried to look after Auden whenever she could, taking him to a department store and insisting that he buy a second suit.[35] After Blücher died in 1970, Arendt gave Auden her late husband's sports jacket: "'I'm wearing a dead man's coat,' Auden would say, chuckling, very pleased that a good thing was not being wasted."[36] And both might have been pleased that they had finally reached a point of compromise with respect to Christian charity: he did not demand the coat, and she did not give him a cloak also.

Arendt, more importantly, did not give herself to him. Auden asked her to marry him in 1970, and she refused. Many years earlier, in 1935, Auden had married Erika Mann to secure her a British passport when the Nazi authorities threatened to take away her German citizenship. Their relationship was never consummated, of course: it was a purely legal arrangement intended to provide safe passage to Mann out of Germany. Nevertheless, they remained married until Mann's death in 1969.[37] Soon after the death of Heinrich Blücher in 1970, Stephen Spender, Auden's friend for many years, apparently began sending out feelers on his behalf, asking Mary McCarthy, "wouldn't Wystan make a good husband for Hannah?" To which she replied, "Are you mad?"[38] Arendt's own reaction to Auden's proposal was no less extreme:

> Auden came—looking so much like a clochard that the doorman came with him, fearful that he might be God knows what. The evening was strange to say the least. (The following just for you [McCarthy], please remember): Said he came back to New York only because of me, that I was of great importance for him, that he loved me very much, etc. I tried to quiet him down and succeeded quite well. In my opinion: Oxford where he hoped to go for good has turned him down (I suppose) and he is desperate to find some other bearable place. I see the necessity but I know that I can't do it, in other words, have to turn him down. I have a hunch that this happened to him once too often, namely being turned down, and I am almost besides myself when I think of the whole matter. But I can't change that; it would simply be suicide—worse than suicide as a matter of fact.[39]

Auden's desperate appearance and Arendt's definitive refusal did not, however, end their friendship. They continued to see each other until Auden found a place for himself in Oxford after all and left New York for good two years later. Their respect for each other expressed itself in numerous publications: in addition to his early review of *The Human Condition*, Auden dedicated *Forewords and Afterwords* to her; Arendt dedicated her essay "Thinking and Moral Considerations" to Auden. He repeatedly quotes from her writings in *The Dyer's Hand* and *A Certain World*; she prefaces her great essay on Bertolt Brecht with some lines from his poem cycle "Thanksgiving for a Habitat," delivers a moving eulogy after his death, and often quotes his poetry in her posthumously published *Life of the Mind*.[40] In addition to these public tributes, they helped and encouraged each other in various, more private, ways, as well. Arendt recommended German translators and had one of her former students, a Korean monk, issue Auden an invitation to his monastery in Minnesota: "It's a good place to be from every viewpoint," she writes him in the summer of 1971, "except weather in the winter."[41] Auden, for his part, tries to persuade Arendt to visit him in Oxford: "I should so love to see you as a visiting Fellow of All Souls," he writes in the summer of 1973, shortly before his death, "even though that would mean enduring A. L. Rowse's lunatic conversations."[42]

Arendt never made it to Oxford. The last time they saw each other, she sensed the seriousness of his frailty: "I also saw Auden before he left for England. For the first time he looks not only unhappy and neglected but sick. I hope it was only exhaustion from packing and leaving, but I doubt it."[43] Arendt's eulogy begins and ends with the immense misery in which he lived his last years. Although she continually refers to his poetry and emphasizes the greatness of his poetic talent, she also recounts intimate details of Auden's life: that he was forced to use the toilet in the neighborhood liquor store when the water in his apartment stopped functioning, for example, or when his stained and overused suit suddenly came apart at the seams—"in brief, whenever disaster hit before your very eyes."[44] Nevertheless, Arendt opens her eulogy with a statement that would lead her auditors to expect nothing of this: "I met Auden late in life at an age when the easy knowledgeable intimacy of friendships concluded in one's youth can no longer be attained, because not enough life is left, or expected to be left, to share with each other. Thus we were very good friends but not intimate friends."[45] With this hairsplitting distinction, Arendt does not so much describe their friendship as preserve one of its most remarkable features: their shared avidity for making distinctions. *The Human Condition* has no more pressing goal than the articulation of the distinctions within the *vita activa*, labor, work, and action; elsewhere, Arendt distinguishes "personality" from "individuality";[46] her early reflections on the course of post-emancipation European Jewry contrasts the Pariah with the Parvenu; and even earlier, her dissertation, following Augustine, seeks out the internal divisions within the phenomenon of love. Throughout his career as poet and critic, Auden, who also had a deep familiarity with Augustine's writings, concentrated on the infinitely delicate, sometimes zany, delineation of love in all its "infinite varieties."[47] And in *The Dyer's Hand*, the zeal for distinctions generates a catalogue of wonderful, inventive, and often humorous oppositions: the Virgin and the Dynamo; Alices and Mabels; Prosperos and Ariels; what is boring and what a bore; geniuses and apostles; the I and the self. One of Auden's major poems reflects the zeal he shares with Arendt in its very title, *The Sea and the Mirror*—where the sea is the place in which distinctions disappear, the mirror the site of their transfiguration.

Comparing Auden's poetry with Brecht's, Arendt includes in her eulogy an even more unexpected distinction than the one between very good and intimate friends: "Auden, so much wiser—though by no means smarter—than Brecht, was aware early on that, 'poetry makes nothing happen.'"[48] A eulogy, unlike a critical essay, is not generally a place for careful distinctions among terms of approbation. Arendt's seemingly pedantic insistence on distinguishing wisdom from intelligence—and compared to Brecht, of all people!—might seem jarring, even inappropriate, if not understood from the perspective of the shared avidity for making distinctions that is a hallmark of their friendship from the very beginning. Auden interrupts his reflections on Falstaff to delineate some distinctions that were absent from *The Human Condition*. And Arendt responds in kind—not only conceding that forgiveness and pardon are indeed different and thereafter detailing a set of corresponding distinctions but also concluding her reflections with a final distinction that parodies her own apparent pedantry: "I better stop. I hope you don't think I am being quarrelsome and, worse, tiresome. But if you do, you will, please, be kind, and forget it."[49] The distinction between *quarrelsome* and *tiresome*, each of which names a state of mind in which one makes too many distinctions, could hardly be more comic. Having written only a few lines earlier, "it is more difficult to ask than to give forgiveness," Arendt—in what must surely be a self-conscious parody of her own letter—does not ask Auden to forgive her for being quarrelsome or tiresome, if either is the case; rather, she bids him "forget it": forget not the previous distinctions, which retain their validity and significance, but whatever in her remarks would undermine their developing friendship. Arendt's comic send-off contains in miniature her understanding of friendship and reverberates with one of Auden's characteristic traits: regardless of her strenuous effort to make decisive political and ethical distinctions among often-conflated terms, Arendt is willing to "forget it" if, under certain circumstances, this effort makes friendship impossible.[50] And Auden, as Arendt writes, is wise enough to understand that, for all his life-long passion and need to create poetry, "poetry makes nothing happen." One of Auden's late poems called "The Common Life" closes with a particularly understated, even prosaic expression of this shared sensibility:

> and always, though truth and love
> can never really differ, when they seem to,
> the subaltern should be truth.[51]

II. Commensurability

The sensibility Auden and Arendt share also finds expression in one of the major addresses Arendt wrote and delivered during the time in which they were first becoming friends, "On Humanity in Dark Times: Thoughts about Lessing."[52] The address to the "free city of Hamburg" is organized around what Arendt calls Lessing's "highly unorthodox opinions about truth": "He refused to accept any truths whatever, even those presumably handed down by Providence, and he never felt compelled by truth, be it imposed by others' or by his own reasoning processes."[53] Arendt's prooftext for her sympathetic exposition of Lessing's celebration of close—but not intimate—friendship is his most famous play, *Nathan the Wise*: "In the end, after all, Nathan's wisdom consists solely in his readiness to sacrifice truth to friendship."[54] As Arendt recognizes, this play enjoys an iconic status: developed out of Lessing's great friendship with Moses Mendelssohn, it represents an ideal image of Christian-Jewish— and Islamic—relations. The imperative under which this image operates is not the Kantian categorical imperative, which, like Christian charity, recognizes no distinctions among persons, but rather the unorthodox, even paradoxical demand that Nathan makes on some of the individuals he meets: "We must, must be friends."[55]

Arendt's address on Lessing amplifies and clarifies her initial letter to Auden and can even be seen to determine its horizon. She has a "prejudice" against Christian charity because it is always unfriendly: friendship is discriminating and makes distinctions, whereas charity cannot do either. But Auden, who has made clear his prejudice in favor of charity, is nevertheless—or for this very reason—a friend: a friend not because he shares her opinions but because, like Arendt, he recognizes that the free and open exchange of opinions is the *conditio sine qua non* of friendship. Whether conscious or not, Arendt and Auden create a friendship in the middle years of the twentieth century that resonates with the friendship that developed between Lessing and Mendelssohn in the middle years of the eighteenth—and is almost as unlikely: just as Lessing and Mendelssohn came from, and for the most part remained within, very different worlds, so, too, do Arendt and Auden. None of this suggests that there is a one-to-one correspondence between these four figures: the Jewish Arendt for Mendelssohn, and the Protestant Auden for Lessing; or, in reverse, Arendt as a modern Lessing, who champions friendship over doctrine, and Auden as a renewed Mendelssohn, who seeks to find a convincing manner in which a religious doctrine can meet the needs and demands of his contemporaries. Rather, in both cases, a friendship developed under improbable circumstances because each of the friends recognized and appreciated the other's "openness to the world,"[56] regardless of any doctrinal allegiances. If ever there arises a conflict between truth and friendship, truth must be, as Auden writes, "the subaltern."

This shared sensibility makes the relation between Auden and Arendt, beyond any personal interaction, into an auspicious place to reconsider the "ancient quarrel" between philosophy and poetry. The famous phrase "ancient quarrel" derives from the tenth book of Plato's *Republic*.[57] After having concluded their discussion of the just city, Socrates and Glaucon return to the topic of an earlier conversation concerning the various forms and functions of poetic language. At the end of this discussion, they decide, after all, that "we can admit no poetry into our city save only hymns to the gods and praises of good men."[58] The quarrel between philosophy and poetry can be decided in favor of the former only under the condition that the two antagonists be commensurable. For Plato, the measure under which both stand is truth. Since philosophy is closer to truth than poetry, which is only the imitation of an imitation of the true world, it is the unambiguous victor. Plato's manner of deciding the "ancient quarrel"—making poetry and philosophy commensurable by measuring them both against the standard of truth—has determined the terms in which the relationship between poetry and philosophy has been cast ever since. The Platonic hierarchy can be altered, of course: the poet can be understood to represent the true world in a more immediate and therefore truer manner than the philosopher. More radically, the poet in the widest sense of the term—the inventor, the fabricator, the falsifier—can be seen to stand closer than the philosopher to the truth of chaos: the paradoxical "truth" that there is, after all, no truth. Nietzsche's "reversal" of the Platonic hierarchy, with which both Arendt and Auden were intimately familiar, decides the "ancient quarrel" in favor of poets because they, unlike philosophers, do not measure themselves against fixed and stable standards but, instead, create anew the very standards for their own creations.[59] And this incessant drive toward innovation makes poetic creations more adequate, more faithful, and thus "truer" to the only true world: the ever-changing and all-encompassing chaos that philosophers since Plato have erroneously sought to capture, stabilize, and bring into order once and for all. Nietzsche's decision of the "ancient quarrel" in favor of the poet issues into a formal paradox akin to the "Cretan Liar's Paradox," for the statement that poetry is truer than philosophy presents itself as a philosophical proposition and must therefore be considered untrue as long as it is true.[60]

The commensurability of Auden and Arendt consists in a shared commitment to a different kind of paradox altogether—an ethical paradox at the heart of friendship. Neither follows Nietzsche and dissolves truth into a powerful error. For both of them, truth remains all-important; it cannot be sacrificed, least of all for the goal of increased power. Yet it must be sacrificed under certain conditions: whenever it makes something like friendship—understood in the widest sense as a relation among singular beings, each of whom remains incommensurable with any other—impossible. Truth, in other words, retains all its prerogatives; but it must nevertheless be the "subaltern" as well. Respect for this paradox does not mean, for Auden and Arendt, that they welcome aporias for their own sake; rather, both carefully confront paradoxical conditions, circumstances, and formulations without either the sanguine-optimistic attitude that all impasses will be overcome or the melancholic-pessimistic attitude that nothing can be done, for all paths lead nowhere in the end. While remaining committed to discovering and disclosing the truth, both are equally prepared to relinquish a claim to having captured a truth, however large or small, if this claim destroys the possibility of becoming friends. Such is the force of Arendt's memorable words in her letter to Auden: "I hope you don't think I am being quarrelsome and, worse, tiresome. But if you do, you will, please, be kind, and forget it."

One of the surest signs of both Auden's and Arendt's respect for this ethical paradox is their renewed appreciation of *doxa* (opinion). As an unqualified champion of *epistēmē* (knowledge), which orients itself toward universals, Plato had little regard for the "it seems to me" (*deiknumai*) in which individuality announces itself.[61] Nietzsche's reversal of Platonism promotes competing perspectives, each of which struggles for greater height, which is to say, increased power. What is lost in this "perspectivism" is the common world through which viewpoints become perspectives in the first place; without a common world onto which different perspectives open, any talk of *perspective* is misplaced. Because Arendt and Auden never lose sight of this common world, they never fall into the formal paradox of perspectivism: if there are only perspectives and no common world, there can be no perspectives in the strict sense of the term. Arendt and Auden therefore keep perspectives "doxic," and this creates a corresponding—ethical—paradox: each *doxa* or opinion claims to be true, and yet these claims must be abrogated if any one of them destroys the doxic condition of plural perspectives on a world held in common. A grateful appreciation of *doxa* permeates all of Arendt's work and leads, for example, to her praise of Lessing: "Lessing's greatness does not merely consist in a theoretical insight that there cannot be one single truth within the human world but in his gladness that it does not exist and that, therefore, the unending discourse among men will never cease so long as there are men at all."[62] For Auden, a commitment to, and celebration of, the "it seems to me" manifests itself with exceptional clarity in the concluding words of his "commonplace book," *A Certain World*:

> What the poet has to convey is not "self-expression," but a view of a reality common to all, seen from a unique perspective, which it is his duty as well as his pleasure to share with others. To small truths as well as great, St. Augustine's words apply. "The truth is neither mine nor his nor another's; but belongs to us all whom Thou callest to partake of it, warning us terribly, not to account it private to ourselves, lest we be deprived of it."[63]

This clear recognition and appreciation of the original sense of *doxa* is even more succinctly expressed in a haiku by Auden that Arendt quotes as the epigraph to the opening section of *The Life of the Mind*:

> Does God ever judge
> us by appearances? I
> suspect that he does.[64]

That neither Arendt nor Auden claims access to the true world consolidates their commensurability. Plato not only *decided* the "ancient quarrel" between philosophy and poetry but *created* this quarrel by subjecting these otherwise incommensurate occupations to a single standard—that of truth. Without a standard under which both contestants are judged no quarrel can even begin. The relation between Auden and Arendt cannot be understood as a quarrel not only because they were in fact friends but also—and this is a significant dimension of their friendship and motivates their common concern for friendship—because the commensurability of their work does not consist in mutual subjection to a single standard. Nor, however, does their commensurability consist in a relation of subjection whereby the accomplishments of one become the standard and point of orientation for the other. Such relations are not uncommon among poets and philosophers. Schelling and Hegel, for example, received guidance from Hölderlin in their joint attempt to overcome the limits of Kantianism.[65] The English romantics were guided by developments in British political and social philosophy.[66] Or, to cite a case in which the direction of guidance cannot be determined, Heidegger and Celan acted out a failed friendship over many years.[67] By contrast, for all their immense respect for, and appreciation of, each other, neither Arendt nor Auden finds a guiding voice in the other. In one sense, this is not surprising, for, as Arendt notes in her eulogy, they met late in life—after both had established the basic contours of their thought and had already published many of the major works by which they were known. Their chronological maturity, moreover, mirrors their intellectual maturity. Not only do they not, as representatives of poetry and philosophy, engage in a quarrel—ancient or modern—they do not even recognize each other as potential rivals who would be measured by a single standard. Instead of subjugating themselves to such a standard for the purpose of winning over the other, they put their trust in a common world upon which their perspectives converge. In her eulogy for Auden, Arendt

calls such maturity "sanity."[68] In "'The Truest Poetry is the Most Feign-
ing,'" Auden calls it "reticence."[69]

Auden's and Arendt's commensurability, in short, paradoxically precludes any attempt to measure them against a single standard. Accordingly, this study of their work measures them neither against such a standard nor against each other. Instead, it measures them against the
demands imposed by a phenomenon like friendship: the recognition that
their perspectives are necessarily singular and incomplete (otherwise,
they would not be perspectives) and the imperative that they remain
open to other perspectives, other *doxai*, and other "opinions" (otherwise,
there could be no common world). As advocates of the doxic condition,
Arendt and Auden invite readers to view them from perspectives other
than their own. A study of the precise manner in which they chart—and
champion—this condition demands, moreover, that they not be treated
in isolation. Concerned almost exclusively with works written before
they came to know each other, this study does not further pursue the
story of their friendship. And the relation between their respective works
can best be described by the phrase with which Arendt summarizes the
nature of their friendship: "very close but not intimate." For intimacy
does away with the "interspaces between men in all their variety."[70] Both
Arendt and Auden cherish these interspaces and turn their attention to
the disclosure of the—paradoxically—doxic condition of human affairs.
This condition is most acutely apparent when it is absent—when, as
Arendt writes, "One Man of gigantic dimensions" replaces a plurality of
perspectives.[71] The catastrophic movements of the mid-twentieth century
give urgency to their corresponding attempts to expose, dignify, and preserve the fragile condition in which one can legitimately speak of perspectives. And this is the basis of their commensurability. The study of
their work undertaken here thus begins with, and orients itself toward
their powerful accounts—one philosophical, the other poetic—of those
regions in which the doxic condition is replaced by a single, nonperspectival, and therefore monstrous vision.

III. "Regions of Sorrow"

It is a measure of Auden's subtle brilliance that he responds to Arendt's
account of forgiveness in *The Human Condition* by reflecting on *Measure for Measure*. Judicial pardon serves as an alternative to retributive

justice signaled by the principle that informs the play's title: " . . . death for death. . . . and Measure still for Measure."[72] Forgiveness, by contrast, does not operate within the calculus of crime, punishment, and judicial pardon. As Auden writes with characteristic lucidity: "The law cannot forgive, for the law has not been wronged, only broken; only persons can be wronged. The law can pardon, but it can only pardon what it has the power to punish."[73] Arendt's reply to these remarks forms the gravitational center of her initial letter to Auden: "You are entirely right (and I was entirely wrong) in that punishment is a necessary alternative only to judicial pardon. I was thinking of the absurd position of the judges during the Nuremberg trials who were confronted with crimes of such a magnitude that they transcended all possible punishment."[74] The crimes to which Arendt refers—and Auden is doubtless also thinking of them as he interrupts the gaiety of Falstaff with the somberness of Angelo—are so immense that there is no measure for them and no adequate measure to be taken against their perpetrators. As Arendt writes in "The Image of Hell," which is a review of *The Black Book: The Nazi Crime Against the Jewish People* and *Hitler's Professors*, "It is as necessary to punish the guilty as it is to remember that there is no punishment that could fit their crimes. For Goering the death penalty is almost a joke, and he, like all his fellow-defendants at Nuremberg, knows that we can do no more than make him die but a little earlier than he would have anyhow."[75]

The classical topos for the place where crimes are punished without any hope of forgiveness is hell. Near the beginning of *Paradise Lost* Milton calls the stations of this place, which "Eternal Justice" has prepared for those who rebel against divine governance, "regions of sorrow": " . . . where peace / And rest can never dwell, hope never comes / That comes to all."[76] The places about which Arendt writes in "The Image of Hell" not only differ from the infernal regions Milton describes—those consigned to the Nazi death factories are not there because of anything they have done but only because of what they are classified to be—they also transform in retrospect prior representations of the worst possible conditions. Neither Dante, nor Milton—nor either of their respective divinities—finds himself in the "absurd position" of the Nuremberg judges: rendering verdicts concerning crimes that transcend "all possible punishment." As Dante famously writes, in lines to which Milton clearly alludes, the words inscribed on the entrance to hell proclaim this place a work of great love:

PER ME SI VA NE LA CITTÀ DOLENTE,
PER ME SI VA NE L'ETTERNO DOLORE,
PER ME SI VA TRA LA PERDUTA GENTE.
  GIUSTIZIA MOSSE IL MIO ALTO FATTORE;
FECEMI LA DIVINA PODESTATE,
LA SOMMA SAPÏENZA E'L PRIMO AMORE.

  Through me the way into the grieving city,
Through me the way into eternal sorrow,
Through me the way among the lost people.
  Justice moved my high maker;
Divine power made me,
Highest wisdom, and primal love.[77]

For all the hopelessness of its inhabitants—and the last line of Dante's next stanza is even more famous, "LASCIATE OGNE SPERANZA, VOI CH'INTRATE [Abandon every hope you who enter]"[78]—the hell imagined by Dante and Milton is nevertheless not without hope. It is hopeful at the very least because it *can* be imagined: darkness is made visible in supreme acts of poetic imagination, which, in turn, generate an abundance of pleasure. Aesthetic pleasure may even increase as the imagination reaches its limits and collapses into enjoyable incoherence. Such is the force and function of the sublime, which received a new reservoir of images from Milton's great epic.[79] But the hell about which Arendt writes is unimaginable in a completely different manner. That it cannot be imagined, moreover, means that its unimaginable horrors should not be made into an aesthetic image—or even imagined in terms of aesthetic failure. The unimaginable character of this hell is aptly captured in the following remarks from Auden's *Secondary Worlds*:

> It is necessary that we know about the evil in the world—about past evil that we may know what man is capable of and be on the watch for it in ourselves, and about present evil so that we may take political action to eradicate it. This knowledge it is one of the duties of the Historian to impart. But the Poet cannot get into this business without defiling himself and his audience. To write a play (that is, to construct a secondary world) about Auschwitz, for example, is wicked; author and audience may try to pretend that they are morally horrified, but in fact they are passing an entertaining evening together in the aesthetic enjoyment of horrors.[80]

Auden's remarks should not be confused with Adorno's famous dictum: "To write poetry after Auschwitz is barbaric."[81] What Auden calls "wicked"—and implicitly distinguishes from evil—traverses the distinction between culture and barbarism, however "dialectical" its presentation. As Arendt notes, reflecting on the same milieu in which Adorno's dictum achieved its prominence, "the very word 'barbarism,' today frequently applied by Germans to the Hitler period, is a distortion of reality; it is as though Jewish and non-Jewish intellectuals had fled a country that was no longer 'refined' enough for them."[82] For Auden, Adorno's concern with culture is beside the point; poetry becomes not barbaric but, rather, wicked whenever it fails to acknowledge its limits. The classical topos of hell is not one of those limits; on the contrary, it is by courageously stepping into its obscure but well-articulated regions that Dante, following Virgil and thereafter giving guidance to Milton, establishes himself as a major poet. By contrast, the topic of Auden's sober comment in *Secondary Worlds* is not a region of sorrow. His comment should not be understood to suggest, however, that the poet—isolated from the facts of history, happy in a world of his own making—must somehow remain oblivious to the horrors to which Auden alludes. Nor should poets try to guarantee that poetry remain "undefiled" by keeping their poems free of any reference to, reflection about, or contact with these horrors. Keeping language free of corruption remains, for Auden, the paramount duty of the writer, and this demands that distinctions be made—between, for example, the "regions of sorrow" brought to light by a Dante or a Milton, and the hell that should not be made into the subject-matter of poetry. Critical urgency accrues to this distinction whenever a poem seeks to disclose a region of sorrow in remembrance of those places that cannot be adequately described as regions of sorrow—and cannot be adequately described at all. Such is the case with the poems by Auden chosen for this study. *The Age of Anxiety* is the first major poem in English that touches on the extermination camps: "When bruised or broiled our bodies are chucked / Like cracked crocks onto kitchen middens," says the Jewish character named Rosetta at the poem's climax.[83] The *like* in this line—and with it, the understanding of the poem as a mirror in which distinctions are transfigured—enters into a crisis that the poetic achievement barely survives. There is no gateway to this region, no guide for its exploration, and no hope that hopelessness can be made into the material of poetry. Instead, the *like* risks defiling the poem, poet, and reader alike. And this risk presents itself as a demand that the poem be read with renewed seriousness, skepticism, and sobriety—not so that it, or we, be rescued from the risk of defilement but so that the ethical fragility of the situation as a whole be exposed.

IV. Overview of the Argument

At the center of Arendt's *Origins of Totalitarianism* is a short but trenchant analysis of wide-scale statelessness that serves as a synecdoche not
only for the book as a whole, but also for her entire political thought. And
it is with this analysis that my book begins: the significance of the extreme
phenomenon of statelessness for Arendt's work can be measured by one of
the most powerful statements she makes in the *Origins*: "Man, it turns
out, can lose all so-called Rights of Man without losing his essential quality as man, his human dignity. Only the loss of a polity itself expels him
from humanity."[84] Beginning with this extreme displacement of the stateless, this book identifies a number of other spatial tropes that Arendt discovers in the course of writing her study. And it places these tropes in a
kind of descending order toward the total collapse of spatiality that takes
place in the destructive movement of totalitarianism—what Arendt will,
in a chilling phrase, call "the abyss of the 'possible.'"[85] Each of these spatial formations, as I argue, is constitutively linked to a specific linguistic
mode of expression according to an implicit but nevertheless rigorous
rule: the greater the displacement, the less meaningful the language. As
Arendt writes of the displaced persons she places at the center of her
study: "Their freedom of movement, if they have it at all, gives them no
right to residence which even the jailed criminal enjoys as a matter of
course; and their freedom of opinion is a fool's freedom, for nothing they
think matters anyhow."[86] Meaningful language, for Arendt, demands an
identifiable place from which to speak, and displaced persons, therefore,
can emit only less than meaningful signals. This bitter insight gives to *The
Origins of Totalitarianism* its particular form as an essay in the relationship
of language to spatiality. Throughout her discussion of the appearance of
totalitarianism as a novel form of government, Arendt explores a bewil-
dering and queasy sequence of spatial distortions in which centers are
evacuated as peripheries expand, and she describes the complex manner
through which the mendacity of ideology comes to infuse the space of this
coordinated evacuation and expansion. The first chapter of this book thus
traces the progressive despatialization that both characterizes the motility
of totalitarian movement and makes its "language" into the most extreme
expression of meaninglessness: a "murderous alphabet."[87]

The Age of Anxiety can be similarly understood as an exploration of the
strangely vertiginous spaces of generalized displacement. But as the title

of the poem indicates, and this study seeks to demonstrate, Auden's poem is centrally concerned with temporality—more exactly, the temporal distortions that structure its compositional strategy. The poem depicts four characters during the Second World War, but the age of anxiety cannot be simply identified with "war-time," and even "war-time," as the narrating voice defines it, cannot simply be measured by the duration of military conflict. The "age of anxiety" is generated by totalitarianism, but the end of this age does not coincide with the cessation of the war. The anxious temporal distortions of the poem extend into the structural elements of the poem itself and are expressed in the resurrection of an archaic metrical form: the alliterative four-stress line of Anglo-Saxon epic poetry. Auden's magisterial organization of language does not, however, simply exult in its dazzling virtuoso display but rigorously reflects on the status of all systematic forms of organization. While the four characters are drawn to the bar as a place of refuge from the "universal disorder" of the war, the poem as a whole gravitates toward utopias as places—or nonplaces—of systematic order. But the desire for utopias in which contingency would give way to necessity is, as the poem proceeds to show, the paradoxical source of the disastrous historical disorder. In the most spectacular, and spectacularly difficult, section of the poem, the four characters seek a solution to this dilemma in a regressive return to a "state of prehistoric happiness which, by human beings, can only be imagined in terms of a landscape bearing a symbolic resemblance to the human body."[88] "The Seven Stages." progresses as an exploration of this symbolic body, and Auden's principal guide to its symbolic significance is, as he indicates, the central treatise of Jewish mysticism, the *Zohar*.[89] As the four characters travel over this enigmatic terrain, the movement of their regressive quest begins to disconcert the sense of both space and time to such an extent that neither common experience nor any theory of temporality can capture their place in time. But the most extraordinary and compelling temporal distortion that occurs in *The Age of Anxiety* is the messianic motif of "the ragged remnant" that unexpectedly irrupts in the speech that concludes the body of the poem. Delivered by a character who reveals herself to be Jewish, this stunning speech places at its center what Arendt calls "the true central institution" of totalitarian rule—the concentration and extermination camps. Yet this meditation does not express despair or resignation; nor does it find satisfaction in the thought of a utopian future. The messianic dimension of *The Age of Anxiety* finds expression in the phrase by which the same character comes to describe her own radically displaced status: "anxious hope."

The book continues to explore this messianic dimension by turning to Arendt's *Human Condition* and arguing that her continual use of the language of salvation and redemption should be taken seriously. At the conclusion of Arendt's chapter on action, the messianic language is particularly dense:

> The miracle that saves the world, the realm of human affairs, from its normal, "natural" ruin is ultimately the fact of natality, in which the faculty of action is ontologically rooted. . . . It is this faith in and hope for the world that found perhaps its most glorious and succinct expression in the few words with which the Gospels announced their "glad tidings": "A child has been born unto us."[90]

For all the complexity of this reflection, Arendt could hardly be more explicit, and as the book seeks to show, her use of messianic language and redemptive motifs has a long and distinguished tradition in German-Jewish scholarship. Perhaps the most famous text of this tradition is Walter Benjamin's "Theses on the Concept of History," a collection of fragments that Arendt helped save from destruction.[91] Where Benjamin speaks of a "*weak* messianic force," Arendt develops an account of the *vita activa* that organizes itself around the weak redemptive power of action—weak because action, for all its redemptive potential, is precisely not sovereign strength. Arendt's insistence on the weakness or "frailty" of action can thus be understood to correspond to the messianic reflections that give shape to her argument. For Arendt, the messianic does not enter the world as an independent force and is certainly not embodied in a salvational figure but remains, instead, a schema with three distinct dimensions: action as a whole saves the world of the human artifice from its inherent ruin; in the act of promising, action remedies its own inherent unpredictability; and in the act of forgiveness, it redeems its irreversibility.

Because the act of forgiveness is an action in its own right, the redemptive schema of action issues into an abyss: forgiveness interrupts and puts an end to action's unforeseeable and irreversible consequences and thereby makes possible the resumption of action beyond the automatic reaction of revenge; but since forgiveness is itself an action, it, too, must be forgiven, and this act of forgiveness, in turn, must be forgiven, *ad infinitum*. The chapter closes with a consideration of two responses to the abyssal structure of action: goodness and love. Both of these responses

collapse the "in-between" that constitutes the "'web' of human relationships,"[92] and neither can secure a ground for the redemptive power of human action: goodness must radically conceal itself; and although love may
be limitless enough to conform to the *ad infinitum* of the abyssal structure
of action, for this very reason it expels those who love—and, for Arendt,
love is "one of the rarest occurrences in human lives"[93]—from the world.
For all its reliance on the discourse of redemption, *The Human Condition*
is emphatically not an eschatological treatise; indeed, it analyzes the cost
of early Christian eschatology: flight from—not hope for—the world. But
The Human Condition is nevertheless deeply concerned with ends, especially with the predominance of the end in the means-end schema. A
world given over entirely to this schema is at its end, even if automatic
processes continue to run. And it is from this perspective that the language of "miracles" first appears: the interruptive, redemptive power of action is miraculous to the extent that it is unprecedented, uncaused, and
impossible to anticipate. Against the ever-recurring cycles of nature and
the end-dominated world of the human artifice, action is always new.

Taking up the thought of novelty pursued in *The Human Condition*,
the fourth chapter reads in detail one of Auden's most difficult, formally
complex, and generally neglected poems, "Canzone," and interprets this
poem's central concern—the nature of the will—in light of Arendt's late
reflections on the faculty of willing. "Canzone" is modeled after a form invented and used only once by Dante for his poem "Amor, tu vedi ben che
questa Donna" in which only five rhyme words are used to end more than
sixty lines of poetry. Whereas for Dante the novelty of the form serves as
compensation for the nonreciprocation of his love, for Auden the repetitions in the form serve to chastise the will as it seeks to master both the
poet's own emotions and the affections of another. Repetition precludes
willing, because willing demands an open future—one determined not by
a past that returns in ever-repeating cycles, but by the will itself. But the
closed, repetitive form of Auden's "Canzone" locks the (word) *will* into a
pattern of return. Thus frustrated, the will finds itself "caught in reflection
on the right to will."[94] One precise measure of the intellectual affinity between Auden and Arendt can be found in the fact that Arendt, too, is
drawn into a reflection on the rightness, more exactly, the legitimacy, of
the faculty of willing from the perspective of its competing faculties,
above all, thinking. And Arendt's reflections in *The Life of the Mind* revolve around the same temporal conundrums that give Auden's poem its

definitive shape: the faculty of willing is discovered when the classical idea of eternal return is no longer taken for granted, and it becomes a central category of philosophical reflection when the idea of cyclical temporality gives way to eschatological hopes. Scholastic philosophy, which Arendt places at the center of her investigation, conceives of its duty as the reconciliation of will with intellect, hence, the reconciliation of the cosmic, cyclical time of Platonic-Aristotelian thought—which honors necessity— with the demands of a temporality marked by an absolute beginning in divine creation and an equally absolute endpoint: the eschatological vision of the future. And Dante, for Auden as well as Arendt, serves as a figure in whom these two conceptions of temporality achieve a tenuous, but ultimately impossible, reconciliation. Auden's "Canzone" registers the impossibility of this reconciliation: it neither accepts eternal return nor places its hope in an eschatological vision. It must, instead, discover the new in repetition, as it opens up a space for a will that does not seek sovereign satisfaction in achieving the aim of its own willing. The disclosure of a space for an ever-renewed faculty of willing coincides with the irruption of a new mode of speaking: praise. Whereas the poet of "Amor, tu vedi ben che questa Donna" laments his helplessness—his inability to make the lady love him—the poet of "Canzone" bids his "fellow-creature" praise the condition of helplessness, for this condition alone makes possible fellowship (in Arendt's terms, plurality) and creatureliness (in Arendt's terms, contingency). Plurality and contingency save a world otherwise consigned to reactive repetition.

The conclusion takes its point of departure from two simple and sober sentences discovered in the course of the book: the imperative "We must try to get on" (Auden)[95] and the statement that the act of forgiveness makes it "possible for life to go on" (Arendt).[96] "Getting on" and "going on" may appear as unambitious proposals, yet they both constitute powerfully concentrated responses to anxieties generated by the catastrophic events of the twentieth century. Their modesty may be understood in contrast to the "saving solution" presented by totalitarianism, which seeks to eradicate the "miracle" of action—and therefore responsibility— by replacing the human condition of plurality with "One Man of gigantic dimensions."[97] Action itself responds in opposition to totalitarianism's efforts to reduce plural human beings into "bundles of reaction."[98] But action is by no means a "saving solution," for it cannot escape accusations of its own irresponsibility: every action necessarily alters beyond its control the "'web' of human relationships." The vicissitudes of action find remedy and redemption in two of action's own potentialities: promising, which can remedy action's unpredictability, and forgiveness, which can redeem it of its irreversibility. But the redemptive power of forgiveness— which allows action to resume—generates and discloses the abyssal structure of action as a whole. The book concludes by arguing that the act of praising joins promising and forgiveness as a third internal potentiality of action. Praising does not remedy or redeem one of action's predicaments; rather, it brings to light the sheer conditionality of action. Auden, as Arendt emphasizes, conceives of the poet's duty in terms of praise, and nowhere, perhaps, in his work is this duty more explicitly formulated than in his magnificent poem, "In Praise of Limestone." The conclusion of the book thus traces a few elements of this poem. Its elaborate syntax and suddenly shifting verbal patterns correspond to the ever-changing topography of the region described. Auden's limestone landscape is the image of promise and forgiveness, and his minute exploration of its complex surfaces and hidden interiors provides a model for praise that comprehends, without trying to change, the abyssal structure of action and therefore lays the faulted ground for the "miraculous" resumption of action—or, in less exalted terms, "going on."

V. What's Missing

This study concentrates on a limited number of its subjects' works and therefore leaves out some of their major achievements. In the case of Auden this limitation is particularly apparent, for his poetic productivity is as remarkable for its extraordinary range as for its technical virtuosity.[99] Equally adept at lyric, dramatic, and meditative modes of writing, Auden was a master of myriad complex poetic forms, ranging from all variety of songs, ballads, and limericks to some of the most solemn, somber, and technically difficult poems written in the English language.[100] Known to delight in writing intricate verse forms of great technical difficulty (such as Englyns, Drott-Kvaetts, and Sestinas), he was perhaps best known, and most beloved, for the dexterous quality and sheer beauty of his light verse. Also absent from this study is an explicit discussion of Auden's complicated commitment to Christianity, which he, against his own critical principles,[101] once, and only once, made into the direct subject matter of his poetry: in his "Christmas Oratorio" of 1944 entitled *For the Time Being*.

Similarly omitted from this study, although less conspicuously, are some
of Arendt's well-known writings on politics: *On Revolution* and the essays
that constitute *Crises of the Republic*, for example, with their analyses of re-
publicanism and the nature of democracy, do not appear in any significant fashion. There is also little discussion of the peculiar or even uncate-
gorizable genre with which Arendt continually experimented and in
which she developed an inimitable critical voice: what might be called her
"portraits" of famous and infamous figures ranging from Pope John XXIII
to Adolf Eichmann. None of these portraits is more penetrating and perplexing than her first, *Rahel Varnhagen: The Life of a German Jewess from
the Romantic Era.*[102]

Something is missing from *For the Time Being*, and the same is true of
Rahel Varnhagen. Auden's "Christmas Oratorio" is a poetic account of the
time and conditions of redemption. Amidst a multitude of diverse yet
wonderfully consonant poetic forms, two voices come to define these conditions: the angelic verse dialogue between Gabriel and Mary called "The
Annunciation" on the one hand, and the tortured prose monologue of
Herod entitled "The Massacre of the Innocents" on the other. The setting
of Auden's poem is the world of the Roman Empire, but as the Roman
world begins to bear unmistakable traits of the modern world, the time of
redemption undergoes a kind of radical concatenation, dilation, and collapse: "These are stirring times for the editors of newspapers," says the
Narrator, "History is in the making; Mankind is on the march. / . . . Our
great empire shall be secure for a thousand years."[103] Entirely absent from
the poem is the child whom Gabriel announces and about whom Herod
worries. This absence casts the whole poem—dedicated to the memory of
Auden's mother[104]—into the mood of mourning: the concept of time that
Auden illuminates in *For the Time Being* runs counter to every conception
of history in which it could be understood as "in the making" or humanity understood as "on the march." The only access to time no longer understood in terms of making and marching is in the experience of mourning. And mourning describes both the mood and the formal conditions of
Arendt's *Rahel Varnhagen* as well. What's missing from this strange and
stunning portrait is an account of the time and conditions of its composition: what Arendt describes in the book's preface (written twenty years after the last chapters were completed) as "the doom [*Untergang*] of German
Jewry."[105] The body of this book is completely silent about the *Untergang*
of European Jewry, but only in light—or in the darkness—of this doom

does Rahel's life become an historical subject in a strict sense. As Arendt insists in the preface, "it should never be forgotten that the subject matter [of this book] is thoroughly historical and that today not only the history of the German Jews but also their specific problematic is a matter of the past."[106] To be unable to forget that something is "thoroughly historical" and a "matter of the past" is to be in mourning.

Neither *For the Time Being* nor *Rahel Varnhagen* represents those who have been lost and for whom they mourn. In both cases, the central concerns of these otherwise incomparable works—the brutal destructions and annihilations that were being organized and executed as the texts were being written—are never mentioned. Nor is any figure of redemption represented. And in these works, which are intimately related to their most personal experiences, no one whom they ever met appears. What's missing is what touches them most dearly. This study does not speculate on these matters. Yet it is likely that both Arendt and Auden would appreciate a remark Wittgenstein made about the work in which he believed he had brought philosophy to its definitive end: "I wanted to write [in its preface] that my work consists in two parts: of the one which is here, and of everything which I have *not* written. And precisely this second part is the important one."[107]

§ 1   The Spaces of Anxiety

Arendt's "Origins of Totalitarianism"

"The unacknowledged legislators of the world" describes the secret
police, not the poets.
> —W. H. Auden, "Writing"

I. Displacement—Declaration

In the final central sections of *The Origins of Totalitarianism,* Arendt describes the new phenomenon of statelessness. What is new is not of course
forced migration, ritual exile, or in any case the loss of a home in which
one can establish "a distinct place in the world"; rather, "what is unprecedented is . . . the impossibility of finding a new one."[1] The novelty of
Arendt's analysis consists in her explication of the plight of the stateless in
relation to a declaration that was intended to do away with the consequences of statelessness: the Declaration of the Rights of Man. She sees
the novel appearance of wide-scale statelessness and the hitherto unknown
discovery and declaration of inalienable human rights as closely correlated
phenomena—so closely correlated that, against all appearances, they reinforce each other. Far from pointing the way to the solution of a problem,
the Declaration prepares the way for the expansion of the problem to unprecedented proportions. The ineffectiveness, hollowness, and indeed
emptiness of the Declaration correspond to the placelessness of those who
no longer harbor the possibility of having a home, and this correspondence is rooted in the "object" about which the Declaration authorizes itself to speak: a homeless and thus always displaced object; the human being in general; hence, the human being who by definition is unable to
find a home.[2]

Arendt is not a thinker who seeks out paradoxes for their own sake, as
though the task of thought were either to eliminate paradoxes or embrace
them as the forms that demonstrate the absurdity of life; she is not, in

other words, drawn either toward Russellian logistics or Sartrean existentialism, and yet, she is drawn to this word when she begins to analyze the
affinity between statelessness and the statement that the human being as
such is endowed with rights: "From the beginning the paradox involved
in the declaration of inalienable human rights was that it reckoned with
an 'abstract' human being who seemed to exist nowhere" (291). As Arendt
formulates this paradox something of the very same perplexity attaches to
her formulation: "from the beginning" is almost as abstract as the language of a declaration that speaks of a human being who cannot even be
said to exist nowhere but only "seem[s] to exist nowhere"—and, indeed,
seems to no one in particular. Everything in Arendt's thought runs
counter to the abstractness of a universal declaration: if there is a categorical imperative to which her writing is responsive, it is the imperative that
appears throughout her work to articulate specificity, distinctions, and
distinctness. The *Origins* describes the disastrous destruction of discrete
spaces and the attendant vanishing of distinct individuals—"as though
their plurality had disappeared into One Man of gigantic dimensions"
(466); *The Human Condition* is concerned with articulating distinctions
within the *vita activa* and, still more, with articulating distinctness as the
actualization of the human condition of plurality—the fact that "not one
man, but men, inhabit the earth."[3] And yet, the paradox that Arendt
identifies as she speaks of the Declaration—a declaration that proffers
rights to an abstract and homeless human being—has the power to insin-
uate itself into her own discriminating language. In a certain sense, this is
not surprising: throughout her writings, Arendt enters into the voices of
those about whom she speaks—most remarkably in the strange ventriloquism first developed in her biography of Rahel Varnhagen, but also notably employed in the various portraits collected in her volume *Men in
Dark Times*; and this technique is carried over to studies like the *Origins*,
the voice of which is for the most part that of an independent, critical
scholar. When she adopts, therefore, the voice of the Declaration of the
Rights of Man, her language tends toward emptiness. But the paradox of
the Declaration goes beyond any questions of technique and touches on
the central concerns of the *Origins*, if not all of her writings: language in
the eminent sense is possible, and sentences, including those of the Declaration, can be meaningful solely on the condition that human beings are
conditioned, which means, at the very least, spatially conditioned—that
is, that they can claim an identifiable place from which to speak.

Despite its baroque architectonic, the *Origins* as a whole constitutes an essay in the relationship of spatiality to language. To every spatial formation that Arendt analyzes there corresponds a specific mode of expression: massive displacement is correlated with the Declaration of the Rights of Man; the fringe of society with an inarticulate sign language; imperial expansion with arbitrary decree; the depths of the soul with pseudomystical humbug; the layered character of totalitarian organization—which she brilliantly presents in terms of an onion—with the lies of totalitarian rule; and the despatialization that occurs in totalitarian "movement" with a "murderous alphabet." Whenever she speaks of spatial formations, Arendt not only describes and analyzes the language of those who speak from within the parameters of these formations, she also alters her own language in turn. It is because of her particular sensitivity to the relation between the topological and tropological dimensions of language that the analyses of literary works Arendt undertakes in the *Origins* are not mere embellishments or examples but integral investigations into specific correlations of language and spatiality. Even when she does not directly link her analyses to spatial formations—as she does in her remarkable reading of the relation of center to fringe in Proust[4]—such formations serve as the ordering framework for her inquiry into linguistic phenomena: Kipling can become the author of imperialism's foundation legend, according to Arendt, only because limitless expansion beyond the borders of a nation could not take place without a narrative that, like ancient ones, would "promis[e] safe guidance through the limitless space of the future" (208). For the phenomenon of wide-scale and massive displacement, however, Arendt pursues her analysis without reflecting on any literary corpus, unless her own body of work, including the *Origins* itself, is to be understood in these terms. Arendt gives no indication in the *Origins* that she, too, is among those who sought refuge from the calamities of displacement. But from the time she left Berlin—where she had been jailed for her work with Kurt Blumenfeld's Zionist organization—and crossed the Czech border at Karlsbad, fleeing from the Nazis in 1933, until she received U.S. citizenship in 1951 (which coincides with the publication of the complete text of the *Origins*) Arendt moved through Prague, Geneva, and Paris; was interned in a camp in Gurs in 1940, escaped to Montauban, passed into Lisbon, and reached New York in 1941, where she resided as a "stateless person" for ten years.[5] And it is in the context of her analysis of statelessness in the *Origins* that the correlation of language to spatiality comes to a critical juncture: permanent displacement eliminates the possibility not so much of language as such but of language in the eminent sense—language, that is, in which utterances are not only meaningful according to grammatical and logical criteria but, above all, significant to other speakers who are able to speak meaningfully in return. The paradox Arendt uncovers as she discusses the Declaration concerns nothing so much as the possibility of such speech; it is a paradox in the original sense of the word—that which confounds *doxa* ("opinion")[6]—because those who are permanently displaced, the stateless, are precisely the ones who are robbed of the possibility of *doxa* and whose opinions, therefore, are confounded even before they are ever articulated.

The Declaration itself confounds opinion inasmuch as it speaks of abstract and placeless beings who are deprived of the possibility of opinion because of their abstractness and placelessness. To be without the possibility of opinion is thus to be dispossessed of rights:

> The fundamental deprivation of human rights is first and above all in the deprivation of a place in the world which makes opinions significant and actions effective. . . . People deprived of human rights . . . are deprived, not of the right to freedom, but of the right to action; not of the right to think whatever they please, but of the right to opinion. (296)

And the Declaration is paradoxical in another manner as well: it not only confounds *doxa* but also expresses a general historical condition in which *doxa* is confounded. Against the emptiness of the language of the Declaration, Arendt is struggling to protect the ability to speak meaningfully, such that meaning—in contrast to the long philosophical tradition that seeks to overcome mere "opinion" and arrive at knowledge—is correlated to *doxa*. The relation of *doxa* to *epistēmē* ("knowledge") is not, for Arendt, so much partial as it is spatialized, positioned within a field of other *doxai*. In *doxa* language is combined with space; more exactly, *doxa* is spatialized language or the articulation of a specific spatiality: "taking a stand" and "having a point of view" are the ineluctable expressions through which *doxai* are articulated. Such expressions can supplement every opinion, just as, according to Kant, the "I think" can accompany every representation.[7] Furthermore, every phenomenon, for Kant, is conceptualized sensibility, and space itself is nothing other than the form of outer sense; similarly, every *doxa*, for Arendt, is spatialized speech, and our experience of the world is formed by common sense: "Even the experience of the materially and sensually given world depends upon my being in contact with other men, upon our *common* sense which regulates and controls all other senses and without which each of us would be enclosed in his own particularity of sense data which in themselves are unreliable and treacherous" (475–76).[8]

It is therefore the duty of thought, for Arendt as for Kant, not to allow appearances—or the "it appears to me" of *doxa*—to be superseded by a supposedly "higher" instance of rationality or systematicity: concepts entirely removed from the possibility of spatial instantiation or language that has nothing to do with the specific spaces of those who speak. For both Kant and Arendt the supersession of appearances and the collapse of spatiality can result only in isolation, which, in both cases, leads away from what Kant calls the "land of truth."[9] This land is the space of possible agreement and also possible disagreement about a world held in common. And just as, for Kant, the first, but not last, duty of philosophy is to reflect on the sources—sometimes he uses the word *origins*[10]—of knowledge in the equiprimordial faculties of sensibility and conceptuality, for Arendt the investigation of origins cannot proceed without a scrupulous investigation into the sources of opinion in space and language. If the comparison with Kant is valid, the new phenomenon of statelessness constitutes something like a null-point in her analysis: language and space are disjointed not combined or—to use the Kantian vocabulary—schematized. The new phenomenon of wide-scale statelessness destroys space itself— not, however, in a cartographic sense (there is still physical space between people) nor in the sense of the "lived space" explored by phenomenologists; statelessness destroys the specificity of spaces understood as necessary conditions for the possibility of perspectives and position-taking, expressed in the language of points of view.

Those who are stateless, therefore, are not only not allowed to stay in one place but are also unable to make a meaningful statement or state an opinion that matters:

> [Although the stateless] may have more freedom of movement than a lawfully imprisoned criminal or . . . enjoy more freedom of opinion in the internment camps of democratic countries than they would in any ordinary despotism, not to mention in a totalitarian country . . . , their freedom of movement, if they have it at all, gives them no right to residence which even the jailed criminal enjoys as a matter of course; and their freedom of opinion is a fool's freedom, for nothing they think matters anyhow. (296)

These two elements of statelessness—being unable to claim a home or articulate a meaningful opinion—are closely related to each other: having a point of view—where the word *have* cannot be immediately understood in terms of either possession or appurtenance—depends on having a place from which to view a world held in common. And the very idea of a point of view, which is to say, the idea of opinion, implies a multiplicity of points and thus a plurality of perspectives: it depends on others also having places from which to articulate individual points of view, and these places must, like language itself, be articulated; that is, they must be distinct, discrete, and divisible. Statelessness, in short, issues into state(ment)lessness. In contrast to the perpetual mobility with which the stateless are threatened, those who are able to state an opinion and thus take a stand occupy a place of relative stability—a condition of stasis or, in other words, a "state," to draw on the etymology of the political sense of the word.[11] Like the state, opinion is in every sense *relatively* stable. Relative to contemplation, which fixes on absolutely stable forms, opinion is as mutable as its objects; for this reason, it has been denigrated in favor of immutable knowledge. But relative to the sheer expression of emotion, opinion is nevertheless stable. If it is to count as a stance from which one articulates a point of view, it cannot be merely the expression of a momentary whim; opinion may not run directly counter to the vicissitudes of temper, as contemplation is supposed to do, but it cannot surrender itself entirely to the motility of emotion either. Arendt devotes only a short section to the problem of statelessness, but it serves as a synecdoche not only for the *Origins* but also for her entire political thought. The designation "DP"—one who can never enjoy a state of relative stability—may be bureaucratic jargon (a thoughtless category), but, for Arendt, it names a fundamental philosophical-political problem. Arendt's thinking about the displacement of DPs is exemplary: the thoughtlessness with which this designation took hold is itself an aspect of the task to be thought in the *Origins*. And in order to think the nature of displacement and statelessness, Arendt must develop a political philosophy of space in which the relative stability of opinion takes precedence over the absolute stability of contemplation, which—by disregarding individuals in favor of the forms under which they fall—is strangely in league with both the abstractness of the Declaration and the arbitrariness of bureaucratic jargon that creates and identifies the phenomenon of displacement in order to deal with those who, having lost their individuality, merge into a "huge and nameless crowd" (287).

The namelessness of the crowd corresponds to the anonymity of those whom the Declaration of the Rights of Man addresses as it seeks to redress acts of violence. Such acts would have been violations of identifiable criminal codes if only the enforcement of these codes had extended to the growing percentage of Europe's population that since the end of the first World War, "lived outside the pale of the law" (277). Because it treats mankind rather than distinct individuals as its object, the Declaration generalizes the human being and throws it back onto its "natural givenness" or "mere differentiation" (302). Individuality, therefore, no longer consists in the ability to take a stand or express an opinion within the parameters of a political space but on the "abstract nakedness of being human" (299). In this way, the Declaration is not only an expression of the reduction of human beings to "specimen[s] of an animal species" (301–02) (Arendt goes so far as to compare the rhetoric of abstract human rights with the arguments of animal rights activists[12]), but it also contributes to this very reduction, for it sets in motion the "emancipation" of human beings from both nature and history by seeking the tautological and therefore empty formulas that would make humanity into its own guarantor. "This new situation, in which 'humanity' has in effect assumed the role formerly ascribed to nature or history, would mean in this context that the right to have rights, or the right of every individual to belong to humanity, should be guaranteed by humanity itself" (298).

Arendt does not rest content with the identification of the paradoxical character of the Declaration of the Rights of Man—"that it reckoned with an 'abstract' human being who seemed to exist nowhere." Rather, she closes the section on "The Perplexities of the Rights of Man" with an analysis of a more basic philosophical-political paradox, one of whose derivatives is the paradox she identifies in the Declaration:

> The paradox involved in the loss of human rights is that such loss coincides with the instant when the person becomes a human being in general—without a profession, without a citizenship, without an opinion, without a deed by which to identify and specify himself—*and* different in general, representing nothing but his own absolutely unique individuality which, deprived of expression within and action upon a common world, loses all significance. (302)

Without a relatively stable space in which individuals can appear to one another *as* equals, there can be no individuality, or rather, there is nothing but naked individuality.[13] This *as* is the telos of institutions founded on a principle of justice: "Our political life rests on the assumption that we can produce equality through organization, because man can act in and change and build a common world, together with his equals and only with his equals" (301). Equality, which is coeval with the "public sphere," is the condition for the possibility of an individuality that can articulate itself as individual. Conversely, the constantly mobile and permanently stateless condition of nonequality and naked individuality is one in which everyone is paradoxically equal—equally insignificant and finally superfluous. And this condition cannot be consigned to some prehistoric or fictitious "state of nature," a concept which, as Arendt explains in her piercing excursus on Hobbes, does not describe anything but instead predicts the condition for the politics that is absorbed into bourgeois society.[14] It is not the threat of reversion to the state of nature that is an ever-present possibility—and thus justifies according to a Hobbesian principle the maintenance of a state. The irrepressible possibility is, rather, that naked individuality can "brea[k] into the political scene as the alien," which is to say, as the figure of one who, alienated from both nature and history, is the putative subject of all discourse on inalienable rights. Arendt is not being histrionic when she dramatizes the alien as the figure who irrupts on the political stage and disrupts the play of equals that is acted out in the public sphere; the arrival of the alien is the paradoxical appearance of the disappearance of the public sphere as such. If, for Kant, "intuitions without concepts are blind,"[15] for Arendt, mere givenness without opinion is the opacity in which all points, especially points of view, vanish:

> [T]he dark background of mere givenness, the background formed by our unchangeable and unique nature breaks into the political scene as the alien which in its all too obvious difference reminds us of the limitations of human activity—which are identical with the limitations of human equality . . . [and] the limitations of the human artifice. (301)

By representing the darkness in which all points of view and all perspectives vanish, the alien reveals the artificial character of equality. Arendt is by no means an extremist; but, as her reflections on the alien demonstrate, she recognizes the revelatory character of the extreme. Only in view of the extreme, not the average, can certain dimensions of a situation, and often the most basic or significant ones, make themselves known. This is particularly true of statelessness, which distinguishes itself from criminality in the modern sense of the term to the precise extent that the stateless, unlike the criminal, is not simply outside the law but, as Arendt repeatedly writes, "outside the pale of the law" (277, 286, and 296). The extremity of statelessness can be measured by comparing this condition with ancient slavery, for the stateless could not even claim the oppressive place conferred on slaves in the ancient world: "Even slaves still belonged to some kind of human community; their labor was needed, used, and exploited, and this kept them within the pale of humanity" (297). Nor are those who are stateless outside the pale of the law in the same sense as the outlaw of the ancient and medieval worlds; the acts of expulsion through which individuals were transformed into outlaws doubtless meant "civil death," but outlaws could still find places for themselves in which they could live: the world was not yet "One World," and humanity was not yet "completely organized" such that "the loss of home and political status become identical with expulsion from humanity altogether" (297). Being "outside the pale" is therefore a condition of being not only exterior to a territory defined by a particular set of poles or stakes, which is one sense of *pale*, but also beyond a specific legal order—a Pale[16]—and thus, in the end, beyond every conceivable jurisdiction:

> Something much more fundamental than freedom and justice, which are rights of citizens, is at stake when belonging to the community into which one is born is no longer a matter of course and not belonging no longer a matter of choice, or when one is placed in a situation where, unless he commits a crime, his treatment by others does not depend on what he does or does not do. This extremity, and nothing else, is the situation of people deprived of human rights. (296)

The extreme of statelessness occupies the center of the *Origins* in accordance with Arendt's peculiar methodology, which seeks to understand a phenomenon from the perspective of its extreme instance or element. Because Arendt orients herself toward the extreme, the use of the term *methodology* is problematic insofar as the purpose of any methodology is the reduction of unusual, exceptional, and extreme cases to standard instances obedient to a general pattern, rule, or law. Instead of undertaking a systematic ordering of phenomena according to a set of axioms or basic principles, and instead of seeking to discover average phenomena by applying more or less rigorous statistical methods, which would then stand in need of some explanatory principles—instead, in short, of the opposing methodological principles of rationalism and empiricism that define the parameters of research on the phenomena Arendt discusses[17]—the *Origins* takes its point of departure from extreme situations like that of wide-scale statelessness, and it never lets these extremes out of its sight by integrating them into a seamless web of explanation. One characteristic of the extreme is that it alone makes it possible to recognize and measure the specific space of which it is the limit. Another characteristic of the extreme is that it defeats rationalism and empiricism to the extent that it remains both irreducible and incredible. Arendt takes her point of departure from phenomena at the limits of human comprehension that, under no condition, can be represented by means of traditional topoi or accepted axioms. And Arendt accordingly eschews the arrogance of total comprehension whose dangers she articulates as she introduces her own project: "The conviction that everything that happens on earth must be comprehensible to man can lead to interpreting history by commonplaces. Comprehension does not mean denying the outrageous, deducing the unprecedented from precedents, or explaining phenomena by such analogies and generalities that the impact of reality and the shock of experience are no longer felt" (viii). The extreme situation of massive displacement, in short, cannot be understood with reference to a commonplace. Arendt could be seen to develop an insight Kierkegaard articulates in *Repetition*: "The exception explains the universal and himself, and if one really wants to study the universal, one only needs to look around for a legitimate exception, [for] he discloses everything far more clearly than the universal itself."[18] But for Arendt, it is not only the exception—and certainly not primarily the "legitimate exception"—but also extremes of illegitimacy and illegality that have a power to reveal the nature and limits of universality, especially the supposed universality claimed by the Declaration of the Rights of Man. And nowhere perhaps are the lines between legitimate and illegitimate exceptionality more acutely drawn than in Arendt's analysis of the figures of the "exception Jews" who uneasily occupy the fringes of *fin-de-siècle*, bourgeois society.

II. Fringe—Sign Language

Arendt's mode of procedure brings marginal phenomena into the center of analysis. In hindsight, there is nothing particularly noteworthy about beginning an investigation into the origins of totalitarianism with a discussion of anti-Semitism, since, of course, anti-Semitism played a decisive role in the machinery and ideology of Nazi power. But this very fact—that so marginal and insignificant a phenomenon as anti-Semitism should occupy a central place in the operations of totalitarianism—constitutes, for Arendt, a problem: not least, a problem of methodology. When she begins the *Origins* with a study of anti-Semitism, she is mirroring the systematic anomaly she seeks to understand; that is, the movement of a fringe phenomenon into the center: "It must be possible to face and understand the outrageous fact that so small (and, in world politics, so unimportant) a phenomenon as the Jewish question and antisemitism could become the catalytic agent for first, the Nazi movement, then a world war, and finally the establishment of death factories" (viii). And this movement from fringe to center is repeated throughout the *Origins*. Arendt does not seek out marginal phenomena for their own sake; nor does she try to resurrect or habilitate generally overlooked historical phenomena or forgotten people; nor does she seek to demonstrate that certain things that had hitherto been considered marginal play a decisive historical or structural role after all. Instead, Arendt chooses to concentrate on precisely those fringe phenomena that have unquestionably become central to the events she analyzes. Few cases would be clearer in this regard than that of Dreyfus, whose "case" occupied the center of attention for a European-wide audience, even though it is impossible to identify anything particularly extraordinary about his accomplishments, abilities, or supposed crimes. Something similar can be said of Disraeli: his achievements were hardly meager, of course, but what drives Arendt's analysis is not the extent or depth of his skill or achievements but the fact that this baptized Jew understood from the beginning of his career that he had to emphasize his "exoticism, strangeness, mysteriousness, magic, and power drawn from secret sources" (69) in order to bring himself into the center of British power; in other words, he had a lucid, although not particularly articulate, sense that, if he wished to occupy the center of both power and attention, he had to present himself as marginal, even alien. Arendt articulates Disraeli's insight—not, of course, in order to follow him into the seat of power but to understand the historical, political, and social conditions that made self-marginalization a viable and indeed highly successful strategy.[19] Instead of allowing marginal figures or phenomena simply to occupy a central position by virtue of hindsight, from the very beginning of her study Arendt emphasizes their marginality, as she seeks to make the movement from margin to center comprehensible—and comprehensible in all its outrageousness.

What drove the Jews away from the fringes and into "the storm center of events" (87) was a specific set of political forces, but the extremity of violence that came to define this storm was, according to Arendt, more the result of social than of political factors: "Social factors . . . changed the course that mere political antisemitism would have taken if left to itself, and which might have resulted in anti-Jewish legislation and even mass expulsion but hardly in wholesale extermination" (87). These social factors do not, however, simply reveal themselves to the observant investigator; indeed, they are "unaccounted for in political or economic history, hidden under the surface events, never perceived by the historian and recorded only by the more penetrating and passionate force of poets or novelists (men whom society had driven into the desperate solitude and loneliness of the *apologia pro vita sua*)" (87). Of all the social factors determining the violence that attended the movement of Jews from the fringes to the center of society, none is so decisive as the appearance of "the Jew" as a fantastic figure—attractive or repulsive or both at the same time—who was defined not by any relationship to Judaism but, instead, characterized by "certain psychological attributes and reactions, the sum total of which was supposed to constitute 'Jewishness'" (66). And of all the *apologiae pro vita sua*, none, according to Arendt, reveals more about the ultimate stakes of this transformation than Proust's *A la Recherche du temps perdu*.[20] For Proust, who was both a Jew and a homosexual, took upon himself the task not only of presenting a virtually exhaustive image of society but also of describing everything in social terms so as to make sense of, and thereby justify, his painful passage from complete immersion in society to complete withdrawal from all social intercourse.

Arendt's *Origins* is less a strategic narrative like Disraeli's *Sybil* in which the author solidifies the image of the Jew as a mysterious and even phantomlike alien, than an *apologia* akin to Proust's *A la Recherche* where the conditions and mechanisms by which this alien comes to occupy the center of attention—if not of power—are presented and analyzed with exacting rigor. Proust was "born on the fringe of society" (80); but the fringe, and indeed, the very society, into which he was born was decisively not the same as that in which, a century earlier, Rahel Varnhagen had established her famous salon. Although Rahel's salon, too, "was established on the fringe of society" (59), the relation of fringe to center had, by Proust's time, altered in such a way that marginal characters were no longer able to establish a social space by virtue of their "natural" or at least readily recognized differences from the politically dominant aristocracy and their educational differences from other "ordinary Jews" (65); instead, they were valued for the very extremity of their marginality. The "exception Jews" from whose midst Rahel Varnhagen emerged were first of all exceptions among the Jews, for they enjoyed certain social privileges that were denied to the Jewish people as a whole.[21] But this straightforward sense of exception, which could operate only within a political realm founded on the principle of privilege rather than right, developed into a significantly more complex designation at precisely the moment in which the idea of universal rights began to appear self-evident. Jews could still be exceptions, but no longer simply among Jews; they were additionally compelled to present themselves as—and here Arendt is thinking specifically about the decisive case of Heine[22]—"exceptional specimens of humanity" (58). The exceptional thus made the universal visible and lent it its amplitude; to guarantee this visibility of the universal, the exceptional had to be seen as exotic, alien, almost otherworldly. Thus did the eighteenth century's search for "new specimens of humanity" discover these "foreign" specimens "in their age-old neighbors" (57), who thenceforth were cast into the role of demonstrating the unity of humanity by being artificially, even dramatically other than their compatriots. None of this would have been of any significance, however, if Jews had not become precisely that: compatriots. With the emancipation of the Jews in France after the Revolution and then in Prussia after the Napoleonic conquest, the original idea of the "exception Jew" no longer made sense: "The dark poverty and backwardness against which 'exception Jews' of wealth and education had stood out so advantageously was no longer there" (60–61)—not because there was no longer poverty, but because wealth and education ceased to issue into social privileges and therefore "psychological self-respect" (61). But exceptionality did not then cease to characterize Jews. Under the social conditions that developed out of their political emancipation, the Jews as a whole, not individual "exception Jews," began to appear as exceptions: " 'Exception Jews' were once again [after political emancipation] simply Jews, not exceptions from but representatives of a despised people" (61). And once this contempt was revived for the Jewish people as a whole, it could then go so far as to revile each Jew as an exception from humanity as such.

"Proust describes at great length how society, constantly on the lookout for the strange, the exotic, the dangerous, finally identifies the refined with the monstrous and gets ready to admit monstrosities—real or fancied" (82). According to this ratio—the more exotic, the greater the force of attraction, the higher the degree of attractiveness—Jews could no longer enter society simply by being exceptional among Jews and thus assimilable in some fashion but instead had to go farther and cast themselves into the role of the "utterly alien" (83): Swann, therefore, who because of his immense wealth would have belonged to the class of "exception Jews" had he appeared in a novel written a hundred years earlier, is doubtless socially acceptable, but, as Arendt emphasizes, it is Bloch, the lower-class Jew with the recognizably Jewish name, whom society "more enthusiastically embrace[s]" (83). Whatever else Proust's "truthful record" (80) of society may accomplish, it grants access to an otherwise unrecorded phenomenon: the "exception Jews," who wanted at all costs to be considered legitimate exceptions—perhaps even *the* legitimate exceptions through which the universal could express itself—had to transform themselves into figures of "necromancy" (82) in which nothing was expressed other than their own illegitimate extremity: "'as if'"—Proust writes and Arendt quotes—"'they really were creatures evoked by the effort of a medium'"(82).[23] The principal feature of all those about whom one could entertain the thought that they might be exceptions from humanity is not only that they are barred from belonging to society—this is true of all lower orders—but also that they can never belong to any specific place on the globe. Like the abstract human being of the Declaration, the apparition of "the Jew" is an alien both created and discovered by social discrimination, a generalized type who can lay no claim to belonging to a particular place:

> Social discrimination, and not political antisemitism, discovered the phantom of "*the* Jew." The first author to make the distinction between the Jewish individual and the "Jew in general, the Jew everywhere and nowhere" was an obscure publicist who had, in 1802, written a biting satire on Jewish society and its hunger for education, the magic wand for social acceptance. (61)

Proust's *apologia pro vita sua* takes the form of a gigantic satire not, however, on Jewish society, but on post-emancipation bourgeois society as a whole, a society in which both "the Jew" and "the invert" play constitutive roles precisely because this society cannot consolidate itself without an intricate, and sometimes violent, process of "discrimination" in both senses of the term: making distinctions among individuals is not only implicated in excluding individuals of one reified type, the former process is grounded in the latter. And the only guarantee that a society has an innermost core—or, in Proust's terms, a "côté de Guermantes"—around which society as a whole can be organized is the existence of fixed types whose members are "vicious" by nature and therefore would be excluded as such from society if they were ever to display their "'innate disposition'" (84). The controversy surrounding Dreyfus, as it plays itself out in Proust's novel, provides the opportunity to fill out the empty category of "viciousness" as the designation of that type which, however close it approaches the central figures of society, like Madame de Guermantes, nevertheless remains excluded in principle: the vicious one is the traitor. But the traitor Jew is admitted, and indeed admitted into the very heart of the Faubourg Saint-Germain, to the consternation of certain non-Jewish and especially bourgeois members of society. As Arendt emphasizes, however, the admission of Jews to society does not indicate a revised attitude about the Jews—that they are no longer seen as among the vicious—but rather, it indicates a revised attitude toward vice.[24] The Jews whom Proust describes respond in turn by displaying themselves as though they *could* be members of society, while everyone who belongs to society understands from the beginning that, in fact, because of their ineradicable nature, they remain excluded even as they are included. Jews and homosexuals do not simply enter into society as visible representatives of the "vice" of Jewishness or homosexuality; rather, they undertake ever more convoluted performances of self-display combined with self-concealment, for it is only the shameful fact of their "Jewishness" or homosexuality—as if something like "Jewishness" were ever a fact, or homosexuality an "abnormality"—that makes them attractive in the first place: "The salons of the Faubourg Saint-Germain consisted of such an ensemble of cliques, each of which presented an extreme behavior pattern. The role of the inverts was to show their abnormality, of the Jews to represent black magic ('necromancy')" (85).[25] The "magic wand" of education used by the "exception Jews" becomes the "black magic" of Jewish self-obfuscation in whose darkness the political sphere disappears.

Social discrimination makes distinctions, but these distinctions are never those of *doxa* or points of view. Whereas *doxai* are distinguished from one another insofar as each one claims a perspective on a common world of diverse perspectives and therefore renounces in advance anything like a claim to being at, or even oriented toward, the center, social discrimination demands and produces a central point from whose enigmatic, even mystical presence the sphere of society radiates. The lack of diverse perspectives entailed by the structure of society has linguistic consequences, and these, too, make themselves apparent in Arendt's reading of Proust: instead of being speakers in the eminent sense—ones who are capable of statements that are meaningful to other speakers—the characters in *A la Recherche*, for all of their captivating loquacity, fail to speak; they manufacture and manipulate signs according to society's "silent demands" (84).[26] This is particularly true of the Jewish characters who invent a "mysterious sign-language" that is all the more mysterious because it does not communicate any knowledge: "Jews us[e] this sign-language only to create the expected atmosphere of mystery. Their signs mysteriously and ridiculously indicat[e] something universally known: that in the corner of the salon of the Princess So-and-So [sits] another Jew who [is] not allowed openly to admit his identity but who without this meaningless quality would never have been able to climb into that corner" (85). The "corner," for Arendt, names the central point of society, and it is accessible to an alien on the following conditions: the alien must be a product of "alienation" (84) from the community out of whose midst it emerged; it must also be drawn into extreme behavior patterns, which are nothing more than meaningless social hieroglyphs; and it must ultimately be made into an alien in the extreme—one who represents nothing but the dark background of mere life outside of the public sphere and arouses "dumb hatred, mistrust, and discrimination" (301). Social symbolism—of which sign language is an amusing, but, as both Arendt and Proust know, hardly innocent, version—can take a form in which the alien as such, in its very physicality, represents a vague, inarticulate, and unarticulated threat: "The 'alien' is a frightening symbol of the fact of difference as such, of individuality as such, and indicates those realms in which man cannot change and cannot act and in which, therefore, he has a distinct tendency to destroy. . . . [The alien] has become a specimen of an animal species called man" (301–02). This threat appears in Proust's world as the fringes of society are drawn into the center: it is the *frisson* that "virtue" draws from "vice."

III. Expansion—Decree

"The main point about the role of the Jews in this *fin-de-siècle* society," Arendt notes near the conclusion of her analysis of Proust, "is that it was the antisemitism of the Dreyfus Affair which opened society's doors to Jews, and that it was the end of the Affair, or rather the discovery of Dreyfus' innocence, that put an end to their social glory. In other words, no matter what the Jews thought of themselves or of Dreyfus, they could play the role society had assigned them only as long as the same society was convinced that they belonged to a race of traitors. When the traitor was discovered to be the rather stupid victim of an ordinary frame-up, and the innocence of the Jews was established, social interest in Jews subsided" (86). This description goes well beyond Proust's novel and even beyond *fin-de-siècle* France, for it touches on a constitutive feature of bourgeois society as a whole: it seeks to ally itself with lawless elements, not only with traitors to the state, but also with the mob. That this alliance with lawlessness is a constitutive feature of bourgeois society is one of the guiding insights of Arendt's analysis of imperialist expansion. Imperialism, for Arendt, is to be understood, not as it was by Lenin, as the highest and therefore the last stage of capitalism, but rather, as the "first stage in political rule of the bourgeoisie" (138)[27]—a bourgeoisie, moreover, whose rule is intimately and inevitably tied to the mob: "The society and the politicians of the Third Republic, its scandals and affairs, had created a new class of *déclassés*; they could not be expected to fight against their own product; on the contrary, they were to adopt the language and outlook of the mob" (109). Expansion would not be possible were it not for the inclusion of the excluded—this time not the Jews who inhabit the fringes of society, but the *déclassés*, who are expelled from all classes of society. But just as academic historians, according to Arendt, are unable to gain insight into the social character of anti-Semitism—and this motivates her turn to Proust—pessimistic historians like Burkhardt who lament the fall of western culture into mob rule are similarly unable to grasp the significance of the inclusion of those who are excluded in the fundamental operation of bourgeois society. And although it is only in passing, Arendt turns to a telling image from Goethe's *Wahlverwandtschaften* (Elective Affinities) to present a connection that eludes the conceptual grasp of philosophically trained historians of culture:

> [W]hat they [historical pessimists from Burkhardt to Spengler] failed to understand was that the mob is not only the refuse but also the by-product of bourgeois society, directly produced by it and therefore never quite separable from it. They fail for this reason to notice high society's constantly growing admiration for the underworld, which runs like a red thread through the nineteenth century, its continuous step-by-step retreat on all questions of morality, and its growing taste for the anarchical cynicism of its offspring. (155)

Ottilie's red thread, which, within the context of Goethe's *Elective Affinities*, serves as a sign of unlikely psychic continuity in a world that threatens to break apart,[28] becomes for Arendt the blood-soaked image of an illegitimate continuity—one that finds expression in the alliance of lawless elements with the arbiters of national legislation in a world that is discovering a principle of unification even as it undergoes a process of competitive and racist dissolution.[29]

For capital to expand beyond any given limit—and this, for Arendt as for Marx, is simply the internal law of capital—it cannot abide anything like a legal order (*das Recht* or *le droit*), because it is in the nature of any such order that it provides and is itself a limit. Capital, therefore, along with its agents, the bourgeoisie, cannot fail to ally itself with lawless elements in whatever guise they present themselves. The inclusion of the excluded—the incorporation of the *déclassés* into the class system—and thus the alliance of capital with lawlessness has as much right to be considered a fundamental law of capitalist development as the Marxist doctrine that the rate of exploitation increases as a result of technological innovation.[30] This, for Arendt, is the material basis for the specific coordination of the bourgeoisie as agents of capital and the mob as the "class" of society that has emancipated itself not only from law, but from class interest in the classical sense:[31]

> [T]he concept of unlimited expansion that alone can fulfill the hope for unlimited accumulation of capital, and brings about the aimless accumulation of power, makes the foundation of new political bodies . . . well-nigh impossible. In fact, its logical consequence is the destruction of all living communities, those of the conquered peoples as well as the people at home. For every political structure, new or old, left to itself develops stabilizing forces which stand in the way of constant transformation and expansion. (137–38)

Hope here is obviously not to be understood as a psychological category, but as something like an objective expression of the law of capitalist expansion, for how could any living being hope for the destruction of its community? Only anonymous forces could raise and maintain such hope.

Yet, for all Arendt's reliance on Marxist interpretations of imperialism (of the four major interpreters on whom she draws, only Hobson does not refer to himself as a Marxist[32]) Arendt does not adopt the decisive Marxist term *Mehrwert* ("surplus value") in her analysis of capitalism. Her reluctance to use this term cannot be traced to any allegiance to the kind of economic theorization that developed near the end of the nineteenth century and that, according to certain Marxists, should be understood as a manifestation of the ideological superstructure of capitalism in its imperialist stage. Arendt, in other words, does not seek to eliminate the classical political-economic ideas of wealth, "real price," or value and replace them, as Jevons, Menger, and Marshall did, with categories such as "marginal utility" and "exchange ratio."[33] Instead, Arendt takes over and transforms the thought to which the concept of *Mehrwert* owes its origin: the thought of *Mehrheit*, "moreness," or to use her term, "superfluousness." Classical political economy, unlike modern economics, can speak of superfluousness because it conceives of life, particularly political life, as essentially limited, and the nature of these limits sets the parameters of the discussion.[34] For Marx, who inherits the conceptual framework of classical political economy and who therefore derides those who propound Say's law,[35] the surplus of surplus value lies in the excess beyond what is needed to reproduce the original conditions of production: within a feudal mode of production, it presents itself in the form of *corvé*; within the capitalist mode of production, this excess presents itself in the form of value.[36] For Arendt, by contrast, who does not dream of the classless society,[37] the term *superfluousness* applies to whatever or whoever fails to fulfill a generally recognizable social function:

> Only the fortunate coincidence of the rise of a new class of property holders and the industrial revolution had made the bourgeoisie producers and stimulators of production. As long as it fulfilled this basic function in modern society, which is essentially a community of producers, its wealth had an important function for the nation as a whole. The owners of superfluous capital were the first section of the class to want profits without fulfilling some real social function—even if it was the function of an exploiting producer. (150)

In the late nineteenth century, bourgeois society, which always considered political institutions only from the perspective of private interest, begins to demand protection for its overseas investments and therefore completely alters its attitude toward state power: instead of being a hindrance to the exploitation of the working class, it becomes a necessary instrument in the process of undertaking a new and equally violent "primitive accumulation of capital."[38] Arendt combines two insights into the origin and structure of imperialist expansion: those of Hilferding and Luxemburg. For Luxemburg, the capitalist mode of production cannot exist without other modes of production from which it derives its sustaining impulse, and imperialism becomes necessary when the noncapitalist modes of production within a particular geographical space have been thoroughly eliminated: the "historical process of the accumulation of capital depends in all its aspects upon the existence of noncapitalist social strata," so that "imperialism is the political expression of the accumulation of capital in its competition for the possession of the remainders of the noncapitalistic world."[39] For Hilferding, imperialism is a stabilizing force insofar as it equalizes the national profit rate and serves as a cohesive national interest for a national body deeply divided by class: "Socially, expansion is a vital condition for the preservation of capitalist society."[40] An "elective affinity" therefore develops between superfluousness, whether of wealth or of human beings, and lawlessness, because whatever does not fulfill a social function—whatever exceeds, therefore, the limiting structures of a legal order—finds opportunities for itself in those places where recognizable and enforceable legal codes are diminished, suspended, or, better yet, unknown. And it is on those spaces that imperialism depends and into those spaces that both superfluous wealth and "superfluous working power" (150) are drawn. Superfluousness thus becomes the ironic law of lawlessness to the point where the individual as such is superfluous and replaceable at every moment by iron laws of progress. These laws express "forces of history" for which no one is responsible, and progress, therefore, can no longer be measured in terms of freedom:

> The eighteenth-century notion of progress . . . culminated in the emancipation of man. But this notion had little to do with the endless progress of bourgeois society, which not only did not want the liberty and autonomy of man, but was ready to sacrifice everything and everybody to supposedly superhuman laws of history. "What we call progress is [the] wind . . . [that] drives [the angel of history] irresistibly into the future to which he turns his back while the pile of ruins before him towers to the skies." (143)

In this last quotation from Benjamin, which Arendt takes from its original manuscript version, it seems remarkable that she leaves out the striking phrase, "a storm blows from paradise."[41] But her omission is well-considered since the only paradise she allows within the context of imperialism is the "paradise of parasites" (151), which defines the expanding space of imperialism: Eden, unlike imperialism's paradise, was limited, even more so after the Fall when *cherubim* and "the fiery ever-turning sword" (Gen. 3: 24) guarded the entrance; this new Eden of Arendt's analysis is so far from being limited that its owners enlist not *cherubim* but well-armed "superfluous men" to expand its limits.

Arendt understands that the "entirely new" and "central" political idea of imperialism—that expansion, which is distinct from conquest, should be understood as "a permanent and supreme aim of politics" (125)—demands an entirely new form of governance: a government of bureaucrats who shun the stability of laws for the flexibility of rule by decree. Whereas law includes a constitutive separation between principle and application—a separation that testifies to the need for judgment by someone in particular who is henceforth responsible for the application of the law—decrees exist only in their application, are without an identifiable source, and are therefore irresponsible: "Legally, government by bureaucracy is government by decree, and this means that power, which in constitutional government only enforces the law, becomes the direct source of all legislation. Decrees moreover remain anonymous (while laws can always be traced to specific men or assemblies) and therefore seem to flow from some over-all ruling power that needs no justification" (243). Imperialism, which originated in the realm of business speculation, together with the new bureaucracy that developed for its maintenance leave behind the imperatives of capital and subordinate them to the logic of a limitless expansion that is its own justification. So unconditioned is this new form of government that it is not even limited by the unbounded finitude of the globe and, as Arendt suggests throughout the "Imperialism" section of the *Origins* from its epigraph onward, the telos of imperialist expansion is space itself. Arendt quotes Rhodes, who gives voice to the limitlessness of expansionist ambitions: "'I would annex the planets if I could'" (124). Rhodes, who as Arendt points out "'felt himself a god—nothing less'" (215), seeks to expand into outer space not to exploit the potential resources of a Venus or a Mars—successful expansion is its own inherent justification—but to find a perspective beyond all perspectives: the perspective, in other words, that was traditionally reserved for a deity, an angel, or even a philosopher. Contemplation is always oriented toward a grasping and naming of the whole; so, too, the nonperspectival program of imperialist expansion. Being as such, what Aristotle calls *to on*, lies in expansion or, to use Rhodes's words as he articulates imperialism's moving principle, "Expansion is everything" (124). It was not, however, the extravagantly vain Rhodes but rather the "overmodest" (214) Lord Cromer—recognized by Arendt as the "first imperialist administrator" (211)—who inadvertently, and even unconsciously, discovered the rationale for the godlike perspective from which imperialist expansion originates and to which it aspires: gods do not obey laws. And so, Lord Cromer not only eschewed all laws but also went so far as to eliminate all written traces of his decrees: "Thus does the bureaucrat shun every general law, handling each situation separately by decree, because a law's inherent stability threatens to establish a permanent community in which nobody could possibly be a god because all have to obey a law" (216). Every situation under conditions of expansion is exceptional, and according to the Kierkegaardian logic of exceptionality, the exception gives way to a universal. But here, the universal is precisely not a man-made law under whose protection everyone can live but is the universe itself. The unlimited space of imperialist expansion expresses itself, therefore, in decrees from above: secularized miracles, which suspend general laws, and secret signs, which can be understood only by those who have abandoned themselves in "magic identification . . . with the forces of history" (216).

IV. Depth—"Humbug"

Whatever and whoever does not obey laws is exceptional, and the exception can be understood as that which is capable of, or indeed calls out for, "romanticization." For Arendt, who takes her point of departure from Carl Schmitt's *Politische Romantik*,[42] romanticism is a mode of conceptualizing the relation of the exceptional to the universal such that the exceptional never gives way to the universal. In turn, everything can be made—in thought, in poetry, but of course not in reality—into an exception. Such universal exceptionalism—being exceptional for its own sake—can be summarized in the imperative that Novalis articulates in a fragment of 1798 and that Arendt quotes to introduce her discussion of the romantic figure of the genius: "The world must be romanticized to bestow a high sense upon the common, a mysterious appearance upon the ordinary, the dignity of the unknown upon the well-known."[43] The purpose of such romanticizing or, to coin a term, exceptionalizing, is to remove things and individuals from the sphere of law—the laws of nature in the case of things and juridical principles in the case of people. Romanticism, then, does not so much register an attraction to lawlessness, although bourgeois society sought to romanticize itself by embracing criminality in the form of vice, as make lawlessness in all its forms the central point around which everything in the world of culture ironically gravitates. And nothing is more attractive than the unstable multiplicity of points called "personality." The lawlessness of personality, which stands in the starkest opposition to "the juridical person," makes personality into the object of worship. Arendt's investigation into the "personality-worship" (168) and "genius idolatry" (332) of romanticism serves as an introduction to her analysis of racism because the constitutive indeterminacy of personality removes it, and everyone who stakes a claim on this unstable ground, from the world of appearances. Personality is an initial movement from the visible world of determinate spaces and points of view into the chthonic depths of interiority and "pseudomystical nonsense" (226).

For the early German romantics, the process of romanticization was still tied, however tenuously, to opinion. In their revolt against philosophy in its classical form—the last, and highly ambiguous representatives of which were Kant and Fichte[44]—opinion was rescued from its subservient position with respect to philosophical knowledge and valued for its flexibility and motility: opinions, unlike knowledge, change, and change, for the early romantics, was good for its own sake. Opinions, however, were not then understood in terms of perspectives or points of view; they were spontaneously, and therefore ironically, manufactured according to a process of ever-increasing romanticization:

> The ruthless individualism of romanticism never meant anything more serious than that "everybody is free to create for himself his own ideology." . . . Because of this inherent "relativism" the direct contribution of romanticism to the development of race-thinking can almost be neglected. In the anarchic game whose rules entitle everybody at any given time to at least one personal and arbitrary opinion, it is almost a matter of course that every conceivable opinion should be formulated and duly printed. (168)

For a later generation of German romantics who rallied around the Prussian struggle against Napoleon—Arendt discusses Clemens von Brentano in particular[45]—personality was no longer, as it was for Novalis and the young Friedrich Schlegel, a potentially endless multiplicity of profiles; it was, rather, something "innate" (169) and therefore as unchangeable as opinions for the early romantics were changeable. And the idea of "innate personality," in turn, conjured up images of nobility, which could then be utilized to distinguish two basic and eternally opposed types of human beings: the superior and the base. The consequences of this development within romanticism—the replacement of the juridical person by unstable "personality" and the reification of personality in "innateness"—were

considerable: in the "secret conflict" (230) that characterizes the relationship between state and nation from the French Revolution onward, the
romantic disposition was not only to favor the nation over the state but
also to take the idea of the nation along the same path that the concept
of personality had already trod—into quasireligious depths that express
themselves in cloudy sentiments. If the dominant image of lawlessness
for the early romantics was the child in all its unadulterated "freshness,"[46]
the dominant image of that which is beyond the law for the later romantics—and all those who inherited their attitudes and figures of speech—
was the soul:

> The practical outcome of this contradiction [between the Rights of Man and
> the state on one hand and national sovereignty and the nation as a whole on
> the other] was that . . . human rights were protected and enforced only as na-
> tional rights and that the very institution of the state . . . lost its legal, rational
> appearance and could be interpreted by the romantics as the nebulous repre-
> sentative of a "national soul" which through the very fact of its existence was
> supposed to be beyond or above the law. National sovereignty, accordingly,
> lost its original connotation of freedom of the people and was being sur-
> rounded by the pseudomystical aura of lawless arbitrariness. (230–31)

Romanticism is not responsible for racism, but it gives race-thinking an
expressive form of its own—or, more exactly, a parody of religious forms
of expression. Just as overseas imperialism produces a "paradise of parasites," the expansionist tendencies on the continent, which find their organizing principle in the tribal nationalism of the pan-movements, produce a parasitical language of paradise. Like any talk of paradise, this
parodic language includes the attendant possibility of a fall, and falling
takes place whenever individuals loosen their contact with the supposed
source of their being: "The individual, therefore has his divine value only
as long as he belongs to the people singled out for divine origin. He for-
feits this whenever he decides to change his nationality, in which case he
severs all bonds through which he was endowed with divine origin and
falls, as it were, into metaphysical homelessness" (234). The paradise of the
continental pan-movements is that of the "national soul" whose redemption, already prophesied, is the work of the future: "In contrast to overseas
imperialism, which was content with relative superiority, a national mis-
sion, or a white man's burden, the pan-movements started with an absolute claim to chosenness. Nationalism has been frequently described as

an emotional surrogate of religion, but only the tribalism of the pan-movements offered a new religious theory and a new concept of holiness" (233). Of course there is nothing new in the idea of "chosenness": but whereas for the Jews election wants nothing to do with "the heretical immanence of the Divine" (242), such immanence is the point of departure and the decisive conclusion for everything involving the "national soul." And whereas, according to the Hebrew Bible, the dominant idea of prophecy is that of a wrathful god who chastises his people for its failures, the new religious theory that develops in the context of continental imperialism promotes a version of prophecy that consists in forecasting the triumph of the "exalted inner qualities" (227) of a national essence, irrespective of historical achievements or institutional phenomena. Prophecy, then, gives expression to a "Slavic, or Germanic, or God-knows-what soul" (232). And metaphysical homelessness—which was rooted in the "territorial uprootedness" (236) of the people who were attracted to the quasireligiosity of the pan-movements—becomes not only the state of those who fall out of the pan-movements' paradise of the soul but the defining feature of the pan-movements themselves. These movements never directed their efforts at emancipation of a determinate political space but instead sought once and for all, as if in an apocalyptic finale, to unite a dispersed and chosen people by conquering large parts of the earth.

The independence of the "national soul" from visible institutions and the phenomenal world in its entirety invites pseudomystical utterances that are no longer recognizable opinions but tend more and more toward inarticulate outpourings of suffering and exalted images of resplendent glory: "The whole texture of life and world assume a mysterious secrecy and depth. There is a dangerous charm to this aura because of its seemingly inexhaustible richness; interpretation of suffering has a much larger range than that of action for the former goes on in the inwardness of the soul" (245). What Kant playfully satirized in *The Dreams of a Spirit-Seer, Illustrated by the Dreams of Metaphysics*—the independence of "spirit" from phenomenal instantiation[47]—is anything but playful in the context of romantic exceptionalism as it sets the stage for racial tribalism. In the middle of Kant's short but not inconsequential polemic against Swedenborgian mysticism he quotes Heraclitus's dictum, "when we are awake, we have a common world, but when we dream, everybody has his own."[48] Racism, rooted in the territorial and metaphysical rootlessness of the soul and independent of all visible institutions or occurrences, does not leave everyone to his or her own dreams but instead makes each individual into an epiphenomenon—even a dream—of "the mythical, unidentifiable Man" (234).

The pan-movements, as particularly extreme manifestations of the "secret conflict between state and nation," had no use for the rule of law—or indeed, even for the idea of lawfulness: the holy is by definition beyond the law even if it institutes it. But the institution of the law on the basis of the holy is not an experience of the pan-movements; without the apparatus of constitutional government and without the geographical separation between home and abroad that characterizes overseas imperialism, continental imperialism is characterized by "open disregard for law and legal institutions and ideological justification of lawlessness" (243); its leadership has no time for "legal niceties" (244), and for all the differences between continental and overseas imperialism or between the British idea of government service and the Slavic idea of "holy Russia" on one decisive point they converge: the rule of law must be replaced with rule by decree. But it is only where bureaucratic rule by decree is acknowledged as the legitimate form of government, as in Russia and Austria, rather than despised as the imported intrusion of a colonial force, that it can "create the atmosphere of arbitrariness and secretiveness which effectively hid[es] its mere expediency" (244). Instead of the interpretation of law, which has its limit at the point of application; instead, therefore, of the intermediary stages of political reasoning and forensic argument that separate the rule of law from its application, the issuance of a decree—which exists only in its application as the "brutal naked event itself" (244) and which presents itself as a secular miracle enacted from above—generates a limitless field of interpretation. Freed from the rational interpretation of any concrete document, the range of interpretive speculation about an event—and every event is undergone in suffering rather than initiated by action—is limitless. With limitlessness, moreover, comes secrecy, for the truth of the event is hidden, and with hiddenness comes profundity or, as Arendt writes, "the 'depths' of suffering" (245).

The romanticization of suffering, according to Arendt, characterizes the literary attitude of all Russian prerevolutionary literature. Suffering is particularly susceptible to romanticization when it is the result of unseen, unforeseeable, arbitrary, and therefore "fated" events: the less lawlike the event, the more its exceptionality gives the impression of being the way of the world rather than an ironic whim of the author. Russian literature in the context of the *Origins* is romanticism without irony, and it is all the more attractive to those who have scorned the idea of law because its profundity is supposedly rooted in the mysteriousness of ineluctable fiat or fate: "In an unending stream of literary variations the Pan-Slavs opposed the profundity and violence of Russia to the superficial banality of the West, which did not know suffering or the meaning of sacrifice, and behind whose sterile, civilized surface were hidden frivolity and triteness" (246). Whereas early German romanticism still kept a place open for an ever-changing multiplicity of opinions, the romanticization of suffering promulgated by the pan-movements endlessly repeats the same indecipherable scene. Instead of manufacturing opinions, therefore, the "depth" of quasireligious suffering finds its form of expression in what Arendt calls "profound humbug" (245), which, as an extreme version of nonsense, does not rise to the level of a point of view but remains immersed in the opacity of its own interiority.

Humbug is the expression of any government bureaucracy invested with the power to rule. Its decrees are immediate—without any intervening forensic argument—and an aura of magical acts surrounds their immediacy, opening onto a space of endless, entirely futile, and indecipherable interpretation: "And it is this pseudomysticism that is the stamp of bureaucracy when it becomes a form of government" (245). No one, according to Arendt, was better able to demonstrate the link between pseudomysticism and bureaucracy than Kafka—not as one who indulged in the enchantment of suffering, or as one inspired by the "profound humbug" of Austrian bureaucracy, but rather as one who parodied the parody of religion that characterizes the imagery and discourse of the pan-movements and thus "became the humorist and critic of the whole matter" (245). When Arendt approaches the conclusion of her discussion of the quasireligiosity of bureaucracy, her tendency toward ventriloquism reappears as she once again assumes the language of her subject: for Arendt, however, it is not the decree that is miraculous; it is rather Kafka's ironically failed achievement.[49] Kafka did not mirror reality, nor did he invent an altogether different world. According to Arendt, he did not so much prophesy the transformation of imperialism into totalitarianism as see, without claiming to be a seer, that the latter was embedded in the former:

> He exposed the pride in necessity as such, even the necessity of evil, and the nauseating conceit which identifies evil and misfortune with destiny. The miracle is only that he could do this in a world in which the main elements of this

atmosphere were not fully articulated; he trusted his great powers of imagination to draw all the necessary conclusions and, as it were, to complete what reality had somehow neglected to bring into full focus. (246)

In the world of *Das Schloß* (The Castle), which, as Arendt writes in a footnote, "reads like a weird travesty of a piece of Russian literature" (246),
only K., as a foreigner to the village, is unaccustomed to rule by decree.
As a land surveyor, he is concerned with nothing so much as limits. And
when a particularly odious decree is enacted—when Amalia is given an
obscene note by Sortini[50]—only K. worries over its content: "In K.'s view,
'it's unjust and monstrous, but [he is] the only one in the village of that
opinion'" (246)—or indeed of any opinion for that matter. Instead of
opining, the villagers *belong*, and this belonging includes the "opinion"
that someone like Amalia, who makes gestures of not belonging, is in the
wrong. Yet for all his exceptionality, K. is precisely not a romantic figure:
he is a miracle within the context of extreme exceptionalism insofar as he
can still speak of and form opinions about injustice and monstrosity, each
of which implies in its own way an idea of law.

V. Layers—Lying

The villagers in *Das Schloß* do not belong to their village; the village,
rather, belongs to the castle, and so, too, do the villagers themselves. This
condition, for Arendt, corresponds to that of Austrian bureaucracy in
which imperial power had little to do with the specifics of any locality. But
the relationship Kafka presents between the village and the castle also
points to another, more general, and more troubling condition—not that
of belonging to a place from which one could take a stand and thus develop and articulate an opinion but, instead, the condition of belonging
to an abstraction, a "castle," whose "positions" one adopts and expresses
in general and as a matter of course. Expressions of "opinion" become
functions of loyalty, and the test, indeed the truth, of loyalty is found in
the steadfastness of one's position. Within a context whose parameters are
defined by loyalty's demand for constancy, opinions cannot fail to appear
fleeting, fickle, and, therefore, treacherous. Whereas romanticism values
opinions because of their mutability, loyalty, or loyalism, dismisses opinions for precisely the same reason. But there is nevertheless a continuity
between these two apparently opposing assessments of opinion: in both
cases the relative stability of opinion is rejected and even derided in favor

of something absolute and unassailable. For early romanticism, the exceptionality of genius is something like a universal premise from which follows a potentially endless proliferation of perspectives; for race-thinking, the election of the race is the incontrovertible presupposition on whose basis pseudomystical humbug is generated; for "total loyalty" (323)—the idea of faithfulness taken to its extreme—the absolute is contained in its very formulation.

Since total loyalty necessarily determines the "opinions" of the faithful, these opinions are once again completely mutable: they change according to the vicissitudes of the one genius who has insight into the historical process. If the underlying attitude of the pan-movements could be understood as romanticism without irony, this is all the more true of total loyalty, because any trace of irony would imply a reversible perspective from which the one who commands loyalty could be viewed. As Arendt writes, Goebbels was entirely "sincere" in his "conviction that 'the greatest happiness that a contemporary can experience today' is either to be a genius or to serve one" (332). As the demand for loyalty intensifies, the space of opinion contracts. Total loyalty depends on and contributes to the destruction of those spaces in which diverse perspectives could appear:

> [It] can be expected only from the completely isolated human being who, without any other social ties to family, friends, comrades, or even mere acquaintances, derives his sense of having a place in the world only from his belonging to a movement, his membership in the party. Total loyalty is possible only when fidelity is emptied of all concrete content, from which changes of mind might naturally arise. (323–24)

The only home of the uprooted and isolated individuals who, for Arendt, constitute the masses is a despatialized one: the temporal progression of history. Suffering from the vicissitudes of accident, which, however, have lost any of the mystical aura associated with romantic exceptionalism, the masses are susceptible to the propaganda of totalitarian movements. This propaganda, Arendt emphasizes, not only answers to the condition of homelessness but also exploits precisely the same characteristic of the human mind that, according to Kant, gives rise to the dreams of metaphysics and leads into "the ocean of illusion"[51]—conceptual and imaginative consistency without regard for the world of appearances:

> Totalitarian propaganda thrives on this escape from reality into fiction, from coincidence into consistency. . . . In other words, while it is true that the

masses are obsessed by a desire to escape from reality because in their essential homelessness they can no longer bear its accidental, incomprehensible aspects, it is also true that their longing for fiction has some connection with those capacities of the human mind whose structural consistency is superior to mere occurrence. (352)

The "fiction" of totalitarian propaganda, for Arendt, has precisely the same character as the "transcendental illusions" that, according to Kant, are generated whenever reason allows its systematizing function to operate without concern for possible experience: both the fictions of propaganda and the illusions of metaphysics are objective, and both establish independent worlds "fit to compete with the real one" (362). What Kant identifies as "the dire need" for metaphysics[52] appears for the modern masses as the longing for a home: "Totalitarian movements conjure up a lying world of consistency which is more adequate to the needs of the human mind than reality itself; in which, through sheer imagination, uprooted masses can feel at home and are spared the never-ending shocks which real life and real experiences deal to human beings and their expectations" (353).

Whereas the illusions of metaphysics collapse like a house of cards upon critique, the fictitious world of totalitarian propaganda leaves no place for critique and instead exploits the emptiness of the future by making it into the decisive sphere for all possible experience. In other words, totalitarian propaganda expresses itself in the language of scientific prophecy: its scientific character appears to depend on the distinction between truth and falsity, which, however, its prophetic character then denies. No one who hears the predictions of totalitarian propaganda will be alive to verify their fulfillment. The prophetic language of propaganda thus acquires the convoluted status of redoubled humbug: in replacing the space of opinion with the empty and indeterminate sphere of the future, propaganda precludes the possibility of all opinions—including the opinion that any prophetic pronouncement is merely auratic or pseudomystical humbug. The disregard, distrust, and outright contempt for the visible world of experience means that only the genius, by virtue of his incontrovertible exceptionality, can interpret the universal laws of historical progress.

> To the propaganda assertion that all happenings are scientifically predictable according to the laws of nature or economics, totalitarian organization adds the position of one man who has monopolized this knowledge and whose principal quality is that "he was always right and will always be right." . . .

The leader is always right in his actions and since these are planned for centuries to come, the ultimate test of what he does has been removed beyond the experience of his contemporaries. (383)

If the purpose of lying has always been understood in terms of deception, then there is something new about the lies of totalitarian propaganda—so much so that the term *lying* can be misleading, as if propaganda's function were to change opinions in an underhanded manner. The lie of a Jewish world conspiracy has been promulgated for centuries, and the Dreyfus Affair, along with the publication of the "Protocols of the Elders of Zion," gave new life and a decided virulence to anti-Semitic propaganda around the turn of the century.[53] But the Nazis divested this lie of any association with opinion and made it into an immutable axiom: "Nazi propaganda was ingenious enough to transform antisemitism into a principle of self-definition, and thus to eliminate it from the fluctuations of mere opinion" (356). In this way, predictions about the future came to serve as "retrospective alibi[s]" (349) for the immediate establishment of the fictitious world—a *Volksgemeinschaft*—in which the masses find a home. The purpose, therefore, of totalitarian lies cannot be sought in their putative subject matter, removed as they are from the sphere of competing opinions. Instead of promoting ideological content—and this is what, for Arendt, makes the lies of totalitarian propaganda completely unprecedented and takes them out of the range of traditional discourses on "the right to lie"[54]—they foster organizational forms: "The true goal of totalitarian propaganda is not persuasion but organization" (361).

Lying issues into layering, and layering supports lying. Arendt emphasizes that the creation of front organizations and the multiplication of offices generates a spatial configuration that is sharply distinguished from the stable vertical ranking of traditional authoritarian rule: the onion. With this striking image, she captures the layered character of totalitarian organization, which serves the dual function of fooling the outside world about the character of the totalitarian movement and the movement about the character of the outside world:

> The front organization functions both ways: as the façade of the totalitarian movement to the nontotalitarian world, and as the façade of this world to the inner hierarchy of the movement. Even more striking than this relationship is the fact that it is repeated on different levels within the movement itself. As party members are related to and separated from the fellow-travelers, so are

the elite formations of the movement related to and separated from ordinary members. (367)

Whereas romanticism promotes an endless proliferation of opinions, which results in the dissolution of opinion, totalitarian organization creates ever-new layers within its own peculiar hierarchy, which serves to destroy any notion of generally recognizable rank. The pattern of layering by which this "onion-like structure" (413)[55] is produced has the advantage over traditional principles of rank in that "it can be repeated indefinitely and keeps the organization in a state of fluidity which permits it constantly to insert new layers" (368). Totalitarian organization "create[s] a perfect world of appearances in which every reality in the nontotalitarian world [is] slavishly duplicated in the form of humbug" (371). The lying language of totalitarian propaganda, translated into reality in the form of organizational layers, does not, however, appear as humbug in the eyes of a population capable of developing and articulating opinions but constitutes its own self-enclosing world of illusion—a world of immanent humbug.

VI. Movement—"Murderous Alphabet"

The state of fluidity is a constitutive feature of totalitarian rule. But, as the phrase "state of fluidity" itself indicates, there is something paradoxical, even contradictory, about totalitarianism as it develops from a movement, like that of the pan-movements, into a form of domination. What was a conflict between state and nation in the contexts of both bourgeois imperial expansion and the continental pan-movements becomes a conflict with both state and nation, for they both limit the mobility of the movement: "The danger to the movement lay in the fact that, on one hand, it might become 'ossified' by taking over the state machine and frozen into a form of absolute government, and that, on the other hand, its freedom of movement might be limited by the borders of the territory in which it came to power" (389). Power itself exposes totalitarianism to a dangerous paradox, because, according to Arendt's concise formulation, "power means a direct confrontation with reality" (392), yet the fictitious world of totalitarian organization is essential to its very existence. The paradoxes of a Heraclitean flux cast into the form of a state that exists by virtue of its systematic avoidance of that which makes power possible, do not, however, give rise to an ironic or otherwise self-reflective "logic" of inconsistency in which paradoxes would be welcome; on the contrary, and paradoxically, the paradoxes of totalitarianism in power solidify a demand for unassailable logical consistency, which Arendt compares to arithmetical operations. About such operations, there can be absolutely no opinions, and the mental movements of deductive reasoning—which can be endlessly accelerated but which can never demonstrate the slightest spontaneity—come to replace not only self-generating movement and the space in which such movement could take place but also the corresponding motility and spontaneity of opinion.

The motility of totalitarian movement destroys the idea of law insofar as law is understood to mark a limit—first of all as a demarcation of the space in which human beings act and then as a limitation on the spontaneity of human beings as they relate to one another within such spaces. As long as the law is understood in terms of limits, it establishes a fundamental distinction between those "within the law" and those "beyond its pale." This distinction, without which western political thought would be bereft of its subject matter and every hitherto-known form of government would be unable to function, is no longer valid for totalitarian rule; more exactly, as Arendt writes, totalitarian government "explode[s] the very alternative on which all definitions of the essence of governments have been based" (461). Totalitarian rule can do this since it neither subjects itself to positive law nor does it dissolve into the anarchy of lawlessness; instead, it releases the function of law from all human spontaneity or action within a common world and submits itself to the law of movement, above all, the movement of history:

> It is the monstrous, yet seemingly unanswerable claim of totalitarian rule that, far from being "lawless," it goes to the sources of authority from which positive laws received their ultimate legitimation, that far from being arbitrary it is more obedient to those suprahuman forces than any government ever was before, and that far from wielding its power in the interest of one man, it is quite prepared to sacrifice everybody's vital immediate interests to the execution of what it assumes to be the law of History. (461)

Law is thus effectively despatialized and cast into purely temporal terms. And if, as Kant writes, time is nothing other than the mere form of *inner* intuition, everything that legitimizes itself by appeals to temporal progress can be only indifferent, if not hostile, to the stable and discrete spaces defined by positive law—spaces that are, as Arendt emphasizes in her discussion of the perplexities of the Rights of Man, the necessary ground of human spontaneity.

All of the *Origins* turns on this momentous, and terrifying, reversal: law, which originally served as a limit on the mobility of human beings in their plurality, becomes the very principle of movement, and the freedom of movement, which, according to Arendt, is "the one essential prerequisite of all freedom" (466), can no longer be ascribed to human beings but only to totalitarian movement itself. This reversal has a vertiginous quality, for it is a reversal in which space disappears into time. Arendt hears what is at stake in the word *movement*, which is not simply totalitarian jargon but strikes at the core of what had been hitherto assumed about human beings: that there is something "essential" about their "nature." The extremity of totalitarian motility—"which stands or falls with . . . [its] true central institution" (438), the concentration and extermination camps—has its own perverse revelatory power: It makes apparent that there is nothing universally human, "that human beings can be transformed into specimens of the human animal, and that man's 'nature' is only 'human' insofar as it opens up the possibility of becoming something highly unnatural, that is, a man" (455).

Just as the contempt of totalitarian movements for positive law does not mean that they embrace something like anarchism, neither does their reduction of human beings into specimens of an animal species make them into representatives of what Nietzsche calls nihilism.[56] For totalitarian movements destroy even the space in which nihilism finds its uncanny home: the desert. Without mentioning his name, Arendt refers to Nietzsche's most famous pronouncement not only about nihilism but also about the movement of history that issues into contemporary European reality: "Die Wüste wächst [the desert grows]".[57] For Arendt, the desert does not grow—on the contrary: in the same gesture with which totalitarian movement undermines the discrete spaces posited by "positive" law, it also destroys the lawless and anarchic space of the desert, which because of its lawlessness has always also been the place of spiritual renewal. The desert, too, is swept into movement and is therefore no longer even a place for those who have left or been cast out of the world defined by "the fences of laws" (466): "It seems as if a way had been found to set the desert itself in motion, to let loose a sand storm that could cover all parts of the inhabited earth" (478). This sand storm is the image of despatialization, because, as the desert ground is swept up from under, there are no longer any discernible dimensions, any points of orientation, or any visibility— and yet, there is none of the negative potential that comes with poetic blindness either.

For totalitarian movement to keep itself in motion, it must evacuate every independent "emotion" and arrest every spontaneous turn of thought. The evacuation of emotion is terror. When Arendt uses this word, it can no longer be understood along the lines of those *pathei* that Aristotle or Quintilian analyze in the course of describing the relationship between public discourse and political action.[58] For terror is nothing less than the absorption of all emotion into the single motion of totalitarian movement: "Terror is the realization of the law of movement" (465). Terror is so little a matter of persuasion within a public forum that Arendt even identifies it as that which precludes the possibility of raising one's voice—or even speaking with "the single voice of one unexchangeable person" (476). It substitutes for the "channels of communication" a "band of iron" that so destroys the spaces between individuals it is as though they were absorbed into "One Man of gigantic dimensions" (465–66). Just as terror destroys relationships among individuals, ideology destroys the relationship to reality by making every stable phenomenon into a matter of movement. Isolation, which concerns only the disappearance of political space, becomes loneliness when the common sphere of the human artifice likewise disappears into the vortex of perpetual motion. And with the loss of any world held in common, the individual loses even the reality of a self: "For the confirmation of my identity I depend entirely upon other people" (476).

With this total evacuation of self and world, the only remaining function of the human mind is the empty progression of logicality. This function can scarcely be considered a matter of language as long as language is understood to be composed of statements made within a field of common sense and articulated by individuals who draw on an open lexicon in which rules not only facilitate usage but also prepare a place for innovation. Totalitarian despatialization expresses itself therefore in a destroyed and destructive language—in the nonlanguage, or even antilanguage, for which Arendt invents the chilling phrase "murderous alphabet": "You can't say A without saying B and C and so on, down to the end of the murderous alphabet" (472). This alphabet corresponds exactly to the paradoxical and yet utterly unironic contradiction of totalitarian rule: its ordering is both entirely arbitrary and rigorously lawful. Nothing could be further from language in the eminent sense.

VII. Abyss—Anxiety

Totalitarianism is opposed to "common sense" in every sense of the term: not only the utilitarian principles under which the term "common sense" is generally interpreted but also the commonality of sense that, according to Arendt, is the basis of all our senses and without which each of us would remain locked in the privacy of unreliable sensation. This opposition runs deeper than that of nihilism, because the desert of nihilism, as a space of individual freedom and anarchic initiative, can even be considered the most commonsensical place of all: "What runs counter to common sense is not the nihilistic principle that 'everything is permitted,' which was already contained in the nineteenth-century utilitarian conception of common sense. What common sense and 'normal people' refuse to believe is that everything is possible" (440–41). These last words, which are drawn from Rousset's *Univers concentrationnaire* and serve as the epigraph to the "Totalitarianism" section of the *Origins*,[59] indicate the depths of totalitarian movement's opposition to common sense. Arendt tries to capture this depth of opposition in the image of the abyss: an abyss separates us from the central institutions of totalitarianism, namely the concentration and extermination camps, but it does not separate us from totalitarianism as such. There is nothing profound about this abyss, and it does not serve as a natural buffer or a line of demarcation with which we could separate ourselves from totalitarianism, because totalitarianism—and this is the anxiety—has not been eradicated such that we could gaze over the site of its downfall and, in a sublime gesture, marvel at our own capacity to withstand the sight of a threatening chasm: "Totalitarian solutions may well survive the fall of totalitarian regimes in the form of strong temptations which will come up whenever it seems impossible to alleviate political, social, or economic misery in a manner worthy of man" (459). Yet the abyss—and this inverts its image—nevertheless serves as a partition: it is a barrier to communication.

The abyss cuts two ways, and in both cases it threatens to swallow up the capacity for speech.

On the one hand, those who survive the camps bear the "abyss of the 'possible'" (437) within themselves. Where everything is possible, the "preparation of living corpses" (447) can proceed through the murder first of the juridical, then of the moral, and finally, of the individual subject, who is henceforth fabricated into the limitless and shapeless subject-matter of a monstrous experiment conducted on specimens. Arendt seeks to capture this terrifying condition with reference to Lazarus, who, although declared not to have a "sickness unto death," nevertheless did die and was resurrected: "The reduction of a man to a bundle of reactions separates him as radically as mental disease from everything within him that is personality or character. When, like Lazarus, he rises from the dead, he finds his personality or character unchanged, just as he had left it" (441). Lazarus told no one, not even the inspired writer of the Gospel of John, what he experienced in the abyss between death and life, and Arendt suggests that he could not have spoken to anyone, not even himself, about this "terrifying abyss" (441), for the desperation of this condition is "outside the realm of human speech" (446). And the very fact that Arendt is compelled to draw on the analogy with Lazarus indicates the extent to which the horrors of the camps defy straightforward reportage, even as they demand it all the more desperately. Therefore, the tradition of the *figura*—in which the image of Lazarus participates and from which the ideas of the abyss departs[60]—remains in effect even as the realities they try to express make the appeal to this tradition deeply dubious.

On the other hand, and as a direct consequence, historical memory, too, is traversed by an abyss. The Nazi experiment in the possible sought not only to exterminate human beings but also to eliminate all traces of their ever having existed—and to deposit them into ever-widening "holes of oblivion" (459). The "organized oblivion" (452) around which, as Arendt repeatedly emphasizes, totalitarian movement is itself organized can under no condition be alleviated or overcome by fostering a spirit of free and open exchange, even among those who survive the worst. Such exchanges, Arendt writes, "can communicate no more than nihilistic banalities" (442)—which amount to the pessimistic sigh that "everything is permitted." That everything is *possible*, by contrast, paradoxically makes the project of historical memory impossible. And this is the anxiety out of which the *Origins* originates.

～

Anxiety belongs neither to the register of hope nor to that of hopelessness. Like terror, anxiety is associated with speechlessness. But anxiety is precisely not terror; its speechlessness responds to totalitarianism's "murderous alphabet." Anxiety is responsive to this destroyed and destructive "language" inasmuch as it does not react to the defeat of Nazi Germany in a mood of self-confident elation, as if totalitarianism were put behind us for good, nor does it react to the appearance of totalitarianism in the center of Europe during the twentieth century in a mood of resigned melancholia, as if the destiny of humanity had finally made itself known. As Arendt writes in her "Preface to the First Edition" of the *Origins*, "This book has been written against the background of both reckless optimism and reckless despair. It holds that Progress and Doom are two sides of the same medal; that both are articles of superstition, not of faith" (vii).[61] Throughout the many changes that the *Origins* underwent,[62] Arendt preserves the original preface "in order to indicate the mood of those years" (xxiv), and thus to indicate that, for better or worse, moods may change. This mutability of moods is nowhere better expressed than in her very slight, but telling, transformation of the phrase with which Tacitus prefaced his *Annals of Imperial Rome*: "With the defeat of Nazi Germany, part of the story had come to an end. This seemed . . . the first chance to try to tell and to understand what had happened, not yet *sine ira et studio*, still in grief and sorrow and, hence, with a tendency to lament, but no longer in speechless outrage and impotent horror" (xxiii). *No longer* in speechlessness and *not yet* "without anger and partiality"[63]—the implication of the slight qualification of Tacitus is that a time may come, or that we may already live in such a time, when the terror of totalitarianism would not elicit either rage or partisanship, when, in other words, this terror would be understood as nothing more than another outbreak of the kind of tyrannical mayhem that Tacitus describes. Anxiety is located between the "no longer" and "not yet," between being struck dumb by the "murderous alphabet" and subduing both anger and partisanship in a gesture of "liberal rationalizations" (440); that is, it persists in lamentation. It is no accident that Arendt responds to totalitarianism's "murderous alphabet" with an allusion to *Lamentations*, which is ordered as an acrostic according to the letters of the Hebrew aleph-bet.

In anxiety, the inadequacy of language is recognized, and the recognition that language can approach, but never measure, the "abyss of the 'possible'"—that the horrors of the camps "can never be fully reported" (444)—further intensifies anxiety. This intensification is itself constitutive of anxiety, because anxiety is tempted to speak and make sense of terror in order that common sense not be destroyed or severely damaged after all;[64] yet this "temptation" to speak is the source of further anxiety, since, as Arendt writes, one cannot explain "the intrinsically incredible" (439) without explaining it away—and thus contributing to the erasure of the concentration and extermination camps. One cannot retrieve the specificity of that which the victims of totalitarian experimentation "experienced" in the camps, because the reduction of these people to "bundles of reactions" destroyed experience, too. But the inability to give *some* account of these camps would also be a triumph for the forces of terror, for the organization of totalitarianism around these central institutions assigns entire peoples to "the holes of oblivion." To speak is thus a temptation that results in erasure, but the refusal of the temptation also leads to a form of oblivion that would contribute to totalitarianism's triumph. Hence—and this is the bitterest of Arendt's paradoxes and the ultimate source of anxiety—totalitarianism cannot lose even when it loses.[65]

§ 2 "Time Tormented"

Auden's "Age of Anxiety"

I. Order and Odors: "Prologue"

In Auden's *Age of Anxiety: A Baroque Eclogue*, anxiety takes place away from, yet in relation to, the theater of war. Written between July 1944 and November 1946, the poem returns to the space in which Auden set his earliest and perhaps most famous treatment of the Second World War "September 1, 1939": the bar scene. The latter poem—among the most consequential of the twentieth century—cannot be found in the *Collected Poems*, which contains, as its editor notes, "all those poems that W. H. Auden wished to preserve."[1] For, over a long period, Auden altered, excised, and finally rejected "September 1" as "the most dishonest poem" he had ever written.[2] *The Age of Anxiety* can be understood as one of the places in which Auden engaged some of the difficulties of "September 1" and came to realize not so much the dishonesty of a particular poem as what is at stake for a poem, even one that culminates in the memorable lines "our world in stupor lies," to resist the dishonesty of a world that lies in stupor. Drunk people in a bar provide the poet with a foil with which to relate stupefaction to lying. Whatever "honesty" may mean in Auden's dismissal of "September 1"—and his own explanations are less than fully satisfactory[3]—it does not mean either pathos-ridden sincerity or mimetic accuracy. And whatever finally motivated his decision to excise it from his collected works, he felt sufficiently compelled by the bar scene in which "September 1" takes place to make it into the setting for his last major long poem.[4]

The Age of Anxiety distinguishes itself from "September 1" in at least three ways: First, it is not written in the rhythms and lexicon of the American vernacular but, rather, in highly contrived and unquestionably artificial verse-forms based on Anglo-Saxon epic poetry with heavy employment of words and meanings that cannot be found in any standard American dictionary;[5] second, although both titles make reference to temporality, *The Age of Anxiety* cannot be identified with any moment in calendar time; finally, the poem does not center on a lyric "I" but, instead, distributes its voice among four distinct characters whose discourse is punctuated by the vapid interjections of a radio and the not altogether trustworthy comments of an anonymous narrator.[6] Each of these distinctions reflects a series of strange temporal contortions. Perhaps the most subtle dimension of this distortion in *The Age of Anxiety* results from the poet's departure from the lyric "I": the narration varies between present and past tense—"EMBLE says" or "EMBLE said," for example—and this variation, which is not correlated to shifts from experience to memory, cannot be comprehended in terms of the self-transformation of an ego as it reflects on itself.[7] This oscillation between past and present verb tenses, moreover, is reproduced in one of the most obvious and puzzling features of *The Age of Anxiety*: Auden's resurrection of the Anglo-Saxon line for a poem about four characters in mid-twentieth century New York—as if the beauty and brutality of *Beowulf* had returned to haunt a modern city. As one of its more disquieting dimensions, *The Age of Anxiety*, completed in 1946 and published in 1947, suggests that the war has not come to an end, or less dramatically, that its conclusion has not altered in any fundamental manner the character of the age. A less subtle poet might thus have set the poem immediately after the war to suggest that, despite the triumph for the Allied side, the world is still beset by anxiety—emphasizing that the hostilities of the war have ceased, but the underlying tensions nevertheless remain unresolved. Something of this suggestion can be heard in the vast outpouring of books on existentialism that appeared in English between 1947 and 1948.[8] Despite their atmosphere of despair, primers on existentialism exhibit a triumphal spirit: the darkness of these visions is the expression of disappointment, which is itself the consequence of outsized hopes regarding the prospect of victory. *The Age of Anxiety*, by contrast, is utterly nontriumphal. The odd—almost Brechtian[9]—tone of the narrating voice is a measure of this nontriumphalism: it reassures anxious bar owners that they need never "worry" (449), since there is no possibility that failure and loneliness, which are the conditions under which the bar business succeeds, will ever be overcome. By setting *The Age of Anxiety* not after but during the course of the war, Auden indicates that war somehow inhabits anxiety. The characters reflect on the war from a distance of thousands of miles; the poem is completed in reflection on the war from a momentous historical distance, and the terror of the war in reflection determines the basic shape of *The Age of Anxiety*—and, the poem suggests, any age of anxiety.

One further distinction between "September 1" and *The Age of Anxiety* should be emphasized: whereas it is perhaps all too easy to understand the force of the former, the latter is an almost intractably difficult poem. Not least of its difficulties derives from the fact that the repetitive Anglo-Saxon-inspired line makes the various characters of this "Baroque Eclogue" sound alike, as if the poet wished to obliterate individuality in a quest for poetic virtuosity. Complaints to this effect have been voiced ever since the poem was first published. Yet there is no doubt that the poem is deeply concerned with the plurality of individual perspectives: the section entitled "The Seven Ages," which immediately follows the "Prologue," seeks to capture—from four very different perspectives—the genesis and structure of the individual; the following section, "The Seven Stages," explores in reverse the enigmatic process of de-individuation; and the poem as a whole stages an eclogue in which the characters cannot or will not play out their traditional parts. Any attempt to grasp the poem requires, therefore, a poetics that is rich enough to encompass this apparent contradiction between the uniformity of the poetic line and the development, and envelopment, of a plurality of perspectives in the course of the poem. One such poetics is Hölderlin's, the epitome of which can be found in an ode that Auden repeatedly quotes, "Sokrates und Alcibiades." What is at stake in this short poem is not only the attraction between opposites— wisdom in the shape of Socrates, beauty in that of Alcibiades—but also the dynamic character of the poetic process as such: the thematic opposition between wisdom and beauty corresponds to the poetological opposition between the "basic mood" (*Grundstimmung*) of a poem and its "art character" (*Kunstkarakter*).[10] And the course of the poem, according to Hölderlin's enormously complicated theory of "tonal modulation" (*Wechsel der Töne*) is the dialectical dissolution of this opposition—a dissolution, however, that does not result in an identity of opposing elements. To quote Auden's rendition of the last line of "Sokrates und Alcibiades," which appears in his "Letter to Lord Byron" (1937): "Und es neigen die

weisen zu schönem sich [And the wise incline toward the beautiful],"
which is *not* to say—indeed, it is to deny—that either the wise become
beautiful or the beautiful wise.

Some of the more intractable features of *The Age of Anxiety* can be understood in light of Hölderlin's theory of poetic composition. Few poems
exhibit a more powerful contradiction between their "art character" and
their "basic mood." In *The Age of Anxiety* the former, which Hölderlin
also calls the "appearance" (*Erscheinung*) of a poem, is uniformity; the latter, which corresponds to the poem's "meaning" or "significance" (*Bedeu-
tung*), is plurality. A comparison with *The Waste Land* is in this regard illuminating: whereas the fragmentary form of Eliot's poem is identical to
its principal theme, the invariant form of Auden's is antithetical to its basic mood. According to Hölderlin, a poem should not have the same "appearance" as its meaning; otherwise, it cannot properly convey its meaning—or, as he says, it cannot be "feelable" (*fühlbar*). The initial opposition
between art character and basic mood makes the progressive emergence of
the latter recognizable *as* the meaning of the poem in contrast to its immediately perceptible form. The uniformity of the poetic line in *The Age
of Anxiety* prevents its readers from immediately perceiving the individuality of its characters, and the plurality of perspectives is recognizable
because of this uniformity—recognizable as a dynamic, unpredictable
plurality that positively rejects any standardization, formalization, or automation. And this contrast between the appearance and meaning of *The
Age of Anxiety* develops in at least three other dimensions of the poem as
well. Just as the antiquity of the verse form contrasts with the modernity
of the setting, so does the insistent formality of the meter and its require-
ment that each line have three alliterations oppose the unformalizability
of its events: certain characters assume the task of directing the others, but
in every case this task goes awry. And in the poem as a whole, which is
supposed to be an eclogue, no consummation takes place. In the word
baroque one can hear *broke*, and *The Age of Anxiety*, by pushing the opposition between uniformity of appearance and plurality of meaning to the
extreme, presents itself as a broken eclogue—fragmented not despite but
in light of the unbroken uniformity of the poetic line.

Although the monotonous character of the poetic line tends to obscure
the differences among the poem's four principal characters, they are, nevertheless, initially distinguished through the prose description of the narrating voice. Emble, a sailor in the Navy, is a dropout from a Midwestern

university; Quant, a clerk in a shipping office, is an immigrant from Ireland who was forced out as a child by a violent, class confrontation; Malin, a Medical Intelligence officer, is on leave from the Canadian Air Force; and Rosetta, a department-store buyer, may be American but dwells in her imagination on the English countryside and, in her final meditation, reveals herself to be a Jew who understands her condition as that of exile.[11] Questions about Rosetta's nationality—is she American or English after all?—echo some of the questions that swirled around Auden at the time he was writing *The Age of Anxiety*.[12] And the displacement of all four characters resonates with Auden's peripatetic movements from the time he graduated from Oxford until he settled, for a time, and in his own way, in New York. In the period from 1928 to 1939, Auden traveled in Germany, Scotland, Belgium, Switzerland, Czechoslovakia, Denmark, Portugal, Iceland, Spain, France, Egypt, Hong Kong, China, and various places in the United States.[13] And during the two-and-a-half years he spent writing *The Age of Anxiety* Auden lived on 52nd Street in New York, taught at Swarthmore, joined the United States Strategic Bombing Survey—during which time he traveled all over Germany—took up residence on Jane Street in New York, moved to 57th Street, stayed on Fire Island, taught at Bennington for a semester, and returned to New York, this time to an apartment on Cornelia Street. The narrating voice of *The Age of Anxiety* emphasizes, however, that the condition of displacement cannot simply be assessed by an objective record of movement; displacement, rather, is a function of time. And "war-time"—which itself cannot be simply assessed by seemingly objective criteria such as peace treaties, victorious armies, or conquered peoples—is defined as the era "when everybody is reduced to the anxious status of a shady character or a displaced person" (449).

The specific spatiality of the bar is predicated on its categorical distinction from an outside world. In peacetime, the bar is distinguished as a space for the private play of the intoxicated imagination; in wartime, however, the ability of the bar to separate itself from the rest of the world as an "unprejudiced" (449) and therefore artificially neutral space gains a qualitatively new function—even if that separation is only an imaginary one: "In comparison to the universal disorder of the world outside," the barroom becomes a place of relative order and "seems as cosy and respectable as a suburban villa" (449). The appearance of order in the bar exists in inverse relation to the turmoil of "the world outside." And as the war intensifies, the relative order of the bar seems to acquire the absolute order of a utopia: a world redeemed not only from loss but the possibility of loss and, thus, from chance and contingency. Just as the four characters are attracted to the bar as a place of refuge, *The Age of Anxiety* as a whole gravitates toward utopias, as places—or nonplaces—where the god of chance is deposed, and "universal disorder" gives way to systematic order. As these utopias are projected into both past and future, the temporal contortions that characterize the formal aspects of *The Age of Anxiety* gain a new dimension: nonanxious ages—radically different pasts and radically different futures—haunt every moment in the age of anxiety. And in the first use of the term *utopia* in the poem, this sense of haunting is both explicit and acute:

> . . . for the ego is a dream
> Till a neighbor's need by name create it;
> Man has no mean; his mirrors distort;
> His greenest arcadias have ghosts too;
> His utopias tempt to eternal youth
> Or self-slaughter. (452)

Malin's opening monologue, which moves from the stability of nature to the restless daring of human beings, thus concludes with two different kinds of dreams: that of the solitary ego and that of an ordered and ageless world. The first responds to the opening verse of the poem in which Quant reflects on his own image in the mirror and discovers its distortion: "that land of glass / Where song is a grimace" (451); the second, to the disastrous disorder of the world at war. The impossibility of the ego independently transforming itself into reality makes the utopian landscape dubious. "Man has no mean" for Malin, because a mean would stabilize human beings in such a manner that the ego would no longer need another individual—a specific neighbor—to be itself.[14] An image in the mirror distorts to the extent that no mirror image can confer that name without which the ego remains, as it is, a mere pronoun: an *ego*. And the stability of a utopia cannot be dissociated from the destruction of the being who is without a mean, namely the self. Thus, the "or" in the final lines—"His utopias tempt to eternal youth / Or self-slaughter"—designates more an amplification (*sive*) than an alternative (*vel*). Of this intricate reflection on selfhood and utopia, Malin articulates only a residue in his later sarcastic proposal of possible topics for conversation among the four in the bar:

> Here we sit
> Our bodies bound to these bar-room lights,
> The night's odors, the noise of the El on
> Third Avenue, but our thoughts are free . . .
> Where shall they wander? To the wild past
> When, beaten back, banished to their cirques
> The horse-shoe glaciers curled up and died,
> And cold-blooded through conifers slouched
> Fumbling amphibians; forward into
> Tidy utopias of eternal spring,
> Vitamins, villas, visas for dogs
> And art for all; or up and down through
> Those hidden worlds of alien sizes
> Which lenses elicit? (462–63)

This speech recalls the famous opening lines of "September 1": "I sit in one of the dives / On Fifty-Second Street."[15] But the recollection is even stronger than a repetition of situation, and even of opening verbs, for it seems as though Malin directly responds to the lyric "I" of "September 1." The opening stanza of the earlier poem closes: "The unmentionable odour of death / Offends the September night." And Malin, accordingly, does not mention death when he, too, speaks of "the night's odors." Under Malin's direction, *The Age of Anxiety* might have reproduced the general movement of "September 1," in which a lyric "I" appears to diagnose the historical situation *in situ* and in the order of his own choosing. But the interjection of the narrating voice reminds us that the only choices in a bar are among "physiological aids to the imagination" (449) and that Malin's talk of "free" thoughts is predicated on these meaningless choices: the ellipsis after the word *free* is long enough to contain the remainder of "September 1" as it moves from "exiled Thucydides" to "mad Nijinsky." And this omission, in turn, reveals the emptiness of the conceit of "September 1" according to which a lyric "I" could diagnose present ills with reference to world history and thereby suggest a—dishonest—cure: "We must love one another or die."[16]

Unlike the lyric "I" of "September 1," Malin is not given univocal authority to direct the action of the poem, and he immediately encounters objections to his initial proposal. Quant, who, according to the narrating voice, has acquired some familiarity with mythology, wants nothing to do with the investigations of science ("Those hidden worlds of alien sizes /

Which lenses elicit"); Emble, whose youthfulness is consumed by "anxiety about himself and his future" (451), balks at images from times so re-
mote as the Ice Age ("the wild past"); and Rosetta, whose daydreams tend
toward nostalgic images of an idyllic childhood, declines to discuss Malin's vision of the future ("tidy utopias"). But Rosetta's rejection cannot
simply be understood as a feature of her nostalgic character, for she has already been assaulted by an image of utopia that resonates with Malin's
own description of "vitamins, villas, and visas for dogs"—but with far
greater attention to the menacing quality of this antiseptic future. Malin
intuits the connection between the "night's odors" and a utopian future
that is so under the dominance of a will-to-order that it must control even
creatures identified with a keen sense of smell ("visas for dogs"). This
utopia leaves no room for the anarchy of sensation and welcomes the slogan "art for all" presumably because art is understood to be nothing but
the ordering of sensation. Whereas Malin is merely sarcastic when he
speaks of the well-ordered world of the future, Rosetta dwells on its
threatening character:

> Four who are famous confer in a *schloss*
> At night on nations. They are not equal:
> Three stand thoughtful on a thick carpet
> Awaiting the Fourth who wills they shall
> . . .
> Lord of this life. He looks natural,
> He smiles well, he smells of the future,
> Odorless ages, an ordered world
> Of planned pleasures and passport-control,
> Sentry-go, sedatives, soft drinks and
> Managed money, a moral planet
> Tamed by terror: his telegram sets
> Grey masses moving as the mud dries. (458)

Rosetta's speech does more than present an imaginary version of a meeting among four "famous" characters, one of whom, as the undisputed
leader, has the power to mobilize armies; it comments on the setting of
the poem and contains in miniature an entire aesthetics.[17] Although
Rosetta begins her interior monologue with no reference to the scene in
which she finds herself and moves in her imagination to an imaginary
home—"I see in my mind a besieged island / That island in arms where

my home once was" (457)—her concluding thoughts develop out of the material of her concrete situation. The four in the *Schloß* replicate the four in the bar; the coziness of the former, with its "thick carpet," dovetails with the comfort of the latter, which, as a "suburban villa," protects its inhabitants at the very least from the chaos and grit of the urban world. By superimposing the scene in the *Schloß* onto the otherwise unrelated bar scene, Rosetta makes the definitive connection between order and odor: the four in the *Schloß* may, like those in the bar, be seeking to escape some generalized social or political anomie, but this escape takes the form of planning a sanitized world, which results in the eruption of a global war. The imperative to impose universal order, which is meant to do away with odors, generates the "universal disorder"—and the "odour of death"—from which the four in the bar are seeking escape. The will to absolute order, figured as "odorless ages," is thus the paradoxical source of the odor of a disastrous disorder.[18]

The images Rosetta conjures are not identical with the world from which they are drawn; the relation is, instead, analogical. The famous four are not blended into the customers in the bar, as if all characters were fundamentally the same—only circumstances different. On the contrary, the differences between the two sets of four characters becomes apparent by virtue of the unlikely analogy: the "suburban villa" into which Emble, Quant, Malin, and Rosetta retreat is even more sharply distinguished from the *Schloß* within which plans for attack are advanced. Rosetta's speech thus spells out the terms of an aesthetic resistance to the pretense of mimetic accuracy. The uncanny phrase "He looks natural" is at the core of this aesthetics. The unnaturalness, indeed, the artificiality, of the analogy between the four in the castle and the four in the bar, runs counter to the program of naturalization that animates and gives direction to the dangerous utopianism that seeks to eradicate in reality the disorder of uncontrollable odors. Such eradication—if this is the right word—should be reserved for the realm of art. By saying that "he looks natural" and thus making clear that he is not, Rosetta opens up a space of aesthetic resistance to the reduction of human beings to an undifferentiated natural kind and the identification of the artificial images that characterize ordered artworks with the disorder of reality.

Not only does the "lord of this life" look natural, he also "smells of the future." This formulation would seem to be paradoxical insofar as "the future" cannot generally be understood to emit a smell, and its paradoxical character becomes even more emphatic, since, as Rosetta proceeds to say, the future is "odorless." The smell of the future can therefore only be perceived as the absence of smell. Rosetta's reflections on the war—her nightmare world of an odorless future—are, like the thoughts of the other three characters, stimulated by the report on the radio in which a catalog of horrors commands their attention:

> *Now the news. Night raids on*
> *Five cities. Fires started.*
> *Pressures applied by pincer movement*
> *In threatening thrust.* . . . (454)

It is no accident that "grey masses" are set into movement by the telegraphic and therefore styleless speech of an odorless leader. And it may be that the radio's similarly staccato announcements are no less tendentious: like the telegram imagined by Rosetta, the radio's speech comes from afar, is unidirectional insofar as it allows for no exchange of views, and pretends to do without rhetoric. Whereas the radio news seeks to be purely descriptive, however, a telegram that mobilizes armies is purely prescriptive. But such pure descriptions and prescriptions are nevertheless embedded in a wider context where they become indistinguishable from one another. For the telegram, this context is defined by totalitarian propaganda in which "grey masses," and not simply armies, are made into the matter of a movement; for the radio news, it is defined by "democratic" advertising. And the advertising on the radio, like the "ordered world" of Rosetta's vision, promises an odorless world:

> *Definitely different. Has that democratic*
> *Extra elegance. Easy to clean.*
> *Will gladden grand-dad and your girl friend.*
> *Lasts a lifetime. Leaves no odor.*
> *American made. A modern product.* . . . (462)

Odorless ages are not simply the distant goal of totalitarian organization as it uses the instruments of terror to desensitize the world; the absence of smell is itself a primary goal propagated over the very same instrument that incites Rosetta's reflections on the horrors of this absence. The anxiety of *The Age of Anxiety* thus consists in the immanence of the distant horrors of the war, present as the product's odorlessness, in the familiar worries associated with the characters in the bar. Although Rosetta similarly introduces the horrors of war into her surroundings by figuring the four at the bar as the four in the *Schloß*, she never loses sight of the figural dimension of this superimposition. The radio, by contrast, implicitly claims to communicate an undistorted representation of reality. Rosetta and the radio thus map out two radically opposing versions of the relationship between image and reality: whereas Rosetta understands the relation as analogical, the radio assumes it to be identical. And *The Age of Anxiety* as a whole works out the stakes of this opposition.

II. Propaganda and Paradise: Toward Auden's Poetology

When the radio first breaks into the bar scene, the narrating voice indicates the degree to which the radio's implicit claim to undistorted representation is compromised, presenting its report as an "official doctored message" (454). As the term *doctor* suggests, the message is as much a prescription as a description. This confusion of prescription and description is then intensified in the advertisements that follow the news, deliver "tidings of great joy" (462), as the narrating voice says, and thus replace the message of messianic evangelism for which it makes no sense to distinguish prescription and description. And the relation to evangelism is even closer insofar as the word of advertising, like that of the Gospels, has the magical power to create the reality of which it speaks. In prescribing remedies to anxiety, especially those concerned with cleanliness, advertisements produce the very anxiety they purport to cure. This paradoxical linguistic process guarantees a certain infallibility of advertising even if each of the products it prescribes is rejected, for advertising is still able to create the anxiety it describes. As the narrating voice indicates when it introduces Malin's speech about "the night's odors," all the characters in the bar are consumed by anxiety whenever they hear the "noise" of the radio, and the explicit "object" of this anxiety is the advertising itself: "Matter and manner set their teeth on edge" (462). The theory of advertising contains in reverse the theory of poetry, for poetry, according to Auden, is the opposite of advertising—not in the sense that the two are opposed to each other as negative and positive but because poetry is precisely not what advertising is: magic. Such is the import of Auden's dictum: "Poetry is not magic. In so far as poetry, or any other of the arts, can be said to have an ulterior purpose, it is, by telling the truth, to disenchant and disintoxicate."[19]

Advertising, by contrast, is a species of what Auden calls "black magic." The point of such magic, as Auden explains in "Words and the Word,"[20] is to use enchantment for the purposes of domination. Advertising over the radio is particularly conducive to such enchantment inasmuch as it "does not ask for a free response to [its] spell; [it] demands a tautological echo"[21]: anxiety resonates with descriptions of remedies for anxious conditions. Whatever else the radio's promotional messages may accomplish in *The Age of Anxiety*, they exemplify Auden's theory of propaganda:

> In all ages the technique of the black magician has been essentially the same. In all spells the words are deprived of their meanings and reduced to syllables or verbal noises. This may be done literally, as when magicians used to recite the Lord's Prayer backwards, or by reiterating a word over and over again as loudly as possible until it has become a mere sound. For millions of people today words like communism, capitalism, imperialism, peace, freedom, democracy have ceased to be words, the meaning of which can be inquired into and discussed, and have become right or wrong noises to which the response is as involuntary as a knee reflex.[22]

Thus the first product advertised is described according to the incongruous combination of "democracy" and "elegance": "*Has that democratic / Extra elegance.*" Even if a case can be made that democracy and elegance are consonant terms, there is no place for the adjudication of such questions in the nonreciprocal framework of a radio broadcast. In this way, there is an unexpected continuity not so much between the advertisements and the news about the war as between the advertisements and the war itself: "Propaganda, like the sword, attempts to eliminate consent or dissent, and in our age magical language has to a great extent replaced the sword."[23] In "Words and the Word" Auden acknowledges the relative innocuousness of advertising as a form of propaganda:

> Most commercial advertising . . . is comparatively harmless. If advertising conditions me to buy a certain brand of toilet soap, provided that the law prevents the sale of a substance that poisons my skin or leaves me dirtier than I was before, it makes no difference to my body or my soul which brand I use. Political and religious propaganda are another matter, for politics and religion are spheres in which personal choice is essential.[24]

In *The Age of Anxiety*, however, matters are far less clear, since the cleanliness promised by an anonymous and indeed unnamed product that *"leaves no odor"* is closely associated with "odorless ages" and "tidy utopias"—both of which are inseparable from totalitarian telegrams on the one hand and the threat of "self-slaughter" on the other. Within the economy of *The Age of Anxiety*, the elimination of smells is not so different from the elimination of all spheres in which consent, dissent, opinions, and choices are possible.

The general rejection of the "manner" in which the advertisements are broadcast is easily comprehensible within the terms of the narrating voice's description of the language of the radio: "banal noises" (454) that proceed "blandly" and "inexorably" (462). The reasons for rejecting the "matter" of the broadcast, however, are not so easily comprehensible, especially in the cases of Rosetta and Malin. Indeed Malin is so irritated by the radio that he proposes that the four in the bar replace its "noises" with their own voices. For Malin, who, as a medical intelligence officer, is in fact an official doctor strangely parallels the task of the radio news to deliver an "official doctored message"; he likewise holds a position equivalent to that of the unnamed product of the radio advertisement: just as he serves the military in his capacity as a scientist, the product *"serves through science"* (462). And insofar as Malin is drawn toward "laboratories and lecture halls" (450), he cannot be understood to reject out of hand the promise of order and odorlessness contained in the advertisements. Similarly, Rosetta, who most acutely recognizes the menacing connection between order and odor, is anything but a partisan of disorder; her job consists in ordering goods for a department store, and her nostalgic daydreams concerning the English landscape with its "meadowlands / And sedentary orchards" (453) is motivated by an aversion to the messiness of her adopted home: "Yes, America was the best place on earth to come to if you had to earn your living, but did it have to be so big and empty and noisy and messy?" (450). Even if she might then have little sympathy with appeals to such attributes as *"American made"* and even less for slogans like *"A modern product,"* the same is certainly not true of other attributes and slogans, especially *"Easy to clean"* and *"Leaves no odor."* Malin and Rosetta both long for and recoil from images of tidiness and messages of "good tiding." Both characters are in this sense caught in an unresolvable dilemma: They cannot simply embrace the "green arcadias" to which they are drawn by their attraction to well-ordered spaces; nor, in reverse, can they welcome the disorder, chaos, and sheer messiness that, as they both recognize, generate and are generated by the will to make reality into a "tidy utopia." Poetry, for the Auden of *The Age of Anxiety*, consists in the disruption of this dilemma.

At the end of a complicated, almost algebraic meditation on the idea of order that Auden published just a few years after the publication of *The Age of Anxiety*, he comes to the following conclusion: "Every poem, therefore, is an attempt to present an analogy to that paradisal state in which Freedom and Law, System and Order are united in harmony. Again, an analogy not an imitation. . . . Every beautiful poem presents an analogy to the forgiveness of sins, an analogy, not an imitation."[25] The distinction between analogy, which operates on a principle of proportion, and imitation, which operates on the principle of identity, stands at the basis of *The Age of Anxiety* and of Auden's poetry and poetology as a whole. For this reason, Auden is repeatedly drawn into reflection on images of reflection—most notably in *The Sea and the Mirror* but also in other poems and prose works, both early and late, where images of the mirror, Narcissus, and the self-reflective ego propel Auden's texts in the direction of the structure of a *mise-en-abîme*. The centrality of this concern in *The Age of Anxiety* is evident from the speed with which it is introduced: the narrating voice presents the first of the four characters as one who catches "his reflection in the mirror" (449), and in his opening soliloquy, Quant wonders about the world his mirror image inhabits. The same concern expresses itself in, among other early parts of the poem, Malin's reflections on the distortions of the mirrors of "man" and Rosetta's superimposition of the four in the *Schloß* onto the four in the bar. Each of these reflections on reflection revolves around the distinction between analogy and identity. One of the conspicuous reasons for this distinction is spelled out in the final paragraph of "Nature, History and Poetry":

> The effect of beauty, therefore, is good to the degree that, through its analogies, the goodness of created existence, the historical fall into unfreedom and disorder, and the possibility of regaining paradise through repentance and forgiveness are recognized. Its effect is evil to the degree that beauty is taken, not as analogous to but identical with goodness, so that the artist regards himself or is regarded by others as God, the pleasure of beauty taken for the joy of Paradise, and the conclusion drawn that, since all is well in the work of art, all is well in history. But all is not well there.[26]

The poem thus finds itself in a precarious position: it must sustain the possibility of "paradise" as a real—and not, to use Auden's term, "chimerical"—possibility and yet must not pursue or play into projects in which this possibility is supposed to be realized. Within the context of "Nature, History, and Poetry," Auden defines *paradise* as "a perfect order" in which *order* is understood as the realization of "a community in a social system."[27] Whereas a "social system" is defined as a set of elements whose "self-love" is subordinated to the self-love of the set taken as a whole, a community is understood as a set of elements whose membership in the set lasts only as long as all elements share "a common love for something other than themselves."[28] The perfection of order takes place under the condition that the system or, as Auden also calls it, the "society" in which a community is embodied has no other function than the embodiment of this community. To the terms *community* and *system* or *society*, Auden adds *crowd* to designate a set without any principle of order; as these terms indicate, Auden's theoretical reflections concurrently cover both the interconnectivity of poetic elements and the relationality among human beings. Just as a set of human beings is "ordered" to the extent that it has overcome the tendency of the crowd toward chaos and at the same time has transformed the principle of self-preservation, which characterizes society, into one of love for something other than itself, so too are the elements of a poem:

> The transformation of a crowd of feelings into a community is effected by translating the former into words that embody the latter. The poem itself is a linguistic society or verbal system. . . . It is not possible to say of a poem that it is true or false for one does not have to go anywhere except itself to discover whether or not it is in fact an order, a community of feelings truly embodied in a verbal society.[29]

The point of developing a theory of human relationality and poetic interconnectivity alongside each other is the opposite of what it might appear, for Auden seeks in this manner to demonstrate the ineluctable distinction between the two: order among poetic elements is not identical with order among members of human society. And yet, Auden's complicated algebraic formulations seek to ensure that "the linguistic society" of the poem not be relegated to an aesthetic realm utterly unrelated to human society—as if the purpose of poetry were to produce entirely self-contained and self-referential artifacts. Auden's theoretical reflections around the time of *The Age of Anxiety* thus exhibit a paradoxical feature that corresponds to the precarious position to which they assign the poetic text: at the same time as these reflections seek to demonstrate that there is a *categorical* distinction between the order of poetry and that of human beings, they nevertheless make no *categorial* distinction between the two kinds of sets; both are described according to the same categories, even as the distinction between them admits of no exceptions, however great the poetic achievement may be.

The fundamental, although by no means sufficient, condition for any poetic accomplishment is the translation of a "crowd of feelings" into a "community of feeling." This translation cannot take place without a "love" that each of the members share. Such a love in the case of a poem is the underlying feeling in which the community of feelings subsists. In "Nature, History and Poetry," Auden does not elaborate on the character of this love nor does he try to name it, but in the revised version of this essay, which he includes in *The Dyer's Hand* under the provocative title "The Virgin & The Dynamo," he proceeds further: "The subject matter of a poem is comprised of a crowd of recollected occasions of feeling, among which the most important are recollections of encounters with sacred beings or events."[30] This revision responds to a series of reflections Auden undertakes in the previous essay in the collection, "Making, Knowing and Judging."[31] Without attempting anything like the algebraic exactitude of "Nature, History and Poetry" and indeed with an insistence on the "private" nature of his reflections—"Herewith, then, what I might describe as a literary dogmatic psalm, a kind of private *Quicunque vult*"[32]—Auden specifies the underlying love, emotion, or "impulse" through which a community of otherwise disordered feelings comes into being:

> The impulse to create a work of art is felt when, in certain persons, the passive awe provoked by sacred beings or events is transformed into a desire to express that awe in a rite of worship or homage, and to be fit homage, this rite must be beautiful. This rite has no magical or idolatrous intention; nothing is expected in return. . . . In poetry, the rite is verbal; it pays homage by naming.[33]

The feeling of awe, which includes a multitude of *pathei*—"from joyous wonder to panic dread"[34]—is passive to the extent that it cannot be generated by an autonomous subject but only by a sacred object, the encounter with which cannot be anticipated. But this object is itself not a possible subject of articulate discourse. The poetic "rite" is exhausted in "naming" and does not proceed to predication precisely because, as Auden suggests in "Nature, History and Poetry," there is "no sacred language" in which sacred objects would find adequate expression—no numinous words in which the presence of these objects could be contained. Poetry can bear witness to a sacred being only insofar as its language remains "indirect and negative,"[35] and indirection is thus a categorical imperative for the construction of any poetic "linguistic system."[36] Not sacred objects themselves, but only the awe they elicit is left for the poet to order into a community of feeling embodied in a community of words.

Analogy is the term by which Auden seeks to capture the referential character of the poetic text: a poem is an analogy to paradise, but this analogical relationship inheres in the ordered relation of words, not in anything these words represent. The order of the words is like the perfect order of paradise insofar as both orders reach beyond a system whose self-love is all-embracing and self-contained. To the extent that a community of recollected feelings is aptly embodied in a linguistic system, a poem is an order analogous to that of paradise. Thus, without ever being in a position to specify the means by which paradise may be regained, poetry nevertheless keeps open this sheer possibility. In *The Age of Anxiety*, the act of recollecting feelings and the possibility of regaining paradise converge in the project of resurrecting an archaic poetic form: the alliterative measure of the four-stress line characteristic of Anglo-Saxon epic poetry. *The Age of Anxiety* is distinguished from the latter insofar as it almost always alliterates on the stressed syllables of any word and thus makes stress into an additional principle of construction.[37] By organizing the alliterations around the stresses, the poem gains an added formal dimension; and by further ordering the stresses themselves according to the placement of the caesura separating the first half-line from the second, each line becomes a demanding complex of formal organization. Since alliteration depends on the association of words based on the accident of shared consonants, the additional constraints placed on each line of the poem intensifies the tendency of alliterative lines to produce improbable combinations, impenetrable utterances, and sound-patterns that verge on meaninglessness. In short, the structure of *The Age of Anxiety* is so systematically ordered that it threatens to turn the "linguistic system" it orders into a crowd of words that is incapable of embodying any community of feelings whatsoever.

Sensitive critics have responded to this threat by simply rejecting the poem as unworthy of Auden. No one has done so with as much passion as Randall Jarrell, who presents the author of *The Age of Anxiety* as little

more than an "automaton" or "rhetorical mill grinding away at the bottom of Limbo. . . . Page after page the poem keeps saying: *Remember, the
real subject of poetry is words.*"[38] Whatever else Jarrell's motives may have
been in dismissing *The Age of Anxiety* with such violence, his comments
clearly register a constitutive feature of the poem: for all the technical virtuosity of its articulation, this poem sometimes verges on inarticulateness.
The sustained, almost overwhelming, use of alliteration, which Jarrell
likens to the "obsessive behavior" of a compulsive versifier, creates a dazzling—or to use Auden's term, "baroque"[39]—pattern of sounds that diverts
attention from the semantic dimensions of the text and calls attention, instead, to the sheer materiality of the verbal icon. The fluency of the alliterative resonance thus flows into the inarticulateness of stuttering repetition,
or chatter.[40] In this way, the poetic form exhibits its own analogical function: its constant alliterative stresses so stress the poetic line that the lines
as a whole come to reflect not the awe elicited by a sacred object but the
self-reflective tension of alliteration itself. Poetic speech thus tends toward
speechlessness. If poetry, for Auden, is "memorable speech"[41]—made
memorable, in part, through ordering devices such as alliteration—then
the transformation of alliterative speech into inarticulate stuttering reveals
the manner in which a poem is haunted by the specter of speechlessness.[42]
To the extent that a poem is inhabited by speechlessness, moreover, it can
no longer be understood simply as an analogy to paradise but begins to assume the burden of another analogy. This other analogy cannot achieve the
status of an independent poetic order and can have no other formal designation for its analogue than the opposite of paradise, or hell.[43] About this
latter analogy Auden says very little in his critical writings, but it gives
shape and direction to *The Age of Anxiety* not only in terms of its formal
features—above all in the persistent use of alliteration—but also in the
feeling named in its very title. For just as the memorable speech of poetry
presents an analogy to paradise, the speechlessness of anxiety stands in an
analogical relationship to hell. Randall Jarrell unwittingly touches on this
disturbing dimension of the poetic form when he pictures Auden "grinding away at the bottom of Limbo"—the first circle of *Inferno*.

III. Omission and Opposition: "The Seven Ages"

"The Seven Ages" immediately follows the "Prologue." The bilious vision of the seven ages of man that Jaques articulates in the second act of

As You Like It has no other aim than dis-individuation: everyone—regardless of rank, talents, or station—follows the same, well-worn, inevitable, and futile path from birth to death. The affect of Auden's "Seven Ages," by contrast, is not so easily identified; it is distinctly nongeneric and constantly changing: from wistful to raucous, self-pitying to sanguine, abject to bellicose. Nevertheless, these shifting humors can be understood as modifications of a single, dominant affect: anxiety and, specifically, the anxiety of individuation. The title of the poem invites this interpretation. As the four main characters present four contrasting versions of the seven ages, their descriptions enact the very process they describe. Each character strives to become recognizable as a distinct individual by distinguishing his or her conception of individuation from those of the others. The struggles of the four characters are reproduced in the struggle of the reader to distinguish among them, since the regularity of the metrical line runs in the opposite direction—toward a form of tyrannical uniformity that would prohibit individuating speech altogether.

Malin begins "The Seven Ages" by describing in dense philosophical detail a corresponding prohibition through which the infant first "joins mankind" (465). This prohibition marks the threshold between speech and speechlessness. The infant of whom Jaques speaks in his bitter account of the seven ages—and the single stage of the world—is, as the etymology of the word indicates, "without speech" (*in-fans*), for its primary oral activity, other than "puking," is inarticulate "mewling."[44] And Malin's infant is even more *in-fans*, since it does not make any sound. This absolutely infantile condition is correlated with the affect of dread:

> Behold the infant, helpless in cradle and
> Righteous still, yet already there is
> Dread in his dreams at the deed of which
> He knows nothing but knows he can do,
> The gulf before him with guilt beyond,
> Whatever that is, whatever why
> Forbids his bound; till that ban tempts him;
> He jumps and is judged: he joins mankind,
> The fallen families, freedom lost,
> Love become law. (465)

The infant is dumb but is definitely not deaf: it hears and understands a "ban" without understanding the specific acts that are banned. All that the infant understands of the ban—a word that is etymologically cognate with the *fans* of *in-fans*—is that the uncomprehended word *is* a ban, not a bidding but a forbidding: it says "no" to an act about which the infant knows nothing. This "no," which inhabits the infant as the *in* of *infans*, negates speech (*fans*), including the speech act "no!" When the infant violates the ban and thus negates the negation of speech, it negates itself, as *infans*, and falls into the realm of speech, which, for Malin, is coeval with the realm of law. The ban cannot be expressed in the language that the infant comes to speak as anything other than a law, which, however, the infant creates at the very moment it negates the ban. For the same reason, the infant can be described as "righteous" even before it knows anything of right. By violating the law, in short, the infant creates the law, and despite its fall into speech—or more accurately, if paradoxically, *because* of this very fall—it is unable to articulate the all-important difference between the ban and the law. The dread in which the infant finds itself consists in the incomprehensibility of the "content" of the ban: all the infant understands is the "gulf before him with guilt beyond." As long as the ban is understood to be law—and this "as long as" lasts, for Malin, beyond the seventh age—dread not only cannot be overcome but extends itself into every word of the non-*infans*.

Malin's account of the infant makes it seem as though the infant escapes from dread by entering the world of speech. But, this account is generated by the anxiety in the very bar—if not the ban—in which Malin finds himself, even though his presentation of infancy, like all his expositions of subsequent ages, gives the impression of being a self-contained, clinical analysis of an abstract and generalized "he." If the infant begins in dread, it is because, according to Malin's earlier suggestion concerning a topic of conversation, dread is an unavoidable fact and constitutive element of human nature. His account of the infant is, from this perspective, a retrospective explanation for the current condition in which human beings as a whole, without regard to place or age in any sense, find themselves. And if, as he says, "man" has the power "to explain every / What in his world but why he is neither / God nor good" (463), Malin, without saying so explicitly, marks his own position as somehow inhuman, for his account of the infant seeks to explain why the infant has fallen away from goodness, if not from God. Malin describes this guilty and inarticulate condition as the "insoluble final fact" for "man" which embraces all dimensions of his existence:

>   . . . infusing his private
>   Nexus of needs, his noted aims with
>   Incomprehensible comprehensive dread
>   At not being what he knows that before
>   This world was he was willed to become. (463–64)

"Incomprehensible comprehensive dread" is precisely what Malin seeks to comprehend in his subsequent speech. His theory of dread, which seems to elude dread's comprehensiveness, can be distilled into a paradoxical formulation: speech, which is the infant's escape from dread, sends it into a dread for which it has no articulate explanation. Dread for "man" derives from his inability to suppress the sense that he should have been otherwise, and his corresponding inability to articulate this sense derives from the fact that he is bound to express himself as he is and not as he should have been. In order to express this thought, which seems to break the bounds of articulate expression, Malin exploits the grammatical distinction between "I" and "Me"—without, however, ever speaking of *himself*:

>   His pure I
>   Must give account of and greet his Me,
>   That field of force where he feels he thinks,
>   His past present, presupposing death,
>   Must ask what he is in order to be
>   And make meaning by omission and stress,
>   Avid of elseness. (463)

By making a grammatical distinction into an ontological one, Malin can separate the self into two distinct beings: the "pure I" and the implicitly impure "Me." The self—which, as Kierkegaard explains in *The Concept of Dread* and even more forcefully in *The Sickness unto Death*[45]—consists in nothing other than the relation between these two beings; it furthermore knows itself to be "absconded" (463) and thus in dread only on the basis of this distinction—not, for example, on the basis of an independent revelation concerning the nature of the creator and his relation to his creatures. Of this latter relation Malin remains conspicuously silent. In Malin's Kierkegaardian revision of the self-positing I as it was conceived by German Idealism,[46] the "pure I" does not simply posit itself, as if it were an infinite being that falls into finitude the moment it knows itself as something in particular; rather, the "pure I" comes across a ready-made "Me" whom it is constrained to justify and "greet." When Malin proceeds to speak of the self in terms of the "power to place" (463), it is abundantly clear that this power is precisely not the power to posit anything, not even itself, for a caesura takes place in the line, and in place of the object to be placed, Malin speaks of explaining: "a fallen soul / With power to place, to explain . . . " (463). The being of the "pure I" is so far from being absolute and thus self-grounding that its sole ground lies in the question it poses about itself: "Must ask what he is in order to be." And since the "pure I" thus verges on complete groundlessness—Quant echoes this sentiment when he describes the topic of conversation Malin proposes as "HOMO ABYSSUS OCCIDENTALIS" (464)—it is not only incapable of making its world, or even only positing its "Me"; it cannot even make its world or its "Me" meaningful by any self-positing or positive action. Instead, it can "make meaning" only by acts of omission and by stressing, in a variety of tones, what has already been posited: "And make meaning by omission and stress." The groundlessness of the "pure I," in turn, perpetually propels it elsewhere: To use the terminology Heidegger employs in *Sein und Zeit* (Being and Time) and that Auden quotes in *The Age of Anxiety*,[47] the "I" is "thrown into being" (500), or to use Malin's own words, it is "avid of elseness."

Malin's impressive exposition of Kierkegaardian existentialism is itself structured by omission and stress. It stresses the despairing condition, as it simultaneously omits the discontinuous movement of faith; instead of a "leap of faith," there is a "jump" into the fallen condition in which one is "judged."[48] As a correlate to this omission, Malin also omits any discussion of God, even as he speaks of "what he was willed to become." And in this formulation, like all his others, he also omits something else: his own self. For the "he" stands for the abstract subject "man" and makes no reference to Malin's own life. Less conspicuously, Malin does not even replace himself with a pseudoself, as Kierkegaard does when he signs many of his texts, including *The Concept of Dread*, with a pseudonym.[49] Malin's omission of himself does not go unremarked in *The Age of Anxiety*; the epigraph to "The Seven Ages" suggests a radical critique of any figuration of the condition of dread that makes no reference to the dread of the one who is seeking to figure this condition:

> A sick toss'd vessel, dashing on each thing;
> Nay, his own shelf;
> My God, I mean myself.
>
> George Herbert, *Miserie* (465)[50]

But Malin makes a series of further omissions. In a discourse that is so recognizably Kierkegaardian, it is remarkable that he makes no mention of repetition, which, for Kierkegaard, is doubtless a manner of describing the movement of faith, but which also describes every faithless movement of existence as well, including the movement that "geniuses," as opposed to "apostles," undertake as they produce poetry.[51] When Malin speaks of the self "mak[ing] meaning by omission and stress," he is stressing the impossibility of the self positing itself and, in turn, making the world in which it finds itself. But he is also passing over, consciously or unwittingly, the art of poetry, which, for Auden, is not to be confused with the divine act of *creatio ex nihilo* but is nevertheless a genuine instance of making:

> the poet's activity in creating a poem is analogous to God's activity in creating man after his own image. It is not an imitation for, were it so, the poet would be able to create like God ex nihilo; instead, he requires pre-existing occasions of feeling and a pre-existing language out of which to create. It is analogous in that the poet creates not necessarily according to a law of nature but voluntarily according to provocation.[52]

Malin's omission of poetry is particularly ironic inasmuch as the line through which it becomes recognizable—"And make meaning by omission and stress"—comes close to describing this very line and indeed the prosody of the poem as a whole: it is organized around stresses, which are themselves ordered according to interruptions, or caesuras, in the flow of the line. But Malin further omits any reference to the third distinctive feature of the poetic line: alliteration, which is the intralinear mode of poetic repetition. And he passes over alliteration in precisely that line in which the alliteration would welcome him—or, at least, his name: *Má*lin.

Malin's decision to speak of a nonindividuated "he" in his description of the seven ages can be understood as a response to his own understanding of the specific age in which he finds himself: the fifth. According to his account of this age, the two principles through which a self experiences the individuating anguish of selfhood—sexuality, which occupied every previous age since the first, and death, which closes "The Seven Ages"—are, if not entirely repressed, equally distant. The former "fever" has become largely a matter of memory, while the latter is present only as a vague presentiment in the vocabulary of mourning:

> He fairly blooms; his fever almost
> Relaxes its hold. He learns to speak

> Softer and slower, not to seem so eager;
> His body acquires the blander motions
> Of the approved state. His positive glow
> Of fiscal health affects that unseen
> Just judge, that Generalized Other
> To whom he thinks and is understood by,
> Who grows less gruff as if gravely impressed
> By his evident air of having now
> Really arrived, bereaved of every
> Low relation. (474)

The "Generalized Other" assumes the role Malin earlier attributed to the "neighbor" whose "need" first draws the ego out of its initial dreamlike condition by "naming" it (452). Malin's generalized "he" corresponds to the "Generalized Other" who acts as the "judge" under whose power "he" has been thrown ever since he "jumped" in the first age. And this Other thus assumes the position that, according to Jaques, defines the fifth age of man: "then the justice, / in fair round belly with good capon lined."[53] Malin's "he" is never capable of being, or even only playing, the judge; instead, *ordine inverso*, he is the one judged. The capitalization of the "Generalized Other" indicates that only now, when "he" has established himself as a financial success, does the judge appear with a proper name— even if the name does not single out an individual. Although the relationship between the "he" and the "Generalized Other" seems to be one of reconciliation, there is at least one indication that this relationship is less harmonious than it appears, and this disharmony inheres in the ungrammatical formulation through which their relationship is determined: "that Generalized Other / To whom he thinks." The only possible value of the propositional function "think to" is *self*: I can think to myself, but I cannot think to another. It is as though Malin were thinking of an activity he does not want to admit into his discourse—praying, for example—and therefore replaces it with an activity with which he himself is reconciled, namely, thinking.

At this point, although not around this topic, Malin's omissions become a topic of conversation in *The Age of Anxiety*. Emble's response to Malin's description of the fifth age—"Why leave out the worst / Pang of youth?"—marks the breakdown of the structure of "The Seven Ages." As the youngest of the four, he is not in a position to proceed past the fourth age, and he does not want his most acutely imagined fears to be omitted—that, despite his sexual attractiveness, some Generalized Other will never want him:

> To be young means
> To be all on edge, to be held waiting in
> A packed lounge for a Personal Call
> From Long Distance, for the low voice that
> Defines one's future. The fears we know
> Are of not knowing. Will nightfall bring us
> Some awful order—Keep a hardware store
> In a small town. . . . Teach science for life to
> Progressive girls—? It is getting late.
> Shall we ever be asked for? Are we simply
> Not wanted at all? (474)

In Emble's almost abject objection to Malin's account of an age in which one has established a place for oneself, the "Generalized Other" is refigured as the "Personal Call" that may never come. As the term *call* conspicuously indicates, Emble, like Malin—although perhaps with less awareness of what he is doing—makes use of a theological trope, but neither of the callings he imagines, neither hardware-store manager nor girls' school teacher, is in any way associated with an apostolic vocation. The absence of a "Personal Call" de-individuates the subject of Emble's speech: the subject is always a "we" or a "one," never an "I" or a "me." Emble's recognition that the call, should it arrive, would come "From Long Distance," indicates that none of his "neighbors" in the "packed lounge" has the power to "name" and thereby bring one another out of the dreamlike condition that, in this case, has a nightmarish quality. The fears of youth, according to Emble, are those of permanent displacement: among its many other connotations, waiting in a "packed lounge" suggests large crowds in transition as might be associated with liminal spaces like military depots, docks, and railroad stations. The absence of knowledge that defines the condition of youth is presented as ignorance with respect to one's future whereabouts, which, in turn, is understood as a function of one's place in the world. And the phrase that describes the condition of potentially permanent displacement is "to be all on edge": to be without secure footing, to live in the vicinity of a precipice, or, once again—to invoke Quant's description of the basic theme of the discussion as a whole—to be "HOMO ABYSSUS."

But Quant objects to Emble's interpretation of the characteristically abyssal condition of human beings that he had himself identified as all four characters were "set on edge" by the long distance and deeply impersonal transmission over the radio. Although Malin presents the fifth age as one of reconciliation of the self with the world, as it is figured in the Generalized Other, the fifth age in *The Age of Anxiety* is the most contentious of all: Malin's speech is rejected by Emble, Emble's speech by Quant, Quant's by Rosetta, and Rosetta's by Quant again. None of the characters recognizes any other as an other to whom he or she could be reconciled. Quant's response to Emble ironically gestures toward a kind of reconciliation—not with an other, even a Generalized Other—but with a completely anonymous and autonomous system. From Quant's perspective, Emble's recognition of *homo abyssus* does not go far enough: Emble makes placelessness into a problem of youth rather than seeing it as a function of the infinite replaceability of everyone within a capitalist economy. Quant foresees a time in which Emble will develop a class-consciousness, but this consciousness—or as Quant says, "acknowledgment"—will absolutely not coalesce into a feeling of community with the oppressed, dispossessed, and displaced on the basis of which a revolutionary movement could be generated:

> Well, you will soon
> Not bother but acknowledge yourself
> As market-made, a commodity
> Whose value varies, a vendor who has
> To obey his buyer, will embrace moreover
> The problems put you by opposing time . . . (474)

Quant's opposition to Emble, and the entire dynamic of opposition that characterizes the fifth age, centers on the problem of "opposing time." Emble opposes the mordant manner in which Malin passes over the problems of youth; Quant opposes Emble's inability to recognize that the problems of youth do not confine themselves to the time of youth; Rosetta opposes Quant's "unprivileged time" (475); and Quant categorically opposes Rosetta's assertion that "Time flies" with the declaration, "No, Time returns" (476). The first problem of "opposing time" occurs in the interpretation of the sentence in which this theme is originally articulated: Time may be oppositional by nature, which is to say, it places itself against everything that appears "in" time; or it may be that Emble, as the one to whom Quant speaks, is the one who has chosen to oppose time, which is to say, resist its flow. According to the latter interpretation, Quant would be proposing something like a linear and unidirectional conception of time: if only one "embraces" the flow of time, it will cease to pose problems. According to the former interpretation, however, Quant presents a far more problematic conception of time: it runs counter to everything and everyone to the point where it leaves no stable place for anything or anyone in particular. All things that appear in time are therefore instances of eternal types, and every appearance of something or someone is only a reappearance of the type. Although the two interpretations doubtless oppose each other—and they are for the most part distributed between the two speeches Quant makes in the fifth age—they also reinforce each other: the words of wisdom Quant directs at Emble are embedded in a vast, cosmic conception of time as oppositional. And the unifying element of these two interpretations is Quant's theory of revolution, which is nothing less than a refutation of the possibility of revolution in the modern sense of the term:[54]

> One revolution
> Registers all things, the rise and fall
> In pay and prices, peregrinations
> Of lies and loves, colossal bangs and
> Their sequential quiets in quick order. (476)

Malin's opposition to the idea of the self-positing "I" finds expression in his theory of meaning by means of omission, whereas Quant's opposition to the very same idea makes itself known in his conception of "revolutionary" or circular time. For Quant, not even God is capable of the titanic act of self-positing, as his parodic rendition of certain gnostic tales of creation testifies:

> For Long-Ago has been
> Ever-After since Ur-Papa gave
> The Primal Yawn that expressed all things
> (In His Boredom their beings) and brought forth
> The wit of this world. (477)

Quant's own "wit" is incessantly creative. Throughout the poem, and especially in "The Seven Ages," he creates new mythological creatures out of the material contained in the contemporary world. The sobriety of his first speech in the fifth age, which is dominated by Marxist vocabulary, gives way in his second speech to his characteristic mythopoetic jocularity:

> William East is
> Entering Olive as Alfred West
> Is leaving Elaine; (476)

Although Quant's exuberant use of proper names seems to indicate that he is speaking of distinct individuals, these names are only elements of elaborate, and often lascivious, jokes. And the point of these jokes is that the supposed individuals he names are interchangeable: East and West are arbitrarily designated points on a compass, just as William East and Alfred West are interchangeable and their sexual objects arbitrary. The historical world, which, as Auden indicates in his poetological writings, is defined by singularity of occurrence, becomes indistinguishable from the world of logical and mathematical principles. The distinction between the contingent and temporally defined truths of fact and the necessary and eternal truths of reason vanishes before the eyes of those who pay attention to the visible world:

> And who runs may read written on walls
> Eternal truths: "Teddy Peterson
> Never washes." "I'm not your father
> You slobbering Swede." "Sulky Moses
> Has bees in his bush." "Betty is thinner
> But Connie lays." (476)

The lack of connection among these "eternal truths" finds a correlate in Quant's failure to connect his tendency to engage in Marxist modes of analysis and his tendency to indulge in parodic mythopoesis. This failure—and *failure* is the word Quant uses to describe himself (478)—is never more apparent than in his two speeches in the fifth age: his response to Emble presents a dismal image of class-consciousness without hope for working-class solidarity, to say nothing of revolution; the first part of Quant's second speech in this age generalizes his conception of Emble's replaceability and issues into his theory of cosmic "revolution"; and the second part of the second speech—which is introduced by a conspicuous dash—opens onto a vast parody of Greek, Roman, Jewish, and Christian mythology.

Quant's "opposing time" is strangely nonoppositional: he opposes himself to each of the other characters but does not express a political opinion opposed to the system in which he has clearly found no place for himself; instead, he articulates a joking, often raucous, mythological vision with respect to the cosmos as a whole. For Quant, the failure of Marxism to sustain the hope of overcoming a system in which things are defined by their infinite replaceability creates the conditions in which mythology and mythopoetic imagination flourish. From the very beginning of *The Age of Anxiety*, the narrating voice suggests a close connection between Quant's class-consciousness and his interest in mythology and also indicates that this relationship escapes Quant's own awareness: "He had come to America at the age of six when his father, implicated somehow in the shooting of a landlord, had had to leave Ireland in a hurry. . . . Then, again, in early manhood, when unemployed during a depression, he had spent many hours one winter in the Public Library reading for the most part—he could not have told you why—books on Mythology" (450). By the fifth age, however, it is quite clear that Quant's attraction to mythology is born of political hopelessness: instead of participating in working-class organization, which would be one obvious response to unemployment during the depression, he secludes himself in a public place and immerses himself in systems of thought governed by the principle of immutability—or, to use Quant's own formulation, "Long-Ago has been / Ever-After."[55]

The hopelessness of Quant's formulation comes to dominate the tenor of the sixth age: it is an age defined by longing, but the object of longing is a "Long-Ago" in which "belonging" (476)—and this is the word Rosetta stresses as she closes her speech in the fifth age—does not pose the kinds of problems generated by "opposing time." The reconciliation with the "Generalized Other" that Malin describes in the previous age gives way to recollections of childhood conflicts from which "he" has never recovered: "The bruise of his boyhood is as blue still, / Horrid and hurting, hostile to his life" (477). In earlier ages, according to a principle Malin develops at length, injuries give rise to either violent actions or violent fantasies, and both Quant and Emble verify this principle from their own experiences.[56] In the sixth age, by contrast, Malin registers a change in the "he" for whom wrongs issue into retribution. The "bruise of his boyhood" generates instead a fantasy of paradise in which the "he" disappears and is replaced by a "they" to which he has never belonged and for which the term *reconciliation* would therefore be misleading:

He pines for some
Nameless Eden where he never was
But where in his wishes once again
On hallowed acres, without a stitch
Of achievement on, the children play
Nor care how comely they couldn't be
Since they needn't know they're not happy. (477–78)

Point by point this "Nameless Eden" contrasts with the condition of the infant before its fall, as Malin describes it in the first age: unlike the infant, the inhabitants of the Edenic world as envisioned in the sixth age are not alone; they exhibit no trace of righteousness; and they are not defined by knowledge, especially not self-knowledge. These children, moreover, run counter to Malin's initial account of the manner in which the ego is released from its original dreamlike state. Whereas, according to this earlier account, it is the neighbor's need that "creates" the ego by naming it, the Eden of Malin's later speech is bereft not only of names but also of needs—and therefore, bereft of neighbors as well: the community envisioned is without the dialectic of self and other in which the idea of "achievement" is rooted.

Quant and Emble, each in his own way, draw on their own experiences to substantiate Malin's description of the first age; in response to Malin's description of the "Nameless Eden" of the sixth age, they are similarly motivated to elaborate on Malin's speech, even if each is confined to describing his inability to envision the same condition in any detail. For Quant, this Eden appears to him only after an elaborate quest through mythological places of his own invention and then only for a moment: "I got one glimpse of the granite walls / And the glaciers guarding the Good Place" (479). The characteristic jocularity of Quant's mythopoeisis does not vanish from his parodic romance, but the names of the places through which he must pass—"Torture Tower" and "Twisting Ovens" (478)—are too close to the images of war for them to be funny. For Emble, the "Good Place" that Quant cannot enter appears as a garden to which he has lost access. But Emble, unlike Quant, gives no prelude to his similarly bleak vision of an inaccessible paradise:

I have lost the key to
The garden gate. How green it was there,
How large long ago when I looked out,

> Excited by sand, the sad glitter
> Of desert dreck, not dreaming I saw
> My future home. It foils my magic:
> Right is the ritual but wrong the time,
> The place improper. (480)

The interplay between the speeches of Quant and Emble might be called "from failed romance to failed ritual"—as an inversion and negation of the book that inspired "The Waste Land," according to Eliot's own account, namely, Weston's *From Ritual to Romance*.[57] From Quant's reference to "Wastewood" and his recognition that "A storm was brewing" (478) to Emble's talk of a "desert" and a "key" (480), the sixth age assumes the imagery of Eliot's poem, particularly of its final section, "What the Thunder Said." The thunder, for Eliot, intones ritual formulas drawn from Vedic texts; for Quant, by contrast, the storm has nothing to say: "Thunder thudded" (478). Whereas the lyric "I" in the last section of "The Waste Land" experiences the inexplicable presence of another being—"Who is the third who walks always beside you?"[58]—Quant experiences the opposite: "(But someone important, / Alas, was not there.)" (478). And Emble's vision precisely opposes the one that arises between the thunderous words, "*Dayadhvam*" and "*Damyata*":

> I have heard the key
> Turn in the door once and turn once only
> We think of the key, each in his prison
> Thinking of the key, each confirms a prison.[59]

In "The Waste Land," the key locks the "I" into a prison, and thought orients itself toward this key. In Emble's speech, the key locks the "I" out of the place in which water is abundant and life flourishes. And whereas the imprisonment in "The Waste Land" is apparently a matter of sheer fate—which sharply contrasts with Dante's account of Count Ugolino from which these lines are drawn[60]—Emble faults himself for his exclusion from the garden and suggests a reason: the excitement generated by the vision of the desert throws him out of the garden. The desert not only glitters with the possibility of sexual arousal, its "glitter" is "sad" and therefore all the more attractive: for Emble, as for a tradition as old as Aristotle and as recent as Eliot, melancholia is a mark of distinction.[61]

Rosetta's speech, which is situated between those of Quant and Emble, does not concern itself with either ritual or romance, nor does it present itself as a refinement of Malin's overarching narrative. Instead, from the beginning of "The Seven Ages," Rosetta pursues an altogether opposing narrative: that of the "dolls" who, as she says in the sixth age, are "tearless, timeless" (479) and therefore cannot be integrated into Malin's schemata. Rosetta's narrative technique is also opposed to that of Malin's: while Malin is careful to maintain a distance between the "he" whose life he narrates and his own experiences, Rosetta moves seamlessly between third-person narrative and a strange ventriloquism through which the dolls are animated. And Rosetta's insouciance with respect to Malin's lead—she seems deaf to the description he proffers—is reflected in her account of the doll:

> On picnic days
> My dearest doll was deaf and spoke in
> Grunts like grandfather. (466)

The first property of the doll stands in sharp contrast to the original characterization of the infant. Whereas the latter is inseparable from its ability to hear the ban that tempts it, the former cannot hear at all. The second property of the doll is even more subversive with respect to Malin's project, for it is a complete inversion of the narrative of the seven ages from which he takes his lead. In Jaques' speech, the correlation of infancy and dotage occurs as the final two ages, when "his big manly voice" turns into "childish treble" and the scene returns to "second childishness."[62] The dolls, by contrast, are forever "frühalt"—to use the word Rilke invents as he, too, seeks to come to terms with the uncanny character of dolls.[63] And indeed Rosetta's imagery is as marked by Rilke as Quant's and Emble's are by Eliot. This is especially true of Rosetta's speech in the sixth age where she sets out to specify the space in which they exist:

> Yet holy are the dolls,
> Who, junior forever, just begin
> Their open lives in absolute space,
> Are simply themselves, deceiving none. (479)

The openness of the dolls' lives is a function of their existence in "absolute space." This latter term is drawn from the philosophical lexicon and in particular alludes to the conception of space Newton developed for the purposes of defending the conception of gravitation he proposes in his *Principia Mathematica*.[64] But, Rosetta invokes this term in a context that could hardly be less Newtonian. If, as Blake famously argued—and Auden made into the subject of both poetic and poetological reflection[65]—Newtonian modes of thought destroy the possibility of poetry by making the world into an indifferent and mechanical cosmos, the absolute space Rosetta describes is the exact opposite to that described by Newton, for it is precisely the place in which poetry flourishes:

> O Primal Age
> When we danced deisal, our dream-wishes
> Vert and volant, unvetoed our song. (479)

Newton speaks of an absolute space in order to secure an inertial framework with respect to which one can maintain that something revolves around something else and not vice versa. Such a cosmology describes the ascendancy of an eminent or privileged space. In the same vein, Rosetta—who, as she exclaims to Quant, "refuse[s] to accept / Your plain place, your unprivileged time" (475)—seeks to assert a privileged space by adopting the Newtonian term, but she uses it to subvert Newtonian principles: the privileged space Newton ascribes to God becomes the space she accords to dolls and creatures—in Rilkean terms, "das Offene."[66]

Absolute space is prior to any reflective distinction between inner and outer; it is "God's sensorium,"[67] to use Newton's famous formula, and not a forum for human modes of apprehension. The subversive brilliance of Rosetta's allusion consists in her proposal that absolute space is the sensorium of nonhuman, nondivine, and—at least according to the view of sober adults—inanimate beings. For the dolls, everything is both absolutely exterior and absolutely interior to everything else. The word that captures this primordial spatiality, which corresponds to the "Primal Age" in which the dolls live, is *openness*: the dolls exist in the open. This mode of existence, which is even less a matter of self-positing than the one Malin describes as he begins "The Seven Ages," resides in sheer self-exposure or even self-expositing: being "simply themselves, deceiving none." The dolls do not fall from this state of unadulterated simplicity; instead, they run down. And this slight alteration is enough to sharpen the principle of accusation under which "The Seven Ages" as a whole—to say nothing of "HOMO ABYSSUS OCCIDENTALIS"—has proceeded. Nothing could be more ambiguous than the depleted sentence in which this running down is both expressed and enacted: "I wronged" (479). This sentence could mean "I did wrong" or "I was wronged" or both at the same time: I did wrong, because I was wronged—Malin's principle of retribution—or, more radically still, and as a massive critique of Malin's entire mode of thinking, the "I" is simply "wrong."

That Rosetta may be seeking to oppose Malin in the most rigorous manner possible can be seen in her appropriation of one of his principal words: *neighbor*. She draws the *neigh* out of *neighbor* and makes it into a term that expresses not negation—"nay," or the primal word, "no"—but its exact opposite: absolutely affirmative, yet not self-affirmative, joy. This transformation of Malin's discourse takes place at the close of a startling temporal inversion in which a vision of the "Primal Age" combines conventional images drawn from fairy tales with the prophet Isaiah's images of the messianic kingdom with which history comes to an end:

> For crows brought cups of cold water to
> Ewes that were young; unicorn herds
> Galumphed through lilies; little mice played
> With great cock-a-hoop cats; courteous griffins
> Waltzed with wyverns, and the wild horses
> Drew nigh their neighbors and neighed with joy
> All feasting with friends. (479)

The first of these images can be understood as an elaboration of the reconciliation of all creatures with one another that Isaiah envisions; the second image is drawn straight from childhood fantasies; the third playfully suggests the famous verses from Isaiah, "The wolf also shall dwell with the lamb, the leopard shall lie down with the young goat, the calf and the young lion and the fatling together" (Isa., 11: 6);[68] the fourth returns to the world of the fairy tale; and the fifth offers an image in which the landscape of children's stories, especially the fourth section of *Gulliver's Travels*,[69] blends into an exalted depiction of the messianic kingdom. Rosetta's radical opposition to Malin, signaled by the key word *neighbor*, is, however, mediated by common omissions: like Malin, Rosetta omits herself from her speech, and both characters omit references to God in contexts where the divine presence is nonetheless palpable—contexts such as Kierkegaard's theological writings and the prophetic books of the Bible. Also like Malin, Rosetta shares an impulse to depict the paradise for which all of them "pine." But despite the analogical status of Rosetta's representation of the "the Primal Age," her construction of this analogy unravels as she identifies herself with the dolls, and this collapse of analogy into identification, in turn, interferes with her representation of a paradisal age: the Rilkean world of creatures and things assumes the dubious position of Malin's Generalized Other from whom we want recognition. Her horses are scarcely disguised stand-ins for human beings who have reconciled with one another. The trope is transparent, which may be appropriate for the "Primal Age," but in other ages, including an age of anxiety, or indeed any of the "Seven Ages," the transparency of tropes is paradoxically deceptive, because it gives the mistaken impression that one can attain direct insight into the landscape of paradise.

IV. Backward and Backside: "The Seven Stages"

The imagery Rosetta develops as she envisions the "Primal Age" is regressive: she returns to the iconography of her childhood, some of which is taken from fairy tales, some from children's books, and still others from childlike reinterpretations of famous prophetic sayings. At the end of "The Seven Ages," after each of the characters has reflected on the inevitability of death, Quant asks Rosetta to lead all the characters on a quest back toward the landscape she has just described:

> O show us the route
> Into hope and health; give each the required
> Pass to appease the superior archons;
> Be our good guide. (483)

The terms *hope* and *health* are the simplest descriptions of the destination of a journey that will proceed in the opposite direction from that of "The Seven Ages." But, as the next line makes clear, the journey will be anything but simple, for it will take the characters through an arcane, even gnostic, setting in which the world from which they are escaping is nevertheless hiding in ambush: the appeasement of gnostic deities is, apparently for Quant, the path to peace in their time. The simplicity of the terms *hope* and *health* are misleading in another manner as well: whereas, as Malin indicates, there is "little to say" (481) about the end of "The traveller through time" (463) who progresses through the seven ages—"So their discussion concluded" (481)—much is said about the goal of the journey for which Rosetta has been chosen as leader. And even when in "The Seven Ages" the characters avoid the term *death*, the subject of their discussion—or silence—is never in doubt; when, by contrast, they speak of this other terminus as the goal of the seven stages, there remains an abiding question: are the characters speaking of the same thing after all? This question is intensified each time a new name for paradise appears: "Nameless Eden," "the Good Place," "the Primal Age," "the garden," and "The Quiet Kingdom." The first in this list of names already begs the question, for Eden, of course, *is* a name, indeed, *the* name of biblical paradise, and so Malin must mean that *this* name is somehow still insufficient, less a proper name than a general, and not particularly revealing, common noun. If, moreover, anxiety is correlated with speechlessness and repetitive, inarticulate chatter, then in a paradoxical manner, talk of paradise in *The Age of Anxiety* is more anxious than even talk of death: the multiplication of names for what seems to be the same thing interferes with the semantic function of naming. The superabundance of names does not guarantee, and may even destroy, the possibility of communication. Nowhere is this interference more clearly evident than in the name Rosetta chooses for the goal of their common journey, for there is no indication that the other characters would understand this fairy-tale name as a term for paradise: "may our luck find the / Regressive road to Grandmother's House" (484). Whatever the fairy-tale phrase "Grandmother's House" may symbolize, the journey toward it proceeds in the opposite direction from the one Malin chose for "The Seven Ages": it is not a journey of the ego's progressive self-formation broken off only by death but a regressive journey, undertaken in common, in which the "I" does not die but gradually dissolves. Whereas "The Seven Ages" shows the conditions of plurality against the dark vision of Jaques' melancholic speech, "The Seven Stages" brings into view the dissolution of individuality against the luminous splendor of the *Zohar*.

The departure from the narrative schema of "The Seven Ages" is apparent from Rosetta's response to Quant's suggestion that she act as guide through "The Seven Stages":

> What gift of direction
> Is entrusted to me to take charge
> Of an expedition any may
> Suggest or join? For the journey homeward
> Arriving by roads already known
> At sites and sounds one has sensed before,
> The knowledge needed is not special. (484)

The stages are thus distinguished from ages on at least one small, but critical, point: anyone can participate in the complete journey; that is, the kind of dissension that characterized the fifth age in particular—generated by gender, class, religious, and generational differences—cannot occur during any of the stages. The formation of an "I" that stands in a dialectical relationship to a Generalized Other travels on as many paths as there are selves; by contrast, the regressive movement toward paradise has only one path, although every "I"—precisely because it is an "I"—views the path from a different perspective and therefore cannot fail to mark this path with different names. But the proliferation of names tends to undermine the presupposition that there is only one regressive path. Only on one condition, then, can "The Seven Stages" proceed, and this condition is the subject matter of the narrating voice's first major intervention since it introduced the poem as a whole: everyone has to be drunk.[70] The narrating voice intervenes between Rosetta's final speech in "The Seven Ages" and the reintroduction of the four characters in the "Seven Stages" with two coordinated theses. The first of these theses gives a theory of drunkenness on the basis of which the presupposition of a single regressive path can be justified: all function "as a single organism." And the second thesis indicates the space through which the regressive movement occurs: "So it was now as they sought that state of prehistoric happiness which, by human beings, can only be imagined in terms of a landscape bearing a symbolic resemblance to the human body" (484).

The strange obscurity of this thesis has troubled critics who have tried to understand the symbolic structure of "The Seven Stages" according to a variety of often contradictory schemas.[71] Auden, however, provides a definitive account of both the structure and the source of the corporeal landscape explored in "The Seven Stages" in a letter to Alan Ansen:

> It begins in the belly, the center of the body, goes on to the general region around the heart, then to the hands (symmetrically, two by two), then to the nose and throat (the capital), then north to the eyes where Rosetta goes in and the others describe it from outside, then to the forehead complex (the museum), the ears (garden) through which one receives spiritual direction, the hair (woods), and finally they look down the back, the desert—there's nothing farther. . . . It's all done in the Zohar.[72]

The regression to the "Primal Age" takes place as an exploration of this symbolic body and a gradual diminution of self-awareness—the transfor-

mation of self-consciousness into the communal alertness of a "single organism": "The more completely these four forgot their surroundings and
lost their sense of time, the more sensitively aware of each other they became, until they achieved in their dream that rare community which is
otherwise only attained in states of extreme wakefulness. But this did not
happen all at once" (484–85). Only a singularly complex poetic program
allows such a "rare community" to manifest itself. "The Seven Ages" elaborated the opposition between a basic mood of plurality and a uniform art
character. "The Seven Stages" makes this opposition internal to its own
movement: the art character of "The Seven Stages" tends toward an even
greater uniformity than that articulated in "The Seven Ages," for the characters begin to act as a "single organism." Nevertheless, the perspectives
on the landscape through which the four characters travel are even more
diverse, even more perspectival, than those expressed in the previous section of the poem. Indeed, the perspectives in "The Seven Stages" diverge
to such a degree that it is difficult, if not impossible at times, to discern
the common landscape. Only one thing is known: the landscape is that of
a gigantic body. If this body were equivalent to the "single organism,"
Auden's poem would flirt with a particularly pernicious image: that of the
"One Man of gigantic dimensions" through which totalitarianism consolidates its vertiginous movement.[73] Under this premise, the raucous plurality of "The Seven Ages" would collapse into a disturbing unanimity in
"The Seven Stages." But such is not the case, for the "single organism"
and the body it encounters are not the same; on the contrary, the body is
divine, while the characters remain decidedly human. Auden captures
this disparity between the subject and the object of exploration with the
term *symbol*. This term is often used to construct an unproblematic con-
nectedness between the symbolic and the symbolized. For Auden, however, *symbol* indicates an insuperable distinction: the landscape may bear
a "symbolic resemblance to the human body," but it is for this reason,
taken by itself, something other than the body of a man or a woman.
"The Seven Stages" does not therefore present a self-made man creating
himself in a movement of self-deification; rather, the characters come together in a "rare community" only to the extent that all of them, each in
his or her own way, explore that which is radically other than themselves.
In search of a guide for this otherness and in response to the war against
the Jews, Auden turns to the central text of Jewish mysticism. The *Zohar*
grants him access to an experience of the divine body, the *Adam Kadmon*,

that is on the hitherside of all political projects to erect "One Man of gigantic dimensions."

Only under two conditions can the exploration of the divine body undertaken by the author of the *Zohar* represent God without violating the commandment against graven images: the essence of God—the infinite nothingness of *En Sof*[74]—must remain at all times unrepresented; and the human being, whose body serves as the point of orientation for this exploration, must be understood in accordance with the opening of Genesis (1: 27) as a living, nongraven image of God. Each part of the human body is thus able to symbolize an attribute of God. The exploration of the body of an absolutely prehistoric *corpus mysticum* can then present itself as a privileged method of representing the unity of the singular God, even as the unfathomable essence of divinity retreats from view. Something similar takes place in "The Seven Stages": the exploration of a symbolic landscape "imagined" in terms of a human body represents something—call it "Nameless Eden," "Grandmother's House" or the "state of prehistoric happiness"—that retreats from all direct representation. But the exploration undertaken in the "The Seven Stages" diverges from that of the *Zohar* insofar as the landscape under exploration cannot be immediately recognized as a human body: whereas the *Zohar* famously speaks of the hands, nose, and even beard of God—to mention only three parts of the *Adam Kadmon*[75]—"The Seven Stages" refrains from invoking any bodily terms as markers of its landscape. The landscape is therefore doubly symbolic: its many and varied sites must first be interpreted as symbols of the various parts of the human body before, in turn, these parts can offer themselves as symbols of the paradisal order. The landscape thus becomes a symbol for what the landscape symbolizes—health and hope—and the restless dynamics of the double symbolism of "The Seven Stages" makes this "dream" of "extreme wakefulness" into an interpretive nightmare.[76]

The difficulty of interpreting "The Seven Stages" is so severe that even certain aspects of the *Zohar*, which is often invoked as the interpretive enigma *par excellence*, seem straightforward by comparison. In the kabbalistic text, the exploration of the divine body, which is undertaken without any apparent direction and guided only by the order of the liturgical calendar, is itself a representation of God. Because this exploration is everywhere at its end, the idea of a quest makes no sense; least of all does the author of the *Zohar* seek a path that would lead to the infinite and infinitely empty essence of God, or, the *En Sof*. Written in the manner of an extended midrash to the *Torah*, the *Zohar* defers to the authority of Talmudic sages and thus precludes any interpretation of its mapping of the divine body as a heroic quest of an independent self seeking the key to salvation. "The Seven Stages," by contrast, grows out of the Eliotic quest motif that Malin, Quant, and Emble develop in their speeches in the sixth age and that Quant and Rosetta confirm when they define the terms of the journey of the four characters through "The Seven Stages." As they explore this doubly symbolic landscape, the four characters become a "single organism" that constructs certain forms of reciprocal commonality sharply distinguished from those explored in "The Seven Ages"—forms that were based on the relation of the doubting self to an other whose existence it doubts, yet nevertheless needs. As long as they maintain themselves in a quest, however, the four characters cannot unburden themselves of the anxiety generated by the "righteous" self-assertion that proceeded from the inarticulateness of infancy. The self paradoxically preserves itself in the form of a quest for a place where its constitutive anxiety disappears. All of the characters have a reason—the indubitable reason of self-preservation—to maintain themselves in the role of searchers after something that they can neither describe nor name; once they arrive at their goal, they disappear as the characters whose lives were recounted in "The Seven Ages." If, as Rosetta says, many fail in their regressive journey to "Grandmother's House," it is because failure is well rewarded—with the prize of self-assertive selfhood. The quest for a place whose name and nature remain elusive thus interferes with the ability of the four characters to interpret the space through which their quest proceeds—with the result that each of the seven stages, unlike the seven ages, cannot be described by any of the characters who move through them and must instead be marked by a narrating voice, which, however, remains external to the action and silent about the relation of the stages to the parts of the symbolic body symbolically represented in them.

Orienting oneself in the landscape of the seven stages is further complicated by the apparent anarchy of the stages themselves: they do not establish a one-to-one correspondence with parts of the body. Rosetta speaks of the "Seven Stages" in her response to Quant's suggestion that she be their "good guide," and the narrating voice adopts her numerology, as it, in contrast to Malin's practice in "The Seven Ages," marks off each of the stages only *after* the four characters have completed them. The number seven has almost innumerable associations. In the *Zohar* alone—to say

nothing of such significant literary predecessors as Dante's *Purgatorio* with
its seven cycles of purgation[77]—sevens proliferate: along with the seven
days of creation, which serve as the model for its first description of the
Godhead, there are seven firmaments, seven lower realms, seven ordeals,
seven abysses, and seven windows in "The Hall of the Tabernacles"
through which the Messiah passes.[78] But, the actual structure of "The
Seven Stages," with its many sudden shifts in movement and the apparent
randomness of the numerological designations, contravenes the mystical
aura of the number seven: as the characters enter the seventh stage, something dramatic should happen—be it purgation, as in Dante, or rest, as in
the sabbatical day and the Days of the Messiah. Instead, the seventh stage
grows, divides into two, and eventually occupies more than one-third of
"The Seven Stages" as a whole, until the number seven seems completely
artificial. The four characters travel through three vastly different landscapes corresponding to three different parts of the body; the narrating
voice strains to contain all the action in the single remaining stage and is
forced to break the stage into two parts to avoid designating an additional
stage. The seventh stage, moreover, begins as though the quest had
reached its goal, since the four characters, coming together again after an
interlude of erotic disappointment and disturbance, finally arrive at a
place that bears one of the names of the paradise they have been seeking
all along.

   "The garden" (480) appears in the seventh stage transformed into a
multiplicity of "hermetic gardens" (504) that seem to be only remnants of
the age they are seeking: "They gaze about them entranced at the massive
mildness of these survivals from an age of cypresses and cisterns" (504).
The speeches of the four characters conform to a single poetic pattern
even as the subject matter of the speeches is distinguished according to the
characters' individual perceptions: Rosetta speaks of the ornate and fra-
grant setting of "Italian gardens" (504); Emble speaks of a boyhood
heaven complete with a "miniature railroad" (505); Quant, of a "theater"
where his intellect is no longer impotent, thus a place "where thought becomes act" (505); and Malin, of a precipitous site in which the fall he recounts in the first age is inverted, and the faithless jump into judgment
turns into the faithful—and Kierkegaardian—leap of love: "Tense on the
parterre, he takes the hero's / Leap into love" (505). Yet, the characters are
unable to remain at the gardens, for they cannot unburden themselves of
the deeds for which each alone is responsible, and they consequently go

their separate ways through a "labyrinthine forest" (507). Having achieved the apparent goal of their regressive quest on reaching the gardens, they return to the condition that first set the quest in motion: "a sad unrest" (484). And thus, to complicate matters further, the seventh stage restages the initial movement of "The Seven Stages" as a whole.

The direct opposite of the landscape described as the "hermetic gardens" is that of the open, apparently endless desert with which the four characters are confronted as they approach the "last half" of the seventh stage. Poised between these two opposing symbols concatenated into a single stage, the double symbolism of "The Seven Stages" approaches a critical point in which the very idea of the symbol threatens to collapse. As the traditional symbol of *kenosis*—an emptying that may also prepare the way for fulfillment[79]—the desert is the setting for this symbolic crisis and this crisis of the symbol. A modern echo of the ancient conception of the barren lands beyond the bounds of city and civilization can be found in Nietzsche's exposition of nihilism in terms of values and in his memorable exclamation: "Die Wüste wächst: Weh dem, der Wüsten birgt [The desert grows: woe to him who contains deserts]."[80] With less pathos and no words of warning, Quant describes the desert in Nietzschean terms: "vacant of value" (509). In the overall context of "The Seven Stages," however, the desert appears not only as a symbol of *kenosis* but also as a place that "bear[s] a symbolic resemblance" to a part of the supernal or paradisal body: the back. If the back is understood as nothing more than an unambiguous sign of departure and rejection—as in the expression "turning one's back on"—then the double symbolism perfectly converges: being deserted is the condition in which divinity turns its back on human beings, and vice versa. If, however, the back is understood otherwise, then the two orders of symbolism diverge to the point where the experience of the characters on a symbolic landscape clashes with the landscape in its symbolic resemblance to the divine body. And within the allusive context of "The Seven Stages," there is reason to hesitate before resolving this ambiguity, for the *Zohar* repeatedly refers to the theophantic moment *par excellence*—the moment when Moses, while crossing through a desert that will prepare his people for a promised land of cypresses and cisterns, is allowed to see God's back: "And the LORD said, 'See, there is a place near Me. Station yourself on the rock and, as My Presence passes by, I will put you in a cleft of the rock and shield you with My hand until I have passed by. Then I will take My hand away and you will see My back" (Exodus 33:

21–23). The back can thus symbolize the exact opposite of departure and rejection: by showing Moses his back, God both reveals himself and lovingly protects his most obedient servant from the obliteration that would result from any unmediated, direct, or face-to-face revelation. If the back is indeed a sign of love rather than a gesture of rejection, then it should be interpreted and even experienced as a space of delicate revelation—not of desertion. And since the four characters appear to experience the last landscape through which they travel as nothing other than a deserted place, "vacant of value," the two orders of symbols in "The Seven Stages" so completely diverge that its symbolism as a whole begins to break apart.

In association with its multiple presentations of the theophany around which the entire Hebrew Bible revolves, the *Zohar* makes one further reference to the dynamics of the back. And it is conceivable that this reference is responsible for the entire symbolic landscape of "The Seven Stages":

> As the good shepherd saves the sheep from wolves and lions, so does the good shepherd of Israel save them from pagan nations, from judgement here below and from judgement above, and prepares them for the life of the world to come. Just such a faithful shepherd was Moses. . . . [A]s R. Jose remarked, " . . . Although Jethro was a 'priest of Midian', that is to say a pagan, yet because he was kind to Moses, the latter served him well and tended his flock with all due care in good and fat pasture." AND HE LED THE FLOCK TO THE BACK OF THE WILDERNESS. Said R. Jose: "From the time when Moses was born, the holy spirit never left him. He discerned by means of the holy spirit that the desert was sanctified and prepared by God as the place for Israel's acceptance of the yoke of the Kingdom of Heaven (the Sinaitic Law), therefore 'He led the flock to the back of the wilderness'—not to the wilderness, as he did not wish them to tread that spot."[81]

It is easy to imagine Auden's eyes, as they perused the English volumes of the *Zohar*, being caught by the capitalized formula: "BACK OF THE WILDERNESS." With characteristic audacity, Auden presents the wilderness *as* the supernal back. The back is protective: Moses, as shepherd of sheep, protects the wilderness by leading his flock only to its back; Moses, as shepherd of the Israelites, having dared to lead the Israelites into the desert itself, experiences divine protection when God shows him His back. The back as wilderness makes danger into protection and protection into danger. By means of this concentration of linguistic and symbolic elements, Auden gives a solid shape to the landscape of "The Seven Stages" and an ironic goal to its quest: not the front or center but the back. The inherent ambiguity of the back—desolation, protection—plays itself out in its interpretation by the four characters, none of whom has the authority of a Moses, even if they anoint one or the other as their shepherd. Quant's initial, negative reaction does not therefore last. On the contrary, as the section proceeds, the back as wilderness begins to assume the function of "the good shepherd": to save the sheep from wolves, lions, judgment below, and judgment above.

The narrating voice introduced "The Seven Stages" by indicating that, as their journey advances, the four characters slowly come to approximate that state of mutual reciprocity that characterizes a "single organism." By the last stage, this process, without having reached completion, nevertheless stamps the closing moments and prepares for the unified voice that animates the subsequent "Dirge." The speeches of the four characters as they survey the supernal back are less expressions of their individual perspectives than parts of a single soliloquy. Quant's sober, utterly literal description of the desert where they reunite goes against his ordinarily mythopoetic character. And the subsequent speeches register a progressive, and paradoxical, de-realization of the dreamscape in which Quant's prosaic vision first becomes, the subject matter of Malin's reflection on the mind's self-reflective capacity to distort time and on certain travelers' tales of "unbelievable leaps" (510); then moves toward Emble's narrative of a child so divided from itself that it gravitates, against its will but according to its wish, toward the "original chasm" of the world; and concludes with Rosetta's haunting vision of a completely different "last landscape" made of "solid ice" (511). In contrast to Quant's simple indicative declarations, Rosetta's sentences are articulated entirely in the interrogative mood. These questions unfold the compact question with which Malin, alluding both to the Lord's Prayer and The Apocalypse of John, closes his speech: "'Do I love this world so well / That I have to know how it ends?'" (510). What begins as a quest ends with a series of questions, each of which is as enigmatic as anything in *The Age of Anxiety*—or perhaps even in all of English poetry:

> Does the Moon's message mean what it says:
> "In that oldest and most hidden of all places
>   Number is unknown"? (511)

The appearance of the moon in Rosetta's speech completes the paradoxical process of de-realization and indicates at the very least that the
back of the divine body may be something other than a place of desertion:
the bright, solar landscape Quant describes gives way to a frozen region
dominated by a lunar presence. The Moon of which Rosetta speaks is also
at the furthest remove from Quant's prosaic description insofar as it—capitalized and capable of speech—seems to be a creature of personification.
Rosetta's question, which may be rhetorical, concerns the rhetorical status
of the apparently personified moon's message. Within the Zoharic context
of "The Seven Stages," the routine manner by which a literal moon is distinguished from its personification suffers radical transformation, indeed
reversal: discourse about the Moon—as the feminine dimension of the
Godhead, otherwise known as the *Shekinah*—is literal, whereas all talk of
the moon remains figural, since this moon is nothing but a derivative image of the Moon.[82] According to the *Zohar*, moreover, the Moon is the basis of all numerical reckoning, while numbers themselves are rooted in a
"certain point"—the *En Sof*—that is "unrevealed and unknowable."[83]
With reference to a verse from Genesis, the author of the *Zohar* can then
emphatically assert: "Great is our Lord, and of great power; His understanding is without *number*."[84] Not only does Rosetta's speech make reference to one of the *Zohar*'s central theosophical principles—the Moon as
Shekinah—it also proceeds to draw on Zoharic vocabulary as it offers a
place for the Moon to speak. Even if a capitalized Moon were not the
source of the message Rosetta ponders, this message would still invite a
kabbalistic treatment, because it draws on a name for God that is common in the literature of Kabbalah but unknown in Christian tradition:
"The Ancient Unrevealed Holy One."[85] The antiquity of God is thus correlated with his hiddenness—until the days of the Messiah. According to
a remarkable verse of Isaiah, the moon will not always be inferior to its
cosmic counterpart: "the light of the moon shall be as the light of the sun"
(Isa. 30: 26).[86] On the authority of this prophetic pronouncement, the author of the *Zohar* proceeds to describe the dawn of the messianic day in
terms of a progressive opening-up of the seven windows that constitute
"The Hall of the Tabernacles": after the fourth window, associated with
cypresses, and the fifth window, named "The Cistern," are opened, the
sixth and penultimate window—*Nagha* or "Brightness"—breaks open, allowing the moon to assume a position equal to that of the sun. And this
glorious event in which the *Shekinah* returns from exile "will then cause

the seventh window to open to the whole world, whose star is the 'Star of Jacob.'"[87]

Rosetta's imagery could hardly be more enigmatic, and since everything she says is cast in the form of a question, nothing certain can emerge from her speech. Yet, the strange tranquility of her questions suggests that the four characters are at a point where they finally begin to give up the quest and recognize the symbolic landscape through which they have been traveling as a supernal body. The desert promises to be precisely what it should be within the symbolic ordering of "The Seven Stages": the back of God. In a poem that mentions Moses twice—and only one other biblical character by name[88]—this part of the divine body has an especially strong resonance. The promise of the desert as something other than a space of desertion and therefore as something that cannot be seamlessly symbolized by a desert unfolds, however tentatively, in Rosetta's speech. The redoubled ambiguity of the doubly symbolic landscape strains the symbolism of "The Seven Stages" to a breaking point. This breakdown of the symbolism may, however, be the disclosure of something other than poetic failure insofar as a new symbolic order could be reestablished in which the back—as both the site of desertion and the place of revelation—rather than any journey backward would provide the schema for symbolic representation. But before this can happen, the "world from which their journey has been one long flight" (512) breaks in: the characters encounter a storm in the desert, which displaces everything so completely that the desert ceases to be a desert. Nothing symbolizes anything anymore, and this lack of symbolic order is then expressed in Rosetta's last speech: *everything* becomes a "symbol, the signature / Of reluctant allegiance to a lost cause" (514). The transformation of the desert into an utterly disorienting and violent storm is the effect of the "perpetual fury" (512) that directly opposes the tranquility toward which Rosetta's description of the "last landscape" tends. The violent storm is not merely a symbol of the war; it destroys the symbolic body as surely as war destroys physical bodies

At the beginning of the poem, having tried to forget the war by reflecting on themselves, the four characters are brought back to the reality of this fury by the radio "breaking in with its banal noises" (454). Having tried to forget the radio by reflecting on the seven ages of life, the characters arrive at the banality of universal mortality. Having tried to forget mortality by engaging in a regressive movement toward the "Primal Age," the characters finally enter an enigmatic landscape of utter desertion that may nevertheless contain an equally enigmatic promise, but the war breaks in once again and destroys their dreamscape. No one can therefore answer Rosetta's haunting question: "Are our dreams indicative?" (511).

V. Assimilation and Simile: "The Masque"

In response to the collapse of "The Seven Stages"—its failure to reach the final place of "prehistoric happiness"—the four characters try something new. Compensating for this collapse, they jointly stage a coupling: under the direction of Malin and Quant, Emble and Rosetta are to be joined. Auden chooses a traditional title for such a staging: "The Masque." It is as if the failure of the four to form themselves without any exertions of will into "a single organism" were replaced by a willful effort to fuse two of them in the presence of the others. That the two who are to be joined happen to be the virile young man and the only available woman corresponds to the ritual character of masques: everyone who appears on stage plays an artistically and socially predetermined role. A return to traditional roles—or perhaps more accurately, a reimposition of established norms—follows on the disorienting experience of "The Seven Stages." Since, however, none of the four characters can be contained by the roles they assign themselves, "The Masque," too, is doomed to failure. And the failure of this compensation for the failure of "The Seven Stages" prepares the way for something altogether new: Rosetta's final speech, in which she reveals herself on the hitherside of all roles and yet in tense relation to a particular tradition.

In the introduction to "The Seven Stages," the narrating voice suggests that the belief in the unity and efficacy of a group acting as "a single organism," like all the beliefs of intoxicated people, is clouded by delusion. But in "The Masque," the narrating voice makes clear that the "euphoric state" in which the path to paradise appears to be blocked by nothing more than "some trifling and easily rectifiable error, improper diet, inadequate schooling, or an outmoded moral code" is sheer delusion "induced" not only by alcohol but also by "lust, fatigue, and the longing to be good": "Just a little more effort, perhaps merely the discovery of the right terms in which to describe it, and surely absolute pleasure must immediately descend upon the astonished armies of this world and abolish for ever all their hate and suffering" (523). And the delusion of the four characters is inversely proportional to the clarity of their common vision of paradise. The paired lovers, Rosetta and Emble, begin the process of representing the "millennial Earthly Paradise" with prophetic descriptions of a renewed, and newly cleansed, world:

Then EMBLE:
Nor money, magic, nor martial law,
Hardness of heart nor hocus-pocus
Are needed now on the novel earth.

ROSETTA:
Nor terrors, tides, contagion longer
Lustrate her stables: their strictures yield
To play and peace. (523)

Once again assuming the role of leader, Malin joins the lovers in the representation of paradise, and in the only unambiguous use of symbolism within this section he provides the principle on which the process of regeneration is based. The desert gives way to a fertile season, as eroticism, represented by the mythological figure of Venus, makes a covenant with creation as a whole:

. . . Venus has now
Agreed so gladly to guarantee
Plenty of water to the plants this year,
Aid to the beasts, to all human demands
Full satisfaction with fresh structures
For crucial regions. (524)

Responding to Malin's provocation, the four characters chime in with successive examples of "full satisfaction," none of which is more than three lines long, and all of which sound strangely like "Vitamins, villas, visas for dogs / And art for all"—and still more troubling, like "Odorless ages, an ordered world / Of planned pleasures and passport control." Emble's remark, "The Visa-Division [will] vouch for all" (523) may indicate a benign version of passport control and canine visas, but the structure of surveillance remains intact. The presupposition of the four characters' prophetic and "euphoric" pronouncements is that each individual can be defined by a single, clearly perceived, and entirely transparent desire that can be satisfied by an unambiguous object: "Places of silence / For real readers" (Emble); "A room with a view / For a shut-in soul" (Rosetta); "Vast museums / For the acquisitive kind to keep tidy" (Quant); "Spigots to open for the spendthrift lot, / And choke-pear choices for champion wills" (Malin). The general principle of these formulations is this: to each his or her own. Malin's concluding contribution is almost a *reductio ad absurdum* of this principle, for it imagines a world in which the range of choices is open for some and closed for others—and the choice of the range of choices is each individual's prerogative. But beyond the disturbing resonances and less than perfectly rational character of these pronouncements, something else renders the principle on which they are based dubious: the complicated sexual dynamics of the four characters. If the preparation for paradise takes place under the consoling iconography of Venus, and if eros, in turn, makes possible a direct—rather than an ironic, analogical, or symbolic—representation of "Earthly Paradise," then sexuality must be the outstanding arena in which desire, wholly transparent to itself, can find "full satisfaction" in a completely recognizable object and under altogether determinable conditions. But the mere fact that Malin and Quant join in the revelry as erotic coaches and voyeurs indicates that something is amiss. And, from the very beginning of the poem, the contours of sexual desire have been anything but straightforward. Emble, the young romantic hero whose wooing of Rosetta constitutes the subject matter of the masque for which Quant and Malin serve as audience, is, as the narrating voice indicates, "fully conscious of the attraction of his uniform to both sexes" (451). But Emble is, from the beginning, oddly miscast as a young and virile suitor, for, despite his "succession of sexual triumphs" (451), his own sexual desires seem oddly anemic, even asexual: all his eroticism is absorbed into a concern about himself as an object of the unrequited desires of others. The narrating voice's description of Emble's affect—"slightly contemptuous when he caught an admiring glance, and slightly piqued when he did not" (451)— finds an echo in Malin's own observations about the young man: "Girlishly glad that my glance is not chaste, / He wants me to want what he would refuse" (504).

Malin's reflections on the sexual dynamics of the situation in which he finds himself paired off with Emble in the middle of "The Seven Stages," contrast with his impersonal account of the emerging sexuality of the "he" whose travels Malin narrates in "The Seven Ages." Unlike the other three characters, each of whom recounts more personal moments in their sexual histories, Malin—who may not be an analyst but who nevertheless assumes the position of the "subject who is supposed to know"[89]—exhibits a kind of detached and sovereign relation to the vicissitudes of desire. Left alone with the young and attractive Emble, however, Malin begins to acknowledge his own desire and recognize the mythological and therefore mendacious character of so-called Platonic love:

> . . . my hunger for a live
> Person to father impassions my sense
> Of this boy's beauty in battle with time.
>
> These old-world hamlets and haphazard lanes
> Are perilous places; how plausible here
> All arcadian cults of carnal perfection,
> How intoxicating the platonic myth. (503)[90]

Malin seeks to sanctify one of these "arcadian cults of carnal perfection" as he builds "a little altar of sandwiches" to the "Queen of love" (519), and Quant contributes to this cultic practice by pouring out "a libation" in honor of "the local spirits" (521). If "The Masque" were published separately, as was "The Dirge,"[91] Malin and Quant's performance might be understood as the good-natured and disinterested facilitation of young and heterosexual romance; but Malin's earlier uneasiness with respect to Emble and everything surrounding Quant casts doubt on this judgment. Masques constitute ritualized systems of desire in which there are only two kinds of elements—shepherds and shepherdesses—and these two kinds relate to each other according to a set of conventional patterns that are supposed to appear natural.[92] And *The Age of Anxiety*, as "A Baroque Eclogue," is cast in the pastoral mold.[93] But it is Quant who first introduces the pastoral motif into the poem when, at the end of "The Seven Ages," he describes Rosetta as a "peregrine nymph" whom he charges to "delight your shepherds" (483). Of the four characters, Quant may be the most difficult to integrate into the conventions of pastoral—not, however, because, as many critics have asserted,[94] he is gay but because his desires are so hilariously disordered and deliciously varied that they resist incorporation into any system of desire; to use Auden's poetological terminology, Quant's desires constitute a crowd. The crowded character of sexual desire stands against the utopian pronouncements made in "The Masque," all of which presuppose that desire can be organized into a system. The complicated situation in which the four characters find themselves, in other words, contradicts the simplicity of their formulas for the paradisal condition. And this is especially true of Quant. Beginning with his vision of a woman in a restaurant as a "siren with six breasts" (468), passing through his raucous adventures in the "bath house" on "Venus Island," where "burghers mixed / With light-fingered ladies and louche trade" (470), and concluding with his extraordinary counternarrative to Malin's account of the "Ages of Man," in which the first six ages are correlated with six male sexual positions and practices, Quant's singular ability to sexualize his own mythopoesis almost overtakes "The Seven Ages" as a whole. Venus's genitalia are imagined as an "indolent ulcer" (479), while the anality of the gnostic demiurge becomes the subject matter of the first counterstage Quant sings to the phallic tune, "*With That Thing*":

> Let me sell you a song, the most side-splitting tale
> Since old Chaos caught young Cosmos bending
> With his back bare and his braces down,
> Homo Vulgaris, the Asterisk Man. (480)

In the dreamscape of "The Seven Stages," Quant, like Malin, exposes the strains to which the pretense of disinterested facilitation of Emble's and Rosetta's drunken courtship are subject; in the last speech in which Quant and Rosetta are alone together, he presents his sexual failure in the vicinity of Rosetta in terms of "a dying man dreaming of a daughter-wife" (504). From a certain perspective, Rosetta's presence in the schema of *The Age of Anxiety* seems as though it were the result of a conventionalization of desire that runs through the genres of eclogue and masque: the woman is the standard sexual object. But Rosetta is, at best, a deeply ambivalent object of desire: Quant's self-designation as "Miss ME" and "Tinklebell" (533), Malin's definite, if attenuated, attraction to Emble, and Emble's own sexual indifference all contribute to a sense that Rosetta is out of place— that the entire erotic dynamic of the poem exists as an affair "between men."[95] When Emble passes out before consummating the sexual act that the entire masque seemed to be preparing, Rosetta's out-of-placeness is manifest. And Rosetta's long speech, as she surveys the unconscious Emble, sprawled out on her bed, is an extended meditation on placelessness. It is not, however, an anxious rumination about sexual displacement, as if she were disappointed by Emble's impotence; rather, her reflections surprisingly turn into a meditation on her own displacement as a Jew. There is nothing surprising, however, about Rosetta's resigned and vaguely amused response to the anticlimactic end to her romance with Emble; her attitude toward her own sexuality and sexual expectations has been remarkably sober and clear-sighted throughout the poem. From the beginning, Rosetta recognizes the mismatch between her own desires and those of the men in whom she half-heartedly invests her eroticism: "Though she was not as young as she looked, there were plenty of men who either were deceived or preferred a girl who might be experienced—which indeed she was. But why were the men one liked not the sort who proposed marriage and the men who proposed marriage not the sort one liked?" (450). As the narrating voice proceeds to say, and the rest of the poem substantiates, Rosetta's daydreams, for all their fairy-tale qualities, never turn into romances with princes as prizes: "So she returned now to her favorite daydream in which she indulged whenever she got a little high . . . and conjured up, detail by detail, one of those landscapes familiar to all readers of English detective stories, those innocent countrysides inhabited by charming eccentrics . . . " (450). Rosetta's lack of interest in romantic love is particularly evident in her description of the second age. Everything in her speech seems to prepare the way for a romantic interlude in which she and her "special" companion breathlessly enjoy an erotic adventure against a backdrop of seaside wealth; but, as the last lines of the speech emphasize, Rosetta's adventure is enjoyed alone. The general sexual context of the second age and the secret places she explores strongly suggest that her adventure is the discovery of her own body, and her eroticism self-stimulating:

> . . . but safe in my purse
> I kept the key to the closet where
> A sliding panel concealed the lift,
> Known to none, which at night would take me
> Down through the dark to my dock below,
> A chamber chiselled in the chalk hill,
> Private and perfect; thence putting forth
> Alone in my launch through a low tunnel
> Out to the ocean, while others slept,
> Smiling and singing I sailed till dawn,
> Happy, hatless. (468)

Rosetta's solitude does not mean that, in this "private and perfect" place, she is not thinking of another; on the contrary, as she says, "One was special" (468). Within the orthographical economy of *The Age of Anxiety*, the capitalization of the word indicates that "One" ought not to be confused with "someone," and the specialness of this "One" further indicates that it marks something other than a "Generalized Other." *One* is, however, clearly one of the names for divinity understood in a resolutely monotheistic manner. Rosetta's critical distance from romantic daydreams is thus intimately connected with her Jewishness, and at the dramatic moment of her first kiss with Emble, the same "One" returns—and indeed returns in a recognizably Zoharic formula: "The Outer Owner, that Oldest One whom / This world is with, be witness to our vows" (521). But the drama of *The Age of Anxiety* does not culminate with the consummation of what this kiss promises; instead, the climax of the poem occurs in Rosetta's long meditation in which "that Oldest One" and resolutely not any "pleasant prince" (527) occupies her attention. Indeed, this meditation concludes the body of the poem—so much so that it is the only place in the poem where the words of a character are allowed to close a section without any commentary by the narrating voice.[96]

As Rosetta tells the sleeping Emble to "dream," she remains awake—"Rest for us both" (527)—and quietly returns to the dream imagery she invoked at the critical moment when the seventh stage was interrupted:

> . . . I won't shine,
> In the sobering sun. We're so apart
> When our ways have crossed and our words touched
> On Babylon's banks. You'll build here, be
> Satisfied soon, while I sit waiting
> On my light luggage to leave if called
> For some new exile, with enough clothes
> But no merry maypole. (527–28)

Rosetta does not quite identify herself with the moon when she denies that she will shine with the sun's rising, but the subtle Zoharic allusion to exile contained in the capitalized Moon of her speech in "The Seven Stages" is intensified by her reference to the most powerful image of exile in the Hebrew Bible:

> By the rivers of Babylon,
> There we sat down, yea, we wept
> When we remembered Zion. (Ps. 137: 1)

Because of the imposing precedent of this Psalm, Babylon has long served as a figure of the condition of exile. But, as Rosetta's invocation of the "sobering sun" suggests, her language keeps figurality at bay. One of the marks of her extraordinary sobriety as she addresses her unconscious, would-be prince—and she has been drinking all night—is her commitment to accounting for her concrete conditions: it is not the *Shekinah* in exile but she herself and the Jewish people as a whole.[97] And nowhere in her speech, which is the longest in the poem, does she imagine herself either in a "Quiet Kingdom" or in a "promised land" where the condition of exile will come to an end; instead, her only prospect is "some new exile." When she does refer to a paradisal location—"the Innocent Place" (529)—it is not only to acknowledge that such locations are "mythical scenes" but also to indicate that she does not confuse the stable English scenery of her drunken daydreams with the displacement that characterizes the historical reality of her own situation. If there is a critical consensus about *The Age of Anxiety*, it lies in the contention that the poem somehow turns on Rosetta's final transformation from self-deceptive Anglophile to self-conscious Jew. Her efforts at assimilation—which are supposed to be the substance of her self-deception—take an amusing detour through the English countryside until she confronts the fact that she will never be assimilated into her host country. A recent example of this interpretation clearly articulates the general scholarly assessment of Rosetta's character: "Rosetta's awareness in her final long speech of a need for a paternal deity resolves her self-delusions."[98] However complicated the concept of self-delusion might be, within the context of *The Age of Anxiety*, it would have to be described in relationship to a key comment from the narrating voice as it introduces "The Masque": "Human beings are, necessarily, actors who . . . can be divided, not into the hypocritical and the sincere, but into the sane who know they are acting and the mad who do not" (518).[99] For Rosetta to be self-delusional in a strict sense—and not simply someone who, as the narrating voice says, "indulged" in "day-dreams . . . whenever she got a little high"—she would have to sincerely believe in the role she plays in her "mythical scenes." But since her daydreams never exceed the realm of fantasy, and since her fantasies are most powerfully cast in terms of dolls and not in terms of herself, words like *self-delusion* miss the mark. If self-delusion is understood, furthermore, to be a moral failing, the accusation that Rosetta is self-deluded until the moment when she finally recognizes that she can never be assimilated into Emble's "gentile" (528) world, has the deeply troubling consequence that moral failure is ascribed solely to Rosetta—rather than to the world from which she, as a Jew, is excluded and in which Jews are persecuted. And this persecution—its concrete history and its current reality—more than her relationship to her father, is the substance of her astonishing final meditation.

The centrality of Rosetta's last speech to *The Age of Anxiety* as a whole can be ascertained by the word with which its mood changes: "anxious." The anxiety of which she speaks is unambiguously plural without being generically "human": it is "our" mood—that of the Jews—in contrast to the moods that characterize either pagan or Christian forms of life. And this anxiety is transformed from an expression of personal despair into a vehicle of common hope:

> You'd slip and blame me
> When you came to, and couldn't accept
> Our anxious hope with no household gods or
> Harpist's Haven for hearty climbers. (528)

In its alliance with anxiety, hope, like Rosetta herself, acquires an unexpected sobriety. In Emble's world, as she presents it, "hopes" are nothing more than "light elations" (528). Elation organizes itself around totemic objects, including "the merry maypole" that serves as the phallic standard for the ritual—overseen by Venus and a host of "local spirits"—in which Rosetta was an active participant until Emble passed out. As she observes the sleeping Emble, Rosetta distances herself from all totemic ceremonies by identifying the conditions for the young prince's crowning capacity to "Be at home" (528): the presence of "household gods" and the promise of a "Harpist's Haven." The combination of a future heaven and a protected earth—with no trace of hell—together constitute "Christian Luck" and the "crease" of Emble's "creed" (528). The exilic condition, by contrast, is without the protection of totemic icons or representations of heavenly reward. And yet, this condition is not entirely without promise. But the promise never breaks into fulfillment and thus remains unarticulated throughout Rosetta's speech. When she cites Psalm 137, Zion does not therefore appear as a counterbalance to Babylon and a reward for perseverance. In Rosetta's sober assessment of her situation, and in *The Age of Anxiety* as a whole, the exilic condition is not predicated on the representation of a promise fulfilled in a promised land. And this makes the condition of exile analogous to what, for Auden, constitutes the fundamental predicament of poetry: each keeps faith with the promise of paradise without ultimately succumbing to enchanted representations of an "Innocent Place."

As Rosetta turns away from Emble, she turns toward concrete events in Jewish history—from the expulsion ordered by Ferdinand and Isabella to Shakespeare's *Merchant of Venice*, to the *Leibzoll* of Germanic states, ending with the refugee crisis of the 1930s and the fate of the S.S. *St. Louis* in particular:

> . . . for we are His Chosen,
> His ragged remnant, with our ripe flesh
> And our hats on, sent out of the room
> By their dying grandees and doleful slaves,
> Kicked in corridors and cold-shouldered
> At toll-bridges, teased upon the stage,
> Snubbed at sea, to seep through boundaries,
> Diffuse like firearms through frightened lands,
> Transpose our plight like a poignant theme
> Into twenty tongues, time-tormented
> But His People still. (529)

The language of this meditation contrasts with that of other speeches in *The Age of Anxiety* in which historical events serve as the subject-matter of poetry, for the earlier speeches are dominated by two reciprocal and mutually reinforcing rhetorical figures: the anthropomorphization of nonhuman things and the naturalization of human beings. Jarrell's disgust with the poem is generated largely by this feature of the opening speeches: "If a boat is torpedoed and the men die, it's just one more chance for rhetoric."[100] Malin's naturalization of human bombing expeditions—"But we laid our eggs / Neatly in their nest, a nice deposit" (455)—and Emble's corresponding anthropomorphism in which drowning sailors are "exposed to snap / Verdicts of sharks" (457) are jarring enough that they lend Jarrell's judgment a certain force. But Jarrell is so exasperated by Auden's apparent lack of sobriety in presenting the realities of war that he fails to comprehend the manner in which both the rhetoric of the poem and the function of rhetoric in the poem develop. The earlier rhetorical extravagance, which fully justifies the attribute "baroque," makes the later rhetorical sparseness recognizable as the effect of a deliberate poetic strategy. According to Hölderlin's doctrine of tonal modulation, a well-constructed poem should begin in a manner that opposes its meaning; tragic poems should begin with naïve reveries, lyrical poems with passionate outbursts, and epics with contemplative musings. Auden makes this doctrine his

own in *The Age of Anxiety*: not only does its basic mood of plurality contrast with the uniformity of the poetic line but the literalness of its cli-
mactic speech opposes the figurative flourishes with which it conspicuously begins. Such literalness is, as Hölderlin would say, "feelable" only in
light of the previous figurality.

The power of Rosetta's meditation—which makes use of only those
traces of anthropomorphizing and naturalizing rhetoric that belong to
everyday language—can be measured by its vast distance from the earlier
speeches in which events of the war are recounted. And the exact canon
for this measurement can be found in the specific trope she allows herself:
simile. Simile resists any assimilation of the terms it compares. Unlike
other tropes of comparison, especially metaphor, simile can be mechani-
cally identified by the presence of a single word—*like* or *as*—but the identification of a simile is not therefore assured, for *like* and *as* can simply
serve as nontropological vehicles in which two elements are compared or
one element is singled out as an example of a kind. When Rosetta, speaking of Emble, says "More boys like this one may embrace me yet" (530),
she could scarcely be less rhetorical. By contrast, *like* and *as* enter into the
sphere of tropes only under the condition that they intensify their comparative function and emphasize the distinctness of two registers across
the comparison they establish. When such distinctness rises to the level of
discord, *like* or *as* can be unambiguously understood to mark the occurrence of a simile.

Auden, who experimented with the explosive potential of simile
throughout his poems in the 1930s,[101] discloses a new dimension of *like* by
making it into a controlling feature of Rosetta's speech. When she says
that the Jews are "Diffuse like firearms," her speech does not simply draw
strength from the explosive power of simile; the simile is itself as explosive
as a firearm. And when she says that the Jews "Transpose their plight like
a poignant theme," the political, social, and religious strife that gives rise
to "their plight" oppugns the harmonious atmosphere in which musical
themes develop, and this discord is itself captured in the word *poignant*,
which originally referred to weapons and has come to mean both "pierc-
ingly painful" and "agreeably intense." Whether the simile compares the
"plight" of the Jews to a destructive instrument ("firearms") or a creative
impulse ("poignant theme") is of less importance than the clash it stages
between the reality of this plight and the rhetorical resources available for
its expression.

The clash between reality and rhetoric in Rosetta's discordant similes corresponds to a constitutive tension that traverses her long meditation. Within the perspective of the events of Jewish history on which she reflects, anxiety is not simply a given; it is a "gift": "Time is our trade, to be tense our gift" (529). Within the parameters of Rosetta's domestic setting, by contrast, "peace" appears to be the goal:

> I shan't find shelter, I shan't be at peace
> Till I really take your restless hands,
> My poor fat father. (530)

This discord between the "gift" of tension and the goal of domestic "peace" plays itself out in a struggle between two divergent narratives: one about Jewish persecution and the other about Rosetta's childhood home. The narratives are divergent insofar as Rosetta does not place her childhood within the context of Jewish history. Instead of, for example, describing a household in which Jewish practices are observed or, in a gesture of resolute assimilation, consciously ignored, Rosetta connects her two narratives by way of a powerfully articulated reflection on divine omniscience. And the tension between Jewish history and her childhood experiences is concentrated in a point of convergence marked by the word *like*:

> . . . He won't pretend to
> Forget how I began, nor grant belief
> In the mythical scenes I make up
> Of a home like theirs, the Innocent Place where
> His Law can't look, the leaves are so thick. (529)

Insofar as "His Law" does not apply to their homes, the *like* is as nontropological as the *like* in the phrase, "more boys like this one": Rosetta is imagining a nonkosher household. Insofar as "His Law" is, as the word *look* indicates, a trope for divine knowledge, however, the *like* is a strangely self-subverting simile: "A home like theirs" as she imagines it exists only in the mendacity of myth, since no home on earth has leaves thick enough to obscure "His" vision. Rosetta may present God as a "He," but she never refers to him as God the father, and although she speaks of "His People," she never refers to them as his children. And precisely because Rosetta does not identify God with—or as—her father, the entire structure of the second part of her meditation approaches that of a simile:

her father is being compared with God, who is not a father, and the comparison thus registers a startling discord between the two elements of the implicit simile. Her father is decidedly unlike the God whom she describes not least of all because the latter strikes down all myths, whereas the former lies whenever he sees fit: "You so longed to be liked. You lied so, / Didn't you, dad?" (530). By the time Rosetta defines her father's longing, the word *liked* seems like the residue of the similes that have punctuated her speech.

Rosetta's thoughts turn away from her troubled relation to the world Emble inhabits and concentrate instead on the events of Jewish history in the first part of her meditation; similarly, they turn away from her equally, if more profoundly, troubled relation to her father and return to the history of persecution in the second part. The discord between the tension of Jewish history and the potential peace of her domestic relations is resolved in favor of the former, which is to say, it is resolved in favor of tension. This resolution does not alleviate the tensions of her domestic relations, as if a renewed recognition of her Jewishness would reconcile Rosetta with her father; still less, would the act of embracing her father amount to a resolution of the tensions of Jewish history. The renewed acceptance of the "gift" of tension in Rosetta's speech expresses itself in the seamless transformation of the "We both" that refers to her father and herself into the "We . . . all" that refers to those who are anxious about Moses' admonitions:

> We both were asking
> For a warmth there wasn't, and then wouldn't write.
> We mustn't, must we? Moses will scold if
> We're not all there for the next meeting
> At some brackish well or broken arch,
> Tired as we are. (530)

Rosetta never uses the words *Jew* or *Jewish*; instead, she uses equivalent terms like "His Chosen" and "His People." But she also has a more exact, even technical term for those who are made tense by the thought of Moses scolding: "His ragged remnant." The two basic characteristics of this remnant are extreme vulnerability—"ripe flesh"—and the combination of the preparedness for exile and the humility before God that are both signaled by always having their "hats on" (529). The term *remnant*, a key prophetic term first developed by Isaiah, designates not only those who survive the persecutions to which the people of Israel are subject but also those among the Israelites who remain faithful as the tribulations of the messianic era drive the majority into faithlessness.[102] Immediately after Isaiah begins to describe the Days of the Messiah as those in which "the leopard shall lie down with the kid; and the calf and the young lion and the fatling together" (Isa. 11: 6), he reveals the manner in which the remnant will be recovered: "It shall come to pass in that day, that the Lord shall set his hand again the second time to recover the remnant of his people. . . . He will hold up a signal to the nations and assemble the banished of Israel, and gather the dispersed of Judah from the four corners of the earth" (Isa. 11: 11–12). And in one of the most syntactically complicated sentences of the poem—which introduces the simplest—Rosetta, following Isaiah, elaborates the specific and defining function of the "ragged remnant":

> We'll point for Him,
> Be as obvious always if He won't show
> To threaten their thinking in their way,
> Nor His strong arm that stood no nonsense,
> Fly, let's face it, to defend us now
> When bruised or broiled our bodies are chucked
> Like cracked crocks onto kitchen middens
> In the time He takes. We'll trust. (529)

The task of the remnant is distributed between two stances: pointing-for and trusting. The sentence, "We'll trust," can be so short precisely because it does not need to identify that in which the remnant trusts. The relation of faith that binds remnant and God is utterly simple. The relation of remnant to the majority nonremnant, by contrast, gives rise to an immensely complicated problem of reference, and the sentence in which this referential relation is expressed is correspondingly complex. By pointing "for Him," the remnant serves as a sign of divine presence for the majority—whether the latter is able to read the sign or not. And the question of readability extends to the sentence itself, for it can be read in two radically different and even mutually exclusive ways. On the one hand, the remnant, as the sign of divine presence, can be understood to "threaten" the totemic, mythological, or ideological thinking of the faithless "if He won't show," which is to say, in times of divine absence. On the other hand, *if* in the phrase "if He won't show" can be understood as "even if," and another, perhaps more fluid reading results: the remnant remains "obvious" and therefore continues to serve as his sign even under the condition that God refuses to make his presence known by threatening the idolatrous or protecting the faithful. The doubling of the reading occurs at the precise point where the simile assumes a demonic, even monstrous, ambiguity. The shock of the simile "our bodies are chucked / Like cracked crocks" does not simply derive from the comparison of utterly incongruous elements. Auden seems finally to be straining the coordinating power of *like* to a breaking point. But the real shock of his formulation does not lie in some startlingly new juxtaposition; it lies, rather, in what, on reflection, is the utter lack of strain on the term *like*. In the formulation "Like cracked crocks," against all expectation, *like* is thoroughly nontropological: the bodies of the Jews are "now" being made into the dehumanized matter of which "cracked crocks" are an example. Auden is not responsible for the assimilation of human beings into mere inanimate matter—the monstrous work of the Nazi extermination camps. By putting this assimilation into poetic form—and indeed, into the form of the startling simile for which he was known in the late 1930s—he sets this terrifying historical event, rather than any erotic, psychological, or even religious fulfillment, at the climax of *The Age of Anxiety*. Auden punctuates this moment with a particularly dense poetic line that exactly doubles the standard alliterative pattern of repeating three consonants: "Li*k*e *c*ra*ck*ed *c*ro*ck*s onto *k*itchen middens." Thus the moment the poem touches on the greatest terror, its line comes closest to inarticulate stuttering.

VI. Dumb for Dead

Rosetta and Malin are never alone together in the course of the poem. This might not seem remarkable, but they are the only two characters who never appear as a pair. Instead, the structure of the poem places them in parallel positions. *The Age of Anxiety* has two endings: Rosetta concludes the body of the poem, and Malin gives the final speech of the "Epilogue" in a powerful meditation that invites comparison with Rosetta's. In addition to the paired meditations of these two characters, there are at least two other endings: the narrating voice closes the "Epilogue" after Malin's concluding meditation, and Auden appended an additional poem to copies of *The Age of Anxiety* he gave to friends. Auden published a version of this omitted verse in a privately printed pamphlet and allowed still another version to be published under the title "Anthem" in *Epistle to a*

Godson.[103] This last poem would have been a decisive conclusion to *The Age of Anxiety* as a whole. The world of which it speaks has resolved the potentially murderous dilemma of odor and order. For order is not only *not* odorless; on the contrary, "another" odor is the sign and seal of order:

PRAISE YE THE LORD.

Let the whole creation give out another sweetness,
Nicer in our nostrils, a novel fragrance
From cleansed occasions in accord together
As one feeling fabric, all flushed and intact
Phenomena and numbers announcing in one
Multitudinous oecumenical song
Their grand giveness of gratitude and joy,
Peaceable and plural, their positive truth
An authoritative This, an unthreatened Now
When in love and in laughter, each lives himself,
For united by His word cognition and power
System and order are a single glory
And the pattern is complex, their places safe.[104]

Paradise, for Auden, consists in the perfect order of a system in which the system has no other function than the elegant embodiment of the community. The song of this community is "oecumenical," embracing all the inhabitants of "the human household" (535)—to cite the translation of the Greek term that Malin incorporates into his final meditation. Because of its ecumenical claim, as it resolves the dilemma of odor and order, this poem would also have resolved the unstated and yet unmistakable opposition between the Jewish meditation of Rosetta, which omits the word *Jew*, and the Christian meditation of Malin, which omits both *Jesus* and *Christ*.

None of the voices in *The Age of Anxiety*, however, is in a position to deliver the anthem that Auden omitted from the published version of this text. The narrating voice never breaks out of prose and has given no indication that it is prepared to praise. Emble has passed out, and although Quant has departed on an ecumenical note—"Come, Tinklebell, trot. Let's pretend you're a thoroughbred. / Over the hill now into Abraham's Bosom" (533)[105]—his return to ironic forecasts of a future blessed by proponents of "the Functional Society" (533) runs counter to the serious and straightforward tone of the anthem. Rosetta would utterly destroy the unity of her character if she were to start speaking of an ecumenical song.

The Radio might well speak of "cleansed creatures"[106] but only to create anxiety about cleanliness. And Malin, who seems the most obvious character to assign this poem, opens his final and most impressive meditation with words that directly contradict the talk of "positive truth" in the anthem: "For others, like me, there is only the flash / Of negative knowledge" (534). If Malin were to speak the lines of the anthem, furthermore, this would not only compromise the negative integrity of his character but also detract from the independence and completeness of the others', as if all their speeches were merely preparation for his *Summa theologica.* Any suggestion that Malin is somehow the voice of Auden goes in the same direction.[107] *The Age of Anxiety* is thus effectively left without a definitive ending—suspended between the alternate conclusions of Rosetta and Malin. This endlessness corresponds to the one trait that binds the otherwise opposed meditations of the two: based on an absolute rejection of totemic ritual in all its modern varieties, they both, like the prophets, suddenly shift perspective in the direction of a messianic ending.

Malin and Rosetta do not engage in a dialogue, nor does the fact that Malin's meditation follows Rosetta's indicate that her words are a "paternal" preparation for "the Christian solution"[108]—at the very least because it is Malin alone, and decisively not Rosetta, who casts the relationship between God and human beings in paternalistic terms when he speaks in the last sentence of his meditation of "us" as "His children" (535). Recognizing the integrity of their opposing meditations, Auden does not then seek some "fusion of horizons"[109] that would encompass both, nor does he pose "an ideal speech situation"[110] to resolve the conflict established by the double conclusion of *The Age of Anxiety.* Still less does he resolve this conflict by having them "both say the same thing"[111]—namely, that the solution lies in mystical insight. The messianic is not mystical. The messianic is deeply this-worldly, as are Rosetta's concern with the obviousness of the remnant—"We'll point for Him, / Be as obvious always"—and Malin's worry about the obviousness of "the new locus":

> the place of birth
> Is too obvious and near to notice,
> Some dull dogpatch a stone's throw
> Outside the walls (534)

Without engaging in a dialogue with Rosetta, Malin adopts something she said in an earlier part of the poem as he seeks words for precisely that which he cannot conceive. During the discussion of the sixth age, Rosetta incorporated the magnificent verse of Isaiah concerning the Days of the Messiah—"the leopard shall lie down with the kid; and the calf and the young lion and the fatling together" (Isa. 11: 6)—into her image of the "Primal Age":

> unicorn herds
> Galumphed through lilies; little mice played
> With great cock-a-hoop cats (479)

This incongruous juxtaposition of "unicorn" and "great . . . cats" returns in the sole positive picture Malin is able to draw of what he calls, in the very last words of his final meditation, "His World to come" (535):

> We simply cannot conceive
> With any feelings we have
> How the raging lion is to lime
> With the yearning unicorn;
> Nor shall we, till total shipwreck
> Deprive us of our persons. (533)

Malin thus transposes Rosetta's image from a "Primal Age" to a messianic future, and in so doing, he follows her earlier path. For Malin, messianic reconciliation of opposites is not in itself inconceivable; but no conception of such a future can be meaningful unless it is accompanied by feeling. The very image in which the messianic kingdom is cast names feelings that Malin's conception of reconciliation nowhere betrays: it neither rages against injustice nor yearns for justice but only, at most, bemoans the foolishness, blindness, and stubbornness of human beings in general.

Rosetta's final meditation, by contrast, evinces both rage and yearning. And unlike Malin, she completely rids herself of any positive formulation of the messianic kingdom. The "anxious hope" of which she speaks knows no measure for its fulfillment—least of all a measure in which mythical unicorns are still invested with symbolic weight. What is left for Rosetta are only certain "great . . . cats" whose significance is as difficult to determine as the messianic day is to imagine:

> We must try to get on
> Though mobs run amok and markets fall,
> Though lights burn late at police stations,
> Though passports expire and ports are watched,

> Though thousands tumble. Must their blue glare
> Outlast the lions? Who'll be left to see it
> Disconcerted? I'll be dumb before
> The barracks burn and boisterous Pharaoh
> Grow ashamed and shy. *Sh⁽ma' Yisra'el:*
> *'ᵃdonai ᵉlohenu, 'ᵃdonai 'echad.* (530)

Nowhere is Rosetta more sober in her presentation of the mechanisms of terror; nowhere outside of "The Seven Stages" does a symbol, "the lions,"[112] appear more opaque; and nowhere else in the poem does Auden take the opportunity to write a sentence in another language. This last gesture—which is a common feature not only of Auden's own poetic writings but of the modernist project as a whole since the two anti-Semites, Eliot and Pound, began to publish their work—perfectly integrates the Hebrew *Sh⁽ma'* into the alliteration of the poem's Anglo-Saxon-inspired lines, and it allows Rosetta to conclude her speech, and thus the body of the poem, with the word that has come to punctuate her discourse: *'echad*, "One."[113]

~

  Ever since Rosetta thinks of Babylon, her meditation has moved between biblical exile and the contemporary condition of exile from the promised land—without, however, either draining contemporary reality of its terror by making its events into ever-repeated types or making biblical pronouncements into the guide for confronting contemporary conditions. Having just spoken of Moses scolding those who are unprepared for departure, Rosetta articulates a fundamental imperative that, in both its colloquial form and in its modest content, directs itself more toward contemporaneous events than toward the irruptions of idol worship for which Moses scolded the Israelites: "We must try to get on." Oscillations between divergent times are an unmistakable feature of the messianic passages in the prophetic books. And in these passages, as in Rosetta's meditation, historical time is neither disparaged nor divinized: neither does the loss of paradise in the past make all of historical time unworthy of attention and passionate involvement, nor is the recovery of paradise in the future an inevitable outcome of some providential process.[114] And in the words with which Rosetta prefaces the *Sh⁽ma'*, the oscillation between two tormenting times of exile comes to a stunning conclusion as Rosetta's sole venture in prophecy:

I'll be dumb before
The barracks burn and boisterous Pharaoh
Grow ashamed and shy.

Rosetta describes the "ragged remnant" as "time-tormented," and the temporality—or mood—of her last English sentence is indeed tormented: the subjunctive "grow" is an archaic form that retrospectively conditions the indicative contraction "I'll be." When Rosetta thus speaks of the future, she does not describe paradise, nor does she take the opportunity to proclaim that paradise is inconceivable, nor does she ironically invoke images of an odorless future in a "Functional Society." The future of which she speaks is as modest as her imperative: military installations disappear, and Pharaohs are no longer without shame. Hers is a prophecy in the tradition of Isaiah precisely because the future prophesied, although presented in the indicative, is always traversed by a subjunctive: prophecy, unlike fortune telling, combines exhortation and contingency, both of which are, in English, expressed in the subjunctive. Rosetta refuses to resign herself to a fatalistic conception of the future in which barracks are burned only to be rebuilt and Pharaohs always return to their boisterous ways; in other words, she does not simply forecast the inevitable continuation of horrors beyond the equally inevitable end of her life by proclaiming "I'll be dead before" a messianic kingdom arrives. Instead, she replaces *dead* with *dumb*: she will have lost her voice before the Days of the Messiah arrive. Those days should be days of rejoicing and praise, but even to suggest that the arrival of the Messiah would make good on all the terrible events of history is to deprive historical reality of its suffering substance. The replacement of *dumb* for *dead*, by contrast, maintains the rigor of her sober, disenchanted, and entirely clear-sighted perspective on political and historical reality without succumbing to the pathos of self-pity that would make her death into the central event of her prophecy.

Earlier in Rosetta's meditation she articulates something like a formula for this delicate balance: "anxious hope." With this formula, the entire tenor of *The Age of Anxiety* alters: if the anxiety of the age is hopeful, then the age is not altogether unrelated to that of the Messiah. Hope appears in the last English line of her poem in the images of barracks—not human beings—burning, and Pharaoh ceasing to be boisterous, if not falling silent altogether. Anxiety appears in Rosetta's own comportment: dumbness. Without a voice to embrace in praise and joy the Days of the Messiah, those days cannot be finally fulfilled: the formula "anxious hope" thus operates in both directions. Not only does hope draw anxiety out of the solace of despair, but anxiety, in the form of speechlessness, inhabits the hoped-for world. But even the wholly negative disclosure of the messianic day contained in the idea of "anxious hope" reaches beyond the letter of the poem: petrified, Rosetta is made into a Rosetta Stone—or Rosetta Stein[115]—who provides the basis for the decipherment of a sacred script (*hiero-glyph*) by superimposing one language onto another. But the words of Rosetta's prophecy are rendered uncertain by the disconcerting grammar of the subjunctive formulation in which the end of grief might be announced and "boisterous Pharaoh / Grow ashamed and shy." This grammatical uncertainty casts the shadow of an unarticulated condition on Rosetta's final meditation. And so, with the end suspended in speechlessness and conditionality, the poem resumes—and then ends—without a proper ending: "its adoption, as usual postponed" (536).

§ 3 Arendt's Messianism

"The Human Condition"

> To forgive is not so
> Simple as it is made to sound. . . .
> —W. H. Auden, "Music Is International"

I. "Weak Messianic Force"

Rosetta's meditation opens up a space of novelty in *The Age of Anxiety*. In "The Seven Ages" Rosetta opposes Quant's vision of eternal return by posing her own countervision of a privileged time, or "Primal Age"—a time in which, for the child, the world is new. In her final meditation, however, she enacts another and far more powerful refutation of the Quantian conception of time. Instead of imaginatively recreating a world as it newly reveals itself to the child, Rosetta suddenly inserts something new into the poem for which nothing—or nothing obvious[1]—serves as precedent: the account of "the ragged remnant" that culminates in the imperative, "we must try to get on." Critics of *The Age of Anxiety* have repeatedly noted Rosetta's startling change, and some have found its suddenness so unexpected and implausible that they consider it an aesthetic failure. No one, so the accusation runs, could have known what she is: a Jew. Paradoxically, she goes out of character at the precise moment she reveals herself—beyond character.[2] Without any pretensions to aesthetic inquiry, Arendt captures something of this paradox in a remark she makes in a section of *The Human Condition* on "enacted stories":

> The moment we want to say *who* somebody is, our very vocabulary leads us astray into saying *what* he is; we get entangled in a description of qualities he necessarily shares with others like him; we begin to describe a type or a "character" in the old meaning of the word, with the result that his specific uniqueness escapes us.[3]

The novelty of Rosetta's meditation consists in her self-disclosure, and un-expectedness is the hallmark of novelty. The critical conundrum with re-spect to the closing moments of Rosetta's speech is evidence of the diffi-culty, perhaps even the intractability, of the problem posed by the unprecedented, unprepared, and unanticipated fact of novelty. This prob-lem is so central to *The Age of Anxiety* that it absorbs all Malin's consider-able powers of reflection as he closes the poem. And the same is true for Arendt in *The Human Condition*, which culminates in an account of ac-tion and the ability to begin something new. Malin's thoughts revolve around the inconceivability of "the new locus," and the sole image of what cannot be conceived is the miraculous—but altogether "obvious"—birth of a child. So, too, with Arendt, who closes the section on "Action" in *The Human Condition* by drawing out the consequences of her central insight that "the new . . . always appears in the guise of a miracle" (178):

> The miracle that saves the world, the realm of human affairs, from its normal, "natural" ruin is ultimately the fact of natality, in which the faculty of action is ontologically rooted. It is, in other words, the birth of new men and the new beginning, the action they are capable of by virtue of being born. Only the full experience of this capacity can bestow upon human affairs faith and hope, those two essential characteristics of human existence which Greek antiquity ignored altogether, discounting the keeping of faith as a very uncommon and not too important virtue and counting hope among the evil illusions of Pan-dora's box. It is this faith in and hope for the world that found perhaps its most glorious and succinct expression in the few words with which the Gospels an-nounced their "glad tidings": "A child has been born unto us." (247)

With this citation, Arendt brings together all the many strands of her complex analysis of action with singular, if nevertheless uneasy, rhetorical power and elegance. Taken out of its overall context, however, this para-graph—or at least its final quotation—seems out of character for the au-thor of *Rahel Varnhagen: The Life of a Jewess*, the concluding chapter of which is called "One Does Not Escape Jewishness."[4] In closing her reflec-tions on action, Arendt draws on an age-old tradition of Christian oration in which a startlingly apt quotation from the Gospels serves as the sign and seal of truth: if a discourse ultimately converges with the Word of God, it may have errors, but it certainly cannot be errant. Yet there is something aberrant about Arendt's citation: the "glad tidings" she quotes do not appear anywhere in the Gospels. "A child has been born unto us" is drawn from the opening messianic passages of Isaiah: "For a child has been born to us" (Isaiah 9: 5); "For unto us a child is born" (King James version).[5] Whatever the origin of this mistake—deliberate strategy, parapraxis, mere oversight, or a complex combination of all three—this much is clear: her argument proceeds in accordance with the worldliness of Isaiah as opposed to the otherworldly spirit of *The New Testament*. In a famous essay published soon after *The Human Condition*, Gershom Scholem, attentive at every turn to the interpretative problems posed by this passage from Isaiah, presents the distinction between Jewish and Christian messianism in polemical terms: "Judaism, in all its forms and manifestations, has always maintained a concept of redemption as an event which takes place publicly, on the stage of history and within the community. . . . In contrast, Christianity conceives of redemption as an event in the spiritual and unseen realm, an event which is reflected in the soul, in the private world of each individual, and which effects an inner transformation which need not correspond to anything outside."[6] Unlike Scholem, Arendt is not a polemicist; she does not oppose Jewish and Christian interpretations of the messiah. Neither, however, is she a conciliator, who posits something like a "Judeo-Christian" tradition. Without ever referring to a Jewish messiah in the course of *The Human Condition*, frequently referring to the figure of Jesus, quoting from Isaiah, and attributing this quotation to the Gospels, Arendt makes a surprising and almost totally inconspicuous contribution to—in Scholem's words—"the messianic idea in Judaism."

The "glad tidings" Arendt announces express faith in the world—not in God. And, for Arendt, the *world* is saved—not souls from the world. Salvation of the world from its inherent ruination is at the center of *The Human Condition*; this salvation has nothing to do with any effort to transcend the conditions in which human beings find themselves and is therefore antithetical to the worldlessness of Christianity as Arendt herself presents it. The child appears as a representative of the world and an antidote to ruin.[7] Whether ruination is understood in relation to the traditional Christian doctrine of original sin, the Kiekegaardian transformation of this doctrine under the rubric of despair, the Heideggerian reinterpretation of Kierkegaardian despair as *Ruinanz*,[8] or—more radically still—the Benjaminian image of progress as "one single catastrophe that keeps piling wreckage upon wreckage"[9] is of little importance: *The Human Condition* sets itself the task of showing the manner in which "normal, 'natural' ruin" can be overcome without overcoming the limits of the human condition.

Arendt's concluding paragraph, to quote Malin's words from *The Age of Anxiety*, "makes meaning by omission and stress": it stresses the role of the Greeks and omits any reference to Jews. The omission of Isaiah's name corresponds to the elision of a phrase from the passage in Paul's first letter to the Corinthians to which Arendt clearly alludes: "a scandal to the Jews; foolishness to the Greeks" (1 Cor. 1: 23). Of the Greeks, Arendt has much to say: they dismissed the importance of faith among the list of virtues and considered hope a version of vice. From the perspective of the contemplative life—and this perspective is what Greek philosophers first discovered—both faith and hope are foolish, since, each in its own way, attaches itself to time and thus distracts the thinker from the eternal objects of contemplation. But Arendt gives no indication of how the evangelical announcement of birth might be understood as a stumbling block to the Jews. The idea of a crucified God-man in whom one is supposed to believe is a *skandalon* to the Jews, according to Paul, because they "demand signs" (1 Cor., 1: 22); which is to say, the story of Jesus does not correspond to Jewish conceptions of a this-worldly Messiah who will fulfill the promise articulated by the prophets, gather those who have been dispersed, restore the Davidic kingdom, and usher in an age of peace. The Jews are scandalized, in short, because they refuse to abandon the world for the sake of saving their souls: their hope, if not their faith, rests in this world.[10] From the perspective of Paul, Arendt is less Greek than Jewish, for she finds the otherworldly character of Christian messianism a stumbling block; and for Arendt, Christianity, as a doctrine codified by Paul, derives the otherworldliness she so adamantly rejects from the contemplative life discovered by Greek philosophy.[11] As she gestures in the direction of the Gospels, she nevertheless remains faithful to those traditions of Jewish messianic thought that refuse to abandon hope for this world. And yet, she significantly complicates these traditions by bending faith in the direction of hope: faith, too, remains within the limits of the world. This complication cannot, however, be confused with the transformation of messianic ideas into some version of secular utopianism, for, according to a process Arendt mercilessly dissects in *The Origins of Totalitarianism*, "faith in the world" is precisely *not* faith in the ability of human beings to fabricate their world.[12] And in this regard, Arendt completely agrees with the strictest rabbinic interpretations of the messianic tendency of Judaic texts: we are not called on to build the messianic kingdom.[13] Even as she stretches the tradition of Jewish messianic thought to the breaking point—speaking of "glad tidings" and "faith in the world"—Arendt retains and indeed strengthens one of the elemental features through which the messianic idea in Judaism has been able to keep itself distinct from the messianism inherent in the very term "Christianity": just as an unmistakable message of Jewish messianism is that the Jewish people must actively absorb itself in the world of exile while all along remaining ready to abandon this world for another one in the promised land, Arendt shows that complete commitment to the world demands an equally complete readiness to begin anew in a new one.

Arendt's *Human Condition* belongs to the tradition of Jewish messianic thought. It does not concern itself with the restoration of the Davidic kingdom, and it does not present any images of utopian peace in which "the wolf shall dwell with the lamb" (Isa. II: 6). Nor does it seek to universalize the messianic promise by converting it into some form of revolutionary socialism. Nor does it, like the short-lived German-Jewish tradition inaugurated and completed by Hermann Cohen, seek to show the inner connection between the prophetic conception of the messianic age and the Kantian Idea of the "kingdom of ends."[14] Nor, finally, does it model itself after Benjamin's "Über den Begriff der Geschichte"—which Arendt herself helped save from destruction[15]—and weave together in a fragmentary fashion messianic and materialist critiques of historicist procedures and methodologies. But Arendt's work nevertheless can be understood to draw some of its strength from Benjamin's late reflections, since she charges natality with precisely that "*weak* messianic force" with which, according to Benjamin, "every generation," including our own, has been "endowed"[16]: natality is able to save the world from its inherent ruination. This messianic force is "weak" because natality is the precise opposite of sovereignty: it is self-exposure not self-assertion. As she replaces Benjamin's vague word *generation* (*Geschlecht*) with the technical term *natality*, Arendt goes one step further than her friend in constructing an account of "the human condition" according to models of thought developed within the parameters of Jewish messianic traditions. Unlike his messianism, hers is inconspicuous, since she nowhere calls on a supreme being to abrogate the conditionality of human beings, does not use the term *messiah*, and makes no explicit reference to any figure who might be associated with messianic Judaism—with the peculiar and perhaps even ironic exception of Jesus.

But the very inconspicuousness of Arendt's messianism[17]—and inconspicuousness, too, is a messianic theme—allows her to retain the thought
of salvation without succumbing either to some form of traditionalism
that understands redemption as the act of a transcendent being or to some
version of modernism that neutralizes the messianic idea by representing
the redeemed world as a matter of human fabrication.[18] Quoting Isaiah
under the guise of the Gospels—this is, in miniature, Arendt's procedure
for slipping messianism into a discourse that seems antithetical to its aims.

II. Beginning and Ends

Messianic hope expresses itself in the idea that time is coming to a close.
Although this idea can then be represented in apocalyptic imagery, such
imagery is not only not necessary; it may have little—and, as some have
argued, absolutely nothing—to do with messianism.[19] It is legitimate to
speak of time coming to a close only if a new time has already begun, and
these two times somehow compete with one another. Apocalyptic messianism from The Book of Daniel and The Apocalypse of John to modern
totalitarian ideologies represents this competition in terms of clashing
armies. The violent imagery of a final and decisive battle is in no small
measure the reason for mistrusting anything associated with militant,
apocalyptic messianism. But the presentation of two times in competition
with each other need not adopt any martial imagery, and messianism need
not be confused with millenarianism. The surest way to avoid the casual
association of the messianic with the apocalyptic is to champion newness
over closure—to the point where apocalyptic phrases like "the end of
time" or, to use the Hegelian version, "the end of history" are systematically avoided. And this is precisely what Arendt does in *The Human Condition*.[20] Although her analysis is everywhere sensitive to ends—in both
senses of the word—she closes her account of action not with an announcement to the effect that time is coming to a close but by way of mis-
citation: "A child has been born unto us." Here, too, she adopts the redemptive procedure of "pearl diving" that, as she herself indicates, gives
Benjamin's messianism its extraordinary vitality.[21] And the motif of interruption, which runs throughout Benjamin's lifelong effort to rethink the
category of the messianic and determines his characteristic technique of
quotation,[22] gives shape to her account of the complicated structure of
human temporality:

It is the faculty of action that interferes with this law [of mortality] because it interrupts the inexorable automatic course of daily life, which in its turn, as we saw, interrupted and interfered with the cycle of the biological life process. The life span of man running toward death would inevitably carry everything human to ruin and destruction if it were not for the faculty of interrupting it and beginning something new, a faculty which is inherent in action like an ever-present reminder that men, though they must die, are not born in order to die but in order to begin. (246)

With this concentrated exposition of the interruptive movement of action, Arendt opens up a perspective on the human condition that almost—but only almost—takes leave from this condition as it touches on certain theological themes.[23] Human affairs are not entirely abandoned to death and ruin because of a faculty Arendt likens to "an ever-present reminder" of the purpose of life. This reminder functions in a manner analogous, but opposed, to the *memento mori* of Christian theology, with its many philosophical and literary heirs. Not only does Arendt replace the dismal thought of inevitable death with the idea of beginning; she also inverts the teleological order in which the concept of "in order to" operates: the *telos* of human life is precisely not to reach an end—either in the sense of achieving a purpose or coming to a conclusion. On the contrary, the end is to begin. The oddness of this formulation corresponds to the strangeness of Arendt's invocation of the utilitarian phrase "in order to" as the culmination of her account of that mode of the *vita activa* that has nothing to do with utilitarian concerns, namely action. According to her acute analysis of *homo faber*, both utilitarians and those, like Kant, who oppose utilitarianism on the basis of instrumental schemata make a disastrous misstep when they fail to distinguish purposiveness, expressed by "in order to," and meaningfulness, expressed by "for the sake of": "The 'in order to' has become the content of the 'for the sake of'; in other words, utility established as meaning generates meaninglessness" (154). It is precisely the generalization of the means-ends schema that, Arendt argues, destroys the meaningfulness of human life: "The issue at stake is, of course, not instrumentality, the use of means to achieve an end, as such, but rather the generalization of the fabrication experience in which usefulness and utility are established as the ultimate standards of life and the world of men" (157).[24]

Yet, Arendt does not reject the language of "in order to" when she comes to formulate her most explicit account of why human beings are born. If she were to say something like "human beings are born for the sake of beginning," she would transcend the human condition and claim insight into the meaning of human life as a whole. The use of the more modest, instrumental term "in order to" forestalls any such pretension, even as it seems to participate in the ruinous instrumentality that renders the world utterly without meaning. Kant's solution to the problem posed by "the generalization of the fabrication experience" in which every end immediately becomes just another means is to anoint the human being an "end in itself" and thus lord and master over a constantly devaluing world. But by granting human beings the exalted position expressed by the peculiar phrase "end in itself," which is "either a tautology applying to all ends or a contradiction in terms" (154), the rest of the world is relegated to sheer instrumentality: "The same operation which establishes man as the 'supreme end' permits him 'if he can [to] subject the whole of nature to it,' that is, to degrade nature and the world into mere means, robbing both of their independent dignity" (156). Once human beings are considered the only things exempt from instrumentality, the devaluation is not only *not* stopped but is further accelerated. Arendt, by contrast, paradoxically interrupts this acceleration by extending the use of "in order to" so far that it encompasses all of human life: its end is to break out of the order of "in order to." But this breaking out is always only beginning: it is never completed and certainly never cemented into a "supreme end." As opposed to Kant, Arendt thus places human beings *within* the instrumental order, and she does so in order to make room for something other than human beings outside this very order: the *hyper*-generalization of the "in-order-to" structure thwarts the devaluation that accompanies its generalization. Arendt's formulation gestures—but only gestures—toward the thought that God places every human being on earth in order to carry out a specific purpose. What unites utilitarian, Kantian, and theological modes of thought is precisely the idea of fabrication: creation is understood from the perspective of making, and God the creator fabricates a world populated by human beings who are charged with fulfilling the ends for which they are destined. But by insisting that the purpose of action is immediately fulfilled when it begins—for "the end (*telos*) . . . lies in the activity itself" (206) and "action has no end" (233)—Arendt retains nothing more than the barest residue of the theological schema: the meaninglessness of a generalized "in order to" both interrupts and is interrupted by the meaningfulness expressed in the daring statement that human beings are "born in order to begin."

As she delineates the three dimensions of the *vita activa*—labor, work, and action—Arendt describes their corresponding temporal structures. None of these structures, however, can be straightforwardly identified with a single, consistent temporal mode. During the 1920s Heidegger generally assigned the elements of tripartite structures to what he called the three temporal "ekstases."[25] Arendt, by contrast, refuses to correlate labor, work, and action with past, present, and future—or any other ordering of these modes. Instead, each of the temporal structures makes for a certain uneasiness, the escape from which requires another activity, with a temporal structure of its own. This uneasiness is perhaps clearest in the laboring activity, which conforms to the omnitemporality of nature, as it responds to the immediacy of bodily needs. Arendt begins her subsection "Labor and Life" by emphasizing the transience of those things for which *animal laborans* labors and the immediacy of their incorporation into the life cycle: "The least durable of tangible things are those needed for the life process itself. Their consumption barely survives their production" (96). She closes the same paragraph by describing the eternality of the cosmic cycle that makes itself felt in the "life process"—"the overall gigantic circle of nature herself, where no beginning and no end exists and where all natural things swing into changeless, deathless repetition" (96). Arendt does not, however, leave immediacy and omnitemporality as unrelated poles of the laboring process; drawing on Marx and quoting his striking definition of labor as "man's metabolism with nature" (98), she shows the degree to which the biological life process completely integrates itself into the cyclical character of nature—so much so that the day of the laborer mirrors the cycles of nature.[26]

Whereas labor's products are characterized by their transience, the products of work distinguish themselves by their durability: "they give the human artifice the stability and solidity without which it could not be relied upon to house the unstable and mortal creature which is man" (136). And whereas labor never comes to an end—it only pauses—work is entirely absorbed in its end: "The fabricated thing is an end product in the twofold sense that the production process comes to an end in it ('the process disappears in the product,' as Marx said) and that it is only a means to produce this end" (143). But work and labor are not simply opposed; rather, work

saves *animal laborans* from both immediacy and eternality by constructing a world of "objective" durability in which an individual life can first
appear out of "the life of the species" (8). Individual life "interrupts" the
cycles of natural life and is made possible when individuals are wrested
from their natural environment and enter the world of the human artifice.
To the activity of work thus corresponds the artificiality and *un*naturalness
of human existence. But unnaturalness does not describe something inhuman; it is rather, for Arendt, the mark and condition of human individuality. Even birth and death, as the beginning and end of the lives of
human beings, are unnatural occurrences inasmuch as they entirely depend on the world of the human artifice created by work into which individuals appear and from which they disappear: "Birth and death presuppose a world which is not in constant movement, but whose durability
and relative permanence makes appearance and disappearance possible,
which existed before any one individual appeared into it and will survive
his eventual departure" (97). The durability of work's products, for
Arendt, allows for the recognition of change and therefore the comprehension of time itself. And since the work of art is the most permanent
product of *homo faber* Arendt presents it as the model of thingliness: "Because of their outstanding permanence, works of art are the most intensely
worldly of all tangible things" (167). The permanence of artworks is so
outstanding that Arendt does not shy away from presenting them as intimations of immortality: "It is as though worldly stability had become
transparent in the permanence of art, so that a premonition of immortality, not the immortality of the soul or of life but of something immortal
achieved by mortal hands, has become tangibly present" (168).[27] But immortality is *only* intimated; what the permanence of work actually reveals
is not immortality but mortality.

Death, which first becomes apparent within the human artifice, characterizes all the products of work—from their beginning. Arendt emphasizes that the beginning of any work is determined by its end, and within
the instrumental schemata of work the double sense of the term *end* is
fully justified. The "in order to," as the expression of the purpose or end
of any work, so saturates the process of fabrication from start to finish that
no room is left for the meaningfulness expressed by "for the sake of."
Homo faber cannot overcome the meaninglessness of a world determined
entirely by the means-ends schema and must therefore be saved by another activity—action. But the "products" of action are "even less durable

and more futile than what we produce for consumption" (95). Without work to transform the fleeting and intangible products of action into "the tangibility of things," actions would "lose their reality and disappear as though they had never been" (95). As work saves labor, it simultaneously preserves the products of action. But as it transforms these products into the thingliness of the world, it also, and decisively, ruins them. Arendt seeks to capture the strange destructiveness of work's preservative power with reference to the Pauline designation "dead letter":

> [R]eification and materialization, without which no thought can become a tangible thing, is always paid for, and . . . the price is life itself: it is always the "dead letter" in which the "living spirit" must survive, a deadness from which it can be rescued only when the dead letter comes again into contact with a life willing to resurrect it, although this resurrection of the dead shares with all living things that it, too, will die again. (169)

With reference to the greatest messianic hope and the sublimest apocalyptic image—"the resurrection of the dead"—Arendt paradoxically exposes the law of mortality under which everything in the world is cast: works can give an intimation of immortality, but the only resurrection they can afford is a resurrection unto death. Paul hopes to overcome once and for all the Judaic tradition in which he was schooled by presenting the Hebrew Bible as the "dead letter" of the law. Arendt does not deny the emptiness of everything she places under the rubric of the "dead letter," but she emphasizes that human existence "depends for its reality and its continued existence . . . on the transformation of the intangible into the tangibility of things" (95). Life, insofar as it is human life, can never fully and finally overcome the "dead letter" and persist in something like the sphere of "living spirit." Work preserves by ruining and ruins in preserving. And as a whole, considered entirely within itself, ruin is the norm and "nature" of the world. As Arendt writes in the closing paragraph of her section on action and as she strongly reiterates in "What is Freedom?" the "normal, 'natural'" course of the world is toward "ruin" (247):

> It is in the nature of the automatic processes to which man is subject, but within and against which he can assert himself through action, that they can only spell ruin to human life. Once man-made, historical processes have become automatic, they are no less ruinous than the natural life process that drives our organism and which in its own terms, that is, biologically, leads from being to non-being, from birth to death. The historical sciences know

only too well such cases of petrified and hopelessly declining civilizations where doom seems foreordained, like a biological necessity, and since such historical processes of stagnation can last and creep on for centuries, they even occupy by far the largest space in recorded history.[28]

Ruination is understood, for Arendt, in terms of petrifaction, hopelessness, and decline. All these terms are familiar within the tradition of historical pessimism, perhaps best summarized by Schopenhauer's dictum that "the emblem of history should read: *Eadem, sed aliter* [the same, only different]."[29] And Arendt's talk of a foreordained doom seems to participate in this tradition. But, for Arendt, doom only "seems" to be foreordained from the perspective of hindsight, which is precisely not the perspective of action. The ruin of which she speaks consists in conforming oneself to automatic processes of any kind—including, and especially, the processes of history that both optimistic and pessimistic historians try to capture under laws of progress, cyclicality, or decline. Arendt rejects historical pessimism as thoroughly as she rejects the historical optimism that laid the foundations for the ideological movements of the twentieth century. Yet, the ability of perspicacious historians to recognize the automation to which civilizations fall prey makes the melancholic glance at the historical world understandable: to the extent that laws of historical processes are recognizable, action, which always interrupts these processes, seems outside the range of human capacities. Historical pessimism is thus generated whenever the melancholic glance is generalized for human history as a whole. In *The Human Condition*, Arendt does not, as she does in the *Origins*, call on historical pessimists for this vision of ruination; rather, she returns to one of the books Paul consigned to the region of the "dead letter" and finds a particularly vivid vision of the human artifice abandoned, left to operate entirely on its own:

> The melancholy wisdom of *Ecclesiastes*—"Vanity of vanities; all is vanity. . . . there is no new thing under the sun, . . . there is no remembrance of former things; neither shall there be any remembrance of things that are to come with those that shall come after"—does not necessarily arise from specifically religious experience; but it is certainly unavoidable wherever and whenever trust in the world as a place fit for human appearance, for action and speech, is gone. (204)

For all its durability, the world fabricated in work leaves no room for anything new; it presents everything in terms of the instrumental schema of means-ends, absorbs everything into the temporal dimension of the end, and thus gives rise to the vision of Ecclesiastes. As long as there is "no new thing under the sun," the world can be said—without the resonance of any apocalyptic violence—to be at its end.

III. Beginning Again

Only the possibility of action saves the world from the utter desolation that expresses itself in Ecclesiastes' dismal vision of timelessness combined with eternal return. "All is vanity" does not mean that everything is done for the sake of vanity; rather, "vanity" here describes the irreality—*vanitas, hevel*[30]—of insubstantial, futile, and frail things. And this sense of irreality directly corresponds to a vision in which nothing is done—no action is taken—for the sake of anything, even though works might be produced in order to attain certain ends. In Arendt's daring reading of Ecclesiastes, "no new thing" is thus understood from the perspective of *vanitas*: the only "thing" that could qualify as "new" is an action, for action alone saves the world from the *vanitas* to which it otherwise, "normally" or "naturally," succumbs. The saving power of action does not, however, consist in the transcendence of futility or frailty. "The human sense of reality demands that men actualize the sheer passive givenness of their being, not in order to change it but in order to make articulate and call into full existence what otherwise they would have to suffer passively anyhow" (208). Such actualization, as Arendt proceeds to note, must not be confused with the finite realization of an idea in a finished work. Only an activity that "exists . . . in sheer actuality" (208) is capable of transforming "sheer passive givenness," but this transformation can be only an ontological one: it is the calling into existence by word and deed of an irreal, "vain," and futile world—without, however, altering the fundamental frailty of the world in the least. Arendt's technical term for such an activity is "action."

In contrast to the temporality of Ecclesiastes' irreal vision in which timelessness and eternal return are combined, the temporality of action is suspended between two very different poles: the fleetingness of the action as such and the potentially indefinite duration of the process it initiates. Because of its fleetingness—a temporal characteristic it strangely shares with labor—action does not simply save the world fabricated in work; action is itself made worldly by work. Arendt may therefore compare action with "living spirit," but action has none of the otherworldly substantiality that allows the "spirit" of which Paul speaks to maintain itself without works by the grace of God:

> The materialization they [the living activities of action, speech, and thought] have to undergo in order to remain in the world at all is paid for in that always the "dead letter" replaces something which grew out of and for a fleeting moment indeed existed as the "living spirit." They must pay this price because they themselves are of an *entirely unworldly nature* and therefore need the help of an activity of an altogether different nature; they depend for their reality and materialization upon the same workmanship that builds the other things in the human artifice. (95, emphasis added)

The assertion that thought is unworldly corresponds to the general direction of Arendt's reflections as she articulates the project she pursues in *The Human Condition*, but it comes as something of a surprise to learn early in the book that both speech and action are "entirely unworldly." Action, for Arendt, thus converges with a potent messianic motif: it is decidedly *in* the world but not at all *of* the world—without ever forsaking the world for the sake of otherworldly salvation.

Whereas work is principally determined with respect to its ends, action is defined in terms of beginnings. Every beginning worthy of the name is as unprecedented as it is unexpected, and Arendt therefore strongly associates action with one of the categories that Enlightenment discourse progressively disqualified: the miraculous. The miracle can be witnessed but not explained, and although no miracle that human beings can witness is an altogether absolute beginning, its very appearance bears witness to such a beginning: the miracle of miracles, or *creatio ex nihilo*. But Arendt's prominent invocation of the miraculous does not mean she has given up on Enlightenment thought; on the contrary, her explication of the relationship between action and beginning directly links up with the critical project Kant launched: as both Kant and Arendt emphasize, action is possible only under the condition that it is rooted in, and an expression of, freedom; and both define freedom as the ability to begin something new.[31] Just as the term *ends* displays a double sense—purpose and conclusion—so, too, does the term *beginning*. In most modern European languages, however, the doubleness of beginnings, unlike that of ends, has been effectively eliminated; but in Greek—and in the philosophical and political reflections that stem from early Greek experience—the duplicity of the term for beginning (*archein*) has profound and disturbing consequences, which Arendt summarizes in her account of Plato's attraction to the tyranny of the philosopher-king:

> In Plato himself, the legitimacy of this tyranny in everything pertaining to man . . . is still firmly rooted in the equivocal significance of the word *archein*, which means both beginning and ruling; it is decisive for Plato, as he says expressly at the end of the Laws, that only the beginning (*arche*) is entitled to rule (*archein*). In the tradition of Platonic thought, this original, linguistically predetermined identity of ruling and beginning had the consequence that all beginning was understood as the legitimation for rulership, until, finally, the element of beginning disappeared altogether from the concept of rulership. With it the most elementary and authentic understanding of human freedom disappeared from political philosophy. (224–25)

The phenomenon of beginning is thus absorbed into that of rule, and freedom is consequently equated with sovereignty—not with the ability to start something new. The justification for Plato's legitimation of tyranny and consequent replacement of freedom with sovereignty is the analogy he draws between the city and the individual soul: only those who have sovereign control over themselves have a right to control others. The utopia Plato then projects in the *Republic*—which, as Arendt notes, is "the inspiration of all later utopias" (227)—is conceived according to the model of fabrication. By substituting making for acting, Plato seeks to overcome in one stroke both poles of the temporality of action: its fleetingness on the one hand, which links it with everything ephemeral, and its boundlessness and unpredictability on the other, which correspond to the condition of nonsovereign freedom—namely, plurality. The substitution of making for acting owes its origin to Plato's desire to "bestow upon the realm of human affairs the solidity inherent in work" (225), and this desire is in turn rooted in Plato's principal aim: "to make possible the philosopher's way of life" (14). The utopian Republic is projected in order to preserve the possibility of the *vita contemplativa*, which itself seals the disappearance of nonsovereign freedom by denigrating and devaluing all human activities because of their tense temporalities. The contemplative life demands quiet as it directs itself toward the eternal order of the *kosmos*.

Arendt, unlike both Marx and Nietzsche, does not seek, however, to devalue or "transvalue" (*umwerten*) the value of the *vita contemplativa*; indeed, she frames and punctuates her discussion of the *vita activa* with reference to the undiminished dignity of certain forms of life that cannot be understood in terms of labor, work, or action—not only the *vita con-templativa* but also love and goodness. But the dignity of these forms of life under no condition justifies a utopian structure in which they would be somehow preserved intact and not be exposed to the contingency of human existence. Fabrication so thoroughly animates the utopian impulse that not only would any utopia be itself a fabricated "thing," if one were ever realized; utopias are inconceivable outside of the model of making. *The Human Condition* is thus composed against the tradition of political philosophy as an anti-utopian essay[32]: utopias always miss the multiplicity of activities as they simultaneously fail to acknowledge the plurality of human beings. Arendt resolutely resists any gesture toward utopias and always speaks of them with a certain disdain because, from the beginning and in the end, they make human beings into the material of, and for, fabrication. And as she notes with exaggerated restraint, "Recent political history is full of examples indicating that the term 'human material' is no harmless metaphor" (188).

The utopian desire to replace action with making stems from what Arendt calls the "frustration of action" (220). Making can doubtless be frustrating: materials may be inadequate, tools unavailable, and the end toward which making orients itself may be unattainable. But, in all these instances, the frustration is limited to the particular case and does not extend to making as a whole. If a particular mode of making—or to use Marx's term, "mode of production"—proves thoroughly frustrating for a long enough time, it can be abandoned and replaced by another one. Marx's theory of revolution, as it is articulated in the "Preface" to the *Critique of Political Economy*, derives from a meditation on the "fettering" of productive forces by frustrating modes of production.[33] Action, by contrast, is always frustrating and no mode of action is replaceable by any other one that might prove unfrustrating. For Arendt, the frustrations of action are inherent in the human condition of plurality: the outcome of any action is unpredictable, and the processes actions inaugurate are always irreversible. To each of these disabilities—unpredictability, irreversibility—corresponds a specific ability, which Arendt, drawing from the lexicon of Enlightenment philosophy, describes as a "faculty." None of these faculties can be actualized to the point of overcoming the disability to which it responds, and all the ones Arendt identifies in her account of the "faculty of action" (246), including action itself, are therefore in positions parallel to the one that Kant's great work of "faculty psychology," the *Critique of Pure Reason*, assigns to the "faculty of reason": it responds to—but is unable to overcome the irrationality of—mere givenness. Unpredictability and irreversibility are givens: the latter a constitutive feature of time, the former a direct result of plurality. When Arendt comes to identify those potentialities inherent in the power of action that are able to save action from its "calamities" (220)—powers to the second power, to quote Schelling[34]—she offers a summary account of the tripartite character of redemption through which *The Human Condition* as a whole is structured:[35]

> We have seen that the *animal laborans* could be redeemed from its predicament of imprisonment in the ever-recurring cycle of the life-process . . . only through . . . the capacity for making. . . . We saw furthermore that *homo faber* could be redeemed from his predicament of meaninglessness, the "devaluation of all values" . . . only through the interrelated faculties of action and speech. . . . What in each of these instances saves man—man *qua animal laborans, qua homo faber, qua* thinker—is something altogether different; it comes from the outside—not to be sure outside of man, but outside of each of the respective activities. . . . The case of action and action's predicaments is altogether different. Here, the remedy against the irreversibility and unpredictability of the process started by acting does not arise out of another and possibly higher faculty, but is one of the potentialities of action itself. (236)

Arendt identifies the potentiality of action that remedies its unpredictability as the "faculty of making and keeping promises" (237). Making promises is utterly distinct from making products, and keeping promises is similarly distinct from keeping possessions. Whereas the process of fabrication can be done alone, promises are inconceivable in isolation. And whereas *homo faber* is "indeed lord and master . . . of himself and his doings" (144), those who promise make themselves into servants: they are beholden to the ones to whom they promise. The faculty of promising is, therefore, "the only alternative to a mastery which relies on domination of one's self and rule over others; it corresponds exactly to the existence of a freedom which was given under the condition of non-sovereignty" (244). But there is nevertheless a certain continuity between making products and making promises: they both stabilize what would otherwise disappear. And making promises does make something, according to Arendt; namely, "islands of security" in "oceans of uncertainty" (237). None of these islands, however, resembles Atlantis, the utopian island Plato imagines in the *Critias*[36]: the unpredictability to which islands created in the act of promising are exposed is not a function of scientific ignorance concerning the cyclical rise and fall of the seas but is, rather, a result of, one, the unreliability of human beings "who never can guarantee today who they will be tomorrow" (244) and, two, the impossibility of "foretelling the consequences of an act within a community of equals where everybody has the same capacity to act" (244).

Arendt does not simply contrast the islands created by promising with oceans of uncertainty; she also turns to an image of the wilderness as she presents the unique power of promises. Only the faculty of promising is capable of rescuing human beings from the wilderness in which they otherwise wander, for every act of promising draws human beings out of their isolation and gives direction to their endeavors. Identity, for Arendt, is never a given but is always a result and function of the relationality established in the world through speech and action. Keeping one's identity and keeping one's promises are therefore so closely correlated that Arendt can be understood to touch on the central concern of *The Human Condition*— its "heart," to use her own word—when she considers what it would mean to be "freed" from the bonds of stability forged in the act of promising: "Without being bound to the fulfillment of promises, we would never be able to keep our identities; we would be condemned to wander helplessly and without direction in the darkness of each man's lonely heart" (237). The image of the wilderness reappears when Arendt comes to identify those who discovered the stabilizing power of promising. She first turns toward the inventors of early Roman law, who kept "the eternal city" stable by sanctifying the act of promising; but then, as if to correct herself—and this correction has largely gone unnoticed, perhaps because it approaches or assumes the tone of a Jewish joke—she turns instead to the one who discovered this power by uprooting himself from a stable city and then wandering without help or assurance into the "wilderness":

> [O]r we may see its discoverer in Abraham, the man from Ur, whose whole story, as the Bible tells it, shows such a passionate drive toward making covenants that it is as though he departed from his country for no other reason than to try out the power of mutual promise in the wilderness of the world, until eventually, God himself agreed to make a Covenant with him. (243–44)

In Arendt's brief discussion of promising, which closes the chapter on "Action," she does not mention but nevertheless alludes to a Promised

Land: the wilderness landscape is the place in which the faculty of promising is discovered. In the wilderness, as in the desert, the world of the human artifice is either absent or moribund; the only remaining force of sta-
bilization, however weak, derives from the power of promising. Abraham,
therefore, has to leave the city in order to discover the specific power of
promising. And the stability established in promising never loses the
shadow of a wilderness—whether in the loneliness of the heart or the
emptiness of the world. One of Arendt's central insights, which distinguishes her analysis of promising from the tradition that culminates in
Nietzsche's *Zur Genealogie der Moral*,[37] is that the stabilizing power of
promising is predicated on the interruptive faculty of forgiveness. Against
the traditional ordering of these two faculties, which expresses itself in the
almost irresistible sequence, "promising and forgiveness," Arendt places
forgiveness first: it is as if Abraham could not have set out on his journey
without some sense that he could be forgiven his trespasses, including, of
course, the binding of Isaac. The anxiety surrounding the act of promising, which finds one of its most spectacular expositions in Kierkegaard's
account of Abraham's journey in *Fear and Trembling*,[38] is potentially so
great that this act would issue into a speechlessness that would deprive the
speaker of the capacity to promise—were it not for a prior promise, issued
by another, of forgiveness for failing to fulfill one's promises. The faculty
of forgiveness, therefore, must come first, as it does in Arendt's presentation of the two faculties. And this ordering corresponds to a messianic
schema: the promise of fidelity to another—the promise through which
one first defines oneself and thus gains an identity—is predicated on a
prior promise of this other to release one from one's failure to keep this
very promise. This schema explicates itself in the unpredictable course of
events that Abraham's unprecedented act of promising inaugurates. The
covenant made by Abraham becomes the nucleus of all messianic hope:
the "remnant," by remaining faithful, will thus be allowed to enter into
the land promised to Abraham. Little wonder, then, that when Arendt
comes to identify the "discoverer" of the faculty of forgiveness, she
chooses a well-known messianic figure, Jesus of Nazareth.

Just as promising responds to action's unpredictability, forgiveness
responds to its irreversibility. When Arendt first introduces these corre-
spondences, however, she makes a slight but significant distinction.
Promises "remedy" one of "action's calamities" (220), whereas forgiveness
has the power to redeem another: "The possible redemption from the

predicament of irreversibility—of being unable to undo what one has
done though one did not, and could not, have known what he was doing—is the faculty of forgiving" (237). The redemptive function of forgiveness, for Arendt, consists in saving not acts themselves—such is the
function of work—but the possibility of action after a deed has been
done: "Without being forgiven, released from the consequences of what
we have done, our capacity to act would, as it were, be confined to one
single deed from which we would never recover; we would remain the victims of its consequences forever, not unlike the sorcerer's apprentice who
lacked the magical formula to break the spell" (237). The structural position of forgiveness with respect to action is therefore parallel to that of action with respect to work and work with respect to labor: each redeems
the other. As Arendt proceeds to explain, however, this parallelism breaks
down, since the faculty of forgiveness is not an external and "possibly
higher" faculty but is, rather, "one of the potentialities of action itself"
(236–37). That action can redeem itself without reference to a higher
power is the surprising message Arendt attributes to Jesus, and it is this
message that sets him apart from contemporaneous interpreters of Biblical
texts. As Arendt seeks to understand the relationship between Jesus of
Nazareth and Jewish intellectual, religious, and political debates during
the late Second Temple era, she follows an explosive tradition of German-
Jewish scholarship that begins with Abraham Geiger and finds perhaps its
greatest exemplar in the figure of Martin Buber who, early in his career,
welcomes Jesus as a "great brother."[39] And in the section on forgiveness in
The Human Condition, Arendt likewise resumes the short-lived tradition
of German-Jewish scholarship that, inspired by the depiction of the radical eschatological experience of primitive Christianity in Franz Overbeck's
works and often incited by the young Heidegger's intriguing suggestions
that authentic temporality could be interpreted on the basis of primal
Christian existence, explores with great originality experiences generally
associated with Christianity:[40]

> Jesus maintains against the "scribes and pharisees" first that it is not true that
> only God has the power to forgive, and second that this power does not de-
> rive from God—as though God, not men, would forgive through the
> medium of human beings—but on the contrary must be mobilized by men
> toward each other before they can hope to be forgiven by God also. Jesus' for-
> mulation is even more radical. Man in the gospel is not supposed to forgive
> because God forgives and he must do "likewise," but "if ye from your hearts

forgive," God shall do "likewise." The reason for this insistence on a duty to forgive is clearly "for they know not what they do" and it does not apply to the extremity of crime and willed evil. (239)

At least in the case of trespass, human action can save itself. And in all other cases, which are "rare"—"even rarer perhaps than good deeds" (240)—talk of salvation is misplaced: those who are willfully evil will be delivered over to the Last Judgment, which is characterized not by forgiveness but by just retribution.[41] The Jesus whom Arendt constructs— tentatively and with careful use of the tools of scholarship—is a figure who, by reclaiming the power of forgiveness from God, appears to diminish divine omnipotence and indeed to make it dependent in part on the power of human beings. For this reason, he elicits antagonism from those who want to protect the prerogatives of God. Jesus is not, for Arendt, a figure of salvation; rather, he relieves God of the power to forgive, but not to punish, and, by so doing, he discovers the immanent eschatological possibility contained within the miraculous act of forgiveness itself: the possibility, that is, of "put[ting] an end to something that . . . could go on endlessly" (241). Without relying on means of any kind—immediately and therefore, as Arendt herself indicates with her surprising reference to the sorcerer's apprentice, magically[42]—forgiveness can accomplish an end. Only under the condition that action be able to come to an end can it begin, which is to say, only if one has a prior sense that one can be "released"[43] from the consequences of one's actions can action be released into the world. According to Overbeck's exposition of primitive Christianity, the eschatological mode of life does not properly consist in living with some premonition that the end of the world is near but, rather, in living out one's life from the extreme perspective of its end: only by drawing the sense of life's end into one's life can one live on.[44] According to Arendt's transformation of this historical insight into a messianic schema, only by sensing that the consequences of action can come to an end can action resume and life "go on." The sober imperative Rosetta articulates near the end of her final speech in *The Age of Anxiety*—"We must try to get on"—finds its corollary in the equally sober phrase Arendt employs to designate the ultimate purpose of her inquiry into the saving power of action: to delineate the conditions that "make it possible for life to go on."

[T]respassing is an everyday occurrence which is in the very nature of action's constant establishment of new relationships within a web of relations, and it needs forgiving, dismissing, in order to make it possible for life to go on by constantly releasing men from what they have done unknowingly. Only through this constant mutual release from what they can do can men remain free agents, only by constant willingness to change their minds and start again can they be trusted with so great a power as that to begin something new. (240)

Only if one trusts others to relieve one of one's trespasses can anyone— oneself or others—be entrusted ever again with the power to act. A trust that entrusts is, therefore, the absolute condition of life "going on." But the idea of a self-entrusting trust is not free from paradoxes, one of which is readily recognizable in the redemptive function of forgiveness: forgive- ness makes possible an end to the consequences of action, but forgiveness is itself an action and therefore a beginning, which, for its part, likewise needs forgiveness to occur; since this latter forgiveness is also an action, it, too, is a beginning that needs forgiveness in turn, and so on *ad infinitum*. The redemptive faculty of action thus issues into an abyss. For Arendt, there is no worldly resolution to the abyssal structure that arises from the fact that the power of action is redeemed by one of action's own potential- ities. And yet, there is no other-worldly resolution either: not even trust in a "higher" power who entrusts human beings with the faculty of action could fully resolve its abyssal structure, especially because, as Arendt em- phasizes—and this is the whole point of her excursus on Jesus—the faculty of forgiveness is primarily a human power and only secondarily a divine one. The absence of a resolution does not, however, mean the abyssal struc- ture of action does not solicit responses; on the contrary, two responses ar- ticulate the structural limits of *The Human Condition*.

One extreme response to the abyssal structure of action is love. Another is the performance of "good works" or "good deeds."[45]

Goodness: Arendt never resolves the question whether the activity of goodness should be understood as a work or a deed.[46] If it is a work—and Arendt more frequently speaks of "good works" than "good deeds"—it is the strangest form of work imaginable, since it leaves no trace and indeed must destroy its appearance to preserve its goodness: "It is manifest that the moment a good work becomes known and public, it loses its specific character of goodness, of being done for nothing but goodness' sake" (74). Arendt opens her discussion of goodness by noting that it is an "admit- tedly extreme" phenomenon. And the extremity of this phenomenon leads Arendt into her only discussion within *The Human Condition* of the doctrine of extremes—in Greek, *eschatologos*—that orients itself toward the end of time:

> [T]he otherworldliness of Christianity has still another root [i.e., the activity of goodness], perhaps even more intimately related to the teachings of Jesus of Nazareth, and at any rate so independent of the belief in the perishability of the world that one is tempted to see in it the true inner reason why Christian alienation from the world could so easily survive the obvious non-fulfillment of its eschatological hopes. (74)

After acknowledging that the eschatological character of early Christianity was the primary reason for its antagonism to the *res publica*, she proceeds to indicate that this antagonism could be understood from another perspective: all good works are, in their own way, eschatological. The world held in common comes to an end in good works. The activity of "doing good" has a "ruinous quality" (77) that paradoxically associates it with the ruin to which the world would succumb were it not for the redemptive power of action. As a consistent mode of life, and not simply a fleeting exception, good works ruin the public realm altogether: "Fleeing the world and hiding from its inhabitants, it negates the space the world offers to men and most of all that public part of it where everything and everybody are seen and heard by others" (77). Good works escape the abyssal structure of action to the extent that they do not depend on any promise of forgiveness in order to begin—not, however, because they are good, but because they take place beyond the sphere in which both promising and forgiveness are meaningful. Instead of appearing in the world of plural individuals, they conceal themselves even from those who perform them. Strictly speaking, doers of good deeds do not know who they are or what they do.

Arendt is relentless in tracking down the self-concealing character of goodness. Whereas those who act do not know what they do and therefore depend on forgiveness, those who do good works are so radically ignorant of what they do that acts of forgiveness lose their meaningfulness: there is no revelation of a "who" in good works and therefore no one to forgive. Doers of good works, according to a Jewish legend Arendt pauses to recount, are the solid pillars on which the world of appearances rests, and this world as a whole can be forgiven its trespasses for their sake. Only in her account of this legend—which seems barely related to the line of inquiry she pursues in *The Human Condition*—does Arendt speak of something other than action saving the world: "The same conviction [as Jesus' statement that 'none is good save one, that is God'] finds its expression in the talmudic story of the thirty-six righteous men, for the sake of whom God saves the world and who also are known to nobody, least of all to themselves" (75). The *tzadikim* are not saints: they do not seek out one another in order to establish a "counterworld" (54) on the assumption that the world of appearances is bound to perish; on the contrary, they remain in this world despite—or, paradoxically, because of—the fact that they are completely hidden. Because their hiddenness is absolute, the visible world goes on as before, and this "going on" is itself a sign, perhaps the only sign, of divine approval. The collapse of the common world after the fall of the Roman Empire gave impetus, according to Arendt, to the formation of counterworlds populated by saints and criminals. A similar collapse—"albeit for quite other reasons and in very different, perhaps even more disconsolate forms"—seems to have occurred "in our own days" (54). The talmudic legend of the *tzadikim* offers a subtle counter-image to that of saintly and criminal withdrawal into either monastic or conspiratorial counterworlds. One of the lessons of this legend was spelled out soon after Arendt published *The Human Condition* when it became the subject matter of André Schwarz-Bart's popular novel about the Shoah, *Le Dernier des justes.*[47]

Love: as Arendt presents it in *The Human Condition*, love is like goodness insofar as it ruins the condition of plurality by "destroy[ing] the in-between which relates us to and separates us from others. . . . Love by its very nature is unworldly" (242). But love does not, like goodness, escape the abyssal structure of action; on the contrary, love throws itself into it. Love, for Arendt, is an infinite relation that alone corresponds to the *ad infinitum* character of forgiveness understood as an action in its own right: those who love forgive each other without conditions. This absence of conditions does not abrogate "the human condition," but it does absolutely guarantee that a new beginning—the resumption of love—can occur after any and every trespass. If, however, love is the *only* ground of forgiveness, and forgiveness is possible only on the condition of love, forgiveness, as Arendt notes, would escape the analysis she undertakes in *The Human Condition*: action could not look toward forgiveness but would have to rely entirely on punishment to put an end to its consequences. But in that case, punishment, too, would fail to enable action by providing an end, because even punishment—to the extent that it is distinguished from the automatic reaction of vengeance[48]—is inextricable from the power of forgiveness:

> [M]en are unable to forgive what they cannot punish and . . . they are unable to punish what has turned out to be unforgivable. This is the true hallmark of those offenses which, since Kant, we call "radical evil" and about whose nature so little is known, even to us who have been exposed to one of their rare outbursts on the public scene. All we know is that we can neither punish nor forgive such offenses and that they therefore transcend the realm of human affairs and the potentialities of human power. (241)

Only because love is not the sole ground of forgiveness can forgiveness continue to function within the sphere demarcated by the human condition. Again drawing on Kant, but without naming him, Arendt calls the other ground of forgiveness *respect*: "What love is in its own, narrowly circumscribed sphere, respect is in the larger domain of human affairs" (243). Left to themselves, acts of love would withdraw from the world as thoroughly as good works do: by disregarding any concern with *what* individuals may be and solely acting for the sake of *who* they are, lovers leave the world, which is always defined by the question, "what is?" And love is exposed to the same equivocation as goodness, even if Arendt does not explicitly vacillate between the expressions "acts of love" and "works of love." Since lovers do not simply flee from the world, their love can sometimes produce a product: "As long as its spell lasts, the only in-between which can insert itself between two lovers is the child, love's own product. The child . . . is representative of the world. . . . Through the child, it is as though the lovers return to the world from which their love had expelled them. But this new worldliness . . . is, in a sense, the end of love" (242)—and therefore the end of the only phenomenon capable of corresponding fully and completely to the *ad infinitum* of forgiveness. Arendt's invocation of the child does not seek to invalidate forms of love that cannot issue into parenthood, and in any case, she does not seek to validate or invalidate the phenomenon of love at all. The child is to love as forgiveness is to action: they both break a magical "spell" (237, 242) and thereby initiate a new beginning. Within the general structure of *The Human Condition*, the child functions as the central image of miraculous novelty, but it can fully serve this demanding function only insofar as it includes within itself a corresponding sense of ending: not clashing armies but a child as both beginning and end—this is the image of Arendt's inconspicuous messianism. When Arendt then quotes the "glad tidings" under the sign of Isaiah—"'A child has been born unto us'" (247)—she not only offers a dramatic image of new beginnings, she also indicates, against the grain of the Gospels, that this beginning is also an end: not the end of the fallen world accomplished by a loving God but, on the contrary, the end of love.

~

   Salvation does not come by way of a child, for the appearance of a child is as little capable of resolving once and for all the abyssal structure of action as goodness or love. This structure is constitutively incapable of resolution—so much so that not even divine forgiveness can resolve it, since forgiveness is primarily a human faculty. Redemption, then, remains only a schema internal to the activities of the *vita activa* in relation to one another: this schema cannot be embodied in a salvational figure, nor even can it proceed into the world as an independent force. Nowhere is this impossibility more apparent than in the appearance of a child, for a child is sheer dependence. And with its appearance the anxiety generated by the abyssal structure of action itself changes from a concern with forgiveness for one's own actions to an alertness to one's responsibility for a child—and therefore alertness to one's responsibility for the world to come.

§ 4 "Reflection on the Right to Will"

Auden's "Canzone" and Arendt's Notes on Willing

I. A Season of Melancholia

Arendt opens the section on action in *The Human Condition* with a lengthy quotation from Dante's *De Monarchia*. With reference to this quotation Arendt singles out the underlying intention of every action, regardless of what it aims to accomplish—self-disclosure:

> *Nam in omni actione principaliter intenditur ab agente, sive necessitate naturae sive voluntarie agat, proprium similitudinem explicare; unde fit quod omne agens, in quantum huismodi, delectatur, quia, cum omne quod est appetat suum esse, ac in agendo agentis esse modammodo amplietur, sequitur de necessitate delectatio. . . . Nihil igitur agit nisi tale existens quale patiens fieri debet.*

> For in every action what is primarily intended by the doer, whether he acts from natural necessity or out of free will, is the disclosure of his own image. Hence, it comes about that every doer, in so far as he does, takes delight in doing; since everything that is desires its own being, and since in action the being of the doer is somehow intensified, delight necessarily follows. . . . Thus, nothing acts unless [by acting] it makes patent its latent self.[1]

The translation of *explicare* by "disclosure" marks a telling transformation of Dante's intention when he gives an account of action: whereas *explicare* ("uncoiling" or "unfolding") can characterize a purely internal occurrence—and this indeed is the direction of Dante's thought as he seeks to justify the institution of monarchy[2]—the grammar of *disclosure* demands someone to whom something is revealed. Entirely absorbed with the relation of the agent to itself, the analysis of action Dante undertakes in *De Monarchia*, as might be expected from its title, fails to consider the plurality of agents and thus misses what, for Arendt, is the essential condition of action. Because of this condition, doing cannot be purified of passivity, and its delight cannot be dissociated from suffering: "Because the actor always moves among and in relation to other acting beings, he is never merely a 'doer' but also a sufferer. To do and to suffer are like opposite sides of the same coin."[3] But Arendt does something more daring, and less easily justifiable, than translate *explicare* as *disclosure*. In the last sentence from *De Monarchia* she quotes, she reads *patent* into *patiens*: "Thus, nothing acts unless [by acting] it makes patent its latent self." A more accurate translation of the same sentence runs: "Therefore, nothing acts unless it has the qualities which are to be communicated to the thing acted upon [*patiens*]."[4]

Arendt is transforming Dante in the process of quoting him. By subtracting an *i* from *patiens* and thereby arriving at *patent*, she turns one of the great pleas for an utterly nonplural politics into an exposition of plurality as "*the* condition—not only the *conditio sine qua non*, but the *conditio per quam*—of all political life" (7). The opening of the self presupposes another self to whom it opens, and this other self must be in some manner an equal, not a divinity, since otherwise it would be inappropriate to speak of an opening. Divine eyes, to draw on one of the images with which Rosetta concludes her final meditation, see everywhere. In action, through word and deed, human beings "show who they are, reveal actively their unique personal identities and thus make their appearance in the human world."[5] That identity is "actively" rather than passively revealed corresponds to the making manifest of what in some sense already exists. Arendt's insistence that human beings first appear in the world through action may best be understood as the "making patent" of a "latent" self who is biologically born but must be continually reborn to make its appearance in the world: "With word and deed we insert ourselves into the human world, and this insertion is like a second birth."[6] The active self-disclosure of a continuous and, until its appearance in the world, latent identity thus depends on the discontinuous and startlingly new action through which the agent is disclosed. At the same time, a general condition for action—always a miraculous novelty—is the continuity of the agent: action "would no longer be action" without an agent who "identifies himself as the actor, announcing what he does, has done, and intends to do."[7] Thus, the novelty of action depends on the continuity of the agent, and the continuity of the agent, in turn, depends on the ability of the agent—by promising and in forgiveness—to interrupt its hitherto established course of affairs.

With only the slightest alteration in Dante's text, Arendt makes *De Monarchia* into a plea for a nonmonarchial politics. Reading *patent* into *patiens*, she touches on the essential unity of action as disclosure and the suffering that agents must undergo. "About suffering they were never wrong, / The Old Masters,"[8] Auden famously writes, and the author of *Inferno* could certainly be included among these masters. Although he everywhere suppresses plurality in his account of agency, Dante could hardly be accused of suppressing suffering. And suffering links agency with an elemental feature of poetic production: its ability to make suffering endurable and thus allow life to go on.[9] Without explicitly referring to poetry, Arendt indicates this link by citing Isak Dinesen alongside Dante at the beginning of her section on action: "All sorrows can be borne if you put them into a story or tell a story about them."[10] Many years after the publication of *The Human Condition*, Arendt is again drawn to the same insight expressed in Dinesen's quotation as she writes her memorial lecture on Auden and reflects on the poetry of her dead friend; and in this lecture she gives a new twist to Dante's insight that "the human sense of reality demands that men actualize the sheer passive givenness of their being, not in order to change it but in order to make articulate and call into full existence what otherwise they would have to suffer passively anyhow."[11] Scattered through Arendt's writings is something like a syllogism through which the task of poetry is defined: human beings cannot fail to suffer, regardless of what they do and indeed because of the conditions of their doing; the thought that suffering is inescapable is itself unbearable unless a reason for such sorrow is found; and the production of poetry, as the articulation of suffering, offers a reason for the ineluctability of suffering. Poetry thus appears as the final (but, of course, not efficient) cause—or end—of human suffering, because without suffering poetry would never be called into existence. And because poetry does nothing but make suffering bearable, it is entirely anti-utopian: it does not seek to overcome suffering by altering the calamities of action or any of the conditions of human beings. Arendt's memorial lecture for Auden revolves around the sad recognition that her friend, like the "Old Masters" before him, could be counted among those well-versed in suffering: "Here I think lies the key both to his extraordinary unhappiness and to the extraordinary greatness, intensity, of his poetry. Now, with the sad wisdom of remembrance, he seems to me to have been an expert in the infinite varieties of unrequited love."[12] The greatness of Auden's poetry, according to Arendt, arises from his willingness to open himself to, and nevertheless continue to bear, an incomparable range of sufferings: "[Auden was] somehow convinced, as the bards of ancient Greece were, that the gods spin unhappiness and evil things to mortals so that they may be able to tell the tales and sing the songs."[13]

⁓

Of all the poems born of the "extraordinary unhappiness" Auden experienced in "unrequited love," perhaps none achieves greater intensity of expression than his largely overlooked, enormously difficult, and emphatically peculiar 1942 poem, "Canzone."[14] "Canzone" is peculiar at the very least because its form is unusual—almost unique—in the Western literary tradition and at the time of its composition unprecedented in the English language. Of course, English poets have written canzoni, many on the model of Petrarch, but among the many poetic forms called canzoni, Auden chooses a particularly difficult one, invented and employed only once by Dante in his poem of 1296 or 1297, "Amor, tu vedi ben che questa Donna."[15] Just as Dante serves as Arendt's unwilling predecessor for her account of the ever-new irruption of action, so, too, does his work offer a foil for Auden's exploration of poetic novelty as a specific response to inescapable suffering. "Amor, tu vedi ben che questa Donna" is one of the *rime petrose*, in which Dante gives an account of the frustrations he undergoes at the hands of a cold, unresponsive lady. In this exacting poetic form, there are five twelve-line stanzas, with a *commiato* of six lines, in which each line ends with one of only five rhyme words—*donna, petra, freddo, luce,* and *tempo* (lady, stone, cold, light, and time). The rhyme words appear in an ordered sequence whose repetition and cyclical transition from one dominant word to another corresponds to the transmutation of one element into another and to the transfiguration of something in the natural world into something divine. The poem is itself born of these transformations, as Dante indicates in the final stanza, when the coldness of the lady becomes, for the poet, the cause and condition for the invention of "che non fu mai pensata in alcun tempo [something never thought before in any time]," namely, this novel poetic form.[16]

Dante's final apostrophe to the poem—"Canzone, io porto ne la mente donna [song, I carry in my mind a lady]"—is meant to indicate that the poet's sexual frustration, as a particularly intense form of suffering, can be transformed into the novelty of a hitherto unheard-of song. The poet wants the fulfillment of the will that gives rise to the poem—the will to be loved by the lady. And he implores God to bring about this, the last transmutation of a cold substance into something warm, the final satisfaction of the poet's will. In the meantime, he celebrates the novelty of the thing he *can* master: the poem, song or "canzone." Although poetry is an end-product, unlike action, which is always a beginning, poetic works like "Amor, tu vedi ben che questa Donna" nevertheless share an affinity with actions insofar as they, too, can interrupt a continuum—here a poetic tradition—and begin a new one. But there is a limit to this affinity, and this limit is an integral part of Dante's poem as well as of his treatise, *De Monarchia*: poetic novelty is achieved in isolation. Not only does Dante eschew plurality, he does not even leave a place for duality: the lady exists as a stone. And although he praises novelty, what he really wants remains the same; indeed, he wants nothing less than the return of the same, the reciprocal return of his warm, loving glance. Novelty here functions as compensation; it is a substitute for the moment of final restitution, in Stoic-Christian terms *apokatastasis pantōn*. Once the last holdout, namely, the lady, undergoes an ordered transformation, warms up, and returns his love, all things will have returned to their proper state. The cyclical temporality of the cosmos does not run counter to the linear temporality of human agency; on the contrary, the latter confirms the former, and the novelty of the song, like the stubborn uniqueness of the untransformed, still cold lady, is merely an index of the expectation of final restoration. The satisfaction of the will depends on the possibility that it can produce the conditions of its own fulfillment, that the will can project itself into, and thereby master, a future, bringing that which escapes the will into the ordered course of events. As Auden's "Canzone" repeats Dante's poem, it analyzes the zone of this possibility, this can-zone.

Like the poet of Dante's *rime petrose*, Auden suffered from a lover turned cold, when Chester Kallman announced his infidelity and his decision to end their sexual relationship in the summer of 1941.[17] Auden had planned to write a *Vita Nuova* in which Kallman's unfaithfulness would serve a function analogous to the death of Beatrice, and "Canzone" may have figured into this plan—or served as a substitute for it.[18] Neither the term *cold* nor any of its many synonyms is one of the dominant rhyme words in "Canzone," however, and in fact Auden conspicuously departs from Dante in his choice of rhyme words by avoiding all reference to the natural elements. Nevertheless, Auden preserves, with only the slightest variation, the form Dante specifically devised for "Amor, tu vedi ben che questa Donna."

CANZONE

When shall we learn, what should be clear as day,
We cannot choose what we are free to love?
Although the mouse we banished yesterday
Is an enraged rhinoceros to-day,
Our value is more threatened than we know:
Shabby objections to our present day
Go snooping round its outskirts; night and day
Faces, orations, battles, bait our will
As questionable forms and noises will;
Whole phyla of resentments every day
Give status to the wild men of the world
Who rule the absent-minded and this world.

We are created from and with the world
To suffer with and from it day by day
Whether we meet in a majestic world
Of solid measurements or a dream world
Of swans and gold, we are required to love
All homeless objects that require a world.
Our claim to own our bodies and our world
Is our catastrophe. What can we know
But panic and caprice until we know
Our dreadful appetite demands a world
Whose order, origin, and purpose will
Be fluent satisfaction of our will?

Drift, Autumn, drift; fall, colours, where you will:
Bald melancholia minces through the world.
Regret, cold oceans, the lymphatic will
Caught in reflection on the right to will:
While violent dogs excite their dying day
To bacchic fury; snarl, though, as they will,
Their teeth are not a triumph for the will
But utter hesitation. What we love
Ourselves for is our power not to love,
To shrink to nothing or explode at will,

To ruin and remember that we know
What ruins and hyaenas cannot know.

If in this dark now I less often know
That spiral staircase where the haunted will
Hunts for its stolen luggage, who should know
Better than you, beloved, how I know
What gives security to any world,
Or in whose mirror I begin to know
The chaos of the heart as merchants know
Their coins and cities, genius its own day?
For through our lively traffic all the day,
In my own person I am forced to know
How much must be forgotten out of love,
How much must be forgiven, even love.

Dear flesh, dear mind, dear spirit, dearest love,
In the depths of myself blind monsters know
Your presence and are angry, dreading Love
That asks its images for more than love;
The hot rampageous horses of my will,
Catching the scent of Heaven, whinny: Love
Gives no excuse to evil done for love,
Neither in you, nor me, nor armies, nor the world
Of words and wheels, nor any other world.
Dear fellow-creature, praise our God of Love
That we are so admonished, that no day
Of conscious trial be a wasted day.

Or else we make a scarecrow of the day,
Loose ends and jumble of our common world,
And stuff and nonsense of our own free will;
Or else our changing flesh may never know
There must be sorrow if there can be love.

In Auden's version, this form comprises five stanzas of twelve ten-sylla-
ble lines (with only one line differing in syllable count) and a five-line envoy. The end of each of the envoy's lines is one of the five rhyme words—
day, world, will, know, love—in a sequence (aedcb) determined by taking
the first rhyme word in each of the five main stanzas and maintaining the
same order of rhyme words in each of the successive lines.[19] Whereas the

cyclical pattern of Dante's poem mirrors the transmutations it describes and the transformations for which it pleads, the cyclical pattern of Auden's poem cannot be assigned such a transparent function. In fact, one could say that the poem is continually interrogating the cyclical character of its form. In Dante, the poetic form corresponds to cosmic time (in the sense of both seasonal transformation and the eternal return of the same as it is outlined in Platonic-Aristotelian cosmology). In Auden, by contrast, there is no suggestion of cosmic time, no suggestion of the inevitable return of the seasons, and no indication that, to use the memorable words of Plato's *Timaeus*, time is "the moving image of eternity."[20] On the contrary, in Auden's "Canzone" only words return in a regular fashion, specifically, the five rhyme words that end all sixty-five lines of the poem. And images from the natural world, when they return, do so in wholly unpredictable fashion. Thus, in the first stanza: ". . . the mouse we banished yesterday / Is an enraged rhinoceros today."

The central stanza of Dante's poem is dominated by the word *cold*: water freezes into crystalline stone; the cold expression of the lady freezes the poet's blood. And the relation between these two transformations is that of analogy where the two parts each occupy six lines with the connective, "cosi [just so, thus]." The central stanza of Auden's poem, by contrast, is dominated by the word *will*, and it opens with the poem's sole reference to one of the seasons, and thus, to cyclical time. Not surprisingly, that season, Autumn, is associated not only with the transformation of warmth to cold but also with the melancholic temperament.[21] "Drift, Autumn, drift; fall, colours, where you will." This line reproduces in miniature the problematic character of the poem's form. Instead of the repetition of the seasons, prepared by the repetition of *drift*, what is repeated is a word, *fall*, that, in the dimension of cyclical, seasonal time, would be a synonym for *Autumn*, but is here instead, an imperative—not a recurrence of a natural phenomenon, but an expression of the will. Thus, cyclical time is overtaken by the will, and this word dominates the stanza. For the word *will* not only marks the future as a verb tense; as a faculty the will demands an unforeseeable future, one determined not by a past that returns in ever-repeating cycles but by the will itself.[22] There is no will without the possibility of novelty; it needs an open temporal horizon, but the formal structure of the canzone closes down any such opening. The repetitive character of the poem's form locks the will into a pattern of return. And this return is itself figured in the term *will*, the return of the term.[23]

Although Auden takes over the form Dante invented in order to address a situation similar to that which inspired Dante's invention—the coldness of a lover—Auden's poem does not will the reciprocal affection of the beloved and is not pressed into the service of either satisfaction or mastery. An index of Auden's rejection of these willful projects lies in his use of the term *will* as the central rhyme word in his canzone: *will* does not return at will but in accordance with a set pattern, and this pattern effectively cancels the futurial dimension of the word. As in Dante's poem, the attention of Auden's central stanza is divided into two parts, but these parts are not contained by the first and second sections of the stanza nor are they presented in sequence, and the relation between them is anything but analogical. It is instead a relation of simultaneity, indicated by the adverb *while*. Together, the two parts characterize the bipolar dimensions of the will as it loses the possibility of novelty. The first is dedicated to depression—or as Auden writes, "bald melancholia"[24]—and the second to mania or "bacchic fury."

Melancholia "minces," but it does not mince the world; instead, it "minces *through* the world"; the intransitive use of *mince* means that it must be understood as a term not of affecting but of affectation: melancholia does not act on the world but rather, on itself. It travels "through the world," affecting an excessively refined and delicate manner, displaying itself as decorous, elegant, and polite. (This of course is the intransitive meaning of the word *mince*.) This self-affection is a sign of melancholia's indifference, not toward itself but toward the world and the possibilities it presents. As Auden writes in *The Enchafèd Flood*, "The grand explanatory image of this condition is of course Dürer's Melancholia. . . . What is the cause of her suffering? That, surrounded by every possibility, she cannot find within herself or without the necessity to realise one rather than another."[25] The absence of an objective world on which melancholia can act—absent because no object appeals to it—throws melancholia back on itself: its verbs are intransitive. Even its efforts at elegant self-affection, however, are ineffectual, as it reaches a point of withdrawal in which the grand image of melancholia can be replaced by a series of substitutions: "regret, cold oceans, the lymphatic will." The last of these replacements, "lymphatic will," can be described only as a failure of effectiveness, which, as a sluggish noun, does not deserve an active verb, not even an intransitive one; instead of an active verb, there is only a passive one, indeed *the* verb of passivity, *caught*: "caught in reflection on the right to will." There is so little action, much less transformation, under the sign of melancholia that Auden has the audacity to cite the principal rhyme-word in the corresponding stanza of Dante's canzone: "cold." But this cold does not have the power to change the substantial character of anything; it does not freeze, and the oceans, not transformed to crystalline stone, remain in the same state. Under the weight of the lymphatic will, the poem threatens to collapse; in the critical terms Auden develops in *The Enchafèd Flood*, the ego declines to make any decision and thus allows the self to which it is "predicated" to remain sheer potentiality without any actualization or action (EF, 117–18). And this inaction expresses itself in a verbless sentence. But the line, "Regret, cold oceans, the lymphatic will," can be read in another manner as well. *Regret*, a term for melancholia, is also of course a verb: the oceans are called on, summoned in an invocation to regret the ineffectualness of the will as it is "caught in reflection"; thus to regret the attractiveness of melancholia's passivity at a time when—or as Auden writes "while"—"violent dogs excite their dying day."

This regrettable time is a manic one. The violent dogs, an image perhaps drawn from Nietzsche—who also brings the canine will into relation with Bacchus and especially with the feigned fury of Wagnerian opera[26]— are the opposite of melancholia's self-affection, which ends in ineffectualness and the total absence of affect. But the dogs' excitement, as expectation or provocation of some action that could alter the course of events, must collapse onto itself—explode in "bacchic fury"—because the temporal dimension that would allow the fulfillment of such expectations is foreclosed. The violence of the dogs excites the day to activity, but the only activity of the day is "dying": the now-point passes away, and there is no trace of the future, least of all a futurial use of the word *will*. The teeth are the display of excitement and are in a sense a correlate to the self-display of the melancholic. They do not lack the worldly ambition of melancholia, but they are just as much a demonstration of the failure to will: "utter hesitation." What Riefenstahl documents in her famous 1935 film *Triumph des Willens* is *not* a "triumph for the will." This strange reference to a singularly effective piece of fascist propaganda, made even stranger when one reflects that it was written at the height of Nazi power in Europe, makes sense only if the word *will* can mean something other than the violent exercise of the forces at one's disposal. But here, the line that speaks of hesitation hesitates. And the opening onto this other meaning of the will is caught in the caesura of the line. When the line begins again—"What we love / ourselves for is our power not to love"—it reverts to the interpretation of willing that makes the will enter into manic-depressive phases: the will understood as self-affection or self-love, which can only will negation, "not to love." As the stanza on willing closes, the melancholic and the bacchic become increasingly indistinguishable. A series of chiastic inversions mark the last three lines. Melancholia, the ability "to shrink to nothing," and mania, the ability to "explode at will," are two versions of "what we love ourselves for." So are, reversing the order, the ability "to ruin" (mania) and the ability "to remember" (melancholia)—and here, not remember what we've *done* (for melancholia cannot be said to have done anything) but what we *know*. What we know, however, is described only negatively as that which "ruins" (now describing the melancholic and thus characteristically appearing as a noun rather than as a verb) and "hyaenas" (those violent dogs) "cannot know."[27]

All these complicated inversions serve to reinforce the gnomic utterance that places *power* at the exact mathematical center of the poem (calculated here in terms of syllables): "What we love / Ourselves for is our power not to love." Willing is understood as power, specifically the power not to love. But the melancholic will, as a subject deserving only a passive verb, must convert the question of its power (what can I do?) into a question of its authorization (what am I allowed to do?), and thus it is paralyzed, "caught in reflection on the right to will." The formulation, "right to will," is in a certain sense unprepared; indeed, it is paradoxical, for the concept of right makes sense only in the context of a structure of rights or legal order that is itself an expression of the will. One must be able to will in order to have a right, and any order of right is a function of independent wills as they relate to one another. The phrase "right to will" loses its paradoxical character, however—and in this way, breaks away from the aporias of melancholic reflection—when the term *right* is understood as an enabling condition and "the right to will" is understood as the legitimacy of the faculty of willing with respect to the other faculties; in other words, when the phrase prompts an inquiry into the historicity of the will instead of registering a state of "utter hesitation." "Reflection on the right to will" can thus be understood as a meditation on the condition of willing—its legitimacy in the context of competing faculties, especially that of thought—and thus on its history.

II. A Priceless Gift

The question of the will's history and that of its legitimacy are closely related. For, as Arendt writes in *The Life of the Mind*, "the faculty of the Will was unknown to Greek antiquity and was discovered as a result of experiences about which we hear next to nothing before the first century of the Christian era. The problem for later centuries was to reconcile this faculty with the main tenets of Greek philosophy."[28] This effort at reconciliation has consisted, for the most part, in the demonstration of the limited validity of the will with respect to the faculty of thought. But Arendt herself seeks to find and preserve a specific space *for willing* by investigating its history. In a set of reflections that continually refers to Auden's work (although not to "Canzone"),[29] Arendt seeks to understand the same temporal conundrums that give Auden's poem its definitive shape. And she renews the question of the legitimacy of the will in precisely that philosophical-historical context explored in Auden's poem; the two poles defining "Canzone" are the scholastic debates concerning the will (which reach their artistic pinnacle in Dante's work) and the devastation of the Second World War (the ideological expression of which is aptly formulated in Riefenstahl's phrase the "triumph of the will"). These same two poles guide Arendt's inquiry in *The Life of the Mind*, and for this reason, it grants an auspicious, and perhaps irreplaceable, perspective on the general context of Auden's earlier work.

The starting point for Arendt's inquiry is the fact that the faculty of willing was "discovered" (LM, 2: 3), and indeed discovered well after the inception of classical Greek philosophy. Neither Platonic nor Aristotelian thought knew of any faculty that was correlated to freedom in the same way that thinking was correlated to truth; in other words, they knew no will but at most, a faculty of choice (*proaieresis*) among already given options. Arendt's notes on "Willing" continually refer to the obscurity surrounding the discovery of the specific faculty of willing; nowhere, however, does she have the opportunity to investigate the complicated circumstances of Hellenistic thought in which Aristotle's *proairesis* begins to approximate what would later be recognized under the category of *voluntas*. Arendt takes up the history of the Will only as it becomes a central faculty in the contemporaneous writings of Paul and Epictetus. Of particular importance for Arendt's account of the emergence of the Will as an independent faculty is a massive alteration in the conception of time that accompanies the integration of the biblical story of creation into the philosophical culture of antiquity: Greek philosophy generally conceived of time as cyclical and had no place for a future that was not a repetition of the past. Thus for Arendt, the faculty of willing began to compete with that of thought when the world was understood as beginning at a contingent moment of creation—God might have created any other world or no world at all—and when, in turn, history was felt to open onto a future for which nothing in this world prepared us, the apocalyptic future of the early Christians. And scholastic philosophy, which Arendt places at the center of her investigation, conceived of its duty as the reconciliation of will with intellect, hence, the reconciliation of the cosmic, cyclical time of Platonic-Aristotelian thought—which honors necessity—with the demands of a temporality marked by an absolute beginning in divine creation and an equally absolute endpoint: the eschatological vision of the future. Dante's "Amor, tu vedi ben che questa Donna" can be understood as a poetological version of this reconciliation: the end of time witnesses the ordered transformation of the only hitherto untransformed thing, the lady; in the meantime, there is the novelty of song. Auden, who of course had returned to Christian practice by the time he wrote "Canzone," did not throw himself into a project of reviving a world in which this reconciliation would be meaningful. Nevertheless, he repeats Dante's performance, and the force of this repetition makes itself known in light of Arendt's reflections on the right to will.

The discovery of the Will did not secure its legitimacy, and one of the reasons for the persistence of questions concerning its rightness is the strange circumstance that those who bring it into question, namely, philosophers, have, according to Arendt, something like a professional animus against the Will. For willing displaces the faculty of thinking from its contemplative state: the solitary quiet in which thought may proceed—*otium*—is forced into *nec otium* (negotiation).[30] Viewed from the perspective of philosophers who privilege its competing faculty, thinking, and who, indeed, resent its intrusion into the free functioning of that faculty, the Will presents three principal difficulties: first, it may not exist; second, the freedom without which there is no Will runs counter to the principle of reason; and last—and this includes the other two—the will, as she writes, suffers from the "curse" (LM, 2: 27) of contingency. Oriented as they are toward the enduring present, thinking and its partisans want necessity, however it is conceived—whether under the strictures of the principle of noncontradiction or those of the principle of causation. And until the Will can rid itself of contingency, it cannot be legitimated in the eyes of a contemplation that finds satisfaction only in necessity. Of all the philosophers whom Arendt discusses, ancient or modern, only one defends what she calls "the factor of contingency in everything that is" (LM, 2: 31), namely, Duns Scotus. And she notes that her study of Scotus could serve as "the speculative conditions for a philosophy of freedom" (LM, 2: 146)—something she unfortunately did not live to work out.[31]

Arendt cites more than once Scotus's earthy proof for the existence of contingency: "Let all those who deny contingency be tormented until they admit that it would be possible *not* to be tortured" (LM, 2: 134). The insight of Scotus that guides Arendt, not only in her discussion of the subtle philosopher but in all her reflections on the right to will, is that there must be contingency if there is to be freedom, or, to use a more exacting yet paradoxical formulation: contingency is the price to be paid for the priceless gift of freedom.[32] Arendt closes her discussion of Scotus with a nod to another of his "surprisingly original" (LM, 2: 145) insights, without precedent or sequel in the history of Western thought: that the faculty of Will can be transformed into the sheer activity of love, not, however, by the binding of love with its object or by the transcending of desire through the activity of thinking but by delighting in itself. Because of this delight, love can be emptied of the desire to possess the object of love, while still loving its object. Love is thus the foretaste of blessedness, of "perfect love of God for God's sake," in which the Will "no longer needs or is no longer capable of, rejection" (LM, 2: 144) and hence of choice. But this does not mean, as Arendt points out, that those in a state of blessedness have lost the faculty of saying "yes." On the contrary, Scotus, for Arendt, is better able than even Augustine to make sense of the line that has haunted her work since her dissertation on the doctrine of love in Augustine: "*Amo, volo ut sis* [I love, I will that you be]" (LM, 2: 144).[33]

With the advent of modernity—and this is, in a sense, the meaning of "modernity"—the present takes precedence over the past, and the present ceases to be an enduring present as it seeks its legitimation in the future instead of in the past or in the necessary order of things. In this way, as Arendt proceeds to explain, the Will not only gains a certain legitimacy with respect to the faculty of thought, it progressively, and often under the protection of the imperatives of progress, overwhelms the other faculties. And therefore an attempt like that of Scotus to defend the rights of the will against the claims of contemplation no longer makes sense. Once the Will vanquishes all competitors, which finally happens for Arendt in Nietzsche's work, the only thing that it can will is return, the return of all things. And Nietzsche's doctrine of recurrence, which he understood to be the culmination of a theory of will as the will-to-power—that is, as a will-to-will rather than as a will to accomplish specific tasks—is Arendt's evidence for this ironic reversal. Thus, even though Auden's "Canzone" has no trace of cyclical time, the future in any genuine sense is as foreclosed as it would be if its content corresponded with its poetic form. The reference to the "triumph of the will" and "bacchic fury" underscore Auden's acute ear for the Nietzschean paradox. At the height of willing, there is nothing to will but return, but this will-to-return is the pure form—or formal test—of willingness: can one *will*, not merely bear, to suffer everything all over again? Taking up the wisdom of Silenus, on which Nietzsche based the dynamics of his first book, and retrieving the image of the Dionysian dance to which he is drawn during his last lucid days, Auden writes in "Death's Echo": "Not to be born is the best for man; / The second-best is a formal order, / The dance's pattern; dance while you can" (CP, 153).

Arendt sees this history of the will from its discovery in early Christianity to its apotheosis in Nietzsche with remarkable clarity. Once the will has subsumed all other faculties into itself, it closes the temporal horizon without which there can be no specific act of volition. For Nietzsche, then, the future is given over to those who can pass the formal test of the will, and as Arendt explains as she outlines the two leading "metaphors" of his writings, this test is administered in the precise location where contemplation had once taken place: in utter solitude. The Nietzschean Will hears the residue of thought in the words of a demon who appears out of its "loneliest loneliness" (LM, 2: 166).[34] When fellowship returns—and it is the strange fellowship of a Nietzschean "we" that is one of a kind and not therefore subject to the vicissitudes of plurality—the word *will* is heard everywhere. Arendt is attentive to this resounding return of the word *will* and centers her account of Nietzsche in her notes on his doctrine of return and on a curious aphorism in which Nietzsche hears the word *Wille* in *Welle*, "will" in "wave": "Thus live waves—thus live we who will . . . [*So leben die Wellen—so leben wir, die Wollenden*]. Carry on as you like, roaring with overweening pleasure or malice—or dive again . . . and throw your infinite white mane of foam and spray over them. . . . For . . .

you and I—are we not one of a kind?" (LM, 2: 164–65)³⁵ Hearing the
echo of *Wille* in *Welle*, Nietzsche, who, as Arendt writes, has become an
uncompromising partisan of the willing faculty, reveals the total collapse
of everything, starting with the primal sea, into the will.

In *The Enchafèd Flood*, Auden, like Arendt in her chapter on willing,
traces the problematic character of attempts to open the temporal horizon, to forge a future unencumbered by the past—not by way of a word,
as with Arendt, but in view of a specific iconography, to use the subtitle
of this work, "the Romantic Iconography of the Sea." Auden's study is less
an investigation into the literary movement of Romanticism (although it
does concern itself with Wordsworth and Novalis) than an inquiry into
what he describes as a "rare," "revolutionary change in sensibility" (EF, 2).
Auden prefaces his study by noting that the only precedent for the sudden
appearance of what he writes is "more conveniently than accurately" (EF,
2) called Romanticism is the appearance of *Amor* in the twelfth century.
Romanticism distinguishes itself for Auden by rejecting and repudiating
the city, and this repudiation is revolutionary because it does not seek to
replace the iconography of the city with anything that would serve the
same function; that is, it does not seek to illustrate a space of cultivated
stability.³⁶ When the city *is* integrated into the iconography of Romanticism, as in "the ship of state," it is always only the city in peril, never the
city as the site or promise of an abiding order. The sea, for Auden, is therefore Romanticism's central icon. It is "that state of barbaric vagueness and
disorder out of which civilisation has emerged and into which, unless
saved by the efforts of gods and men, it is always liable to relapse. . . . [It]
is the symbol of primitive potential power" (EF, 6, 9). As Auden develops
his argument, these features of the sea—formlessness, chaos, and power—
make way for another and more trenchant one: the sea is the place to
which one turns as one turns away from contingency, for once one sets
forth onto the sea, having come to the Romantic realization that everything is contingent in civilization, the will of the waves leaves one with no
choices, or, at best, the stark choice of the divided will: to live—that is, to
continue to will—or to let oneself die—that is, to will-not-to-will.³⁷ As
Auden writes near the center of *The Enchafèd Flood*: "Their going to sea
is a commitment to a necessity which, however unpleasant, is at least certain and preferable to the melancholia and accidie induced by the meaningless freedom on shore" (EF, 71).

III. Another Will

"Canzone" is Auden's struggle with the spirit of Romanticism, which sees a virtue in fleeing from contingency or converting it into necessity. The rigid constraints of this poem, which harks back to the revolutionary appearance of *amor*, confine the "chaos of the heart" within the fabricated necessities of the form. Helpless before a lover's refusal to return his love, the poet navigates the treacherous inconstancy of his own emotions and the feelings of his beloved by building a meticulously structured vessel for those emotions, which threaten to get away from him entirely. Auden had conceived of his relation to Chester Kallman as a marriage, and even took to wearing a wedding ring. And Kallman's unfaithfulness was for Auden a catastrophe that drove him almost to the point of murder.[38] Years later, Auden, who did in fact remain wedded in his way to Kallman until his death, described with a combination of dismay and humor the chaos he felt when Kallman betrayed him: "I was forced to know in [my own] person what it is to feel oneself the prey of demonic powers, in both the Greek and the Christian sense, stripped of self-control and self-respect, behaving like a ham actor in a Strindberg play."[39] In this characteristically reverent and irreverent confession from his essay in *Modern Canterbury Pilgrims*, Auden takes up with almost no alteration one of the lines from "Canzone"—"In my own person I am forced to know / How much must be forgotten out of love"—and the poem as a whole displays a violent struggle—not however of the will divided against itself as the will-to-will and the will-not-to-will, but the wholly unpredictable struggle of one will against another will that refuses to be integrated into a project that wants the "fluent satisfaction" of that will: Kallman simply says "no" to Auden's desire. What love first asks of its object is that its projection be reciprocated. What it demands is something it cannot accomplish by means of willing. The question with which the poem opens is, in this sense, concerned with the right to will: "When shall we learn, what should be clear as day, / We cannot choose what we are free to love?"

The concern with learning, the peculiarity of the lyric "we," and the paradoxical character of the question it poses set the opening lines in the philosophical tradition of reflection on the legitimacy of the will, which Auden, like Arendt, seeks to reignite. If we cannot choose what we are free to love, then love must be distinguished from choice, such that the inability to choose the object of love does not imply that love is not free. We must therefore learn *how* to distinguish love from the desire of the will to possess its object; that is, we must learn a love that will not be modeled on the structure of desire.[40] A clear answer to the question—"when shall we learn?"—should be available now or "today," because presumably it is contained in the only activity the poem has yet mentioned: the free act of loving. But the opening question receives no answer, and in place of the free act of loving—in which love would be the intimation of a day when there is clarity about love—the poem presents a series of animal imagery, in which the will, not yet transformed into the delight of loving, threatens to be reduced to sheer appetite. *As* appetite, the hungry and frustrated will is available for "baiting"—in every sense: "Faces, orations, battles, bait our will / As questionable forms and noises will." That which baits "our will" would lure it out of its freedom—and, thus, away from love and toward the "outskirts" of the day. The allure of such things—faces, orations, battles—is that they have the hue of resolution in an atmosphere of chaos: expressions of resoluteness, glorifications of national resolve, and the resolution of conflict through violence. Each of these things is an example of what has a tendency to lure the will away from its freedom and, drawing on the other sense of *bait*, harasses and incites it to violence, namely "questionable forms and noises."[41]

If, however, the same line is read so that the *as* indicates simultaneous action, then the subject of volition changes: while certain things bait *our* will, questionable forms and noises exert *their* will. Among these questionable forms is, of course, the poem, which has been set into motion by a question and whose form, indeed whose very title, begs to be questioned: What is a canzone? Canzone about what? By subtly indicating that "we" are not the only possible *subject* of volition, the poem thus keeps alive, as it were, the possibility that there is another *sense* of willing, especially since it is difficult to imagine that any answer to the question "what does the poem will?" would involve the possession or consumption of an object, even itself. And keeping alive this possibility is particularly important as the poem enters into the second stanza, which, although dominated by the rhyme word *world*, allows only "we"—or "our claim"—to be grammatical subjects and issues into the *knowledge* that "our" appetite is "dreadful": it demands that present, past, and future—that is, "order, origin, and purpose"—not deviate at any point from the "fluent satisfaction of our will." Regardless of how successful "we" may be in establishing a world that satisfies our will—regardless, therefore, of whether we have devised a perfectly mechanized world "of solid measurements" or a perfectly animated, magical world "of swans and gold," our world must nevertheless house otherwise homeless objects—"objects," of course, because they cannot function as subjects, not even as subjects of the stanza's fluent sentences. "We" are required to love these objects, which at the very least means to allow them to inhabit our world. But if love has the potential to reveal its object as independent of our will, then it also has the potential to dispossess us of our world, and if love can dispossess us of our world, it can also displace us from the site through which our will becomes worldly, namely our bodies. If, finally, neither the world nor the will can be said to belong to us; then the only thing that can be claimed as ours is "catastrophe," and with this word, which marks a caesura, preparing the way for "utter hesitation" in the next stanza, the world of the will takes a turn for the worse (*kata strophein*), no longer described in terms of mechanical perfection or mythopoetic dream but in terms of "panic," "caprice," and dread.

As the central stanza works through the dimensions of the catastrophe of our will—a will characterized by hunger and capable of nothing but negation—the lyric "we" breaks apart, "shrink[ing] to nothing or explod[ing] at will." And therefore, if the poem is to survive itself, it must begin anew: this time with a lyric "I" and a lyric "you"—not awaiting a future day of clarity but firmly situated in the "darkness" of the now. The now-point that opens the stanza dominated by the rhyme word *know* is made even darker by the obscurity of the images and syntax through which the "I" begins to inquire into the specificity of its dealings with the "you." Not only does the lyric "I" pose a question to the "you," the question it poses opens onto an almost endless series of questions about itself, which exacerbates the obscurity of this dark stanza: where to place the suppressed *either* that corresponds to the explicit *or*; to whom to ascribe the mirror in which the "I" begins to know; how to understand the juxtaposition of "genius" and "day"; where to locate the missing term of the dissolving hypotactic formulation *if . . . then*; how to read the connective *for*, since it cannot be adequately motivated by a question—to say nothing of the problems presented by the image of the "spiral staircase," which, together with the tower, became central symbols in Yeats's mid to late work (his erection, as it were, of his own patriarchal domicile) or, indeed, by the image of the mirror, which, along with the sea, plays a central role in Auden's poetic production at this time.[42] Whatever else one might say about the complications of this obscure stanza, this much is clear: instead of a will divided against itself, the will, now borne by an "I," is in commerce, or "lively traffic," with a "you." This will, which begins in the darkness of diminished knowledge, seeks to calculate the give and take of itself in relation to another, in whose mirror—and precisely whose mirror remains obscure—knowledge begins again; only this time, not in terms of hunting and haunting, but in terms of counting and negotiating, "as merchants know / Their coins and cities." And because forgetting and forgiving are therefore subject to exact calculation of quantity—*"how much"*—they remain within the economy of getting and giving. The *for* with which for-getting and for-giving begin is as questionable, even dispensable, as the *for* that starts the sentence that closes the fourth stanza.

"Our value," including the value of our terms, is therefore "more threatened than we know." The otherwise endearing terms of address that begin the fifth stanza—"Dear flesh, dear mind, dear spirit, dearest love"—are absorbed into the economics of this giving and getting. Each of these things has a cost, and the most expensive of all is love. Similarly, under the dominance of a hungry will, whose hunger is baited by the scent of the object it desires, time is valued only insofar as it brings the will closer to its final satisfaction; all other time is wasted. As the disgregated character of my will—figured as "blind monsters" and "hot rampageous horses"[43]—emerges, it becomes apparent that the will is caught in cycles of exchange: love for love. The exchange of love for love in which the cost of love can be determined describes the cycles in which the will acquires and calculates value. Hence, for the will, "love gives no excuse," which is to say, it allows no debts of love to be forgiven; and as the will "whinnies" this solemn decree, which extends beyond the actual world to include every possible one, it violates the otherwise perfectly regular syllable count of the line, speaking for two extra syllables in the eighth line of the stanza—precisely the line, moreover, where in the previous stanzas conspicuous caesuras had momentarily gestured toward an opening in which willing, and thus loving, could be understood as something other than ownership, power, and calculation; an opening, that is, onto a space of contingency. The self disintegrates in the penultimate stanza as a result of diametrically opposing positions on forgiveness: the will always says, "no"; the lover, *as* a lover, always says, "yes." The will's final speech, the principal feature of which is hyperbolically extended negations—*no, neither, nor, nor, nor,*

nor—is in anticipation of such an opening: the "horses of the will" shy away from and indeed hesitate before the hint of that which under no condition can be brought under the direction of the will. "Catching the scent of Heaven," they close off the specific lyric space in which an opening had been prepared by means of—and this must be understood ironically—their loquacious noise. "Heaven" names a time as much, if not more than, a space: a future over which the will has no say. Within the economy of the poetic world of "Canzone," the "scent of Heaven" (and one can hear the monetary term *cent* and thus another indication of cost) is comprehensible only as that of the "fellow-creature," whose scent no longer "baits" a hungry will and who, as a creature, is an image of its creator and, as a fellow, inhabits a world in common—but not necessarily in commerce—with the poet. Plurality and contingency, moreover, characterize everything creaturely, for no creature can be a cause of itself, none can be without a beginning, and every one is exposed to its equals. The fellow-creature, who is dear and thus costly to the poet precisely because it thwarts the satisfaction of his will, is the figure of sheer contingency within the space of the poem. Instead of determining the cost of love, the poet confronts what costs his will, more exactly, the paradoxical *price* of a will that is free: contingency. Once a will pays the price for what Arendt memorably calls the "priceless . . . gift of freedom" (LM, 2: 141) and does not therefore try to overcome contingency but, on the contrary, remains conscious of *being tried*, then time cannot be the fertile ground for "whole phyla of resentments": the retrospective evaluation that time was wasted. The time of trial can then be the opening of a time that no longer serves as a substitute for something else—and better: "Or else we make a scarecrow of the day."

Whatever is free, and therefore has no price, is acquitted of the cycles of exchange; its value escapes the calculations of the hungry will. Within the sphere of exchange into which the poem had been drawn since the poet began to speak of himself in terms of an "I" in "lively traffic" with a "you," a *free* will has no ascertainable value, removed as it is from the economy of exchange. Whereas the structure of the poem, as it turns from "we" to "I," develops out of the formula this-*for*-that, the formula that overtakes the poetic voice as it turns to a very different "we"—different at the very least because it is no longer a pretentious extension of the "I"—is not this-or-that, which would be a matter of choice, but, rather, this-*or else*-that. What "our free will" cannot will if it is to be free is necessity.

Only contingency, in other words, is necessary, and the only knowledge of contingency lies in the experience of an unsatisfied will—or, as Auden writes in the poem's last line, in "sorrow": "There *must* be sorrow if there *can* be love." What the will must abandon for the sake of its freedom, therefore, is necessity in all its forms: not only the force of superior power to which weaker objects must submit but also the vessel that, by turning away from the condition of contingency, makes its every move necessary, including, of course, the poetic form of "Canzone." And at the one and only place in which the poem qualifies the will as free—"And stuff and nonsense of our own free will"—it abandons, if only for a moment, the rigorous formal constraints under which it has operated and through which it has sought to bring the "chaos of the heart" under control. Dante's poem closes with a *commiato* of six lines, the order of which is determined by the sequence of the dominant rhyme words in each of the five stanzas, except that the rhyme word of the central stanza, *cold*, is repeated in the middle. "Canzone," by contrast, closes with an envoi of five lines in which the central rhyme word *will* is left alone.[44] Whereas Dante celebrates the novelty of the *thing* he can master—not the lady but, instead, the canzone—Auden bids his fellow-creature to praise the *condition* of helplessness, and he does so without drawing attention to his sole formal innovation: the phrase "our free will" is not paired with any other use of *will*.

Or else it is silently paired with another *will* (and here, I mean the word): a *will* whose dimensions may be understood in terms of the space left open by the missing line. This *will*, which is not incorporated *into* the poem, guarantees that the poem, for all its formal mastery, will remain open to a will (and here, I mean the faculty) about which it does not speak, a will to which this absence at the center of the final "send off" only gestures.

Conclusion

Going On

Changes of heart should also occasion song.
      —W. H. Auden, "Ischia"

Auden is one of the few readers of Arendt's *Human Condition* who responds to the redemptive schema by which it seeks to explicate the *vita activa*. And Auden's review of Arendt's book recognizes that the schema it develops remains only a schema and cannot come forward as a salvational power in its own right, as a formula for future action, or as a solution to the "anxious" condition that characterizes "the age in which we live": "Miss Arendt is not, of course, so foolish or presumptuous as to offer saving solutions. She merely asks us to think what we are doing."[1] In describing Arendt's purpose in writing *The Human Condition*, Auden adopts her own formulation: "What I propose, therefore, is very simple: it is nothing more than to think what we are doing" (HC, 5). The simplicity of this proposal is inversely proportional to the complexity of a thought that seeks to come to terms with "our newest experiences and our most recent fears" (HC, 5): the unprecedented and outrageous fabrication of corpses at the center of totalitarian domination. By dividing the undifferentiated *vita activa* into its constitutive elements—marked by the terms *labor*, *work*, and *action*—Arendt seeks to initiate a rethinking of the human condition outside the perspective developed within the *vita contemplativa*, which sets for itself the supreme goal of overcoming spatiality, temporality, and the plurality of perspectives, as it models itself in solitude after eternal intellect. And Auden recognizes Arendt's mode of proceeding when he describes *The Human Condition* with the unassuming phrase "an essay in Etymology."[2] The simplicity of Arendt's proposal corresponds to the simplicity of the analytic proposition that gives direction, however indefinite, to the power of action: the act of forgiveness "make[s] it possible for life to go on."³ Life going on describes a *weakly* redemptive resumption. Almost the same phrase—and precisely the same thought—guides the culminating, but deeply anticlimactic, moment of *The Age of Anxiety*, as Rosetta, hitherto inebriated, articulates the soberest imperative imaginable: "We must try to get on."⁴ The disarming simplicity of this imperative—allied with its counterpart, "We'll trust" (529)—not only stands out against the extravagant complexity of Auden's "Baroque Eclogue" but also stands against the immense calamities that make Rosetta stutter the lines, "our bodies are chucked / Like cracked crocks onto kitchen middens" (529).

Phrases like "getting on" and "going on" seem poorly matched to the enormity of the events to which both Auden and Arendt are trying to respond. Despite their simplicity, however, these formulations are anything but simplistic: they are not slogans through which political enthusiasms can be generated; nor are they ironic emblems of withdrawal from public life. The degree to which the motif of "going on" traverses Arendt's thought can perhaps best be measured by a story recounted by one of her friends: "Hannah Arendt . . . told of a concentration camp in World War II in which people got together and tried to remember as much of Homer as he or she could, to piece together all the pieces they knew. They did not manage to construct all of Homer; and so their work did not keep Homer going, as it were . . . ; but they did it because it 'kept *them* going,' she said."⁵ Although modest, the phrases Arendt and Auden choose to express the weakly redemptive resumption of "going on" are not meek: they do not register resignation in the face of overwhelming force; nor do they propose a kind of clandestine existence, common to saints and criminals, hidden from public view. And although Auden and Arendt are careful to make intricate and articulate distinctions, their mutually supporting formulations—"getting on" and "going on"—do not give any directions: they are deeply anti-utopian and skeptical even of programmatic statements that hope to capture the course of history; yet, their anti-utopian stances and their well-considered skepticism do not arise from or give rise to anarchic or nihilistic rejections of conditions, limits, or laws—whether political or poetic. "Getting on" does not mean forgetting, and "going on" does not demand forgoing. The imperatives that correspond to these two phrases have nothing to do with oblivion or sacrifice. When Auden writes, "we must try to get on," and Arendt writes that the act of forgiveness makes it possible for "life to go on," they are responding—soberly, with outrage, and yet without bravado—to the calamities and disasters of their age.

~

Totalitarianism is a "saving solution." It seeks to eliminate two of action's inherent frustrations: irreversibility and unpredictability. Unpredictability is a direct consequence of plurality. By eliminating plurality, everything becomes predictable—not for those who live under the condition of totalitarian domination, to be sure, but for the totalitarian movement itself: "Total domination, which strives to organize the infinite plurality of differentiation of human beings as if all humanity were just one individual, is possible only if each and every person can be reduced to a never-changing identity of reactions, so that each of these bundles of reactions can be exchanged at random for any other."[6] Irreversibility would seem to be impossible to cancel insofar as it is a characteristic of temporality as such: time is unidirectional. Totalitarian ideologies, furthermore, want no part of classical ideas of cyclical time in which temporal reversibility could perhaps make some sense. Eliminating irreversibility is, strictly speaking, impossible, but the central institutions of totalitarianism are places where "everything is possible"—including the elimination of an ontological condition of human life: detention, concentration, and extermination camps are all "holes of oblivion"[7] in which people not only disappear but disappear as if they never existed. In place of the miracle of action—and unlike the "old-fashioned method of murder"—the new phenomenon of totalitarianism substitutes its own "miracle": "The murderer leaves behind him a corpse, and although he tries to efface the traces of his own identity, he has no power to erase the identity of his victim from the memory of the surviving world. The operation of the secret police, on the contrary, miraculously sees to it that the victim never existed at all."[8] The murders organized by the secret police miraculously reverse the miracle of birth. In one of the fragments of "Über den Begriff der Geschichte," Benjamin writes: "Only that historian will have the gift of fanning the spark of hope in the past who is firmly convinced that *even the dead will not be safe* from the enemy if he wins. And this enemy has not ceased to be victorious."[9] Arendt takes this anxious thought one step further; totalitarianism cannot lose even when it loses, because even as it loses, it succeeds in creating "holes of oblivion" in "the abyss of the 'possible.'"

Action responds in opposition to totalitarianism's efforts to reduce plural human beings into interchangeable "bundles of reaction," but action

is not a saving solution even if, as Arendt shows, it has the power to redeem the world of the human artifice, and even if one of its own potentialities has the power to redeem action from the predicament that totalitarianism seeks to eliminate altogether: irreversibility. Action is not a
saving *solution* precisely because it is always only a beginning, never a resolution. And action can never attain the finality of a solution because of
its abyssal structure: one of its own potentialities brings an end to the consequences of the act it initiates, but this end is itself an act and therefore a
beginning, similarly in need of an end. Action, for this reason, is fundamentally helpless: there is no higher power that can rescue it from the outside. Helpless, too, is the child—the figure by which Arendt represents the
redemptive resumption that is action. Whereas all totalitarian movements
seek to overcome helplessness with the principle of infallible leadership,
action, as Arendt understands it, continually reignites helplessness without end—and without outside help, although not without hope for the
world. The continual and continually interruptive reignition of helplessness in action is the paradoxical *conditione sine qua non* of responsibility,
for only a free action is able to respond, and not simply react, to the conditions, laws, and limitations of human life.

But, as Arendt acknowledges, action cannot protect itself from accusations of irresponsibility: the freedom to begin an action does not extend
to the freedom to control or even simply guide its consequences. In contrast to Kant, Arendt does not propose a universal formula to guarantee
the rational uniformity of action and secure the responsibility of the agent
by abstracting moral judgment from all considerations of unintended
consequences. Nor does she seek to secure the realm of human affairs by
substituting making for action in which a perfectly constructed world—a
"tidy utopia"—is the end and only consequence that guides any activity
from its beginning. As she writes in her chapter on the traditional substitution of making for acting, "It has always been a great temptation . . . to
find a substitute for action in the hope that the realm of human affairs
may escape the haphazardness and moral irresponsibility inherent in a
plurality of agents."[10] The temptation to overcome the irresponsibility inherent in plurality—and *temptation* is precisely the word Arendt uses for
the attractiveness of totalitarian solutions[11]—is not responsible, however,
but represents the intensification of irresponsibility: responses are abandoned in favor of reactions, until in the end human beings are nothing
more than "bundles of reaction." Responding to this intensification of

irresponsibility, *The Human Condition* insists on the irreplaceable dignity of action, even as it acknowledges action's inherent irresponsibility. Arendt does not lament this condition; she embraces it: plurality is the condition of both action and its predicaments. And although Arendt does not develop a technical term to describe this act of embracing, the book as a whole can be understood as a tribute to the human condition of plurality in all its frailty and with all its frustrations. Auden, for his part, addresses plurality in the simple vocative of "Canzone"—"dear fellow-creature": as a fellow, the creature cannot be sovereign, and as a creature, the fellow can begin anew because of its own beginning in creation and birth. The vocative is in service to an imperative: "praise" (331). Although the object of praise is a god—"praise our God of Love / That we are so admonished"— the aim of the imperative is not to extol this god above all things but to praise it for our lack of sovereignty: for the condition of creaturely fellowship—in Arendt's terms, *plurality*—it created.

Praise is a response to the irresponsibility of action that absorbs into itself this very irresponsibility: it is an activity that does nothing except bring into view the sheer conditionality of action. Praise cannot therefore escape its own frivolity. Promising is a potentiality of action that remedies action's unpredictability; forgiveness, another of action's internal potentialities, redeems action from the irreversibility of its consequences and, in so doing, reveals the abyssal structure of action: there is no final or fundamental action. Praise is an additional potentiality internal to action: it does not remedy or redeem action's predicaments; rather, it has the capacity to conform itself to the abyssal structure of action as a whole and can therefore become a frivolous analogue to action that comprehends, without seeking to overcome, the full range of action and its predicaments. Not all praise, however, remains within these parameters: some forms of praise reach out to extramundane beings; still others exalt individuals, human and divine, along with their individual actions. The form of praise that corresponds to the abyssal structure of action does not commend individuals for their actions but embraces the condition of action such that there can be individuals. If Kantian terms were adequate here, which is doubtful, since Kant praises only duty,[12] the praise that complements promising and forgiveness is a transcendental rather than a transcendent praise: it is concerned with the conditions of the possibility of action, not with exalted agents. The exaltation of "our God of Love" in "Canzone" would seem to align the poem with a tradition in which gods and heroes are the incontrovertible objects of praise, but this god is praised "*that* we are so admonished"—*that* designating the sheer facticity of our condition of createdness, fellowship, and plurality.

Praise is the last word of Auden's famous elegy for W. B. Yeats: "In the prison of his days / Teach the free man how to praise" (249). In this wonderful line, the imperative is teach, not praise. And praise as yet has no object: *what* to praise can arise only out of the process of learning *how* to praise; thus praise remains something to be learned. In *The Life of the Mind*, Arendt gives a brief but powerful account of the historical conditions in which praise has to be learned—or relearned:

> I spoke of the ancient Greek notion that all appearances, inasmuch as they *appear*, not only imply the presence of sentient creatures capable of perceiving them but also demand recognition and *praise*. This notion was a kind of philosophical justification of poetry and the arts; world-alienation, which preceded the rise of Stoic and Christian thought, succeeded in obliterating it from our tradition of philosophy—though never entirely from the reflections of poets. (You can still find it, very emphatically expressed, in W. H. Auden—who speaks of "that singular command / I do not understand, / *Bless what there is for being*, / Which has to be obeyed, for / What else am I made for, / Agreeing or disagreeing?"—in the Russian poet Osip Mandelstam, and, of course, in the poetry of Rainer Maria Rilke.)[13]

In *The Human Condition*, Arendt describes how philosophy almost destroys the articulations within the *vita activa* and thereby contributes to the obliteration of action; in this excursus from her notes on Willing in *The Life of the Mind*, Arendt proposes a similar project: describing how philosophy almost succeeds in destroying praise—not for things, heroes, or gods but for appearances as such and thus for the condition of plurality—and therefore forces poetry to justify itself. The justification of poetry is that appearances demand praise. Poetry, however, does not justify appearances—or anything else.

Arendt makes praise, understood in this manner, into the guiding motif of her memorial essay for Auden. She emphasizes that the praise about which he speaks in the last lines of "In Memory of W. B. Yeats" has no theodicical or otherwise justificatory function: "Praise is the key-word of these lines, praise not of 'the best of all possible worlds'—as though it were up to the poet (or the philosopher) to justify God's creation of it—but praise that pitches itself against all that is most unsatisfactory in man's condition on this earth."[14] Arendt is exact in her phrasing: she does not identify an object of praise; rather, praise is a reflexive activity—it "pitches itself"—that embraces the conditions and conditionality of action. But the exactness of Arendt's wording does not preclude a significant ambiguity, for her phrase "all that is most unsatisfactory" can be understood in at least two ways: from the perspective of *The Human Condition*, action is the fundamental and ineluctable frustration that leaves no place for final or even merely provisional satisfaction; from the perspective of *The Origins of Totalitarianism*, the "abyss of the 'possible'" makes all talk of satisfaction, whether final or provisional, outrageous. The calamities of action and the catastrophes of totalitarian domination are radically opposed to each other, and praise is drawn toward both: to praise the frustrations of action against the infinitely unsatisfactory historical disaster that occupies, and never leaves, the center of both Arendt's and Auden's articulate reflections. Praise, like all actions, is unsatisfactory, particularly if satisfaction is understood in terms of resolution, restitution, or retribution. Praise is certainly not a satisfactory response to the "abyss of the 'possible,'" and it is not even a satisfactory solution to the abyssal structure of action, especially if the adequacy of its responsiveness is measured in terms of responsibility. For praise not only remains, like all actions, irresponsible but draws attention to its inherent frivolity as well.

By the time Auden came to publish *The Dyer's Hand*, he was convinced that praise was the unsurpassable duty of poetry. At the conclusion to the chapter on "Making, Knowing and Judging," he lavishly lists the possibilities of poetry only to insist on its sole necessity: "Poetry can do a hundred and one things, delight, sadden, disturb, amuse, instruct—it may express every possible shade of emotion, and describe every conceivable kind of event, but there is only one thing that all poetry must do; it must praise all it can for being and for happening."[15] The object of poetic praise remains indeterminate. By presenting the object in terms of poetic possibilities— "all it can"—as it simultaneously insists on the poetic necessity of the act of praise, this final sentence considerably complicates the imperative of poetic responsibility: it cannot simply praise anything and everything but must understand itself sufficiently well to know what it *can* praise. And, conversely, only by learning what it can and cannot praise does poetry come to understand itself.

In Auden's elegy for Yeats, he identifies no object of praise. Three years later, in "Canzone," he enjoins his fellow-creature to praise a god not for any act or attribute, but "that we are so admonished." In the anthem that Auden appends for his friends to the "Epilogue" of *The Age of Anxiety*, he seems to return to a more traditional form of praise poetry, as he begins his poem with "PRAISE YE THE LORD"[16]—an understandable formulation, given that the piece was written for a patronal festival. When he republishes this poem in *Epistle to a Godson*, he transforms the opening line into the less liturgical injunction: "Let us praise our Maker."[17] In both versions of this anthem the direction of the praise moves away from the maker and toward, as the last line says, the places and patterns made: " . . . the pattern is complex, their places safe."[18] Throughout all of these poems, the poet is teaching himself through "conscious trial" (331) how to praise. And in teaching himself how to praise, Auden learns what he can praise: not everything, understood in a metaphysical sense, but appearances as such; and nothing that destroys the plural world of appearances, either through mobilization or solidification. Whereas mobilization marks every moment of totalitarian movement, solidification characterizes every utopian impulse. An act of praising that both conforms itself to the abyssal structure of action and responds to the "abyss of the 'possible'" can take as its object only something that remains as frail, as faulty, and as irredeemably faulted as action itself—something very much like a limestone landscape: a safe and complexly patterned place.

When Auden writes "In Praise of Limestone," he finds something he can, and therefore *must*, praise: not a hero, god, or age but an inconspicuous and altogether irregular space, a specific, nonutopian landscape. As he departs from the traditional objects of poetic encomia and touches on the countertradition most famously announced in Erasmus's *Moriae encomium* (The Praise of Folly),[19] his poem exhibits the frivolity of praise. Limestone is not itself abyssal: it is fissured. The act of praising limestone does not ground the abyssal structure of action or seek to take account of, or otherwise memorialize the "abyss of the 'possible.'" Rather, the act of praising absorbs into itself the anxieties generated by these abysses. And limestone—with its "secret system of caves and conduits" (540)—is the landscape of this absorption.

~

The conclusion to "Making, Knowing and Judging," reads as if it were a description of "In Praise of Limestone." The poem explores all the possibilities Auden discovers in poetry: "Poetry can do a hundred and one things, delight, sadden, disturb, amuse, instruct—it may express every possible shade of emotion, and describe every conceivable kind of event, but there is only one thing that all poetry must do; it must praise all it can for being and happening." One of Auden's greatest poems, and one he especially cherished,[20] "In Praise of Limestone" is capacious and generous enough to encompass all of these possibilities as it carries out the sole poetic necessity with unsurpassed lucidity. Like the limestone landscape it describes and after which it models itself, Auden's meditative and stunning poem is unassuming in its praise, even as it "pitches itself against all that is most unsatisfactory in man's condition on this earth." From its evocation of a combined landscape drawn from the Pennines of Auden's childhood and the Ischian home he later adopted, to its marvelous adaptation of the tradition of *paysage moralisé*, to the rich intricacy of its elegant and elegiac form, "In Praise of Limestone" invites its readers to enjoy and explore its terrain in the same manner that the creatures it exhibits— not only human beings but also butterflies, lizards, and fish—inhabit the landscape it describes: not with a synoptic vision but attentive solely to "the short distances and definite places" that "entertain" and house them.[21]

As in *The Age of Anxiety*, "In Praise of Limestone" adopts and adapts a traditional poetic form—not, this time, the epic line of Anglo-Saxon verse but the classical elegiac meter Auden particularly came to admire in the work of Ovid. Whereas *The Age of Anxiety*, following the tradition of Anglo-Saxon epic poetry, is organized around accentual stresses, "In Praise of Limestone" chooses the deliberately constructed ease of the unstressed syllabic line, with its attendant fluency of tone, for its form. The lucidity of the poem's imagery corresponds to the fluidity of lines in which stress has been suspended, and only in one place does this fluidity seem to falter. Near the middle of the poem, the elegiac line is interrupted by an ellipsis:

> So, when one of them goes to the bad, the way his mind works
>   Remains comprehensible: to become a pimp
> Or deal in fake jewellery or ruin a fine tenor voice
>   For effects that bring down the house, could happen to all
> But the best and the worst of us . . .
>   That is why, I suppose,
>   The best and worst never stayed here long but sought
> Immoderate soils where the beauty was not so external,
>   The light less public and the meaning of life
> Something more than a mad camp. (541)

The suspension of metrical stress in the lines does not signal the absence of anxiety from the poem. The ellipsis in these lines marks a moment in which incomprehension gives way to inexpressibility. It seems as though both the best and the worst escape comprehension and are thus both elided in the ellipsis. And this impression is further supported by the parallelism of the contrasting landscapes: granite for the saints, clay and gravels for the Caesars, and oceans for the "really reckless" (541). But as the opening of the sentence indicates, the reassurance that minds remain comprehensible extends only to "the bad"—not, perhaps, because the minds of the good are somehow always comprehensible but because their incomprehensibility does not generate the same degree or kind of anxiety.

"In Praise of Limestone" scrupulously avoids any mention of minds that have gone so bad that they not only take leave of the limestone landscape but recede from human comprehensibility as well. The poem does, however, make allusions to recent historical events: marching "in step," "craters" created by the "blazing fury" of bombs, "armies," "slaves," and, of course, "slamming the door"—a ghastly phrase of Goebbels that Arendt, too, includes in the *Origins*[22]:

> "Come!" purred the clays and gravels,
> "On our plains there is room for armies to drill; rivers
>   Wait to be tamed and slaves to construct you a tomb
> In the grand manner: soft as the earth is mankind and both
>   Need to be altered." (Intendant Caesars rose and
> Left, slamming the door.) (541)

The "abyss of the 'possible'" that Goebbels helped engineer is contained in the statement "soft as the earth is mankind." And the minds that would seek to prove this by mobilizing armies not only remain incomprehensible, but also, and for this very reason, generate an anxiety that expresses itself in the speechlessness of the ellipsis. Equally disturbing are the words that open the final division of the poem, for they acknowledge that the wretched voices of clays and gravels cannot be dismissed as error: "They were right, my dear, all those voices were right / And still are" (542). This last gesture—"And still are"—registers the echo of the door slammed: Auden is so little triumphal that he recognizes the possibility that the World War could resume. And even the defeat of Caesarian armies does not repair the "holes of oblivion" created by the experiment in human malleability that imperial forces conducted. The extraordinary strength of "In

Praise of Limestone"—a strength in which virility is associated not with martial prowess but with "a mad camp"—can be measured by its ability to offer an encomium, against all expectation, to an infinitely malleable landscape.

The poem is everywhere concerned with malleability, from its first line onward. The inconstancy of the limestone landscape soothes an anxiety generated by the inconstancy of a "we" whose precise dimensions the poem never specifies:

> If it form the one landscape that we, the inconstant ones,
>   Are consistently homesick for, this is chiefly
> Because it dissolves in water. (540)

The sole consistency of "inconstant ones" is homesickness for a landscape that is itself inconstant. Presumably—and the poem here invites deductive speculation by virtue of the strongly hypotactic structure of its opening sentence—the desire of the "inconstant ones" is to discover a place that corresponds to their inconstancy because, as long as they are there, they paradoxically need not change and can indeed remain wholly themselves: inconstant, not forced into a rigid or rigorous consistency common to saints and field marshals. And yet, insofar as the limestone remains a *land*scape and is not completely reabsorbed into the sea, it shelters the inconstant ones from the absolutely paradoxical consistency of the "really reckless" who, by allowing themselves to dissolve in water, cannot even retain the constancy of an inconsistent identity. The inconstancy of the "inconstant ones" has something of the negative or otherwise disapproving connotation of infidelity, and the landscape for which untrustworthy lovers longs blunts the accusation of infidelity because it, too, changes in accordance with seemingly unpredictable whims: not only does it dissolve in water, it offers a variety of aspects that constantly alter according to the perspectives and needs of the various creatures who make it their home. But even as the landscape attracts those whom it resembles by virtue of its finite mutability, it does not overcome the anxiety—or homesickness[23]— that drew the inconstant ones to it in the first place. The constancy of this anxiety is itself figured in the grammatical form of the sentence: the poet does not simply affirm the correspondence of the "inconstant ones" with the limestone landscape; this affirmation is conditioned on a hypothetical clause expressed in the subjunctive—"if it form the one landscape." Limestone may not form this "one landscape" because it may not form *one*—

consistent, self-contained, whole—landscape at all: it may, and indeed does, form many landscapes, some of which the poem proceeds to describe in loving detail.

Hypothetical propositions, articulated by if-then schemas, express a degree of uncertainty: the conclusion is secured only under the condition that the premise is true. But the same grammatical form also expresses logical consistency, since the conclusion, as consequence, directly follows from the premise, as ground. "In Praise of Limestone" returns in its concluding lines to the hypothetical-hypotactic form with which it began—as a sign of consistency or as a mark of inconstancy, it is impossible to say. But one thing is certain: inconstancy has been relieved of its negative connotations. Instead of being associated with infidelity, inconstancy reveals itself in the act of forgiveness, which expresses a change of heart:

> In so far as we have to look forward
> To death as a fact, no doubt we are right: But if
> Sins can be forgiven, if bodies rise from the dead,
> These modifications of matter into
> Innocent athletes and gesticulating fountains,
> Made solely for pleasure, make a further point:
> The blessed will not care what angle they are regarded from,
> Having nothing to hide. (542)

In retrospect, the poem can be understood to be perfectly consistent. The limestone dissolving in water is a figuration of absolution, and the "inconstant ones" are anxiously drawn toward this landscape because, knowingly or not, they yearn for a transformative—not a self-annihilating—release: a transformation in which they would not suddenly become constant, or regain innocence, but simply be forgiven. Forgiveness extends itself only to faults, or as Arendt writes, "trespasses," and not to offenses that escape all power of comprehension—least of all to the offense of making resurrection impossible by utterly destroying the bodies of the living and seeking to exterminate the memory of the dead. As the poem indicates with its third and final *if,* moreover, there is nothing simple about the act of forgiving faults; it is no less miraculous and no less transformative than the paramount and paradigmatic messianic moment: the resurrection of the dead. And the grammar of the poem even suggests that with forgiveness comes the redemptive resumption that is—or perhaps is only figured as—resurrection.

"In Praise of Limestone" embeds its reference to the absolute transformation of corpses into living bodies signaled by the term *resurrection* in a prodigious exposition of the relative transformations of various materials into finished forms of those arts, generally defined as "fine," that are "made solely for pleasure." Immediately before turning toward the fact of death and the possibilities of forgiveness and resurrection, the poem discovers the function of music: to "comfort" the anxieties whose litany gives direction to "our Common Prayer" (542). Music can carry out this function because it is purely transformative—so constantly inconsistent and inconsistent in its constancy that it leaves no trace of itself: "And does not smell." The plastic arts, by contrast, as "modifications of matter," give evidence of, but do not themselves participate in, a transformative power. Under the messianic premise of forgiveness and resurrection, however, they gain a surprising new function and are thus able to point elsewhere: toward a condition beyond that of "comfort," indeed toward a correspondingly messianic condition in which anxiety is altogether overcome—the state of blessedness. If the premises of forgiveness and resurrection are accepted, then the plasticity of the plastic arts gives an indication that blessedness will consist in the constant act of self-exposure that is itself exposed in these arts: "The blessed will not care what angle they are regarded from, / Having nothing to hide." Insofar as limestone can be modified into marble, the material of sculpture and architecture, and insofar as it offers a place for shameless self-exposure—"the nude young male who lounges / Against a rock displaying his dildo"[24]—it, too, can be absorbed into the further function that the poem discovers for the plastic arts: to point beyond the spaces and the ages of anxiety.

But the labyrinthine spaces of the limestone landscape and the intricately constructed poem that praises it cannot be entirely absorbed by the expanded function attributed by the poet to the plastic arts; both remain distinct, and distinctly themselves. Like Arendt's two faculties of action, promising and forgiveness, praise belongs to the "'web' of human relationships"[25] that overlays the world of the human artifice. But unlike promising, which establishes islands of security, and forgiveness, which releases agents from the consequences of their actions, praise does not alter this "web"—much less the limestone. Praise is therefore even more intangible and more unworldly than either of the two faculties internal to action that can remedy and redeem its predicaments. If the act of praise is not to disappear altogether, it must seek refuge in a work: the poem.

Strangely enough, however, "In Praise of Limestone" does not offer any direct account of the function of poetry—not even the vaguely comforting function of housing praise. Indeed, the lyric "I" of "In Praise of Limestone" distances itself from the only account of poetry contained in the poem itself: the "earnest habit of calling / The sun the sun, his mind Puzzle" (542). And the "I" distances itself from this account of poetry for the precise reason that it is "made uneasy" by "marble statues"—not the statues in themselves but the statues insofar as they prefigure blessedness under the premise of forgiveness. The poem of praise does not comfort like music; nor is it able to model itself on marble statues; and even as it establishes an analogical relation to paradise, it can never directly represent the state of blessedness. Instead, the "I" is "made uneasy," and the poem, which means "made thing," articulates this uneasiness. Uneasy in two directions at once: anxious with respect to the "abyss of the 'possible'" figured in the malleability of human material; and anxious with respect to the prospect or promise of forgiveness—and therefore resurrection. Resurrection, however, is not an event within the poet's field of knowledge:

> Dear, I know nothing of
> Either, but when I try to imagine a faultless love
> Or the life to come, what I hear is the murmur
> Of underground streams, what I see is a limestone landscape. (542)

Forgiveness, the sole guarantor of which is an absolutely "faultless love," allows life to go on; "the life to come" is a life entirely lived in the movement of going on—after death. The poem concludes by categorically excluding any knowledge of what it would mean to go on in this manner. But the poet—and this may define poetry—can nevertheless imagine what it would be like to go on: it would be like "the murmur of underground streams" and like "a limestone landscape." The inarticulateness of the former expresses the continuation of anxiety; the faulted character of the latter exposes the uncertainty inherent in every aspiration to go on.[26] Without a faultless love, there is no assurance that the next action will not unleash consequences for which there is no remedy or redemption—or that the next step will not plunge one down a precipice. The persistence and ubiquity of faults do not, however, plunge the poet into "bald melancholia" (330); nor does his ignorance with respect to resurrection give rise to recklessness of any sort—whether in the "reckless optimism" (Arendt) expressed in an "antimythological myth" (Auden) or in the "reckless despair" (Arendt) expressed in an "oceanic whisper" (Auden) that offers dissolution in place of absolution.[27] Poetry as praise cannot repair any faults and does not celebrate faultlessness in any form. By praising faulted beings, poetry lays the ground for forgiveness—and this ground is fissured, fluid, and thankfully faulted.

Notes

Introduction

1. See Immanuel Kant, "Beantwortung der Frage: Was ist Aufklärung?" originally published in the *Berlinische Monatschrift* (1784), reprinted in *Gesammelte Schriften*, ed. Königlich Preußischen [later, deutschen] Akademie der Wissenschaften (Berlin: Reimer; later, De Gruyter; 1900–), 8: 35. All translations in this volume, unless otherwise cited, are my own.

2. Hannah Arendt, *The Origins of Totalitarianism* (rev. ed. New York: Harcourt Brace Jovanovich, 1979), vii.

3. Elisabeth Young-Bruehl, *Hannah Arendt: For Love of the World* (New Haven: Yale University Press, 1982), 188.

4. Arendt, "We Refugees," reprinted in *The Jew as Pariah: Jewish Identity and Politics in the Modern Age*, ed. and intro. Ron Feldman (New York: Grove Press, 1978), 61, 63.

5. Arendt, "We Refugees," 59.

6. W. H. Auden, "September 1, 1939," in *Selected Poems* (New York: Vintage, 1979), 86.

7. Humphrey Carpenter, *W. H. Auden: A Biography* (Boston: Houghton Mifflin, 1982), 256. Carpenter's biography is the principal source of information on Auden in this paragraph.

8. Auden and Christopher Isherwood, *Journey to a War* (New York: Paragon House, 1990), 300.

9. Nicolas Nabokov, "Excerpts from Memories," in *W. H. Auden: A Tribute*, ed. Stephen Spender (New York: Macmillan, 1975), 145.

10. Nabokov, "Excerpts," 145.

11. See Carpenter, *W. H. Auden*, 336. According to James Stern, "during these months we were continually together, under circumstances about which I was to

write a book but of which Wystan in the years to come could very rarely be persuaded to speak. He did, however, while awaiting my arrival, write to Tania [Stern's wife] in May 1945: 'The work is very interesting but I am near crying sometimes. . . . The people . . . are sad beyond belief.' The main purpose of this letter, I should add, was to ask Tania, whom Wystan had entrusted with power of attorney, to send a cheque for $100 to the sick wife of . . . a refugee who was in Dachau" (James Stern, "The Indispensable Presence," in *W. H. Auden: A Tribute*, 126). For a copy of the letter, see "Some Letters from Auden to James and Tania Stern," ed. Nicholas Jenkins, *"In Solitude for Company": W. H. Auden after 1940*, ed. Katherine Bucknell and Nicholas Jenkins, *Auden Studies*, Vol. 3 (Oxford: Clarendon Press, 1994), 93–95.

12. When Thucydides analyzes the revolution in Corcyra, he traces the brutality of its violence through the breakdown of language: "To fit in with the change of events, words, too, had to change their usual meanings. What used to be described as a thoughtless act of aggression was now regarded as the courage one would expect to find in a party member; . . . the ability to understand a question from all sides meant that one was totally unfitted for action" (Thucydides, *The Peloponnesian War*, trans. Rex Warner [Harmondsworth: Penguin, 1983], 242.) Just as Thucydides correlates the collapse of the Corcyran *polis* to the systematic alteration of ethical terminology—and Corcyra serves as a synecdoche for Greece as a whole—Sallust traces the decline of the Roman Republic to the collapse of a stable moral vocabulary; see especially Sallust's description of the ineffectiveness of moral language in the preface to *The Jugurthine War*, trans. S. A. Handforth (Harmondsworth: Penguin, 1963), 35–38.

13. See Walter Benjamin, "Notizen über 'Objektive Verlogenheit,'" in *Gesammelte Schriften*, ed. R. Tiedemann and H. Schweppenhäuser (Frankfurt am Main: Suhrkamp, 1977–1985), 6: 60–62. Scholem indicates that Benjamin often invoked the category of "objective mendacity" in his conversations (see G. Scholem, *Walter Benjamin: The Story of a Friendship*, trans. Harry Zohn [New York: Schocken, 1981], 9–10), and Arendt's life-long interest in the relation of lying to politics may owe something to her contact with him.

14. Arendt, *The Origins of Totalitarianism*, 471.

15. Quoted in Anne Fremantle, "Reality and Religion," in *W. H. Auden: A Tribute*, 90.

16. W. H. Auden, "The Fallen City." *Encounter* 13, 5 (November, 1959), 21–31; reprinted without alteration as "The Prince's Dog" in W. H. Auden, *The Dyer's Hand and Other Essays* (New York: Vintage, 1968), 182–208.

17. Auden, "The Fallen City," 28 (*Dyer's Hand*, 200).

18. Auden, "The Fallen City," 29 (*Dyer's Hand*, 202).

19. Although Auden's 1946–1947 lectures on the *Henry* plays and *Measure for*

Measure—preserved in detailed notes by his students at the New School for Social Research in New York—overlap with the Falstaff essay of 1959, his specific concern with the distinction between forgiveness and judicial pardon is developed only in the later article. See W. H. Auden, *Lectures on Shakespeare*, ed. Arthur Kirsch (Princeton: Princeton University Press, 2000). For Auden's admiring review of *The Human Condition*, see W. H. Auden, "Thinking What We Are Doing." *Encounter* 12, 6 (June 1959), 72–76.

20. Critics have often stated that Arendt's letter responds to a (lost) letter written by Auden. There is no need for this supposition. Even a cursory reading of "The Fallen City"—to which Arendt refers as she opens her letter ("I just read the Falstaff piece")—should convince anyone that she is responding to his detailed remarks on *Measure for Measure*. Each of the points in her letter is punctuated by quotes from his essay. When she writes, for instance, "If we are to trust in what 'the Gospels assure us' of, then the 'command to forgive' is not unconditional," the former quote can be found on page 29 of "The Fallen City"; the latter on page 28 (*Dyer's Hand*, 201 and 200).

21. Arendt letter to Auden (14 February 1960; #004864 and #004865); General Correspondence, 1938–1976, n.d.—Auden, W. H.—1960–1975. Hannah Arendt Papers, Manuscript Division, Library of Congress, Washington, D.C. A digitized version of this letter can be found at http://memory.loc.gov/ammem/arendthtml/arendthome.html.

22. Arendt letter to Auden (14 February 1960; #004864); General Correspondence, 1938–1976, n.d.—Auden, W. H.—1960–1975.

23. Auden, "The Fallen City," 29 (*Dyer's Hand*, 201–02).

24. Arendt letter to Auden (14 February 1960; #004865); General Correspondence, 1938–1976, n.d.—Auden, W. H.—1960–1975.

25. Auden letter to Arendt (5 July 1973; #004858); General Correspondence, 1938–1976, n.d.—Auden, W. H.—1960–1975. A digitized version of this letter can be found at http://memory.loc.gov/ammem/arendthtml/arendthome.html.

26. Christopher L. Bowen letter to Auden (28 March 1964; #004853); General Correspondence, 1938–1976, n.d.—Auden, W. H.—1960–1975. A digitized version of this letter can be found at http://memory.loc.gov/ammem/arendthtml/arendthome.html.

27. Auden, *Dyer's Hand*, 218.

28. Carpenter, *W. H. Auden*, 376.

29. See Young-Bruehl, *Hannah Arendt*, 371.

30. Auden, "Thinking What We Are Doing," 72.

31. See Arendt's letter of 27 July 1959, in *Between Friends: The Correspondence of Hannah Arendt and Mary McCarthy, 1949–1975*, ed. Carol Brightman (New York: Harcourt Brace, 1995), 58.

32. See Young-Bruehl, *Hannah Arendt*, 436.

33. Hannah Arendt, "Remembering Wystan H. Auden," in *W. H. Auden: A Tribute*, 182.

34. Arendt, "Remembering Wystan H. Auden," 182.

35. Young-Bruehl, *Hannah Arendt*, 436; see also Arendt, "Remembering Wystan H. Auden," 182; and Carpenter, *W. H. Auden*, 430.

36. V. S. Yanowsky, "W. H. Auden," *Antaeus* 19 (autumn 1975): 107–35; quoted on 116.

37. In May 1935, Erika Mann approached Auden's friend Christopher Isherwood, whom she met through her brother, Klaus. She had been declared a public enemy of the Third Reich and hoped to become a British subject through marriage to an Englishman. Isherwood declined but volunteered to write to Auden, explain the situation, and ask him if he would be willing to marry Mann. Auden wired back a one-word response: "Delighted" (Christopher Isherwood, *Christopher and His Kind: 1929–1939* [New York: Farrar, Straus and Giroux, 1976], 206–07).

38. Arendt and McCarthy, *Between Friends*, 272.

39. Arendt and McCarthy, *Between Friends*, 269–70.

40. See W. H. Auden, *Forewords and Afterwords* (New York: Vintage, 1989) and Hannah Arendt, "Thinking and Moral Considerations: A Lecture," *Social Research* 38, 3 (fall, 1971), 417–46. See also Hannah Arendt, *The Life of the Mind*, where she quotes "Talking to Myself" (1: 60–61), "As I Walked Out One Evening" (1: 212–13), "Precious Five" (2: 92 and 187), and *The Dyer's Hand and Other Essays* (1: 213). As the epigraph to the opening section of *The Life of the Mind*, Arendt quotes one of Auden's "Shorts"; as the epigraph to her essay on Brecht, she quotes "The Cave of Making," which is a section from a longer cycle entitled "Thanksgiving for a Habitat"; see Hannah Arendt, *Men in Dark Times* (New York: Harcourt Brace Jovanovich, 1983), 207. See also W. H. Auden, *A Certain World: A Commonplace Book* (London: Faber and Faber, 1982), 167, 369, and 405.

41. Arendt letter to Auden (15 June 1971; #004888); General Correspondence, 1938–1976, n.d.—Auden, W. H.—1960–1975. A digitized version of this letter can be found at http://memory.loc.gov/ammem/arendthtml/arendthome.html.

42. Auden letter to Arendt (5 July 1973; #004858); General Correspondence, 1938–1976, n.d.—Auden, W. H.—1960–1975.

43. Arendt and McCarthy, *Between Friends*, 323.

44. Arendt, "Remembering Wystan H. Auden," 182.

45. Arendt, "Remembering Wystan H. Auden," 181. The extraordinary character of this distinction—good but not intimate friends—is particularly striking in light of Auden's marriage proposal and Arendt's own behavior after his death. As Elisabeth Young-Bruehl reports: "Arendt met her classes as usual the week after Auden's death on 28 September, but she was haggard and unsure of

herself. . . . [S]he wept when one of them [her students] came forward to offer to accompany her to Auden's memorial service. . . . At the memorial service, dressed in black . . . she was lost in melancholy" (Young-Bruehl, *Hannah Arendt*, 455). The day after Auden died, Arendt wrote a letter to Mary McCarthy in which she worried again about Auden's proposal: "I am still thinking of Wystan, naturally, and of the misery of his life, and that I refused to take care of him when he came and asked for shelter. Homer said that the gods spin ruin to men that there might be song and remembrance. . . . Well, he was both the singer and the tale" (Arendt and McCarthy, *Between Friends*, 343–44). In her memorial essay on Auden, Arendt writes, "he seems to me to have been an expert at the infinite varieties of unrequited love," and she concludes her reflections on Auden's poetry with the same image she uses in her correspondence with McCarthy: "[He was] somehow convinced, as the bards of ancient Greece were, that the gods spin unhappiness and evil things to mortals so that they may be able to tell the tales and sing the songs" (Arendt, "Remembering Wystan H. Auden," 186). Arendt gives no indication in her eulogy that these remarks have anything to do with her personal relationship to Auden.

46. Hannah Arendt, "Karl Jaspers: A Laudatio," in *Men in Dark Times*, 72–73.

47. Arendt, "Remembering Wystan H. Auden," 183.

48. Arendt, "Remembering Wystan H. Auden," 184. Arendt is quoting from Auden's famous elegy, "In Memory of W. B. Yeats," *Collected Poems*, ed. Edward Mendelson (New York: Vintage, 1991), 248.

49. Arendt letter to Auden (14 February 1960; #004865); General Correspondence, 1938–1976, n.d.—Auden, W. H.—1960–1975.

50. In a 1947 letter to Kurt Blumenfeld, Arendt writes, "Nichts auf der Welt zählt wie Freunde [Nothing in the world counts like friends]." *Hannah Arendt and Kurt Blumenfeld, ". . . In keinem Besitz verwurzelt": Die Korrespondenz*, ed. Ingeborg Nordmann and Iris Pilling (Hamburg: Rotbuch, 1995), 43.

51. W. H. Auden, *Collected Poems*, 716.

52. First delivered as a Lessing Prize lecture in Hamburg and published as *Von der Menschlichkeit in finsteren Zeiten: Rede über Lessing* (Munich: Piper, 1960); "On Humanity in Dark Times: Thoughts about Lessing," translated by Clara and Richard Winston for the opening essay of *Men in Dark Times*, 3–31.

53. Arendt, *Men in Dark Times*, 26.

54. Arendt, *Men in Dark Times*, 26.

55. Lessing, *Nathan der Weise*, Act 2, Scene 5: "Wir müssen, müssen Freunde sein" (*Werke*, ed. Karl Eibl and Herbert Georg Göpfert [Munich: Hanser, 1970–1979], 2: 253). This imperative is all the more paradoxical because it seems to contradict the most famous statement Nathan makes—his "theory" of freedom, so to speak: "Kein Mensch muß müssen [no one must have to; no one has

to do anything]" (Lessing, *Nathan der Weise*, Act 1, Scene 3; *Werke*, 2: 219); see Peter Fenves, "Politics of Friendship—Once Again," *Eighteenth Century Studies* 32, 2 (winter, 1998–1999): 133–55.

56. Arendt, *Men in Dark Times*, 26.

57. Plato, *Republic*, trans. Paul Shorey, in *The Collected Dialogues of Plato*, ed. Edith Hamilton and Huntington Cairns (Princeton: Princeton University Press, 1985), 832: "Let us further say to poetry, lest it condemn us for harshness and lack of urbanity, that there is an ancient quarrel between philosophy and poetry" (607b, translation modified).

58. Plato, *Republic* (607a), in *The Collected Dialogues*, 832.

59. In a famous note from 1879 Nietzsche writes: "Meine Philosophie *umgedrehter Platonismus*: je weiter ab vom wahrhaft Seienden, um so reiner schöner besser ist es. Das Leben im Schein als Ziel [My philosophy is reversed Platonism: the farther from the truly being, the purer, the more beautiful, the better it is. Life in mere appearance as goal]" (*Sämtliche Werke: Studien Ausgabe*, ed. Giorgio Colli and Mazzino Montinari [Berlin: de Gruyter, 1967–1977], 7: 199). The first part of Heidegger's *Nietzsche* is devoted to an exposition of this "reversal" of Platonism; see Martin Heidegger, *Nietzsche* (Pfullingen: Neske, 1961), esp. 198–242.

60. Nietzsche is, of course, fully aware of this paradox, and its "solution"—or better yet, its intensification—gives direction to his thought from *The Birth of Tragedy* onward. "Dionysos" is the ever-evolving figure through which this paradox comes to light. For a lucid examination of his writings from the perspective of "life in mere appearance," see Michel Haar, *Nietzsche et la métaphysique* (Paris: Gallimard, 1993). For an analysis of Nietzsche in relation to Arendt, see Bonnie Honig, *Political Theory and the Displacement of Politics* (Ithaca, N.Y.: Cornell University Press, 1993).

61. For a fuller discussion of *doxa*, see the first section of the first chapter and the accompanying endnotes.

62. Arendt, *Men in Dark Times*, 27.

63. Auden, *A Certain World*, 425.

64. Auden, *Poems*, 856; see Arendt, *The Life of the Mind*, 1: 17. For further reflections on this haiku in the context of Nietzschean "suspicion," see the opening pages of my essay, "'Reflection on the Right to Will': Auden's 'Canzone' and Arendt's Notes on Willing," *Comparative Literature* 53, 2 (spring, 2001), 131–50.

65. See the famous essay of Dieter Henrich, "Hegel und Hölderlin," in *Hegel im Kontext* (Frankfurt am Main: Suhrkamp, 1981), 9–40: "Hölderlin gab Hegel als Philosophen den wichtigsten, den letzten prägenden Anstoß [Hölderlin gave Hegel the most important and final push—the one that stamped him as a philosopher]" (38). For an extensive and lively treatment of this topic, see Terry

Pinkard, *Hegel: A Biography* (Cambridge: Cambridge University Press, 2000), esp. 75–81.

66. For an excellent recent exploration of this long-standing connection, see Maureen N. McLane, *Romanticism and the Human Sciences: Poetry, Population, and the Discourse of the Species* (Cambridge: Cambridge University Press, 2000).

67. For an important and influential study of the relation between Heidegger and Celan, see Philippe Lacoue-Labarthe, "Catastrophe," in *Word Traces: The Poetry of Paul Celan*, ed. Aris Fioretos (Baltimore: Johns Hopkins University Press, 1994), 130–56.

68. "There was nothing more admirable about him [Auden] than his complete sanity and his firm belief in the sanity of the mind. . . . The main thing was to have no illusions and to accept no thoughts, no theoretical systems that would blind you against reality" (Arendt, "Remembering Wystan H. Auden," 184).

69. " . . . [L]ove, or truth in any serious sense, / Like orthodoxy, is a reticence" (Auden, *Collected Poems*, 621); see also "Ode to Terminus" in *Collected Poems*, 811 and *Dyer's Hand*, 21.

70. Arendt, *Men in Dark Times*, 31.

71. For the quote, see Arendt, *The Origins of Totalitarianism*, 466. Something similar can be said with respect to thinking: its absence attracts her attention to its conditions. As she writes near the beginning of "Thinking and Moral Considerations," which is dedicated to Auden, "[Eichmann's] total absence of thinking attracted my interest" (4). Another study could be devoted to this absence and its corresponding investigation, especially as they are developed in *Eichmann in Jerusalem: A Report on the Banality of Evil*, rev. ed. (New York: Penguin, 1977). The protocols for such a study, however, would be quite different from the ones pursued here.

72. William Shakespeare, *Measure for Measure*, Act 5, Scene 1, ll. 407–9; reprinted in *The Complete Works*, ed. Alfred Harbage (New York: Viking, 1969), 403–31.

73. Auden, "The Fallen City," 28–29 (*Dyer's Hand*, 201).

74. Arendt letter to Auden (14 February 1960; #004865); General Correspondence, 1938–1976, n.d.—Auden, W. H.—1960–1975.

75. Arendt, "The Image of Hell," originally published in *Commentary*, 1946; republished in *Essays in Understanding: 1930–1954*, ed. Jerome Kohn (New York: Harcourt Brace & Company, 1994), 200. The letter exchange between Auden and Arendt about *The Human Condition*, which begins a close friendship, finds a strange echo in the letter exchange between Scholem and Arendt about *Eichmann in Jerusalem*, which apparently concluded a distant one. Scholem indicates that he was against the execution of the death sentence on Eichmann, to which

Arendt responds: "You say that it was 'historically false,' and I feel very un-comfortable seeing the spectre of History raised in this context. In my opinion, it was politically and juridically (and the last is actually all that mattered) not only correct—it would have been utterly impossible not to have carried out the sentence. . . . Mercy was out of the question, not on juridical grounds—pardon is anyhow not a prerogative of the juridical system—but because mercy is appli-cable to the person rather than to the deed; the act of mercy does not forgive mur-der but pardons the murderer insofar as he, as a person, may be more than any-thing he ever did. This was not true of Eichmann. And to spare his life without pardoning him was impossible on juridical grounds" (*The Jew as Pariah*, 250).

The story of the failed friendship between Arendt and Scholem could be un-derstood as the reverse image of the friendship between Arendt and Auden. Their disagreement over *Eichmann in Jerusalem* repeats an earlier exchange of let-ters initiated by Scholem's outrage over Arendt's "Zionism Reconsidered" (*The Menorah Journal* 33, 2 [October-December, 1945]: 162–65; *The Jew as Pariah*, 131–63). At the conclusion to Arendt's letter in which she responds to Scholem's accusations she writes: "When all is said and done, you are *masculini generis*, and for this reason naturally (perhaps) vulnerable. Please, for God's sake, do not believe, despite this letter, that I am a fanatic for honesty [*Ehrlichkeitsfanatiker*]. Human relationships are, for me, much more important than so-called 'open ex-changes of ideas.' In this case you have attributed to me more provocation than is right and just. Perhaps in this case you could resolve to think as I do: that human beings are worth more than their opinions for the simple reason that human be-ings are *de facto* more than they think or act" (Scholem, *Briefe*, ed. Itta Shedlet-zky and Thomas Sparr [Munich: Beck, 1994–1999], 1: 453–54). An accurate ac-count of the relationship between Arendt and Scholem will have to wait for the publication of their complete correspondence; for a brief but incisive analysis, see Steven E. Aschheim, *Scholem, Arendt, Klemperer: Intimate Chronicles in Turbulent Times* (Bloomington: Indiana University Press, 2001), esp. 65–69.

76. John Milton, *Paradise Lost*, in *Complete Poems and Major Prose*, ed. Mer-ritt Y. Hughes (Indianapolis: The Odyssey Press, 1957), 213; book 1, ll. 65–67.

77. Dante Alighieri, *Inferno*, ed. and trans. Robert M. Durling, *The Divine Comedy*. Vol. 1 (New York and Oxford: Oxford University Press, 1996), Canto 3, ll. 1–6.

78. Dante, *Inferno*, Canto 3, l. 9.

79. Some of Burke's favorite examples of the sublime are drawn from the first book of *Paradise Lost*; see Edmund Burke, *A Philosophical Enquiry into the Ori-gin of our Ideas of the Sublime and the Beautiful*, ed. James Boulton (Notre Dame and London: University of Notre Dame Press, 1968), 61–62.

80. W. H. Auden, *Secondary Worlds* (London: Faber and Faber, 1968), 74–75.

81. Theodor W. Adorno, *Prisms*, trans. Samuel and Shierry Weber (Cambridge, Mass.: MIT Press, 1986), 34. So far as I know, Auden never encountered Adorno. Arendt, for her part, had a very low regard for him; she expressed her dislike in strong words to Jaspers after the revelation that Adorno had tried to ingratiate himself with the Nazis immediately after their seizure of power; see Hannah Arendt and Karl Jaspers, *Correspondence: 1926–1969*, ed. Lotte Kohler and Hans Saner, trans. Robert and Rita Kimber [New York: Harcourt Brace Jovanovich, 1992], especially 634, 644, and accompanying endnotes.

82. Arendt, *Eichmann in Jerusalem*, 58.

83. Auden, *The Age of Anxiety*, in *Collected Poems*, 529.

84. Arendt, *The Origins of Totalitarianism*, 297.

85. Arendt, *The Origins of Totalitarianism*, 437.

86. Arendt, *The Origins of Totalitarianism*, 296.

87. Arendt, *The Origins of Totalitarianism*, 472.

88. Auden, *Collected Poems*, 484.

89. See page 104 in Chapter 2 and corresponding footnotes.

90. Arendt, *The Human Condition*, 247.

91. See note 15 in Chapter 3.

92. Arendt, *The Human Condition*, 183.

93. Arendt, *The Human Condition*, 242.

94. Auden, *Collected Poems*, 330.

95. Auden, *The Age of Anxiety*, in *Collected Poems*, 530.

96. Arendt, *The Human Condition*, 240.

97. Arendt, *The Origins of Totalitarianism*, 466.

98. Arendt, *The Origins of Totalitarianism*, 438.

99. As Orlan Fox reports, Auden "liked to brag that he had written successfully in every known metre" (Orlan Fox, "Friday Nights" in *W. H. Auden: A Tribute*, 175).

100. Auden's remarkable facility with diverse poetic forms by no means exhausts his astonishing range as a writer. In addition to his poetry, Auden's work includes verse plays and other dramatic writings, opera libretti, travel books, critical essays, reviews, short films, and translations.

101. In his "Postscript: Christianity and Art," Auden writes: "I sometimes wonder if there is not something a bit questionable, from a Christian point of view, about all works of art which make overt Christian references. They seem to assert that there is such a thing as a Christian culture, which there cannot be. Culture is one of Caesar's things" (Auden, *The Dyer's Hand*, 458).

102. Hannah Arendt, *Rahel Varnhagen: Lebensgeschichte einer deutschen Jüdin aus der Romantik* (Frankfurt am Main: Ullstein, 1975). None of the English translations reproduces the original title.

103. Auden, *Collected Poems*, 373.

104. The dedication reads "In Memoriam Constance Rosalie Auden, 1870–1941"; *For the Time Being* in *Collected Poems*, 347. The poem, which Auden subtitles "A Christmas Oratorio," was begun shortly after the death of his mother. The epigraph Auden chooses from Romans (and the choice of Romans is itself significant) indicates from the very beginning that the poem is concerned, above all, with a certain speechlessness: "'What shall we say then? Shall we continue in sin, that grace may abound? God forbid'" (*For the Time Being*, in *Collected Poems*, 347). For a remarkable reflection on Auden's elegies in the context of the modernist tradition, see Jahan Ramazani, *Poetry of Mourning: The Modern Elegy from Hardy to Heaney* (Chicago: The University of Chicago Press, 1994), 176–215.

As the subtitle of his poem indicates, Auden expected *For the Time Being* to be set to music and sent it to Benjamin Britten, who, however, ultimately declined to set more than two sections of the poem to music, one of which Auden then removed before publication (see Humphrey Carpenter, *W. H. Auden*, 322–23). Britten's refusal is entirely understandable, as Anthony Hecht notes: *For the Time Being* is much too long "even for the most parsimonious of composers" (Anthony Hecht, *The Hidden Law: The Poetry of W. H. Auden* [Cambridge, Mass.: Harvard University Press, 1993], 242). Something is therefore missing in every reading of the poem: its music. And this absence is perhaps related to the other absences around which the work is organized. (A major abridgment of the oratorio was set to music by the American composer Marvin Levy and was first performed in New York in 1959.)

105. Hannah Arendt, *Rahel Varnhagen: Lebensgeschichte einer deutschen Jüdin aus der Romantik*, 11; *Rahel Varnhagen: The Life of a Jewess*, trans. Richard and Clara Winston, ed. L. Weissberg (Baltimore: Johns Hopkins University Press, 1997), 82. The full quote of this passage runs: "The present biography was written with the awareness of the doom [Arendt translates this as *Untergang*] of German Judaism (although, naturally, without any premonition of how far the physical annihilation of the Jewish people in Europe would be carried)" (German edition, 11; English edition, 82).

106. Arendt, *Rahel Varnhagen* (German edition, 12; English edition, 82).

107. Ludwig Wittgenstein, letter to Ludwig von Ficker, quoted in Ray Monk, *Ludwig Wittgenstein: The Duty of Genius* (New York: The Free Press, 1990), 178. Under the subject heading "Hell," Auden quotes from Wittgenstein's Notebooks to his *Tractatus Logico-Philosophicus*: "Ethics does not treat of the world. Ethics must be a condition of the world, like logic" (Auden, *A Certain World*, 180; Ludwig Wittgenstein, *Notebooks: 1914–1916*, ed. G. H. von Wright and G.E.M. Anscombe, trans. G.E.M. Anscombe [Chicago: University of Chicago Press, 1979], 77).

Chapter 1

1. Hannah Arendt, *The Origins of Totalitarianism*, rev. ed. (New York: Harcourt Brace Jovanovich, 1979), 293. Further references to this work are in parentheses in the body of the text.

2. The consequences of wide-scale statelessness are clear. As Arendt states, "the second World War and the DP camps were not necessary to show that the only practical substitute for a nonexistent homeland was an internment camp" (284).

3. Hannah Arendt, *The Human Condition* (Chicago: The University of Chicago Press, 1958), 234.

4. Arendt's analysis of the relation of center to fringe bears some comparison to recent work in postcolonial studies, especially since, she, like more recent writers, is keenly aware that the perspective from which one can speak of "fringe" or "margin" is that of those who occupy the "center"; see, for example, Sneja Gunew, *Framing Marginality: Multicultural Literary Studies* (Carlton, Vic.: Melbourne University Press, 1994); for a reflection on the possibilities of replacing the image of center/margin with other, less unilateral ones, see Stephen Sumida, "Centers without Margins: Responses to Centrism in Asian American Literature," *American Literature* 66 (December, 1994): 803–15.

5. For an account of Arendt's flight from the Nazis and peregrinations afterward, see Elisabeth Young-Bruehl, *Hannah Arendt: For Love of the World* (New Haven: Yale University Press, 1982), 105–64: "For eighteen years, Hannah Arendt was a 'stateless person.' But this period when she had no political rights—between her flight from Nazi Germany in 1933 and her receipt of American citizenship in 1951—was her most active politically" (113). For one of Arendt's earliest and most bitter reflections on her own displacement, see her 1943 article from *The Menorah Journal*, "We Refugees," reprinted in *The Jew as Pariah: Jewish Identity and Politics in the Modern Age*, ed. and intro. Ron Feldman (New York: Grove Press, 1978), 55–66.

6. According to Liddell and Scott's authoritative account, *doxa* (derived from *dokeo*, which, when used with an object, means "to seem") originally meant "expectation" but came to mean *"notion, opinion, judgement"* after Homer (*Greek-English Lexicon*, rev. ed. [Oxford: Clarendon Press, 1968], 444).

7. Immanuel Kant, *Critique of Pure Reason*, B 131: "It is possible for the 'I think' to accompany all my representations." All citations of Kant are drawn from and refer to *Gesammelte Schriften*, ed. Königlich Preußischen [later, deutschen] Akademie der Wissenschaften (Berlin: Reimer; later, De Gruyter; 1900–), except quotations from the *Critique of Pure Reason*, which, according to scholarly convention, refer to the first ("A") and second ("B") editions of the

text; for a translation, see Kant, *Critique of Pure Reason*, trans. Norman Kemp Smith (New York: St. Martin's, 1965), 152.

8. These remarks from the *Origins* clearly allude to Kant, especially those sections of the first part of the *Critique of Judgment* devoted to a philosophical explication of *sensus communis*. Later in her life, Arendt returns to the *Critique of Judgment* as a principal source for reflection not only on the character of judgment but also on that of *doxa* in general; see H. Arendt, *Lectures on Kant's Political Philosophy*, ed. R. Beiner (Chicago: University of Chicago Press, 1982), esp. 68–72. It would not be possible within the space of a note to analyze the complicated relation of Arendt to Kant—not only in her discussion of practical reason and the problem of evil but also of theoretical reason and the function of judgment. For a recent examination of Arendt's use of Kant's exposition of *sensus communis*, see Andrew Norris, "Arendt, Kant, and the Politics of Common Sense," *Polity* 29 (winter, 1996): 165–91. Norris underestimates the extent to which Kant's exposition of the *sensus communis* in the third *Critique* not only deviates from certain aspects of the "formalism" that guides his investigation into the specific modes of aesthetic judgment (and thus indicates that the reflections on common sense predate those on the aesthetic judgment) but also corresponds to some of the deepest motives for his entire critical enterprise, especially the idea of "consciousness in general" (*Bewußtsein überhaupt*) as it is elaborated in the *Prolegomena*.

9. See the opening section of the "Transcendental Doctrine of Judgment" in the *Critique of Pure Reason*: "This domain is an island, enclosed by nature itself with unalterable limits. It is the land of truth—enchanting name!—surrounded by a wide and stormy ocean, the native home of illusion, where many a fog bank and many a swiftly melting iceberg give the deceptive appearance of farther shores" (A 235; B 294–95).

10. See the opening paragraph of the "Amphiboly of Concepts of Reflection" in the first *Critique*: "Many a judgment is accepted owing to custom or is grounded in inclination; but since no reflection precedes it, or at least none follows critically upon it, it is taken as having originated in the understanding [*das im Verstande seinen Ursprung erhalten hat*]" (A 261; B 316).

11. Arendt credits Machiavelli with introducing the term *state* into political theory; see H. Arendt, *On Revolution* (New York: Penguin, 1963), 39. For a thorough investigation into the etymology and concept of the state in relation to the idea of stasis, see Quentin Skinner, *The Foundations of Modern Political Thought* (Cambridge: Cambridge University Press, 1978). As he indicates in the preface, "I shall seek to show, that the main elements of a recognisably modern concept of the State were gradually acquired. The decisive shift was from the idea of the ruler 'maintaining his state'—where this simply meant upholding his position—

to the idea that there is a separate legal and constitutional order, that of the State, which the ruler has a duty to maintain" (ix–x).

12. "Even worse was that all societies formed for the protection of the Rights of Man . . . were sponsored by marginal figures. . . . The groups they formed, the declarations they issued, showed an uncanny similarity in language and composition to that of societies for the prevention of cruelty to animals" (292).

13. Arendt's use of the word *naked* may owe something to Walter Benjamin's term *bloßes Leben* ("naked life" or "mere life") in his essay "Zur Kritik der Gewalt"; see Benjamin, *Gesammelte Schriften*, ed. R. Tiedemann and H. Schweppenhäuser (Frankfurt am Main: Suhrkamp, 1977–1985), 2: 199–200; for a discussion of this term, which draws on Benjamin as well as Arendt, see Giorgio Agamben, *Homo Sacer: Sovereign Power and Bare Life*, trans. D. Heller-Roazen (Stanford: Stanford University Press, 1998).

14. Arendt's analysis of Hobbes (139–47) prefigures in many ways Macpherson's famous exposition of the author of *Leviathan* under the rubric "possessive individualism"; see Crawford Brough Macpherson, *The Political Theory of Possessive Individualism: Hobbes to Locke* (Oxford: Clarendon Press, 1962).

15. Kant, *Critique of Pure Reason*, A 51, B 75.

16. According to the OED, *pale*, originally a stake (especially one that helps form a fence), came to mean a "district or territory within determined bounds, or subject to a particular jurisdiction, e. g., English pale, the confines or dominion of England, the pale of English law." As Arendt writes, "The law of the city-state was neither the content of political action nor was it a catalogue of prohibitions. . . . It was quite literally a wall" (*The Human Condition*, 63–4); in her notes to this analysis of law in the city-state, Arendt refers to the derivation of *nomos* from *nemein*: "The combination of law and hedge in the word *nomos* is quite manifest in a fragment of Heraclitus: *machesthai chrēton dēmon hyper tou nomou hokōsper teicheos* ('the people should fight for the law as for a wall'). The Roman word for law, *lex*, has an entirely different meaning. . . . but the boundary and its god, Terminus, who separated the *agrum publicum a privato* (Livius) was more highly revered than the corresponding *theoi horoi* in Greece" (*The Human Condition*, 63). For a poetic treatment of Terminus, see "Ode to Terminus" in W. H. Auden, *Collected Poems*, ed. Edward Mendelson (New York: Vintage, 1991), 809–11.

17. Arendt discusses the problems of methodology in "Rejoinder to Eric Voegelin's Review of *The Origins of Totalitarianism*," *Review of Politics* 15 [January, 1953]: 76–85), reprinted as "A Reply to Eric Voegelin" in *Essays in Understanding: 1930–1954*, ed. Jerome Kohn (New York: Harcourt Brace & Company, 1994), 401–08. Benhabib well summarizes the difficulty of accounting for Arendt's mode of procedure when she writes of the *Origins*: "From the standpoint of established

disciplinary methodologies, Arendt's work defies categorization while violating a lot of rules. It is too systematically ambitious and overinterpreted to be a strictly historical account; it is too anecdotal, narrative, and ideographic to be considered social science, and although it has the vivacity and the stylistic flair of a work of political journalism, it is too philosophical to be accessible to a broad public" (Seyla Benhabib, *The Reluctant Modernism of Hannah Arendt* [Thousand Oaks, Calif.: Sage Publications, 1996], 63. Philip Hansen considers the difficulty of describing in any precise manner the methodology of the *Origins* as integral to the significance of the work: "*The Origins of Totalitarianism* is highly suggestive or allusive rather than analytically precise. In my view this quality is not merely accidental, it is integral to Arendt's approach. Neither historicist nor rationalist, neither empiricist nor essentialist, *The Origins of Totalitarianism* is not only an attempt to think and write about a radically new and unprecedented phenomenon. Although not explicitly metatheoretical, it is also an attempt to think in a new way about the political by focusing on a phenomenon which neither the conventional historical record, however extensive, nor conventional rationalist political concepts, however precise or radical . . . , can ever fully illuminate" (Hansen, *Hannah Arendt: Politics, History and Citizenship* [Stanford: Stanford University Press, 1993], 133). With particular sensitivity and insight, Margaret Canovan seeks to understand the *Origins* on the model of categories that Arendt herself developed, including those of "pearl-diving" and storytelling; see *Hannah Arendt: A Reinterpretation of Her Political Thought* (Cambridge: Cambridge University Press, 1992), 4–6 and 94–98. For further reflections on Arendt's methodology, see David Luban, "Explaining Dark Times: Hannah Arendt's Theory of Theory," in *Hannah Arendt: Critical Essays*, ed. Lewis and Sandra Hinchman (Albany, N.Y.: State University of New York Press, 1994), 79–109; and Lisa Disch, *Hannah Arendt and the Limits of Philosophy* (Ithaca, N.Y.: Cornell University Press, 1994), 1–19.

18. Søren Kierkegaard, *Fear and Trembling—Repetition*, ed. and trans. Howard Hong and Edna Hong (Princeton: Princeton University Press, 1983), 227. As Arendt recognizes as early as 1932, Kierkegaard's discussion of the exception is meant as a critique of Hegel: "In Kierkegaard's view, Hegel negates concrete reality, contingency, and therefore the individual when he interprets history as a logically comprehensible sequence of events and a process that follows an inevitable course" ("Søren Kierkegaard," *Frankfurter Zeitung*, no. 75–76 [29 January 1932]: 2; translated as "Søren Kierkegaard" by Robert and Rita Kimber in *Essays in Understanding*, 46). Arendt returns to Kierkegaard's reflections on the category of the "exception" in her later essay, "What Is Existenz Philosophy?" *Partisan Review* 18, 1, 1946 (reprinted in translation from a later German version as "What Is Existential Philosophy?" in *Essays in Understanding*, 163–87). With the same quotation from *Repetition*, Carl Schmitt closes the first chapter of his

Politische Theologie: Vier Kapitel zur Lehre von der Souveränität (1922; rpt. Berlin: Duncker & Humblot, 1990), 22. Arendt, incidentally, discusses Schmitt in several places in the *Origins*, at one point noting that his case was "most interesting" among "German scholars who went beyond mere co-operation and volunteered their services because they were convinced Nazis"; his writings of the 1920s, according to Arendt, still "make arresting reading" (339).

Far more important to Arendt, however, are the methodological protocols of Walter Benjamin's investigation of the German Baroque, *Origin of the German Mourning Play* (1928)—a work that, along with a number of contemporaneous artistic and scholarly projects, altered the predominantly negative evaluation of the Baroque; see Benjamin, *Gesammelte Schriften*, esp. 1: 238–40. Benjamin, who acknowledges Schmitt's precedent, considers the extreme the determining factor for any legitimate "historical-philosophical" mode of reflection and presentation. The mode of proceeding that Benjamin works out for his *Origin* stamps the character of his last text, "Über den Begriff der Geschichte," the sole surviving manuscript of which was in Arendt's possession (all other versions are typescripts; see Benjamin, *Gesammelte Schriften*, 1: 1253). A thorough comparison of Arendt's *Origins* and Benjamin's *Origin*, to say nothing of their other work, is not possible within the confines of a note. For more on Benjamin and Arendt, see the opening of Chapter 3 with its corresponding footnotes.

19. In this way, among many others, Arendt distinguishes herself from the path of another German-Jewish refugee, Henry Kissinger. In his discussion of Disraeli, Kissinger clearly lets it be known that the earlier Jewish conservative "expert" in the field of international diplomacy is a prefiguration of the later Jewish conservative "expert" in the field of international diplomacy: "It is no small irony that the Victorian Tory Party . . . should have produced as its leader this brilliant Jewish adventurer, and that the party of quintessential insiders should have brought to the forefront of the world's stage the quintessential outsider. No Jew had ever risen to such heights in British politics" (Henry Kissinger, *Diplomacy* [New York: Simon & Schuster, 1994], 150); "Both [Bismarck and Disraeli] subscribed to *Realpolitik* and hated what they considered moralistic cant. . . . Neither Bismarck nor Disraeli had any sympathy for the Balkan Slavs, whom they viewed as chronic and violent trouble-makers. Both were given to biting cynical quips, broad generalizations, and sarcastic barbs. Bored with nettlesome detail, Bismarck and Disraeli preferred to approach politics in bold, dramatic strokes" (155–56).

20. At the conclusion of her essay "The Jew as Pariah" Arendt presents Proust as a writer who was singularly able to illuminate "the ambiguity" that "became decisive for the social behavior of the assimilated and emancipated Jewry in western Europe" (*The Jew as Pariah*, 110). For an exposition of Arendt's relation to Proust, see Morris Kaplan, "Refiguring the Jewish Question: Arendt, Proust, and

the Politics of Sexuality," in *Feminist Interpretations of Hannah Arendt*, ed. Bonnie Honig (University Park, Pa.: Pennsylvania State University Press, 1995), 105–33.

21. Arendt first examines the phenomenon of the exception Jews in her brilliant and uncanny biography, *Rahel Varnhagen: Lebensgeschichte einer deutschen Jüdin aus der Romantik* (Frankfurt am Main: Ullstein, 1975); *Rahel Varnhagen*, trans. Richard and Clara Winston, ed. L. Weissberg (Baltimore: Johns Hopkins University Press, 1997).

22. For Arendt's most detailed analysis of Heine, see the section of "The Jew as Pariah: A Hidden Tradition" entitled "Heinrich Heine: The Schlemihl and Lord of Dreams" (*The Jew as Pariah*, 69–75). In a letter to Jaspers in 1946, comparison of Heine's situation with her own leads Arendt to emphasize the significance of language in the question of nationality and therefore spatiality: "Unfortunately, Heine's solution doesn't work anymore. . . . I never felt myself either spontaneously or at my own insistence, to 'be a German.' What remains is the language, and how important that is one learns only when, more nolens than volens, one speaks and writes other languages" (*Hannah Arendt, Karl Jaspers: Correspondence 1926–1969*, ed. Lotte Kohler and Hans Saner, trans. Robert and Rita Kimber [New York: Harcourt Brace Jovanovich, 1992], 70). Arendt repeats this formulation in an interview of 1964; see "'What Remains? The Language Remains': A Conversation with Günter Gauss," translated in *Essays in Understanding*, 12.

23. Marcel Proust, *Remembrance of Things Past*, trans. C. K. Scott Moncrieff and Terence Kilmartin. (New York: Vintage, 1982), 2: 195; *Le côté de Guermantes* (Paris: Gallimard, 1954), 1: 229: "Comme s'il s'agissait en effet d'êtres évoqués par un effort médiumnimique."

24. After it is introduced into Arendt's analysis of Proust, this theme repeats itself throughout the *Origins*: "Society was far from being prompted by a revision of prejudices. They did not doubt that homosexuals were 'criminals' or that Jews were 'traitors'; they only revised their attitude toward crime and treason" (81).

25. At the opening of *Sodom and Gomorrah*, Proust elaborates in extraordinary detail the similarity of "inverts" to Jews: "Their honor precarious, their liberty provisional, lasting only until the discovery of their crime [homosexuality]; their position unstable, like that of the poet one day fêted in every drawing room . . . and the next driven from every lodging . . . excluded even, save on the days of general misfortune when the majorities rally around the victim as the Jews rally around Dreyfus . . . like the Jews again (save some who will only associate with those of their race and have always on their lips the ritual words and the accepted pleasantries), shunning one another, seeking out those who are most directly their opposite . . . having finally been invested, by a persecution similar to that of

Israel, with the physical and moral characteristics of a race, sometime beautiful, often hideous . . . while steadfastly denying that they are a race (the name of which is the vilest of insults. . . .)." (*Remembrance*, 2: 638–39; *Sodome et Gomorrhe* [Paris: Flammarion, 1987], 1: 17–18). The sentence from which these quotations are drawn is the longest one in the entire *Recherche*, as if the exploration of the implicit similarities between "inverts" and Jews, once begun, cannot be stilled.

26. For a global interpretation of Proust's novel in terms of what Arendt calls "sign-language," see Gilles Deleuze, *Proust et les signes* (Paris: Presses Universitaires de France, 1964). Unfortunately, Deleuze does not take notice of Arendt's earlier analysis.

27. See Vladimir Ilyich Lenin, *Imperialism, the Highest Stage of Capitalism*, trans. anon. (Moscow: Progress Publishers, 1966).

28. See Johann Wolfgang von Goethe, *Die Wahlverwandtschaften*, in *Goethes Werke* (Weimarer Ausgabe), ed. Hermann Böhlau et al. (Weimar: Böhlau, 1887–1919), 20: 212. In her "Reply to Eric Voegelin," Arendt uses the Goethean metaphor to describe the unity of her own work: "The elementary structure of totalitarianism is the hidden structure of the book, while its more apparent unity is provided by certain fundamental concepts which run like red threads through the whole" (*Essays in Understanding*, 403).

29. Arendt's *Origins* shows certain affinities with more recent investigations into "culture and imperialism" (Edward Said) and "the location of culture" (Homi Bhabha). In their introduction to *Colonial Discourse and Post-Colonial Theory*, Patrick Williams and Laura Chrisman indicate some of the ways in which Arendt's work anticipates the kinds of investigations into "discourse" and "power-knowledge" that were later undertaken by Foucault and Said, and they indicate that "her insights and methods offer an important resource for future colonial discourse theorization" (*Colonial Discourse and Post-Colonial Theory: A Reader*, ed. P. Williams and L. Chrisman [New York: Columbia University Press, 1994], 7). Despite these affinities, Arendt explicitly concerns herself only rarely with one of the central terms of many contemporary "counter-discourses," namely *culture*. For Arendt's most sustained discussion of the term, see "The Crisis in Culture: Its Social and Political Significance" in *Between Past and Future: Eight Exercises in Political Thought* (New York: Penguin, 1968), 197–226. (It is worth noting that Arendt's only sustained and explicit discussion of the term was occasioned by a conference with culture as its theme; the original version of "The Crisis in Culture" was written as a lecture for the 1958 *Internationaler Kulturkritikerkongress in München*. The lecture first appeared as "Kultur und Politik," *Merkur* 12, 12 [1958]: 1122–45.) Arendt's understanding of the term *culture* is extremely complicated and cannot be undertaken here, but it is striking that such a significant term remains largely absent from all her major works. Although, for Arendt, humanity is a conditioned (not a natural) thing whose

conditions are determined by what can broadly be conceived as human culture, the word *culture* never appears as a significant category in *The Human Condition.* Arendt may consider *culture* inadequate, perhaps even misleading in this context, because, as she writes in a short essay, "Creating a Cultural Atmosphere" (1947), "culture . . . made its appearance rather recently and grew out of the secularization of religion and the dissolution of traditional values" (Arendt, *The Jew as Pariah*, 91). Arendt proceeds to analyze the ambiguous position of European Jewry in the process of acculturation. As she shows in *Rahel Varnhagen*, for Jews, culture (understood as *Bildung*) is nothing less than the abandonment of their Jewishness: "Jews who wanted 'culture' left Judaism at once, and completely" (*The Jew as Pariah*, 92). Having converted, Rahel becomes one of the original champions of the ideal of *Bildung*. An adequate discussion of Arendt's usefulness for what is generally (if still problematically) known as "postcolonial studies" would therefore have to begin with a careful study of "the Jewish question" as it relates to her thought.

30. See section four of the first volume of *Capital*, the results of which Marx vividly summarizes in the section of part five devoted to "General Law of Capitalistic Accumulation": "We saw . . . that within the capitalist system all methods for raising the social productivity of labour are put into effect at the cost of the individual worker; that all means for the development of production undergo a dialectical inversion so that they become means of domination and exploitation of, the producers; they mutilate the laborer into a fragment of a man, degrade him to the level of an appendage of a machine . . . they alienate from him the intellectual potentialities of the labour process in the same proportion as science is incorporated in it as an independent power" (Karl Marx, *Das Kapital: Kritik der politischen Ökonomie* [Berlin: Dietz, 1981], 1: 674; Marx, *Capital: Critique of Political Economy*, trans. Ben Fowkes [New York: Vintage, 1977], 1: 798–99).

31. Arendt is always aware of the material basis of the phenomena she discusses, and this is particularly true of her exposition of imperialism, which she describes, *contra* Lenin, as "the first stage in political rule of the bourgeoisie" (138). Arendt, like Lenin, takes over in large part Hobson's theory of imperialism according to which it is generated by surplus wealth, and she never loses sight of this surplus. Unlike some other more recent interpreters of imperialism, including Edward Said, Arendt does not frame her analysis in ideological terms and is therefore not particularly interested in how "the culture of imperialism" produced images of other cultures that could then facilitate further exploitation and domination; see Edward W. Said, *Culture and Imperialism* (New York: Vintage, 1994). Arendt is much closer in this regard to classical Marxist modes of interpretation in which "the forces of production" have a certain primacy, although of course she does not place any hope in the liberating powers of the European proletariat.

And in a certain sense, Arendt could be understood to be more materialist than most Marxists, if not Marx himself: imperialism is generated when certain people seek to live on interest from investments alone, when, in other words, they seek to remove themselves entirely from the sphere of labor. In antiquity, as Arendt elaborates in *The Human Condition*, absenting oneself from labor was the prerogative of the citizen who, as a slave owner, was able to participate in public life; slaves reproduced the conditions of life so that citizens could enter the sphere of freedom, the realm of the *polis* (see *The Human Condition*, esp. 28–37). In the context of bourgeois capitalism, by contrast, absenting oneself from labor is not done for the purpose of participating in public life. The reproduction of the conditions of life is consigned to the working classes while the bourgeoisie produce nothing and instead consume culture. And it is this elemental condition that, for Arendt, constitutes the relationship between "culture and imperialism."

32. In addition to Hobson (*Imperialism: A Study* [London: Archibald Constable, 1905]), Arendt draws on the work of Lenin (*Imperialism, the Highest Stage of Capitalism*), Rosa Luxemburg (*Die Akkumulation des Kapitals: Ein Beitrag zur ökonomischen Erklärung des Imperialismus* [Berlin: Vereinigung internationaler Verlags-Anstalten, 1923]), and Rudolf Hilferding (*Das Finanzkapital: Eine Studie über die jüngst Entwicklung des Kapitalismus* [Vienna: Ignaz Brand & Co., 1910]). Arendt also makes some marginal use of other, non-Marxist writers in her discussion of imperialism, especially Carlton Hayes, *A Generation of Materialism: 1871–1900* (New York: Harper & Brothers, 1941) and Joseph Schumpeter, "Zur Soziologie des Imperialismen," *Archiv für Sozialwissenschaft und Sozialpolitik* 46 (1918–1919).

33. See the magisterial exposition of Joseph Schumpeter, *History of Economic Analysis* (New York: Oxford University Press, 1954), 825–85.

34. One indication of the finite nature of political life (or life in the *polis*) can be found in the famous remark that Aristotle appends to his discussion of slavery: "There is only one condition on which we can imagine managers not needing subordinates, and masters not needing slaves. This condition would be that each [inanimate] instrument could do its own work, at the word of command or by intelligent anticipation, like the statues of Daedalus or the tripods made by Hephaestus" (Aristotle, *Politics*, trans. Ernest Barker [Oxford: Clarendon Press, 1950] 12; 1253b).

35. First articulated in J. B. Say's *Traité d'économie politique* (1803), Say's Law of Markets has been variously formulated as "supply creates its own demand" or "whatever is sold is bought." See the discussion of Schumpeter, *History of Economic Analysis*, 615–25.

36. As Marx writes in the section of *Capital* entitled "The General Form of Capital," "this increment of excess over the original value I call 'surplus-value.' The value originally advanced, therefore, not only remains intact while in circulation,

but increases its magnitude, adds to itself a surplus-value, or is valorized [*verwertet sich*]. And this movement converts it into capital" (*Capital*, 1: 251–52). For Marx's contrasting analysis of the *corvé*, see *Capital*, 1: 346–48.

37. Arendt presents Marx's "dream of a classless society" as the "last, though utopian trace of the eighteenth-century concept [of progress]" (143).

38. Marx introduces this term in the concluding section of the first volume of *Capital* (see the eighth part, "The So-Called Primitive Accumulation," 1: 873–926).

39. Arendt thus summarizes the "brilliant insight" Luxemburg develops in her *Akkumulation des Kapitals* (*Origins*, 148).

40. Hilferding, *Das Finanzkapital*, 470 (quoted in the *Origins*, 150). Hilferding proceeds to explain that the "politics of expansion unites all the layers of property owners into the service of finance capital" (470).

41. Walter Benjamin, "Über den Begriff der Geschichte," in *Gesammelte Schriften*, 1: 697–98: "ein Sturm weht vom Paradiese her."

42. See Carl Schmitt, *Politische Romantik*, 2nd ed. (Munich: Duncker & Humblot, 1925). In a lengthy footnote to her essay, "What Is Existenz Philosophy?" Arendt discusses Martin Heidegger's political behavior, which she describes as both "comic" and "abysmal," with respect to German Romanticism. And she ironically applies the term "Romantic" to Heidegger's career—ironically, because what she says of Heidegger could of course be said of Schmitt (see *Essays in Understanding*, 187).

43. See the aphorism of "Fragmente und Studien, 1797–1798" that begins with "Die Welt muß romantisiert werden" (Novalis, *Studienausgabe*, ed. Gerhard Schulz [Munich: Beck, 1987], 384–85; Arendt, *Origins*, 167–68).

44. The importance of Kant and Fichte for the development of early German romanticism has often been emphasized but perhaps nowhere with such succinctness and almost algebraic sureness as in Walter Benjamin's doctoral dissertation, *Der Begriff der Kunstkritik in der deutschen Romantik* (1918), reprinted in *Gesammelte Schriften*, esp. 1: 18–40. For Kant and Fichte, practical reason has a decisive priority over theoretical reason, but practice is itself entirely conceived in terms of law, even if the law is something other than positive law. See also Géza von Molnár, *Novalis' "Fichte Studies": The Foundations of his Aesthetics* (The Hague: Mouton, 1970).

45. Arendt discusses Brentano's participation in the anti-Semitic *Christlich-Deutsch Tischgesellschaft*, which was founded as a patriotic society in response to the Napoleonic wars (*Origins*, 61–62 and 169).

46. See, for example, Novalis's exposition of "the first human being" in terms of the child: "Der erste Mensch ist der erste Geisterseher. Ihm erscheint alles, als Geist. Was sind Kinder anders, als erste Menschen? Der frische Blick des Kindes ist überschwenglicher, als die Ahndung des entschiedensten Sehers [The first hu-

man being is the first spirit-seer. Everything appears to him as spirit. What are children other than the first human beings? The fresh glimpse of the child is more superabundant than the intimation of the most decisive seer]" ("Fragmente und Studien," § 47; *Studienausgabe*, 389).

47. In the "Paralogisms of Pure Reason," the term *spirit* is replaced by that of *soul*; see Kant, *Critique of Pure Reason*, A 341–405.

48. Kant, *Dreams of a Spirit-Seer Explained by Dreams of Metaphysics*, in *Gesammelte Schriften*, 2: 342; for an analysis of Kant's motif of dreaming, see Peter Fenves, *A Peculiar Fate: Metaphysics and World-History in Kant* (Ithaca, N.Y.: Cornell University Press, 1991), 72–77. Kant mistakenly attributes Heraclitus's saying to Aristotle; see Hermann Diels, *Die Fragmente der Vorsokratiker*, 4th ed. (Berlin: Weidmann, 1922), Heraclitus, B 89. Arendt also quotes Heraclitus's fragment (and notes that it is similar to one of Aristotle's remarks in *The Nicomachean Ethics*) in *The Human Condition*, 199. The thought expressed in Heraclitus's saying has a long and intricate history, and similar formulations can be found outside Greek thought. As Wendy Doniger writes, "Greek 'common sense' is well expressed by Heraclitus's famous dictum: 'For the waking there is one and the same [literally: common] cosmos, but of the sleeping, each turns away to his own [cosmos, when dreaming].' Indian common sense also asserted that, while dreaming was private, the waking state was 'common to all men' (*vaisvanara*)" (Wendy Doniger O'Flaherty, *Dreams, Illusions and Other Realities* [Chicago: University of Chicago Press, 1984], 39).

49. As Auden writes, "From this follows the paradox that K.'s only guarantee that he is following the true way is that he fails to get anywhere" ("K.'s Quest," in *The Kafka Problem*, ed. Angel Flores [New York: Gordian Press, 1975], 60). Benjamin, too, calls Kafka "a failure," and this verdict finds an echo in Arendt's analysis of Benjamin. In a letter to Gershom Scholem that Arendt includes in her edition of *Illuminations*, Benjamin writes, "To do justice to the figure of Kafka in its purity and its peculiar beauty one must never lose sight of one thing: it is the purity and beauty of a failure. . . . Once he was certain of eventual failure, everything worked out for him *en route* as in a dream" (*Illuminations*, ed. and intro. Hannah Arendt, trans. Harry Zohn [New York: Schocken, 1969], 144–45). And in Arendt's introduction, which in many ways mirrors Benjamin's essay on Kafka (both include a section called "The Hunchback"), it is Benjamin who, having assured his own failure, played out his own life as in a dream. The parallel between Arendt and Benjamin in relationship to Kafka is even stronger than these two essays suggest. Just as Benjamin subtitles his essay on Kafka "On the Tenth Anniversary of His Death," so does Arendt subtitle her "Kafka: A Revaluation" with "On the Occasion of the Twentieth Anniversary of His Death." Arendt, however, closes her essay not with the theme of failure but with that of humility: "He did not care to be a genius or the incarnation of any kind

of greatness" ("Kafka: A Revaluation," first published in *Partisan Review* [1944], and reprinted in *Essays in Understanding*, 80). Arendt's appreciation of Kafka's refusal to be a "genius" is repeated in her Benjamin essay when she discusses the same quality in Benjamin. For further reflections on Benjamin, Kafka, and failure, see Werner Hamacher, "The Gesture in the Name" in *Premises: Essays on Philosophy and Literature from Kant to Celan*, trans. Peter Fenves (Cambridge, Mass.: Harvard University Press, 1996), 294–336.

50. Franz Kafka, *Das Schloß*, in *Gesammelte Schriften in zwölf Bänden*, ed. Hans-Gert Koch (Frankfurt am Main: Fischer, 1994), 4: 229–46 ("Amalias Geheimnis"). Arendt conducts a more extensive reading of *Das Schloß* in her essay, "The Jew as Pariah" (*Jew as Pariah*, esp. 81–90) and in "Kafka: A Revaluation" (*Essays in Understanding*, 69–80). It would be worth comparing Arendt's reading of Kafka to that of her former husband, Günter Anders (formally Stern), whose "Kafka pro und contra" set the terms for many of the early debates about the success and failure of his writings; see Günter Anders, *Mensch ohne Welt: Schriften zur Kunst und Literatur* (Munich: Beck, 1993), 45–131.

51. Kant, *Critique of Pure Reason*, A 235–36; B 295.

52. In the *Prolegomena to Any Future Metaphysics* Kant calls metaphysics "dieser dringende Bedürfnis" (*Gesammelte Schriften*, 4: 367).

53. For a well-informed and thorough treatment of this complicated issue, see the four volumes of *German-Jewish History in Modern Times*, ed. Michael A. Meyer and Michael Brenner (New York: Columbia University Press, 1996–1999).

54. See Kant's famous short essay, "On the Supposed Right to Lie from the Love of Human Beings" (*Gesammelte Schriften*, 8: 25–30). For an analysis of Kant in relationship to Arendt on the question of the right to lie see Tobin Siebers, "Kant and the Origins of Totalitarianism," *Philosophy and Literature* 15 (April 1991): 19–39. Siebers makes a case for the "relevance" of Kant within the context of totalitarianism, but he does not address the specific character of totalitarian lies, which have very little to do with conscious misleading and are therefore not within the scope of Kant's investigations.

55. Arendt develops this image of the onion in "On Authority," *Between Past and Future* (Harmondsworth: Penguin, 1977), 91–141.

56. Arendt's distinction between totalitarianism and nihilism, the dimensions of which were rigorously described by Nietzsche, is elided when the former is collapsed into the latter. An expression of this elision can be found in Hansen: "Totalitarianism at its most extreme is profoundly nihilistic" (Hansen, *Hannah Arendt*, 147).

57. Friedrich Nietzsche, "Dionysis' Dithyramb," one of the songs in *Also sprach Zarathustra*; (Friedrich Nietzsche, *Sämtliche Werke: Studien Ausgabe*, ed. Giorgio Colli and Mazzino Montinari [Berlin: de Gruyter, 1967–1977], 6: 382). A few pages after Arendt speaks of the desert, she writes: "Solitude can become

loneliness; this happens when all by myself I am deserted by my own self" (476). To illustrate a self-desertion in which "the lonely man finds himself and starts the thinking dialogue of solitude" (477), Arendt cites the case of Nietzsche and quotes from two of the poems in *Also sprach Zarathustra*.

58. Arendt attended Heidegger's 1924 lectures on Aristotle's *Rhetoric*, which, however, have not yet been published. In *Sein und Zeit*, Heidegger says of the *Rhetoric* that "diese muß—entgegen der traditionellen Orientierung des Begriffes der Rhetorik an so etwas wie einem 'Lehrfach'—als die erste systematische Hermeneutik der Alltäglichkeit des Miteinanderseins aufgefaßt werden [against the traditional orientation of the concept of rhetoric toward something like a "discipline," it should be understood as the first systematic hermeneutics of the everydayness of being-with-one-another]" (Heidegger, *Sein und Zeit* [1927, reprint; Tübingen: Niemeyer, 1979], 138).

59. The epigraph, taken from David Rousset, runs: "Normal people do not believe that everything is possible."

60. See, for an especially significant instance, Kierkegaard's *Sickness unto Death*, which, as an analysis of despair, takes its title, its opening reflections, and indeed its general orientation from the figure of Lazarus; Kierkegaard, *The Sickness unto Death*, trans. Howard Hong and Edna Hong (Princeton: Princeton University Press, 1980). So widespread is this figure that it reaches far beyond the bounds of theological reflection. In a section of *Capital* on the "industrial reserve army," Marx speaks of the "lazarus-layers of the working-class [*Lazarusschichte der Arbeitklasse*]" (*Capital*, 1: 798); unfortunately, Fowkes eliminates Marx's reference to Lazarus and translates the preceding phrase by the much more banal "pauperized sections of the working class"; see Karl Marx, *Das Kapital*, 1: 673.

61. Like Arendt's invocation of the figure of Lazarus, her use of the term *faith* here recalls Kierkegaard, who contrasted faith with superstition, on the one hand, and despair, on the other: "The opposite of being in despair is to have faith" (*The Sickness unto Death*, 49).

62. For Arendt's description of the changes that the work underwent, see *Origins*, xxiv–xxv.

63. Tacitus, *Histories IV–V, Annals I–III*, trans. Clifford H. Moore and John Jackson (Cambridge, Mass.: Harvard University Press, 1992), 244–45: "Hence my design, to treat a small part (the concluding one) of Augustus' reign, then the principate of Tiberius and its sequel, without anger and without partiality [*sine ira et studio*], from the motives of which I stand sufficiently removed." In her "Reply to Voegelin," Arendt indicates the reason she chooses to cite—and depart from—Tacitus: "I parted quite consciously with the tradition of *sine ira et studio* of whose greatness I was fully aware, and to me this was a methodological necessity, closely connected with my particular subject matter. . . . To describe the

concentration camps *sine ira* is not to be 'objective,' but to condone them" (*Essays in Understanding*, 403–04).

64. As Arendt writes in 1946, "Human history has known no story more difficult to tell. The monstrous equality in innocence that is its inevitable leitmotif destroys the very basis on which history is produced—which is, namely, our capacity to comprehend an event no matter how distant we are from it" (Hannah Arendt, "The Image of Hell," *Commentary*, 2, 3, 1946; reprinted in *Essays in Understanding*, 197–205).

65. For Arendt's later reflections on "holes of oblivion," see the concluding remarks to the section of her report on Eichmann's trial entitled "Evidence and Witnesses": *Eichmann in Jerusalem: A Report on the Banality of Evil* (rev. ed. New York: Penguin, 1977), 232–33. The *Eichmann* book states flatly that "the holes of oblivion do not exist. . . . There are simply too many people in the world to make oblivion possible. One man will always be left alive to tell the story" (232–33). The *Origins* makes clear that totalitarianism cannot lose even when it loses. It would be a mistake, however, to call *Eichmann* "optimistic" or the *Origins* "pessimistic." Neither term is appropriate, and both express the same anxiety: what must be said cannot be said, but there will always be someone who is bound to speak.

Chapter 2

1. W. H. Auden, *Collected Poems*, ed. Edward Mendelson (New York: Vintage, 1991), xvii; all further references to poems collected in this volume are in parentheses in the text.

2. In a letter to Naomi Mitchison, Auden wrote, "The reason (artistic) I left England and went to the U.S. was precisely to *stop* me writing poems like 'Sept 1st 1939', the most dishonest poem I have ever written. A hang-over from the U.K." (quoted in Humphrey Carpenter, *W. H. Auden: A Biography* [Boston: Houghton Mifflin, 1982], 417).

3. In his preface to his collection of poems published in 1966, Auden explained his reasons for eliminating a number of poems from among his collected works: "Some of the poems which I wrote and, unfortunately published, I have thrown out because they were dishonest, or bad-mannered, or boring. A dishonest poem is one which expresses, no matter how well, feelings or beliefs which its author never felt or entertained. For example, I once expressed a desire for 'New styles of architecture'; but I have never liked modern architecture. I prefer *old* styles, and one must be honest even about one's prejudices" ("Preface" to *Collected Shorter Poems 1927–1957*; reprinted in *Collected Poems*, xxv–xxvi.). An anecdote that Stephen Spender recounts may provide some insight into how honesty is distinct from earnestness, even earnestness about

honesty: "On a later occasion in New York, after he had criticized Spender, who then promised to amend, Auden groaned and held his head in his hands. 'Why do you take me seriously?' he asked Spender. 'My only complaint about Americans is that they will take me seriously. I did trust my English friends not to take me seriously'" (Richard Davenport-Hines, *Auden* [New York: Pantheon, 1996], 209).

4. Edward Mendelson suggests that the stimulus for Auden's final decision to excise "September 1" entirely from his collected works was the now infamous Johnson campaign ad of 1964 in which a nuclear explosion suddenly replaces the image of a little girl holding a flower on the television screen and is immediately followed by "Johnson's voice intoning, 'These are the stakes: to make a world in which all of God's children can live, or go into the dark. We must love each other or we must die'" (Edward Mendelson, "Editing Auden," *New Statesman* [17 September 1976], 376). Although, as Davenport-Hines indicates, Auden never directly responded to Johnson's appropriation of his poem, he nevertheless gave some indication of his editorial decision-making process when, shortly after the airing of this ad, Auden wrote to Stella Musulin, "One cannot let one's name be associated with shits" (Davenport-Hines, *Auden*, 319; quotation drawn from Stella Musulin, "Auden in Kirchstetten," *"In Solitude for Company": W. H. Auden After 1940*, ed. Katherine Bucknell and Nicholas Jenkins, *Auden Studies*, Vol. 3 [Oxford: Clarendon Press, 1994], 210). Auden's decision to disavow "September 1" did not prevent it from being used again as a source for the speechifying by others with whom he would surely have disliked being associated. As Anthony Hecht writes of the poem's concluding stanza and its "ironic points of light," "one shrinks to think that Peggy Noonan borrowed them for campaign speeches of George Bush" (Anthony Hecht, *The Hidden Law: The Poetry of W. H. Auden* [Cambridge, Mass.: Harvard University Press, 1993], 169). In his often tendentious "record of the facts," Joseph Warren Beach includes "September 1" among the poems Auden eliminated for reasons that are difficult to ascertain: "In the case of half a dozen poems from which one or more stanzas were omitted in revision, we enter a dubious border region where our speculations as to the author's reasons are more hazardous. . . . The only possible reason one can think of is that the statement is not made here [in "September 1"] in specifically and unmistakably religious terms" (Beach, *The Making of the Auden Canon* [Minneapolis: University of Minnesota Press, 1957], 49–51). For a very funny account of Auden's habit of eliminating poems from already published volumes in the possession of his friends, see Charles Miller, *Auden: An American Friendship* (New York: Paragon House, 1989), 36–37.

5. Of all Auden's single volumes, *The Age of Anxiety* has the largest number of citations in the *Oxford English Dictionary*—64 in all; see Toby Litt, "From 'Acedia' to 'Zeitgeist': Auden in the 2nd Edition of the OED," *The W. H. Auden*

Society Newsletter, 4 (October 1989). According to Litt, Auden has been included in the OED at least 724 times.

6. Unlike Auden's two other major works of the early to mid 1940s, *The Age of Anxiety* does not rely on a particular character to manage or narrate the action. In *For the Time Being*, he provides a character entitled "Narrator," and in *The Sea and the Mirror* he introduces a "Stage Manager." By having his narrating voice remain anonymous in *The Age of Anxiety*, his next major poem, he departs from these precedents. The narrating voice is so completely anonymous that it receives neither an emblematic nor a functional designation and, like a "shady character" (449), hovers over the other characters in the poem.

7. The narration for all the sections of *The Age of Anxiety* other than "The Seven Stages" is in the past tense; "The Seven Stages," perhaps because it is a dreamscape, is narrated entirely in the present tense—with one exception: "EMBLE said" (500).

8. Among the spate of books on existentialism that appeared in English between 1947 and 1948 are those of Jean-Paul Sartre, *Existentialism and Humanism*, trans. Philip Mairet (New York, Philosophical Library, 1947); William Barrett, *What Is Existentialism?* (New York: Partisan Review, 1947); Marjorie Grene, *Dreadful Freedom, a Critique of Existentialism* (Chicago: University of Chicago Press, 1948); Jacques Maritain, *Existence and the Existent*, trans. Lewis Galantiere (New York: Pantheon, 1948); Gaston Berger, *Existentialism and Literature in Action* (Buffalo: University of Buffalo, 1948); Guido De Ruggiero, *Existentialism: Disintegration of Man's Soul* (New York: Social Science Publishers, 1948); and Emmanuel Mounier, *Existentialist Philosophies: An Introduction* (London: Rockliff, 1948). The only significant discussion of existentialism published in English before Auden began to write *The Age of Anxiety* is Paul Tillich's article, "Existential Philosophy," *Journal of the History of Ideas* 5,1 (Jan. 1944): 44–70. Before Auden completed and published *The Age of Anxiety*, Hannah Arendt published two essays on existentialism in journals Auden surely would have read: "What Is Existenz Philosophy?" *Partisan Review* 18, 1 (1946) (reprinted in translation from a later German version as "What Is Existential Philosophy?" in *Essays in Understanding: 1930–1954*, ed. Jerome Kohn [New York: Harcourt Brace & Company, 1994], 163–87) and "French Existentialism," *The Nation* 162, February 23, 1946 (rptd. in *Essays in Understanding*, 188–93). With characteristic wit and elegance, W. R. Johnson identifies the complex relation between Auden's poem and contemporaneous existential philosophy in the context of discussing scholarship on Vergil: "[R. A.] Brooks and, later, Adam Parry seem not to be listening to Eliot but rather to the news from the Left Bank or to Auden's *The Age of Anxiety*, that wild and scandalously neglected masterpiece which captures its era and outlives it" (W. R. Johnson, *Darkness Visible: A Study of Vergil's "Aeneid"* [Berkeley: University of California Press, 1976], 11).

9. Auden admired Brecht's work, particularly his lyric poetry, translated some of his plays, and disliked him personally; see Carpenter, *W. H. Auden*, 85 and 425. As David Constantine remarks, Auden's German poems bear a certain resemblance to some of Brecht's early poetry; see "Six Early Poems," ed. and trans. David Constantine, in *"The Map of All of My Youth": Early Works, Friends, and Influences*, ed. Katherine Bucknell and Nicholas Jenkins, *Auden Studies*, Vol. 1 (Oxford: Clarendon Press, 1990), 2. The ironic identification with the tribulations of the petty bourgeoisie under the conditions of constant war is a common trait of the narrating voice that opens *The Age of Anxiety* and many of Brecht's plays—especially, of course, *Mutter Courage*. Although Arendt distinguishes the two poets by emphasizing Auden's refusal to understand poetry as an accomplice to political action or to treat it as a forum for saving solutions ("Auden, so much wiser—though by no means smarter—than Brecht, was aware early on that, 'poetry makes nothing happen'"), she nevertheless draws a connection between the underlying motivations of Brecht and Auden: "What drove these profoundly unpolitical poets into the chaotic political scene of our century was still Robespierre's *zèle compatissant*, this powerful urge towards *les malheureux*, as distinguished from any need for action, for public happiness, or the desire to change the world" ("Remembering Wystan H. Auden," in *W. H. Auden: A Tribute*, ed. Stephen Spender [New York: Macmillan, 1975], 184). Arendt emphasizes the comparison between the two poets by beginning her essay on Brecht in *Men in Dark Times* with a quotation from Auden: "God may reduce you / on Judgment Day / to tears of shame, / reciting by heart / the poems you would / have written, had / your life been good" (Hannah Arendt, *Men in Dark Times* [New York: Harcourt Brace Jovanovich, 1983], 207; Arendt does not identify the poem in her citation; it comes from "The Cave of Making," a section from a longer cycle entitled "Thanksgiving for a Habitat," *Collected Poems*, ed. Edward Mendelson (New York: Vintage, 1991, 696).

10. See Friedrich Hölderlin, *Theoretische Schriften*, ed. Johann Kreuzer (Hamburg: Meiner, 1998), esp. 63–67 ("Poetologische Aufzeichnungen"). Auden's admiration for Hölderlin's poetry is evident as early as 1937, when he quotes, apparently from memory, the concluding lines of Hölderlin's "Sokrates und Alcibiades" in his "Letter to Lord Byron": "Und es neigen die Weisen / Oft am Ende zu Schönem sich [And the wise are inclined / Often in the end toward the beautiful]" (*Sämtliche Werke*, 1: 260). Auden shortens the quotation to fit a single line of the rime royale stanza he uses, and he introduces some slight spelling errors in the process: "Es neigt die weisen zu schönem sich" ("Letter to Lord Byron" in *Letters from Iceland* by W. H. Auden and Louis MacNeice [New York: Paragon House, 1990], 234). For a concise explanation of Hölderlin's theory of poetic tonality, see Peter Fenves, "Hölderlin," *The Encyclopedia of Aesthetics*, ed. Michael Kelly (New York: Oxford University Press, 1998), vol. 2, 414–22.

11. Beginning with an influential essay of Edward Callan, critics of the poem have often noted that the four characters seem to correspond to the four Jungian faculties on which Auden draws in the section of *For the Time Being* entitled "The Annunciation" (355–58): Malin is supposed to represent thought; Emble sensation, Quant intuition; and Rosetta feeling; see Callan, "Allegory in Auden's *The Age of Anxiety*," *Twentieth Century Literature* 10, 4 (January, 1965): 155–65. Callan's argument depends in large part on the thesis that "The plot of *The Age of Anxiety* reveals, not character development in the conventional sense, but development within the psychic personality" (Callan, 157). By amalgamating the four characters into a single "psychical personality," Callan cannot fail to underestimate the remarkable characterizations of Auden's poem. For another analysis of the poem in Jungian terms, following Callan, see John Fuller, *W. H. Auden: A Commentary* (Princeton: Princeton University Press, 1998), 369–71. So standard is this interpretation that Anthony Hecht can mention it only in passing, as if it were an established truth; see Hecht, *The Hidden Law: The Poetry of W. H. Auden*, 256.

12. Auden, who moved to the United States in January of 1939 and became a citizen in 1946, would answer interrogations about his nationality by saying "I am a New Yorker" (Carpenter, *W. H. Auden*, 281). Auden's responses to the many vociferous attacks made against him for leaving England were confined to private communications with friends; see the letters to E. R. Dodds of 11 March 1940 and to Stephen Spender of 13 or 14 March 1941 in *"The Map of All My Youth,"* ed. Katherine Bucknell and Nicholas Jenkins, 113–15; see also Kathleen Bell's introduction to the letters to E. R. and A. E. Dodds, for a succinct presentation of the arguments made in favor of Auden's return to England, *"The Map of All My Youth,"* 97–98. For additional analyses, see Carpenter, *W. H. Auden*, 290–93; Davenport-Hines, *Auden*, 206–07; and Charles Osborne, *W. H. Auden: The Life of a Poet* (New York: Harcourt Brace Jovanovich, 1979), 184–88.

13. Both Davenport-Hines and Carpenter track Auden's movements. See especially Davenport-Hines, *Auden*, 147–48; and Carpenter, *W. H. Auden*, 179–249.

14. This sentence may be a transformation of the famous question attributed to Hölderlin in his madness: "Giebt es auf Erden ein Maas? Es giebt keines [Is there a measure on earth? There is none]" (*Sämtliche Werke: Stuttgarter Ausgabe*, ed. Friedrich Beißner [Stuttgart, 1943–1985], 2: 372). Instead of denying a "measure" to earth, Malin denies a "mean" to "man." Whereas the text attributed to Hölderlin then turns to the relation between the "lovely blueness" of the heavens and the solidity of the earth for a "measure," Malin's speech turns toward the neighbor as the place or space in which a "mean" is found.

15. W. H. Auden, *Selected Poems*, (New York: Vintage, 1979), 86.

16. Auden, *Selected Poems*, 88.

17. For all their fame, Rosetta refrains from identifying the four characters who meet in the *Schloß* (castle). That she uses the German word indicates, however, that the primary association is a meeting among three Nazi officials and Hitler—"who wills they shall." In Gottfried Benn's introduction to the German translation of *The Age of Anxiety*, he surrounds his citation of this speech (in translation, since, as he admits, he has no access to the original) with the following comments: "Ich finde . . . zahlreiche Verse, die nur antimarxistich gemeint sein können, darunter diese interessanten. . . . Damit kann ja wohl nur die Yalta gemeint sein [I find numerous verses that can only be considered anti-Marxist, including these interesting lines. . . . This can of course refer only to Yalta]" (Auden, *Das Zeitalter der Angst*, trans. Kurt Heinrich Hansen, intro. Gottfried Benn [Wiesbaden: Bechtold & Co., 1954], 14–15. That Benn understands Rosetta's speech as a commentary on Yalta is in a certain sense understandable: since the term *Schloß* would not stand out in a German text, the association with Germany is lost. Yet it is far from clear how Rosetta's ironic remark about "managed money" could refer to anything other than a capitalist regime—especially one, like that of the Nazis, which combined capitalism with terror. Benn's inability to read the poem (in English) corresponds to a more disturbing incapacity: a blindness to his own complicity with respect to the Nazi regime.

18. According to Howard Griffin, Auden said that "All totalitarian societies start out as utopias" (Griffin, *Conversations with Auden*, ed. Donald Allen [San Francisco: Grey Fox Press, 1981], 26).

19. W. H. Auden, *The Dyer's Hand and Other Essays* (New York: Vintage, 1968), 27.

20. W. H. Auden, *Secondary Worlds* (London: Faber and Faber, 1968), 103–27.

21. Auden, *Secondary Worlds*, 112.

22. Auden, *Secondary Worlds*, 112.

23 . Auden, *Secondary Worlds*, 113.

24. Auden, *Secondary Worlds*, 113. Arendt also presents advertising as a subspecies of propaganda and of course, like Auden, considers business publicity relatively harmless in comparison to the techniques of totalitarian propaganda. But, she makes clear that these two versions of propaganda are conceptually and historically related: the Nazis openly admitted to having learned their techniques from American business publicity, and advertising, like totalitarian propaganda, dreams of replacing itself with the sheer exercise of power. "The strong emphasis on the 'scientific' nature of its assertions has been compared to certain advertising techniques which also address themselves to masses. And it is true that the advertising columns of every newspaper show this 'scientificality,' by which a manufacturer proves with facts and figures and the help of a 'research' department that his is the 'best soap in the world.' It is also true that there is a certain element of violence in the imaginative exaggerations of publicity men, that

behind the assertion that girls who do not use this particular brand of soap may go through life with pimples and without a husband, lies the wild dream of monopoly, the dream that one day the manufacturer of 'the only soap that prevents pimples' may have the power to deprive of husbands all girls who do not use his soap. Science in the instances of both business publicity and totalitarian propaganda is obviously only a surrogate for power" (Arendt, *The Origins of Totalitarianism*, rev. ed. [New York: Harcourt Brace Jovanovich, 1979], 345). As she indicates, Arendt uses soap advertising as an example, because it is the example Hitler himself uses in *Mein Kampf* (see "The Image of Hell," *Commentary* 2, 3, 1946; rptd. in *Essays in Understanding*, 197–205). For Arendt, "America" cannot be wholly separated from the appearance of Nazism: American gangsterism and advertising are indispensable schools for Nazi organization and propaganda, just as, in *The Age of Anxiety*, the odorless world of the totalitarian future ominously returns in the apparently innocent advertising slogan, "*Leaves no odor.*"

25. W. H. Auden, "Nature, History and Poetry," *Thought* 15, 98 (September, 1950), 422. Auden rewrites this article in *The Dyer's Hand* under the title "The Virgin & the Dynamo." Although the terms he uses are generally the same, Auden nevertheless introduces the two defining types, "virgin" and "dynamo," and significantly reduces perhaps the most far-ranging and yet enigmatic feature of the earlier essay—the designation of a poem as a "natural, not an historical object" ("Nature, History and Poetry," 422). In "The Virgin & the Dynamo," the poem is said to be "a natural organism" and this more familiar designation is further explicated when Auden says that it is "not an inorganic thing. For example, it is rhythmical" (Auden, *The Dyer's Hand*, 67). But Auden complicates the schemata of his enormously difficult earlier essay, which reads like nothing so much as one of Kierkegaard's "algebraic" writings, especially *The Concept of Anxiety*; he begins the later essay by defining "the Natural World of the Dynamo" as one that is "describable, not in words but in terms of numbers, or rather, in algebraic terms" (*Dyer's Hand*, 61; for the term *algebra*, see Kierkegaard, *The Concept of Anxiety*, ed. and trans. Reidar Thomte and Albert Anderson [Princeton: Princeton University Press, 1980], 113, 128, 137). Auden's essay, regardless of what it says about poetry, thus belongs to the world of the dynamo rather than to that of the virgin and is therefore closer to the natural world than to the historical one.

26. Auden, "Nature, History and Poetry," 422.

27. Auden, "Nature, History and Poetry," 414.

28. Auden, "Nature, History and Poetry," 413.

29. Auden, "Nature, History and Poetry," 418.

30. Auden, *Dyer's Hand*, 67.

31. That Auden's analysis in "The Virgin & The Dynamo" builds on his reflections in "Making, Knowing and Judging" may be deduced from the remarks

he makes in his introduction to the volume: "The order of the chapters . . . is deliberate, and I would like them to be read in sequence" (*Dyer's Hand*, xii).

32. Auden, *Dyer's Hand*, 54.

33. Auden, *Dyer's Hand*, 57.

34. Auden, *Dyer's Hand*, 55.

35. Auden, *Secondary Worlds*, 120. The only uncertainty in this regard, for Auden, concerns the mode of indirection in which "sanctity" can be indicated: "Sanctity, it would seem, can be hinted at only by comic indirection, as in *Don Quixote*" (Auden, *Secondary Worlds*, 122).

36. According to Lucy McDiarmid's persuasive argument, Auden's poetry is always responsive to a value outside itself; as his work develops, she argues, it increasingly orients itself not toward this "outside" but toward the staging of its own frivolity; see L. McDiarmid, *Auden's Apologies for Poetry* (Princeton: Princeton University Press, 1990).

37. For an account of Auden's relationship to Anglo-Saxon epic poetry in *The Age of Anxiety*, see the rather wacky but technically insightful analysis of Christine Brooke-Rose, "Notes on the Metre of Auden's 'Age of Anxiety,'" *Essays in Criticism* 13, 3 (July, 1963): 253–64. Some of Auden's metrical models are almost impossible to accommodate to an uninflected language, including the skaldic meter of Old Norse, the *dróttkvætt*, which serves as the basis of the duet in "The Masque" (519); for a fuller discussion of the *dróttkvætt* (stanzas consist of four couplets; each line has three stresses and ends on an unaccented syllable; the first line of each couplet has two alliterations and an assonance; the second is related to the first by alliteration and also contains an internal rhyme; ordinary names for things are replaced by kennings), see Auden *Secondary Worlds*, 59; see also E. V. Gordon, *An Introduction to Old Norse* (Oxford: Clarendon Press, 1927), 295–96.

38. Randall Jarrell, *Kipling, Auden & Co.: Essays and Reviews, 1935–1964* (New York: Farrar, Straus and Giroux, 1980), 145.

39. *The Age of Anxiety* is subtitled, rather obscurely, "A Baroque Eclogue." Auden describes the Baroque style, saying that it is "the most this-worldly, a visible hymn to earthly pomp and power. At the same time, by its excessive theatricality, it reveals, perhaps unintentionally, the essential 'camp' of all worldly greatness . . . nothing could be further removed from the Christian view of God and Man" (Auden, *A Certain World: A Commonplace Book*. [London: Faber and Faber, 1982], 28). In a contemporaneous review of the poem, M. L. Rosenthal suggests that the subtitle is meant as a play on the bar in which most of the poem's action occurs: "I fear there is a sad pun in that 'baroque,' considering the setting of most of the poem!" (M. L. Rosenthal, "Speaking Greatly in an Age of Confusion," *New York Herald Tribune* 20 July 1947; reprinted in John Haffenden, ed., *W. H. Auden: The Critical Heritage* [London: Routledge & Kegan

Paul, 1983], 364). In despair over the puritanical sterility of the environment around Swarthmore, Auden gives one further indication of what the term *baroque* might mean: "I am, after all, a crook, and need a more baroque and louche habitat to breathe in, than the Quakers provide" (letter to James Stern, quoted in Davenport-Hines, *Auden,* 221–22.

The baroque, for Auden, is clearly a complex phenomenon—both positive and negative. Auden was doubtless familiar with Wölfflin's famous opposition of the baroque to the classical style (see Heinrich Wölfflin, *Principles of Art History: The Problem of the Development of Style in Later Art,* trans. M. D. Hottinger [New York: Dover, 1950]). Although it is unlikely, Auden may also have been familiar with Walter Benjamin's reevaluation of the baroque in his *Ursprung des deutschen Trauerspiels* (1928; reprinted in the first volume of *Gesammelte Schriften,* ed. R. Tiedemann and H. Schweppenhäuser [Frankfurt am Main: Suhrkamp, 1977–1985]). In any case, Auden's decision to cast *The Age of Anxiety*—and therefore the modern world—under the sign of the baroque testifies to an unexamined affinity between the thought of Benjamin and the poetry of Auden. This would be a fitting topic for another study.

40. See Giles Romilly, "The Age of Despair," *The New Statesman and Nation,* 30 October, 1948; reprinted in Haffenden, ed., *W. H. Auden: The Critical Heritage,* 374: "His teeth have chattered and he wants our teeth to chatter. . . . Chattering teeth do not make good poetry even in The Age of Despair." For an extended discussion of such matters, see Peter Fenves, *"Chatter": Language and History in Kierkegaard* (Stanford: Stanford University Press, 1993).

41. W. H. Auden, "Introduction" to *The Poet's Tongue,* rpt. Auden, *Prose: and Travel Books in Prose and Verse,* Vol. 1, in *Collected Works,* ed. E. Mendelson (Princeton: Princeton University Press, 1996), 105.

42. Speechlessness is not the same as silence. Whereas the experience of silence takes place either under the condition that one wills to be silent about something that could be brought into speech or one understands in advance that the object of one's meditation or vision cannot be brought into language, the experience of speechlessness is purely privative: one is robbed of speech and, more radically, of the ability to speak and therefore the ability to say "I am speechless."

43. In "Nature, History and Poetry" Auden defines hell in the following manner: "In the chimerical case of a society completely embodying a crowd there would be a state of total unfreedom, i.e., Hell" ("Nature, History and Poetry," 415).

44. Shakespeare, *The Complete Works,* ed. Alfred Harbage (New York: Viking, 1969), 257; *As You Like It,* Act II, Scene vii, 143–44. According to the OED, "mewl" means "cry feebly, whimper, like an infant; to make a whining noise." Malin's revision of Jaques' speech is also a direct challenge to Wordsworth's

presentation of infancy in Book II of *The Prelude* (Book II, ll. 233–64; *Selected Poems and Prefaces*, ed. Jack Stillinger [Boston: Houghton Mifflin, 1965], 212–13). Both Malin's infant and Wordsworth's blessed "Babe" are "helpless," but the helplessness of the former is aligned with a transgressive righteousness, whereas the helplessness of the latter is a dimension or source of "Poetic spirit."

45. See Kierkegaard, *The Sickness unto Death*, trans. Howard Hong and Edna Hong (Princeton: Princeton University Press, 1980). Kierkegaard's *Begrebet Angest* (1844) was translated as *The Concept of Dread* in 1944 by Walter Lowrie (Princeton: Princeton University Press, 1944); the more recent English edition "corrects" Lowrie's translation and calls it *The Concept of Anxiety*.

46. Of Auden's many discussions and analyses of Kierkegaard, the one in which he most clearly elaborates the Danish writer's distance from the project of German idealism is perhaps the section of a lengthy essay entitled "Søren Kierkegaard" called "Kierkegaard and the Existential" (*Forewords and Afterwords*, [New York: Vintage, 1989], 170–72).

47. Fuller notes that Rosetta's phrase "thrown into being" resonates with Heidegger's term *Geworfenheit*; see Fuller, *W. H. Auden: A Commentary*, 381. Mendelson notes that Auden mentions Heidegger in a review as early as 1942; see Mendelson, *Later Auden*, 316–17.

48. In his essay "Knight of Doleful Countenance," Auden indicates that Kierkegaard created his own version of Manichaeanism by way of omission (*Forewords and Afterwords*, 191).

49. In an article on *The Age of Anxiety* John Boly asserts that in *The Concept of Dread* Kierkegaard "began to put aside the literary presentation of his ideas through dramatic personae in favor of a more systematic philosophical treatment" (Boly, "Auden and the Romantic Tradition in *The Age of Anxiety*," *Daedalus* 111, 3 [summer, 1982]: 170). This assertion would especially surprise the author of *The Concluding Unscientific Postscript* since this massive work is nothing but a lampoon on any pretense at "systematic philosophical treatments" of anything worthy of human life. And the *Concluding Unscientific Postscript* was written after *The Concept of Dread*, which was in fact signed not by Kierkegaard but by a certain character named Vigilius Haufniensis, roughly transliterated as the "watchman of Copenhagen." Boly misunderstands the "algebraicism" Kierkegaard strategically employs in works like *The Concept of Dread* and *The Sickness unto Death* as systematicity, thereby missing the whole Kierkegaardian critique of German idealism.

50. See George Herbert, *The Complete English Poems*, ed. John Tobin (Harmondsworth: Penguin, 1991), 95; ll. 76–78.

51. See Kierkegaard, *Fear and Trembling—Repetition*, trans. Howard Hong and Edna Hong (Princeton: Princeton University Press, 1983).

52. "Nature, History and Poetry," 420–21.

53. Shakespeare, *The Complete Works*, 257; *As You Like It*, Act II, Scene vii, 153–54.

54. For an analysis of the alteration in the term *revolution* from its original cyclical sense (restoration of ancient prerogatives) to its modern meaning, see Hannah Arendt, *On Revolution* (New York: Penguin, 1963), 21–58.

55. Marx himself famously connects capitalism with mythology in one of the opening chapters of *Capital*, "The Fetishism of the Commodity and Its Secret" (see Marx, *Capital*, trans. Ben Fowkes [New York: Vintage, 1977], 163–77). This short chapter serves as the foundation for the analysis of culture undertaken under the banner of "Western Marxism" from Lukàcs's *History and Class-Consciousness* (1924) onward.

56. See, in particular, the speeches of Quant and Emble in the first age (465–66). In the development of his principle of retribution, Malin again echoes the earlier observations of the lyric "I" in "September 1": "I and the public know / What all schoolchildren learn, / Those to whom evil is done / Do evil in return" (Auden, *Selected Poems*, 86).

57. T. S. Eliot, *The Complete Poems and Plays* (London: Faber and Faber, 1969), 50; Jessie Weston, *From Ritual to Romance* (rpt. Gloucester, Mass.: Peter Smith, 1983).

58. Eliot, *Complete Poems*, 48.

59. Eliot, *Complete Poems*, 49.

60. Eliot, *Complete Poems*, 49; for Eliot's note on Dante, see 54; for Dante's presentation of the fate of Count Ugolino, see Dante Alighieri, *The Divine Comedy*, ed. and trans. Robert M. Durling, Vol 1. *Inferno* (New York and Oxford: Oxford University Press, 1996), Canto 33.

61. For an authoritative account of the history of melancholia, including the assertions of Aristotle (or pseudo-Aristotle) to the effect that "great men" are generally of this disposition, see Raymond Klibansky, Erwin Panofsky, and Fritz Saxl *Saturn and Melancholy: Studies in the History of Natural Philosophy, Religion, and Art* (London: Nelson, 1964).

62. Shakespeare, *The Complete Works*, 257; *As You Like It*, Act II, Scene vii, 161–65.

63. See Rainer Maria Rilke, *Sämtliche Werke*, ed. Ruth Sieber-Rilke et al. (Frankfurt am Main: Insel, 1987), 6: 1063. This term occupies a prominent place at the beginning of Rilke's strange meditation of 1913, "Puppe: Zu den Wachs-Puppen von Lotte Pritzel" (*Werke*, 6: 1063–74). What Rilke says of "we" applies with special force to Rosetta: "Wir orientierten uns an der Puppe. Sie lag tiefer von Natur, so konnten wir unmerklich gegen sie abfließen, uns in ihr sammeln und, wenn auch ein wenig trübe, die neuen Umgebungen in ihr erkennen [We are oriented toward the puppet. It lay deeper in nature, so we could imperceptibly flow against it, collect ourselves in it, and, even if only a little opaquely,

recognize the new surroundings in it]" (*Werke*, 6: 1070). Auden quotes Rilke's reflections on dolls in *The Double Man* (New York: Random House, 1941), 88–89. Auden also quotes the eighth *Duineser Elegie* twice (see *The Double Man*, 104 and 150). In this remarkable poem Rilke presents in its most concentrated form the specific spatiality of "openness": "Mit allen Augen sieht die Kreatur / das Offene [With all eyes the creature sees / the open]" (*Werke*, 1: 714).

64. Newton, *Mathematical Principles*, trans. Andrew Motte, rev. Florian Cajori (Berkeley: University of California Press, 1934), 1: 6–7; General Scholium, Definitions 1–4.

65. As Auden writes in "New Year Letter," "Self-educated William Blake / Who threw his spectre in the lake, / Broke off relations in a curse / With the Newtonian Universe" (203). And as Auden writes in *The Enchafèd Flood*, "To Blake, then, the Enemy was the sort of conception of the universe which he associates with Newton" (W. H. Auden, *The Enchafèd Flood: or the Romantic Iconography of the Sea*, [Charlottesville: University Press of Virginia, 1979] 45).

66. See the opening lines of Rilke's eighth elegy in the *Duineser Elegien*; Werke, 1: 714.

67. On the difficult idea of the *sensorium dei* in Newton, see the informative essay of Gerd Buchdahl, "Comments on 'Newton's Achievement in Dynamics,'" in *The Annus Mirabilis of Sir Isaac Newton*, ed. Robert Palter (Cambridge, Mass.: MIT Press, 1970), 136–42.

68. Quoted from the Revised King James Version; all further quotations of the Hebrew Bible within the body of the text are from this version, which Auden would obviously have known intimately; all other quotations are from *Tanakh: A New Translation of the Holy Scriptures According to the Traditional Hebrew Text* (Philadelphia and Jerusalem: Jewish Publications Society, 5746–1985). The two translations are almost identical in all the translations quoted throughout this essay.

69. See Jonathan Swift, "A Voyage to the Houyhnhnms" in *Gulliver's Travels*, in *The Writings of Jonathan Swift*, ed. Robert Greenberg and William Piper (New York: Norton, 1973), 224–60. With enormous subtlety, this reference to Houyhnhnms resumes the thematics of odor and order, for, of course, the chief characteristic of the Yahoos—and what makes them unbearable to the "wild horses"—is their horrific lack of hygiene. In a letter to Stephen Spender, Auden notes the distinctiveness of Swift's satire, even as he indicates that he has little interest in satire as a whole: "Swift is different because he is satirising Mankind and is therefore included himself" ("*The Map of All My Youth*," ed. Katherine Bucknell and Nicholas Jenkins, 65.)

70. The "regressive road" to the unconscious does not, in other words, follow the prescriptions of any analysis—whether Freudian or Jungian—but instead, proceeds according to the age-old and arbitrary steps of intensified intoxication.

The interest of the narrating voice is centered less on the nature of the self than on the existence of the other—and there is no indication that the outstanding other is a father or his substitute, the analyst: "A less noted and a more significant phenomenon [of drunkenness] . . . is the way in which our faith in the existence of other selves, normally rather wobbly, is greatly strengthened and receives, perhaps precisely because, for once, doubt is so completely overcome, the most startling justifications. For it can happen, if circumstances are otherwise propitious, that members of a group in this condition establish a rapport in which communication of thoughts and feelings is so accurate and instantaneous, that they appear to function as a single organism" (484).

71. Bahlke, for example, notes something of the critical confusion surrounding the significance of the body symbolism of "The Seven Stages" and concludes that this symbolism is insufficiently relevant to warrant further reflection: "The disparity between Spears' and Hoggart's general interpretations of the significance of the stages, as well as of the particular part of the body to be assigned to each stage (the third stage, the city, corresponds to the brain, according to Spears, and to the stomach according to Hoggart), suggests that still another interpretation would only confuse the reader further. . . . It seems to me that none of the stages, with the exception perhaps of the conclusion to the fourth stage, where the return to the womb is figured in Rosetta's entrance into the 'big house,' would gain any further significance than they have independent of a body-symbolism" (George Bahlke, *The Later Auden: From "New Year Letter" to "About the House"* [New Brunswick, N.J.: Rutgers University Press, 1970], 196).

72. Quoted in Edward Mendelson, *Later Auden*, 251. Auden also indicates to Ansen that "Yes I used the 5 vol Zohar . . . just picked bits out" (quoted in Fuller, *W. H. Auden: A Commentary*, 378–79). The edition to which Auden refers is the *Zohar*, trans. Harry Sperling and Maurice Simon, 5 vols. (London: Soncino Press, 1931–1934); hereafter, in accordance with scholarly practice, references are to the volume and page numbers of the standard Hebrew-Aramaic edition (which are reproduced in the Sperling and Simon translation). The English edition is incomplete, since Sperling and Simon decided to translate only those parts of the original medieval and pseudoepigraphic-Aramaic text that, in their view, belong to the "*Zohar* proper" (xxix). Of the many parts they omitted, one of the most important is the famous *Idra Rabba*, or "Great Assembly" (3: 127b–145a). This description of an assembly at which Simeon ben Yohai and his companions were present contains the most detailed exposition of the divine body and the Primordial Man in the *Zohar* (for an outline of the entire *Zohar* and a brief characterization of the *Idra Rabba*, see Gershom Scholem, *The Kabbalah* [New York: Meridian, 1974], 214–19; for a complete translation, see *The Anatomy of God*, trans. Roy Rosenberg [New York: Ktav Publishing House, 1973], 48–131).

It is peculiar that Fuller cites the Sperling and Simon edition of the *Zohar* as the principal source for the bodily landscape of "The Seven Stages" but does not mention that the main Zoharic text devoted to the revelation of the *corpus mysticum* is absent from the edition Auden said he used. The *Idra Rabba* would, however, have been readily available to Auden in both English and German translations. In the late seventeenth century, Knorr von Rosenroth published a Latin compilation of Kabbalistic writings, including the "Great Assembly," under the dramatic title *Kabbalah denudata*. S. L. MacGregor Mathers translated Knorr von Rosenroth's volume into English in the late nineteenth century under both its "original" title, *Kabbalah denudata*, and its translation, *Kabbalah Unveiled*; see *The Kabbalah Unveiled [Kabbalah denudata], Containing the Following Books of the Zohar: The Book of Concealed Mystery, the Greater Holy Assembly, the Lesser Holy Assembly* (London: Redway, 1887). Mather's translation was reproduced dozens of times and was widely available in both Great Britain and the United States. Also available to Auden was a widespread German anthology of the *Zohar* produced by a student of Rudolf Steiner, *Der Sohar: Das heilige Buch der Kabbala nach dem Urtext*, ed. and trans. Ernst Müller (1920, revised, 1932; reprinted, Vienna: Eugen Diedrichs Verlag, 1989), see esp. 27–29 and 76–78. Furthermore, Gershom Scholem's groundbreaking work, *Major Trends in Jewish Mysticism*, first appeared in 1941 and was sufficiently well received to be reprinted by 1946; two of its central chapters are devoted to the *Zohar*, including an analysis of the function and symbolism of the *Adam Kadmon*, which, as Scholem demonstrates, assumes increasing importance for the Kabbalah developed by Isaac Luria; see *Major Trends in Jewish Mysticism* (New York: Schocken, 1941), 156–243.

73. Hannah Arendt, *The Origins of Totalitarianism*, rev. ed. (New York: Harcourt Brace Jovanovich, 1979), 466.

74. Near the beginning of the *Zohar*, the—to quote Malin—"comprehensive incomprehensibility" of the *En Sof* ("that which is infinite") is emphasized: "What is within the Thought no one can conceive, much less can one know the *En Sof*, of which no trace can be found and to which thought cannot reach by any means" (*Zohar*, 1: 21a). For an account of the *En Sof* that was available to Auden when he wrote *The Age of Anxiety*, see Scholem, *Major Trends*, esp. 214–19.

One further point is worth noting: the primordial body explored in the *Idra Rabba* and elsewhere is an *Adam Kadmon*, not a Primordial Woman. But the only feature of the body explored in "The Seven Stages" that clearly bears the marks of sexual difference are the breasts ("mountains"), which, strangely enough, Auden leaves out of his account of the section in his letter to Ansen.

75. For an account of the *Adam Kadmon*, in addition to the passages of Scholem's *Major Trends* cited above, see the first essay in Scholem's *On the Mystical Shape of the Godhead*, trans. Joachim Neugroschel (New York: Schocken, 1991), 15–55.

76. For some representative complaints concerning the enormous difficulty of interpreting "The Seven Stages," see Richard Hoggart, *Auden: An Introductory Essay* (New Haven: Yale University Press, 1951), 202–03; and Herbert Greenberg, *Quest for the Necessary* (Cambridge, Mass.: Harvard University Press, 1968), 162–63. Mendelson summarizes the critical despair: "The shape of 'The Seven Ages' is clear enough, but the shape of the Edenic quest in 'The Seven Stages' has baffled even Auden's most sympathetic readers" (*Later Auden*, 250).

77. See Dante, *Divina Commedia*, trans. Charles Singleton (Princeton: Princeton University Press, 1970–1975), *Purgatorio*, Canto 28; Fuller, *W. H. Auden: A Commentary*, 373.

78. For the seven days of creation, see *Zohar*, 1: 34a; seven firmaments, 1: 32b, 1: 34a, 1: 85b, 2: 10b, 2: 164b–165a, 3: 9b, 3: 287a; seven ordeals, 2: 199b, 3: 127a; seven abysses, 2: 228b; seven windows, 2: 172a.

79. See Auden's discussion of the symbol of the desert in *The Enchafèd Flood*, esp. 13–15.

80. Friedrich Nietzsche, "Dionysis' Dithyramb," one of the songs in *Also sprach Zarathustra*; (Friedrich Nietzsche, *Sämtliche Werke: Studien Ausgabe*, ed. Giorgio Colli and Mazzino Montinari [Berlin: de Gruyter, 1967–1977], 6: 382).

81. *Zohar*, 2: 21a; capitalization as it appears in Sperling and Simon's translation. "Back of the wilderness" derives from the following lines: "Now Moses, tending the flock of his father-in-law Jethro, the priest of Midian, drove the flock into the wilderness [*'ahar hamidbor*], and came to Horeb, the mountain of God" (Exodus 3: 1), after which follows the account of the burning bush. The translation in the *Zohar* is more accurate than that of the standard *Tanakh*, since the preposition *'ahar* is cognate with the substantive *'ahor*, "the hinder side, back part." The term is used in the theophantic moment later in Exodus: "I will take My hand and you will see My back [*'ahori*]" (Exodus, 33: 23).

82. The most extensive discussions of the Moon in the *Zohar* can be found in the following passages: 1: 19a–20a; 1: 53a; 1: 248a–250a. For an analysis of the Moon as symbol, see Scholem, *On the Kabbalah and Its Symbolism*, trans. Ralph Manheim (New York: Schocken, 1969), 107–08, 151–53.

83. *Zohar*, 1: 46b.

84. *Zohar*, 2: 171b; emphasis in Sperling and Simon's translation.

85. *Zohar*, 3: 15a. Similar formulations abound throughout the text; see, for example, 1: 6a; 1: 46b; 1: 141b; 1: 145a; 2: 230b. As early as 1941, Auden uses the Zoharic phrase, drawn from Daniel 7, for the highest of the grades of the God-head, "Ancient of Days"; see the concluding stanza of "Atlantis," the last lines of which are "And may the Ancient of Days / Provide for all you must do / His invisible guidance, / Lifting up, friend, upon you / The light of His countenance" (317). For "Ancient of Days" in the *Zohar*, see, for example, 1: 4b; 1: 11a; 1: 130a; 2: 14b; 2: 83a; 2: 134b; 2: 154a; 2: 217b; 3: 15b; 3:20a; 3:105b. Mendelson notes that

the "Ancient of Days" is "the common title of an engraving by Blake that Auden had been given by an admirer" (Mendelson, *Later Auden*, 167).

86. The importance of this verse for "The Seven Stages" can also be measured by the succeeding line: "And the light of the moon shall be become like the light of the sun, and the light of the sun shall become sevenfold, like the light of the seven days, when the Lord binds up His people's wounds and heals the injuries it has suffered" (Isa. 30: 26).

87. *Zohar*, 2: 172b.

88. Quant's final words are "Abraham's Bosom" (533).

89. See Jacques Lacan, *The Four Fundamental Concepts of Psychoanalysis*, trans. Alan Sheridan, volume 11 of *The Seminars of Jacques Lacan*, ed. Jacques-Alain Miller (New York: Norton, 1998), 230–43; Chapter 18, "Of the Subject Who Is Supposed to Know, of the First Dyad, and of the Good."

90. For a more extravagant critique of the pretensions of Platonic love, see "The Platonic Blow, by Miss Oral"—a poem written, but never publicly acknowledged, by Auden and printed in an unauthorized pamphlet (W. H. Auden, *The Platonic Blow* [New York: Fuck You Press, 1965]).

91. See "Lament for a Lawgiver," *Horizon* 17, 99 (March, 1948): 161–63.

92. For a quirky but powerful analysis of the concept and history of pastoral, see William Empson, *Some Versions of Pastoral* (New York: New Directions, 1974).

93. See, for example, Monroe Spears, *The Disenchanted Island: The Poetry of W. H. Auden* (Oxford: Oxford University Press, 1963), 231; George Bahlke, *The Later Auden*, 146; Edward Callan, *Auden: A Carnival of Intellect* (Oxford: Oxford University Press, 1983), 204.

94. Nelson, for example, describes Quant as an "aging homosexual widower" (Gerald Nelson, *Changes of Heart: A Study of the Poetry of W. H. Auden* [Berkeley: University of California Press, 1969], 81).

95. See Eve Kosofsky Sedgwick, *Between Men: English Literature and Male Homosocial Desire* (New York: Columbia University Press, 1985).

96. By giving Rosetta the final soliloquy in the body of the poem, Auden doubtless aligns himself with Joyce—not only with Molly's speech in *Ulysses* but also with Anna Livia Plurabelle's final words in *Finnegans Wake*. In a letter to Auden, Edmund Wilson offers a list of complaints: "I have some very severe criticisms to make of certain of your recent activities. . . . Your regurgitation in *The Age of Anxiety*, in the girl's speech over the sleeping boy, of the last pages of *Finnegans Wake*. This is the only misstep in the poem, in which the influence of Joyce, where it elsewhere appears, is pretty completely absorbed by your own style" (Edmund Wilson, *Letters on Literature and Politics, 1912–1972*, ed. Elena Wilson [New York: Farrar, Straus and Giroux, 1977], 431; for further comments on the relation of *Finnegans Wake* to *The Age of Anxiety*, see Mendelson, *Later*

Auden, 258). Wilson apparently responds to the movement of Anna's meditation from her lover to her father, especially the line "there'll be others but non so for me" (James Joyce, *Finnegans Wake* [Harmondsworth: Penguin, 1978], 626), which finds an echo in Rosetta's remark "More boys like this one may embrace me yet" (530). Anna's cry "And it's old and old it's sad and old it's sad and weary I go back to you, my cold father, my cold mad father, my cold mad feary father . . . " (*Finnegans Wake*, 627–28) resonates with Rosetta's description of her relation to her father, including the term "sad" (530). But for at least two reasons Wilson's complaint seems misplaced: Anna does not present the history of Jewish persecution as she turns from lover to father, and the cyclical conception of history, which seems to support the structure of *Finnegans Wake*, runs counter to the starkly messianic character of Rosetta's meditation.

97. Boly notes that Rosetta refers to exile in speaking of "Babylon's banks" and then proceeds—without any apparent scholarly support—to interpret her speech in terms of the Kabbalah of Isaac Luria: "Within Luria's theogonic concept of *Tsimtsum*, which provides the central form for Rosetta's meditation, limitation and contraction within the divinity precede flowing forth and expansion" (Boly, "Auden and the Romantic Tradition in *The Age of Anxiety*," 165). To this remarkable thesis, Boly appends a footnote to Gershom Scholem's *Major Trends in Jewish Mysticism* but does not indicate that he has any evidence Auden ever read Scholem's book. It is not unlikely that Auden consulted Scholem, since, although Boly, strangely enough, refers to a later edition, it first appeared in 1941 (see note 72 above). But there is no scholarly reason to concern oneself with Lurianic Kabbalah, since Babylon is without a doubt the most famous image of exile in the entire Hebrew Bible. And Auden made it quite clear that he had worked with the *Zohar*—and in the *Zohar* Babylon is repeatedly mentioned as a symbol of exile: "But the exile of Babylon was a real torment for which there was weeping both in heaven and on earth, as it is written: 'Behold, their heroes (angels) cried without, the angels of peace weeped bitterly' (Isa. XXXIII, 7); 'by the rivers of Babylon, there we sat down, yea, we wept, when we remembered Zion' (Ps. CXXXVII, I): yea truly, all joined in the lamentation" (2: 2b); for other significant examples among many more in the *Zohar*, see 1: 96b; 1: 202a; 1: 237b; 2: 6a–9b; 2: 189b; 3: 16a.

98. Fuller, *W. H. Auden: A Commentary*, 374. For similar comments, see Spears, *The Disenchanted Island*, 232–33: "Since she [Rosetta] is the only one who changes, discarding her illusory and accepting her real childhood with all its implications, she is, in a sense, the protagonist." According to Spears, Rosetta "renounces her dream of 'the Innocent Place where / His Law can't look,' of 'a home like theirs.' Abandoning her Innocent Landscape, she accepts her real childhood . . . , her 'poor fat father,' and the fact of her race which she symbolizes" (Spears, 237). By 1968, Jews were no longer considered a race, but

the judgment on Rosetta was the same: "She accepts finally the brick villa . . . and ends her reflections acknowledging her identity as a Jew" (Greenberg, *Quest for the Necessary*, 166). Callan succinctly remarks that Rosetta "finally faces the truth about her father" (Edward Callan, "Allegory in Auden's *The Age of Anxiety*," 162). Justin Repogle is a little more expansive but no more convincing: "Having fulfilled the dialectical conditions, she now understands for the first time that escape from human existence is impossible, and for the first time accepts life as it is" (Repogle, *Auden's Poetry* [Seattle: University of Washington Press, 1969], 80). According to Bahlke, "in an extended soliloquy she expresses her recognition that she, a Jewess, and thus a permanent wanderer, could never realize any meaningful relationship between herself and Emble" (Bahlke, *The Later Auden*, 143). Although the narrating voice indicates that Rosetta daydreams about the English countryside only when she is "high," Nelson concludes that her entire life—until she sees Emble prostrate—is one long fit of self-delusion: "From this point on, the subject of Rosetta's soliloquy is no longer Emble and herself, but herself alone. She sees no hope in self-delusion, for no matter how hard she tries to run, God the Father, like the Hound of Heaven, will pursue. Her lies have been multiple, her life imaginary, yet the real has never really been hidden from the guilt she feels is God" (Gerald Nelson, *Changes of Heart*, 101).

99. See also Auden's more extensive comments on deception in general and self-deception in particular in Howard Griffin, *Conversations with Auden*, 25.

100. Jarrell, *Kipling, Auden & Co.*, 145.

101. In an essay of 1941 Jarrell notes that "One of the conscious devices of the late poems is the use of a simile blunt, laconic, and prosaic enough to be startling" (Randall Jarrell, *The Third Book of Criticism* [New York: Farrar, Straus and Giroux, 1941], 141). This astute observation is amplified by Richard Hoggart: "The common qualities are pungent conciseness and a startling contrast—a shock of surprise at the incongruity of the relationship called up. . . . In the 'thirties the simile was over-used and echoed from one poet to another, mainly under Auden's influence" (Hoggart, *Auden: An Introductory Essay*, 49–50). See also William Logan, "Auden's Images," *W. H. Auden: The Far Interior*, ed. Alan Bold (London: Vision Press, 1985), 108–09.

102. The concept of "the remnant of Israel" (*she'ar* or *she'erit Yisrael*) is first developed in Isaiah: "And it shall come to pass in that day, that the remnant of Israel, and such of the house of Jacob who have escaped, shall no more again rely upon him who struck them; but shall rely upon the Lord, the Holy One of Israel, in truth. The remnant shall return, the remnant of Jacob, to the mighty God" (Isa. 10: 20–21). Jeremiah then introduces the term "remnant of Judah," especially in relation to the Babylonian exile (Jer. 40–44). Of the many later invocations of these terms in the Prophets, none perhaps summarizes the concept of remnant better than the following passage near the opening of the book of

Michah: "I will surely assemble, O Jacob, all of you; I will surely gather the remnant of Israel; I will put them together like sheep in a fold, like a flock in the midst of their pasture; they shall make a great noise because of the multitude of men" (Mic. 2: 12). For a brief but incisive analysis of the phrase, see Nahum Glatzer, "Remnant of Israel," in *Contemporary Jewish Religious Thought*, ed. Arthur Cohen and Paul Mendes-Flohr (New York: Free Press, 1987), 779–83. As Glatzer points out, the term "surviving remnant" (*she'erit ha-pleitah*) gained a new urgency during and after the Second World War.

103. See W. H. Auden, *Litany and Anthem for S. Matthew's Day*, written for the Church of S. Matthew, Northampton, for the Dedication and Patronal Festival, 21 September 1946. According to Bloomfield and Mendelson, the Northampton publisher of this pamphlet, Stanton and Son, printed 500 copies; see B. C. Bloomfield and Edward Mendelson, *W. H. Auden: A Bibliography 1924–1969* (Charlottesville, Va.: University Press of Virginia, 1972), 59–60; A 28. On the last (unnumbered) page of this pamphlet Auden published a poem entitled "Praise Ye the Lord," the first line of which is "Let the whole creation give out another sweetness." (I am consulting the copy in the United Library of the Garrett-Evangelical and Seabury-Western Theological Seminaries, Evanston, Ill.) With the addition of a new first line, "Let us praise our Maker, with true passion extol Him," and with certain minor variations—altered punctuation and the replacement of "itself" for "himself" in the phrase "each lives himself"—this poem was published under the title "Anthem" in *Epistle to a Godson* (see W. H. Auden, *Epistle to a Godson and Other Poems* [New York: Random House, 1969], 62); reprinted in *Collected Poems*, 332. Some of Auden's friends received other versions of the same concluding poem, including Alan Ansen and Benjamin Britten (see Bloomfield and Mendelson, *W. H. Auden: A Bibliography*, 248; J 65–66); in her commemorative essay on Auden, Ursula Niebuhr reproduces the lines he added to the copy of the poem he gave to her and her husband (see "Memories of the 1940s" in *W. H. Auden: A Tribute*, ed. Stephen Spender [New York: Macmillan, 1975], 115). According to Bloomfield and Mendelson, a version of this poem was "originally conceived as the conclusion to Malin's last thought in the last section of AA" (*W. H. Auden: A Bibliography*, 248; J 66).

104. Auden, *Litany and Anthem for S. Matthew's Day*, unnumbered last page.

105. Although the famous phrase "Abraham's Bosom" is derived from Luke (16: 22), Abraham nevertheless figures as an ecumenical figure of the highest order: he is the "father" of three faiths grounded in the Book: Judaism, Christianity, and Islam.

106. This phrase (rather than "cleansed occasions") is the one Auden uses in the version of the poem he appended to the copy of *The Age of Anxiety* he gave to Ursula and Reinhold Niebuhr; *W. H. Auden: A Tribute*, 115.

107. Nelson, like many other critics, equates Malin with Auden; see Nelson,

Changes of Heart, 106: "Malin is the 'voice' of *The Age of Anxiety*. Through him, more than through any other character, Auden speaks." According to Justin Replogle, "Malin, contemplative, intellectual, and Auden's main spokesman, is an Ethical man searching for something higher" (Replogle, *Auden's Poetry*, 78).

108. Fuller, *W. H. Auden: A Commentary*, 385–86: "not only does it [Rosetta's final meditation] show up Rosetta's illusions about her father and all she made him stand for, but it predicates the Jewish God whose omnipresence is a precondition of the Christian solution Auden demands. . . . Part Six, 'Epilogue' (p. 531), demonstrates that although Rosetta's recognition of a paternal deity may reflect an emotional need for God, it is left to Malin (and therefore the intellect) to make the Christian choice." That Judaism is merely a preparatory stage on the way to Christianity is a proposition that may fairly characterize the traditional Christian viewpoint on Judaism, but it certainly does not correspond to Auden's own position. "To love our neighbor as ourselves . . . [means that] we should have with each person the relationship of one conception of the universe to another conception of the universe, and not to a part of it" (Auden, *A Certain World*, 283).

109. See Hans-Georg Gadamer, *Truth and Method*, trans. Joel Weinsheimer and Donald Marshall (New York: Continuum, 1993), esp. 306–07.

110. See Jürgen Habermas, *The Theory of Communicative Action*, trans. Thomas McCarthy, 2 vols. (Boston: Beacon Press, 1984–1987), *passim*.

111. Boly, "Auden and the Romantic Tradition in *The Age of Anxiety*," 165.

112. Within the context of the Hebrew Bible, lions in the plural are generally associated not with Israel but with its enemies. Thus, for example, Jeremiah proclaims "Israel is a scattered sheep; the lions have driven him away; first the king of Assyria has devoured him; and last this Nebuchadnezzar king of Babylon has broken his bones" (Jer. 50: 17); and Daniel is famously thrown into a "den of lions" (Dan. 8–28). The lion in the singular, by contrast, is sometimes invoked as an image of God, especially in Hosea: "As a young lion to the house of Judah; I will tear and go away" (Hos. 5: 14); "They shall walk after the Lord; he shall roar like a lion" (Hos. 11: 10). And the *Zohar* adapts the image in such a way that Judah is itself the lion (1: 236a).

113. The Hebrew sentence Auden quotes, commonly known as the *Sh'ma'*, is first spoken in Deuteronomy, 6: 4. It is traditionally understood to mean "Hear O Israel: the Lord is our God, the Lord is One." This call thus announces a strict monotheism and provides a guide to understanding the nature of the deity. The same sentence, however, could be understood as "Hear O Israel, the Lord [YHWH, the tetragrammaton] is our God, the Lord is our only God," and in this way it announces, instead, monolatry. It is doubtful that Auden was interested in this rather arcane ambiguity known principally to biblical scholars. Translations in prayer books shy away from the second translation, although it

is conceivable that it was the original sense of the *Sh'ma'*. For a scholarly exposition of the problems of translation surrounding the *Sh'ma'*, which Arendt calls "the very essence of Judaism" in her essay on Walter Benjamin (*Men in Dark Times* [New York: Harcourt Brace Jovanovich, 1983], 164), see Moshe Weinfeld, *Deuteronomy I–XI: A New Translation with Introduction and Commentary* (New York: Doubleday, 1991), 328–57. Weinfeld favors the following translation: "Hear, O Israel! YHWH our God is one YHWH" (330; for four additional translations, see 337; for an analysis of *'echad*, see 331–32). For a recent study of the *Sh'ma'* within the parameters of Jewish tradition, see Norman Lamm, *The Shema: Spirituality and Law in Judaism as Exemplified in the Shema, the Most Important Passage in the Torah* (Philadelphia and Jerusalem: The Jewish Publication Society, 5758 [= 1998 C.E.].

114. In the only section of *Litany and Anthem for S. Matthew's Day* that mentions the messiah, Auden makes the following remarks about history: "It is the particular glory of Matthew that he recognises in Jesus the Messiah foretold by the Prophets, that his witness emphasises the Christ who gives to history its meaning, and warns us most clearly against the idolatrous fancies of the gentiles who would either, like the pagan Greeks regard time as the Evil One or, like the romantic apostates, bow down before the historical process. Let us pray especially therefore at this time to be delivered from all such heresies and follies; from making our society or our age the final revelation of the truth, from justifying present sin as a historical necessity that future good may come. May we worship neither the flux of chance, nor the wheel of fortune, nor the spiral of the zeitgeist, but, following the commandment of Christ, take up our cross of the moment on which alone the past is redeemed and the future is set free" (Auden, *Litany and Anthem for S. Matthew's Day*, third unnumbered page).

115. A long series of critics have deciphered Rosetta's name with reference to the Rosetta stone; see, for example, Callan, "Allegory in Auden's *The Age of Anxiety*," 162; Mendelson, *Later Auden*, 247. If one wants to give her a last name, there is no better candidate than the recognizably Ashkenazi-Jewish name, Stein. Stone is so closely associated with Rosetta that the transformation of this association into a last name is almost irresistible. And when the name (Stone) is then translated into another language (Stein), as befits the Rosetta Stone, the result is a name that fits the Rosetta of the poem.

Chapter 3

1. The persistence of certain motifs in Rosetta's speeches and meditations, like those of the "Moon" and the "One," demonstrate that her final thoughts are not entirely without preparation; but the obscurity of the references through which her character maintains conventional continuity indicates that this continuity is

supposed to be recognizable only on reflection: there is no preparation for the reference to Babylon with which Rosetta begins her account of her distinctness from Emble.

2. See note 98 in the previous chapter for attempts on the part of various critics to account for Rosetta's sudden change. Drawing on a quotation from a source whose appropriateness is questionable given the context—the apostle Paul—Boly emphasizes the surprising and perplexing nature of Rosetta's alteration: "The most puzzling aspect of Rosetta's meditation is the suddenness of its unexpected transformation. She returns, finds Emble asleep on her bed, and in less than Paul's 'twinkling of an eye,' the apocalyptic disclosures begin" (Boly, "Auden and the Romantic Tradition in *The Age of Anxiety*," *Daedalus* III, 3 [summer, 1982]: 165). Delmore Schwartz goes even further; for Schwartz, the suddenness of Rosetta's transformation is the last and best confirmation of the overall characterlessness of all four characters in *The Age of Anxiety*: "The characterization of the four persons is blurred or blotted out again and again when each one makes speeches which cannot be said to be out of character because they have nothing to do with character at all. Just before the end of the poem, for example, Rosetta suddenly turns out to be Jewish. . . . nothing whatever in Rosetta's previous remarks has prepared the reader for this revelation about Rosetta's origin and her views of them" ("Delmore Schwartz on Auden's 'Most Self-Indulgent Book,'" *Partisan Review*, September–October, 1947; reprinted in *W. H. Auden: The Critical Heritage*, 369–70).

3. Hannah Arendt, *The Human Condition* (Chicago: The University of Chicago Press, 1958), 181. Further references to this work are in parentheses in the body of the text.

4. Hannah Arendt, *Rahel Varnhagen: Lebensgeschichte einer deutschen Jüdin aus der Romantik* (Frankfurt am Main: Ullstein, 1975), 203–13: "Aus dem Judentum kommt man nicht heraus."

5. I thank Frederick M. Dolan for calling my attention to the provenance of Arendt's quotation and for his generous and insightful comments on the direction of my argument. There is no place in the Gospels where anything like the words "A child has been born unto us" appears. The closest approximation is this announcement of "glad tidings": "For unto us is born this day in the city of David a Saviour, which is Christ the Lord" (Luke 2:11).

6. Gershom Scholem, *The Messianic Idea in Judaism and Other Essays on Jewish Spirituality*, trans. Michael A. Meyer and Hillel Halkin (New York: Schocken, 1971), 1. Scholem sent Arendt a copy of his " Zum Verständnis der messianischen Idee im Judentum" when it first appeared in the *Eranos Jahrbuch* in 1959 and adds in a letter dated 28 November 1960: "I hope that you will have an opportunity to cite me" (Scholem, *Briefe*, ed. Itta Shedletzky and Thomas Sparr [Munich: Beck, 1994–1999], 2: 75). In the same letter he indicates that a mutual

friend had already received a copy of Arendt's *Vita Activa* (the German title of *The Human Condition*) and that he looks forward to receiving his own copy, which he hopes Arendt will inscribe when she visits Jerusalem to report on the Eichmann trial. The publication of *Eichmann in Jerusalem* led to a famous exchange of letters and was the end of their friendship.

7. In *The Life of the Mind*, Arendt discusses salvation in the context of Virgil's famous nativity hymn in the Fourth Eclogue: "It has long been misunderstood as a prophecy of salvation through a *theos sōtēr*, a savior god, or at least the expression of some pre-Christian yearning. But far from predicting the arrival of a divine child, the poem is an affirmation of the divinity of birth as such; if one wishes to extract a general meaning from it, this could only be the poet's belief that the world's potential salvation lies in the very fact that the human species regenerates itself constantly and forever" (Hannah Arendt, *The Life of the Mind*, ed. Mary McCarthy [New York: Harcourt Brace Jovanovich, 1978], 2: 212).

8. In Heidegger's lectures of the early 1920s he uses the technical term *Ruinanz* where he would later—in *Sein und Zeit* and elsewhere—speak of *Verfallenheit*; see, especially, the concluding section of his 1921–1922 lecture, *Phänomenologische Interpretationen zu Aristoteles: Einführung in die phänomenologische Forschung*, ed. Walter Bröcker and Käte Bröcker-Oltmann, *Gesamtausgabe*, Vol. 61 (Frankfurt am Main: Klostermann, 1985), 130–55. At the opening of the section Heidegger explains his terminological choice: "Ihre Leere [the emptiness of the movement made by factical life] ist ihre Bewegungsmöglichkeit. Damit ist ein Grundsinn der Bewegtheit des faktischen Lebens gewonnen, den wir terminologisch fixieren als *Ruinanz* (ruina—Sturz) [Its emptiness is its possibility of movement. A basic sense of the motility of factical life is thus achieved, which we terminologically call *Ruinanz*]" (130). Heidegger comes close to summarizing the motive of the lecture when he says, "Eine *gegenruinante Bewegtheit* ist die des *philosophischen Interpretationsvollzug* [A motility that runs counter to ruination is that carried out by philosophical interpretation]" (153). Arendt was, of course, present during some of the lectures in which Heidegger presented an existential analysis of "ruination."

9. Benjamin, "Über den Begriff der Geschichte," in *Gesammelte Schriften*, ed. R. Tiedemann and H. Schweppenhäuser (Frankfurt am Main: Suhrkamp, 1977–1985), 2: 697: "eine einzige Katastrophe, die unablässig Trümmer auf Trümmer häuft." In Arendt's essay on Benjamin, she translates *Trümmer* as *ruin*: "The angel of history . . . looks at nothing but the expanse of ruins of the past" (Arendt, *Men in Dark Times* [New York: Harcourt Brace Jovanovich, 1983], 165). In a footnote to his essay on "Walter Benjamin and His Angel," Gershom Scholem criticizes Arendt's refusal to read this passage, and Benjamin's "Theses" as a whole, as admitting of a "dialectically sensible, rationally interpretable process." Scholem asserts, instead, that the vision of the angel of history could indeed be

"sensible in spite of the paradox inherent in it" (Gershom Scholem, *On Jews and Judaism in Crisis: Selected Essays*, ed. Werner J. Danhauser [New York: Schocken, 1976], 234). Despite its brevity and critical tone, Scholem's note indicates the premises of Arendt's reception of Benjamin's "Theses." First, she does not act as an exegete—as if the "Theses" constituted a hidden but nevertheless discoverable program for historiography. And second, she does emphasize the inability of dialectics to make sense after all of the "ruins of the past." Another study might show the way in which images, figures, and tropes from the "Theses" continually intersect with Arendt's own concerns and give rise to some of her characteristic formulations. Implicit in her understanding of the function, but not the meaning, of the "Theses" is the paradoxical proposition that contingency "governs" the structure of the "Theses," just as it "governs" the events of history. And even this "just as" is contingent. For a reading of the "Theses" that is compatible with this understanding, see Timothy Bahti, "Walter Benjamin's Theses 'On the Concept of History,'" in *Allegories of History: Literary Historiography after Hegel* (Baltimore: Johns Hopkins University Press, 1992), 183–203. In the course of reviewing and criticizing various competing attempts to turn the "Theses" into definitive historiographical programs, Bahti insists on the radical contingency at the heart of their ungovernable historical effectivity.

10. For an authoritative treatment of Jewish messianism in the Biblical and early post-Biblical eras, see Joseph Klausner, *The Messianic Idea in Israel, from its Beginning to the Completion of the Mishnah* (London: Allen and Unwin, 1956); see also Jacob Neusner, *Messiah in Context: Israel's History and Destiny in Formative Judaism* (Philadelphia: Fortress, 1984). For a succinct but informative review of Biblical conceptions of the Messiah, see the opening paragraphs of R. J. Zwi Werblowsky, "Messianism," in *Contemporary Jewish Religious Thought*, ed. Arthur Cohen and Paul Mendes-Flohr (New York: Free Press, 1987), 597–602: "This basic stratum of the messianic vision—the end of exile, ingathering of the dispersed, that is, territorial reconcentration of the scattered people regardless of those who think of building Jerusalem in every green and pleasant land, and renewed sovereignty under a Davidic king—thus never lost its primacy and was never spiritualized away" (601).

11. See Arendt, *The Human Condition*, 14–16. This reading sets itself against the prevailing interpretation of current Arendt scholarship in which *The Human Condition* is read as a late and particularly odd or incongruous instance of German Grecophilia—what E. M. Butler calls "the tyranny of Greece over Germany" (E. M. Butler, *The Tyranny of Greece over Germany: A Study of the Influence Exercised by Greek Art and Poetry over the Great German Writers of the Eighteenth, Nineteenth and Twentieth Centuries* [Boston: Beacon Press, 1958]). As Seyla Benhabib notes in *The Reluctant Modernism of Hannah Arendt* (Thousand Oaks, Calif.: Sage Publications, 1996), xxv: "There is by now a standard and

widespread reading of Hannah Arendt's work. Placing *The Human Condition* as the definitive expression of Arendt's political philosophy at the center, this view argues that Hannah Arendt is a political philosopher of nostalgia, an antimodernist lover of the Greek polis." Among the scholarship that most strongly supports this reading, perhaps the best known and most hotly debated, is George Kateb's *Hannah Arendt: Politics, Conscience, Evil* (Oxford: Martin Robertson, 1984). Jürgen Habermas, too, may be understood as deriving his three-pronged critique of Arendt's concept of power from the single thought that "[she] remains bound to the historical and conceptual constellation of Classical Greek philosophy" ("Hannah Arendt's Communications Concept of Power" in *Hannah Arendt: Critical Essays*, ed. Lewis P. Hinchman and Sandra K. Hinchman [Albany, N.Y.: SUNY Press, 1994], 214). Even scholars who seek a more nuanced reading of Arendt's work nevertheless tend to read *The Human Condition* as derivative of a Greek conception of political action. Although Maurizio Passerin d'Entrèves argues that Arendt's work is suspended between two conceptions of action in tension (one of which is decidedly not Greek), he nevertheless sees *The Human Condition* as a work in which Arendt "take[s] the Greek model as her exemplar" (*The Political Philosophy of Hannah Arendt* [London: Routledge, 1994], 92). And although Richard Bernstein seeks to read all Arendt's work through her central concern with what he terms "the Jewish question," he nevertheless concedes that the "prevailing bias among many of Arendt's critics and defenders" who see her politics as "based primarily on her (idealized) account of the Greek *polis*" is "understandable if one focuses primarily on *The Human Condition*" (see *Hannah Arendt and the Jewish Question* [Cambridge, Mass.: MIT Press, 1996], 31). Finally, Jacques Taminiaux—in a clean break with those scholars who read *The Human Condition* as an instance of "Graecomania"—has recently proposed that Rome, and not Greece, serves as Arendt's principal point of orientation (Jacques Taminiaux, "Athens and Rome" in *The Cambridge Companion to Hannah Arendt* ed. Dana Villa [Cambridge: Cambridge University Press, 2000], 165–77). Taminiaux unfortunately misses the messianic dimension of Arendt's text; he does not notice that Arendt turns away from the initial Roman orientation of her account of promising and suddenly shifts her attention to Abraham and therefore to a founding that is always only to come. See page 152 below.

12. Hannah Arendt, *The Origins of Totalitarianism*, rev. ed. (New York: Harcourt Brace Jovanovich, 1979), 74: "The most fateful element in Jewish secularization was that the concept of chosenness was being separated from the Messianic hope, whereas in Jewish religion these two elements were two aspects of God's redemptory plan for mankind. Out of messianic hope grew that inclination toward final solutions of political problems which aimed at nothing less than establishing a paradise on earth. . . . The enthusiastic Jewish intellectual dreaming of the paradise on earth, so certain of freedom from all national ties

and prejudices, was in fact farther removed from political reality than his fathers, who had prayed for the coming of the Messiah and the return of the people to Palestine."

13. The renunciation of any active participation in the building of the messianic kingdom is correlated with what Arendt understands as the withdrawal of the Jewish people from an active role in history from the destruction of the Second Temple until the modern era—with the notable exception of the short period during which Sabbatai Zvi was very widely honored as the messiah who would inaugurate the ingathering of the Jewish people. Arendt's knowledge of the Sabbatian movement and its political repercussion is derived from Scholem's pathbreaking work, *Major Trends in Jewish Mysticism* (New York: Schocken, 1941), the second edition of which she reviewed; see Arendt, "Jewish History, Revised," *Jewish Frontier*, March 1948; reprinted in *The Jew as Pariah: Jewish Identity and Politics in the Modern Age*, ed. and intro. Ron Feldman (New York: Grove Press, 1978), 96–105: "From its beginning, Jewish mysticism had tended toward action and realization; but before ending in utter resignation it attained maximum development in the Sabbatian movement, which, in the new picture given by Scholem, appears as the turning point in Jewish history" (104). As Arendt emphasizes in the conclusion of her review, "the three spiritual trends in modern Jewish history—Khassidism, Reform movement and 'political apocalypse,' i.e. revolutionary utopianism,—which one used to regard as independent if not contradictory tendencies, are found to stem from the same mighty source, from mysticism. The catastrophe of Sabbatai Zvi, after closing one book of Jewish history, becomes the cradle of a new era" (105). For a thoughtful analysis of Arendt's review of Scholem, see Richard Bernstein, *Hannah Arendt and the Jewish Question*, 57–62.

14. See Hermann Cohen, *Die Religion der Vernunft aus den Quellen des Judentums* (Leipzig: Fock, 1919); *Religion of Reason from the Sources of Judaism*, trans. Simon Kaplan (Atlanta, Ga.: Scholars Press, 1995), esp. 236–68: "The Idea of the Messiah and Mankind." Cohen develops similar thoughts in the slightly earlier work, *Deutschtum und Judentum*, according to which German humanism rescues the messianic idea from the Jews, who, having been locked away in ghettoes, naturally understood this idea in a narrow manner—as a liberation from their oppression. Having rediscovered and refined the messianic idea, German humanism gives it back to the Jews, who are then able to return to the prophetic tradition of genuine universalism mediated by an equally genuine particularism; see Cohen, *Deutschtum and Judentum* (1915), reprinted in *Jüdische Schriften*, ed. Bruno Strauß (Berlin: Schwetschke, 1924), 2: 237–301. Cohen's unprecedented prestige in the intellectual world of pre-Nazi Germany gave a strong impetus to the renewal of messianic motifs among a large number of thinkers, writers, and intellectuals, including those, like Martin Buber, Franz Rosenzweig, Gershom

Scholem, and Walter Benjamin, who, each in his own way, strenuously objected to Cohen's combination of Platonism, Kantianism, and rabbinic Judaism—and, after the First World War, to the bellicose nationalism that makes texts like *Deutschtum und Judentum* so unpleasant. For a brilliant representation of Cohen's idea, see Kafka's story, "Ein Bericht an eine Akademie," first published in Martin Buber's journal, *Der Jude*; reprinted in *Gesammelte Schriften in zwölf Bänden*, ed. Hans-Gert Koch (Frankfurt am Main: Fischer, 1994), 1: 234–45. Instead of *Deutschtum und Judentum*, Kafka worries about *Menschentum und Affentum* (humanity and apeness).

15. As Young-Bruehl indicates, Arendt's relationship to this now-famous text of her friend is a long and intimate one: "The last time Walter Benjamin saw Hannah Arendt and Heinrich Blücher, in Marseilles, he entrusted to their care a collection of manuscripts, including the 'Theses on the Philosophy of History' which he hoped they would be able to deliver to the Institute for Social Research in New York. They had the honor of being their friend's messenger. While they waited for their ship in Lisbon, the Blüchers read Benjamin's 'Theses' aloud to each other and to the refugees around them. They discussed and debated the meaning of this moment-to-moment messianic hope" (Young-Bruehl, *Hannah Arendt: For Love of the World* (New Haven: Yale University Press, 1982), 162. Tiedemann and Schweppenhäuser note that Arendt alone possessed a manuscript (as opposed to typescript) version of "Über den Begriff der Geschichte" (*Gesammelte Schriften*, 1: 1253).

Arendt's relationship to Benjamin's life and writing is immensely complex and deserves a lengthy study of its own—one that has unfortunately not yet been written. Even more unfortunate is the misleading set of reflections written by Françoise Meltzer under the title "Walter Benjamin and the Right to Acedia," in *Hot Property: The Stakes and Claims of Literary Originality* (Chicago: University of Chicago Press, 1994), 128–56. Meltzer begins with a rather puzzling invitation to her readers: "Let us see what happens when Hannah Arendt and Theodor Adorno try to present the texts of their dead friend, Walter Benjamin, to an American public in the 1950s" (131). Adorno did not write *Prismen: Kulturkritik und Gesellschaft* (Frankfurt am Main: Suhrkamp, 1955) for an American audience; the English-language volume of Benjamin's work, *Illuminations* (New York: Schocken, 1969) edited and introduced by Arendt, was published in 1969; and Arendt's introductory essay to that volume was first published in 1968—after Benjamin's work had achieved a certain fame, as Arendt's opening reflections note. Meltzer continues her analysis:

> [Celan, Adorno, Arendt, and Benjamin] confront the failure of philosophy in the face of the Holocaust, the way in which they do or do not see language as necessarily collaborative after the Holocaust. The extent to which they participate or not in the reconstitution of a homeland and in the real or imagined parameters of such a home-

land—these all serve to differentiate between political and personal stances, within historical limits. . . . Moreover, if we return to the four names mentioned, there are the specific questions of who survives (Adorno and Arendt do; Benjamin and, ultimately, Celan do not). (163)

Benjamin died in 1940, and to speak of his "confrontation" with anything "in the face of the Holocaust" is to deny the historical reality of the destruction of European Jewry that took place between 1941 and 1945. Benjamin did not survive the Shoah, but Meltzer somehow attributes to him the ability to reflect on language "after the Holocaust"; Celan did in fact survive, yet Meltzer inexplicably denies him his survival. Instead of analyzing Arendt's complicated relationship to Benjamin, which began long before she settled in New York, Meltzer "defends" Benjamin's "Right to Acedia" against what she deems Arendt's "capitalist work ethic" (130). As any reader of "Zur Kritik der Gewalt" knows, Benjamin places no stock in supposed "rights." And every careful reader of Benjamin knows that to ascribe to him talk of rights, including the right to "acedia," so thoroughly misunderstands the underlying movement of his work that it is denied its disruptive force. Françoise Meltzer may want the right to acedia, but Walter Benjamin was the greatest theoretician of the general strike since Rosa Luxemburg.

16. Benjamin, "Über den Begriff der Geschichte," in *Gesammelte Schriften*, 2: 694: "Dann ist uns wie jedem Geschlecht, das vor uns war, eine *schwache* messianische Kraft mitgegeben [Our generation, like every other that has preceded us, is endowed with a *weak* messianic force]."

17. Arendt's messianism has been inconspicuous enough to avoid almost all critical commentary, even among those who discuss her relation to the "Jewish question." Jennifer Ring is something of an exception to the extent that she momentarily explicates Arendt's concept of history with reference to the Messiah (understood as the end of history): "Since Arendt nowhere gives evidence of actually believing in a Messiah, one may wonder how this view of history as having an endpoint, symbolized by the expectation of a Messiah, can possibly be associated with her" (Jennifer Ring, *The Political Consequences of Thinking: Gender and Judaism in the Work of Hannah Arendt* [Albany, N.Y.: SUNY Press, 1997], 269). Ring responds to this question by quoting Amos Funkenstein and summarizing the quotation with the comment "We are reminded that Jewish imagery is simply not as concrete and pictorial, as *visual*, as Christian imagery" (269). Ring gives no indication that the messianic idea in Judaism is enormously complicated and that the question concerning messianism and messianic schemata cannot be reduced to a matter of confessing belief in a Messiah. Arendt, according to Ring, is a "Jewish Soul in a German Scholar" (213), and *The Human Condition* is "another indication of her Jewish soul at work" (259). If it is true that Arendt never articulates any "belief" in the Messiah, it is even more

true that she denies the existence of anything like a "Jewish soul": the *Origins* is, in part, an account of the disaster that attends the identification of individuals with racialized, nationalized, or in any case group-functional "souls."

18. Jean-François Lyotard is one of the few commentators to emphasize the "salvationist" character of Arendt's investigation, but for no particular reason he qualifies the term "salvation" with the term "humanism": "I do not claim that this humanistic, salvationist thinking is Arendt's last word. The text [*The Human Condition*] dates from 1958, ten years after the first American edition of "Die Verborgene Tradition" and seven years after the first American edition of *The Origins of Totalitarianism*—works that include the first meditations on the impossible 'Jewish' condition. This condition, as we know, reserves for God alone the power to forgive, that is, to begin anew, and refuses the futile temptation of a restorative humanism" (Jean-François Lyotard, *Toward the Postmodern*, ed. and trans. Robert Harvey and Mark S. Roberts [Atlantic Highlands, N.J.: Humanities Press, 1995], 153). It is entirely unclear how "we" know any of this: the Jewish condition is, for Lyotard, always a "Jewish" condition, which, apparently, has nothing to do with Jews; even if it did, there is no indication that Lyotard is interested enough in Jewish thought and tradition to consider whether "humanism" is the appropriate term to associate with "salvation." And the off-hand assertion of knowledge—"as we know"—hides what is generally unknown: in this case, the complicated character of Jewish messianism.

19. The most forceful voice of those who wish to separate a genuine messianism rooted in the experience of prophecy from everything having to do with apocalypse is doubtless that of Martin Buber; see, for example, "Prophecy, Apocalyptic, and the Historical Hour," in *On the Bible: Eighteen Studies*, ed. Nahum Glatzer (New York: Schocken, 1982), 172–87. Much of Scholem's energy in his 1959 essay on post-Biblical Jewish messianism is directed at Martin Buber's claim that apocalypticism is a "Persian" rather than an authentically Jewish tradition; see Gershom Scholem, "Toward an Understanding of the Messianic Idea in Judaism," first published (in German) in *Eranos Jahrbuch* 28 (1959): 193–239; translated by Michael Meyer, in *The Messianic Idea in Judaism*, 1–36. Descriptions of the controversy unleashed by Scholem's essay can be found in Joseph Dan, "Gershom Scholem and Jewish Messianism," in *Gershom Scholem: The Man and His Work*, ed. Paul Mendes-Flohr (Albany, N.Y.: SUNY Press, 1994), 73–86; David Biale, *Gershom Scholem: Kabbalah and Counter-History* (Cambridge, Mass.: Harvard University Press, 1979), 148–70. Scholem's conception of the messianic idea in Judaism from the perspective of catastrophe means that, for him, every attempt to dissociate messianism from apocalypticism amounts to its neutralization. It is unfortunate that Scholem's decision to break off all contact with Arendt after the publication of *Eichmann in Jerusalem* made it impossible for them to engage in a debate about this issue:

whether it is possible to develop a messianic idea that, while resolutely opposing any hint of apocalypticism, nevertheless refrains from neutralizing messianism.

20. This might be a place for a fruitful analysis of the relation of Jacques Derrida's work to that of Arendt, both of which develop out of a phenomenological tradition and seek to disclose what constitutively eludes Heidegger's historical reformulation of phenomenological inquiry in terms of "the beginning" and "the other beginning" (the Greeks and the Germans). The motif to which both Arendt and Derrida are drawn is that of the messianic: Derrida under the generalized term "messianicity" (Jacques Derrida, *Specters of Marx: the State of the Debt, the Work of Mourning, and the New International*, trans. Peggy Kamuf [London: Routledge, 1994], see especially, 167–69); and Arendt, under the silent sign of "salvation." Reflections on the necessity of these transformations and silences in the formulation of messianism can be found in Werner Hamacher, "Lingua Amissa: The Messianism of Commodity-Language and Derrida's *Specters of Marx*" in *Ghostly Demarcations: A Symposium on Jacques Derrida's "Specters of Marx"*, ed. Michael Sprinker [London: Verso, 1999], 168–212, especially 205–06.

21. See the final section of Arendt's essay on Benjamin entitled "The Pearl Diver" (*Men in Dark Times*, 193–206). Quotations, Arendt writes, have the task of "interrupting the flow of the presentation with 'transcendent force' . . . and at the same time of concentrating within themselves that which is presented. As to their weight in Benjamin's writings, quotations are comparable only to the very dissimilar Biblical citations which so often replace the immanent consistency of argumentation in medieval treatises" (194). Comparable—and yet dissimilar— to both these procedures is Arendt's own decision to attribute a quotation from Isaiah to the Gospels as she analyzes the interruptive character of action.

22. On the significance of interruption in Benjamin and its relation to his technique of quotation, see Werner Hamacher, "Affirmative, Strike," trans. Dana Hollander, in *Walter Benjamin's Philosophy*, ed. A. Benjamin and P. Osborne (London: Routledge, 1994), 110–38; and Carol Jacobs, *In the Language of Walter Benjamin* (Baltimore: Johns Hopkins University Press, 1999), esp. 91–113 (a chapter entitled "Emergency, Break").

23. When Arendt writes that human beings are "born in order to begin," she is both adopting and adapting a proposition from Augustine's *De civitate Dei* that is as central to her thought as Augustine's extraordinary account of love: "*Amo, volo ut sis* [I love, I will that you be]" (see notes 33 and 40 in Chapter 4). Arendt uses this proposition to close the *Origins*: "But there remains also the truth that every end in history necessarily contains a new beginning; this beginning is the promise, the only 'message' which the end can ever produce. Beginning, before it becomes a historical event, is the supreme capacity of man; politically, it is

identical with man's freedom. *Initium ut esset homo creatus est*—'that a beginning be made man was created' said Augustine. This beginning is guaranteed by each new birth; it is indeed every man" (Arendt, *Origins*, 478–79). Arendt returns to the citation from Augustine (*De civitate Dei*, book 12, ch. 20) earlier in *The Human Condition* (177). And she returns again to this passage as she closes her reflections on willing in her last, incomplete work, *The Life of the Mind*: "The purpose of the creation of man was to make possible a *beginning*: 'That there be a beginning man was created, before whom nobody was'—*Initium . . . ergo ut esset, creatus est homo, ante quem nullus fuit*' " (Arendt, *The Life of the Mind*, 2:217). Auden quotes the same thesis of Augustine in *A Certain World: A Commonplace Book* (London: Faber and Faber, 1982), 243.

24. Arendt elaborates these concerns in "The Concept of History: Ancient and Modern," especially in the subsection entitled "History and Politics" (Hannah Arendt, *Between Past and Future: Eight Exercises in Political Thought*, enlarged ed. [New York: Penguin, 1968], 41–90). For an incisive analysis of Arendt's complicated reflections on the means-end schema, see Dana R. Villa, *Arendt and Heidegger: The Fate of the Political* (Princeton: Princeton University Press, 1996, esp. 197–99.

25. See Martin Heidegger, *Sein und Zeit* (Tübingen: Niemeyer, 1979), 329; see also Heidegger's analysis of Kant's transcendental deduction in the first edition of the *Critique of Pure Reason* in terms of the three temporal "ekstases"—past, present, and future; Heidegger, *Kant und das Problem der Metaphysik* (Frankfurt am Main: Klostermann, 1973), esp. 165–81; § 33.

26. Arendt quotes from Pierre Naville's *La Vie de travail et ses problèmes*: "Le trait principal est son caractère cyclique ou rhymique. Ce caractère est lié à la fois à l'esprit naturel et cosmologique de la journée . . . et au caractère des fonctions physiologique de l'être humain, qu'il a en commun avec les espèces animales supérieures. . . . Il est évident que le travail devait être de prime abord lié à des rhythmes et fonctions naturels [The principal trait is its cyclical or rhythmic character. This character is bound up both with the natural spirit and the cosmology of the day . . . and with the character of the physiological functions of the human being, which it has in common with the other superior animal species. . . . It is clear that labor must be principally bound up with natural rhythms and functions]" (quoted at 98).

27. Arendt does not explicitly cite Wordsworth's famous ode, "Intimations of Immortality from Recollections of Early Childhood" (*Selected Poems and Prefaces*, ed. Jack Stillinger [Boston: Houghton Mifflin, 1965], 186–91); but the specific kind of immortality she attributes to works of art points to a critique of the English romantic enterprise as a whole: it is only the durability of tangible works—and not the subjectivity of the human subject—that, for Arendt, allows for a "premonition of immortality."

28. Hannah Arendt, "What Is Freedom?" (first published as "Freedom and Politics: A Lecture," *Chicago Review* 14 [spring, 1960]: 28–46); heavily revised for *Between Past and Future: Eight Exercises in Political Thought*, enlarged edition (New York: Penguin, 1968), 168.

29. Arthur Schopenhauer, *Die Welt als Wille und Vorstellung*, Vol. 2, § 38; reprinted in *Werke in fünf Bänden*, ed. Ludger Lütkehaus (Zürich: Haffmans, 1994), 2: 517: "Die Devise der Geschichte überhaupt müßte lauten: *Eadem, sed aliter*." For an acute analysis of the mentality that gives rise to historical pessimism, see W. R. Johnson, *Momentary Monsters: Lucan and His Heroes* (Ithaca, N.Y.: Cornell University Press, 1987), 123–34.

30. According to Gesenius, *hevel* (the Hebrew term translated by the Vulgate as *vanitas*) originally meant "vapour, breath" and then was applied to "what is evanescent, unsubstantial, worthless, vanity, as of idols." Gesenius explicates the famous phrase in Ecclesiastes, *havel havelim*, as "the fruitlessness of all human enterprise and endeavour" (William Gesenius, *A Hebrew and English Lexicon of the Old Testament with an Appendix Containing the Biblical Aramaic*, trans. Edward Robinson, rev. ed. Francis Brown, S. R. Driver, and Charles Briggs [Oxford: Clarendon, 1951], 210). Arendt indicates something of her own interest in the biblical meaning of *vanity*: "A life without speech and without action, on the other hand—and this is the only way that a life in earnest has renounced all appearance and all vanity in the biblical sense of the word—is literally dead to the world" (176).

31. See Kant's discussion of freedom at the opening of the Antithesis of the Third Antinomy: "Assume that there is freedom in the transcendental sense, as a special kind of causality in accordance with which the events in the world can have come about, namely a power of absolutely beginning a state and therefore also of absolutely beginning a series of consequences of that state" (*Critique of Pure Reason*, trans. Norman Kemp Smith [New York: St. Martin's, 1965], 409; A 445; B 473). For a further explication of the concept of miracle and its relation to action, beginning, and freedom, see Arendt's essay "What Is Freedom?" in *Between Past and Future*, 168–71. Without thematizing the term, Arendt's analysis of "political life" in the *Origins* takes its orientation from the uneasy miraculousness of individuality: "Since the Greeks, we have known that highly developed political life breeds a deep-rooted suspicion of this private sphere, a deep resentment against the disturbing miracle contained in the fact that each of us is made as he is—single, unique, unchangeable" (Arendt, *Origins*, 301).

32. Those who attribute utopian tendencies to Arendt generally fail to pay attention to her own analysis and genealogy of the term. Utopias, for Arendt, are not the opposite of dystopias: the two have a common root. For a particularly revealing example of an interpretation of Arendt as a utopian thinker that ignores her absolutely clear rejection of utopian visions, see John McGowan,

"Must Politics Be Violent? Arendt's Utopian Vision," in *Hannah Arendt and the Meaning of Politics*, ed. Craig Calhoun and John McGowan (Minneapolis: University of Minnesota Press, 1997), 263–96.

33. See Karl Marx, *A Contribution to the Critique of Political Economy*, trans. S. W. Ryazanskaya (New York: International Publishers, 1976), 20–22.

34. See, for example, the extraordinarily rich and complicated doctrine of powers Friedrich Schelling develops in his *Stuttgarter Privatvorlesung* (1810); reprinted in *Sämtliche Werke*, ed. M. Schröter (Munich: Beck, 1927–1954), 7: 421–84.

35. Although it has never been recognized, the structure of this work resembles nothing so much as Franz Rosenzweig's *Stern der Erlösung*. See Franz Rosenzweig, *Der Stern der Erlösung* (rpt. Frankfurt am Main: Suhrkamp, 1988). By undertaking a revision of Schelling's doctrine of powers, Rosenzweig develops an account of creation (world), revelation (God), and redemption (human being) that bears a striking, and as yet completely unexplored, resemblance to Arendt's account of labor, work, and action. Arendt does not discuss *Der Stern der Erlösung* in *The Human Condition*, but she does use his and Buber's translation of the Hebrew Bible (107).

36. See Plato, *Critias*, in *The Collected Dialogues*, ed. Edith Hamilton and Huntington Cairns (Princeton: Princeton University Press, 1985), 1212–24; 106a–121c. See also Auden's poem "Atlantis" (W. H. Auden, *Collected Poems*, ed. Edward Mendelson [New York: Vintage, 1991], 315–17).

37. For Arendt's brief analysis of Nietzsche's famous account of promising at the opening of *Zur Genealogie der Moral*, see *The Human Condition*, 245.

38. Søren Kierkegaard, *Fear and Trembling—Repetition*, ed. and trans. Howard Hong and Edna Hong (Princeton: Princeton University Press, 1983).

39. See Abraham Geiger, *Urschrift und Übersetzung der Bibel in ihrer Abhängigkeit von inneren Entwicklung des Judentums* (Breslau: Hainauer, 1857); Martin Buber, *Two Types of Faith*, trans. Norman Goldhawk (New York: Collier, 1951), 12. For an exposition of this tradition, see Susannah Heschel, *Abraham Geiger and the Jewish Jesus* (Chicago: University of Chicago Press, 1998); for an abbreviated version, see S. Heschel, "1857: Abraham Geiger's Epoch-Making Book *Urschrift und Übersetzung der Bibel in ihrer Abhängigkeit von inneren Entwicklung des Judentums* Disseminates the Jewish Version of the Origins of Christianity," in *The Yale Companion to Jewish Writing and Thought in German Culture, 1096–1996*, ed. Sander Gilman and Jack Zipes (New Haven: Yale University Press, 1997), 193–98. See also Michael Meyer, "Judaism and Christianity," in *German-Jewish History in Modern Times*, ed. Michael Meyer and Michael Brenner, Vol. 2, *Emancipation and Acculturation, 1780–1871* (New York: Columbia University Press, 1997), 168–98.

40. Arendt's dissertation can be understood in this manner; see *Der Liebesbe-*

griff bei Augustin (Berlin: Springer, 1929); *Love and Saint Augustine*, trans. J. V. Scott and J. C. Stark (Chicago: University of Chicago Press, 1996). Like a number of other Jewish students who gathered around Heidegger's lectures in the 1920s, Arendt was attracted to the study of early Christianity. Arendt notes that when she was fourteen she was drawn to Kierkegaard but was unsure how to understand this attraction: "I had some misgivings only as to how one deals with this if one is Jewish . . . how one proceeds" ("What Remains? The Language Remains" in *Essays in Understanding: 1930–1954*, ed. Jerome Kohn [New York: Harcourt Brace & Company, 1994], 9). There are doubtless many reasons for such attractions, but one of them is worth mentioning in this context. 1919 saw the posthumous publication of Franz Overbeck's *Christentum und Kultur: Gedanken und Anmerkungen zur modernen Theologie*, ed. Carl Albrecht Bernoulli (Basel: Benno Schwabe, 1919)—a powerful work of scholarship that seeks to present Christianity not only as indifferent to "culture" as it was celebrated in late nineteenth-century Germany but as starkly anticultural because of its eschatological character: by outlasting its eschatological expectations, Christianity did away with itself. According to Overbeck, whose close friendship with Nietzsche gave direction to his scholarship and stamped its skepticism, the early Christians lived in anticipation of an absolutely unforeseeable future that would descend on them and destroy the world at any moment; for an exposition of Overbeck's work and influence, see the concluding chapter of Karl Löwith, *From Hegel to Nietzsche*, trans. David E. Green (Garden City, N.Y.: Anchor, 1967), 374–85; for Heidegger's own interest in Overbeck, see Theodore Kisiel, *The Genesis of Heidegger's 'Being and Time'* (Berkeley: University of California Press, 1993), esp. 218; during the winter semester of 1923–1924, just before Arendt began to attend his seminars, Heidegger told several of his students, including Löwith, that his next lecture series would trace the history of Christian theology (see Kisiel, 558–59). Other than Arendt and Löwith, young German-Jewish intellectuals who took a strong interest in Christian thematics include Hans Jonas, who concludes his *Gnostic Religion* by noting that his interest in gnostic texts was incited by certain parallels he perceived between their conception of worldhood and Heidegger's; see *The Gnostic Religion*, 2nd. ed. (Boston: Beacon Press, 1963), 320. Also instructive are the cases of Franz Rosenzweig, who seriously contemplated converting (until he reexperienced a Yom Kippur observation) and who reserves a place for Christianity in *Der Stern der Erlösung* that complements the place of Judaism; Ernst Bloch, whose search for traces of hope led him early in his career to write *Thomas Münzer als Theologe der Revolution* (Munich: Wolff, 1921); Erich Auerbach, who concentrates his considerable critical acumen on the idea of the *figura* among Christian poets, especially Dante (see "Figura," in Auerbach, *Scenes from the Drama of European Literature* [1959, reprint; Minneapolis: University of Minnesota Press, 1984], 11–76); and Walter Benjamin, who draws on

Paul's striking image of mute nature mourning the Fall (Rom. 8) in numerous of his writings, including his early and fundamental "Über Sprache überhaupt und über die Sprache des Menschen," in *Gesammelte Schriften*, 2: 154–56. The attraction of certain German-Jews of the Weimar era to the history and thought of early Christianity can thus be understood as something other than an interest in the Christian religion, for the world of German-Jewry was indeed coming to a swift, unexpected, and violent end.

41. In 1960, Arendt writes a letter to W. H. Auden in which she discusses, quoting the Gospels, those offences that are "clearly beyond the power to forgive: 'woe unto him through whom they come. It were better for him that a millstone were hanged about his neck, and he cast into the sea'—it were better for him that he were never born" (Arendt letter to Auden [14 February 1960; #004864 and #004865]; General Correspondence, 1938–1976, n.d.—Auden, W. H.—1960–1975. Hannah Arendt Papers, Manuscript Division, Library of Congress, Washington D.C. A digitized version of this letter can be found at http://memory.loc.gov/ammem/arendthtml/arendthome.html).

42. Not only does Arendt refer to the legend of the sorcerer's apprentice, she also briefly considers the role of Jesus as "miracle-worker" (247).

43. Arendt prefers to translate the New Testament word *aphienai* by "dismiss" or "release" rather than "forgive" (see her lengthy etymological note, 240).

44. See Overbeck, *Christentum und Kultur*, 72–87.

45. Without further comment, Arendt closes her discussion of "Epictetus and the Omnipotence of the Will" in *The Life of the Mind* with a quotation from Augustine in which an "abyss" is said to lie hidden "in the good heart and in the evil heart" (Arendt, *The Life of the Mind*, 2: 84).

46. For "good deeds," see, for example, *The Human Condition*, 74, 76, and 240; for "good works," see, for example, 75, 76, and 78.

47. André Schwarz-Bart, *Le Dernier des justes* (Paris: Éditions du Seuil, 1959). Schwarz-Bart's novel has been republished numerous times and translated into many languages, including English; see *The Last of the Just*, trans. Stephen Becker (New York: Atheneum Publishers, 1960). For a scholarly presentation of this legend, see Gershom Scholem, "The Tradition of the Thirty-Six Hidden Just Men," in *The Messianic Idea in Judaism*, 251–56.

48. As Arendt notes, "forgiveness is the exact opposite of vengeance" (240); punishment is contrasted with forgiveness as its "alternative" but not its "opposite" (241). Arendt's brief analysis of vengeance dovetails with that of Nietzsche, for whom the release from vengeance is hope itself: "For that the human being be *redeemed from revenge*: that is the bridge to the highest hope and a rainbow after much bad weather" (Friedrich Nietzsche, *Also sprach Zarathustra* in *Sämtliche Werke*, ed. Giorgio Colli and Mazzino Montinari [Berlin: de Gruyter, 1967–1977], 4: 128).

Chapter 4

1. Hannah Arendt, *The Human Condition* (Chicago: The University of Chicago Press, 1958), 175; translation and brackets are Arendt's. Arendt, as she notes a little later (208), is quoting from Dante, *De Monarchia*, i, 13.

2. Here, no less than in her quotation of Isaiah attributed to the Gospels, Arendt extracts the citation from its original context. The specific context of Dante's discussion of agency is the justification of monarchy: "The person who is himself capable of being best disposed to rule is capable of disposing others best. . . . But only the monarch can be best disposed for ruling. . . . It is better for mankind to be ruled by one person than by several [*per unum regi quam per plura*], and thus by a monarch who is the only ruler" (Dante, *Monarchy*, trans. and ed. Prue Shaw [Cambridge: Cambridge University Press, 1996], 22, 25). For Arendt's contrasting discussion of *monarchy* and its oppositional relation to action, see *The Human Condition*, 220–30.

3. Arendt, *The Human Condition*, 190.

4. Dante, *Monarchy*, 22.

5. Arendt, *The Human Condition*, 179.

6. Arendt, *The Human Condition*, 176.

7. Arendt, *The Human Condition*, 178–79.

8. W. H. Auden, *Collected Poems*, ed. Edward Mendelson (New York: Vintage, 1991), 179; hereafter, *CP*.

9. Auden finds a similar insight about the function of poetry in Samuel Johnson: "The only end of writing is to enable readers better to enjoy life or better to endure it" (quoted in W. H. Auden, *A Certain World: A Commonplace Book* [London: Faber and Faber, 1982], 418).

10. Arendt, *The Human Condition*, 175.

11. In Arendt's footnote to this sentence she writes: "This is the meaning of the last sentence of the Dante quotation at the head of this chapter" (Arendt, *The Human Condition*, 208).

12. Hannah Arendt, "Remembering Wystan H. Auden," in *W. H. Auden: A Tribute*, ed. Stephen Spender (New York: Macmillan, 1975), 183.

13. Arendt, "Remembering Wystan H. Auden," 186.

14. All citations of "Canzone" are from *CP*, 330–31. Citations of "Canzone" itself will not be marked, since all can be found on these two pages of *Collected Poems*.

As far as I know, "Canzone" has not been the subject of any sustained interpretive efforts. Blair calls the poem "Perhaps [Auden's] most dazzling piece of virtuosity" but does not proceed beyond a description of its form (John G. Blair, *The Poetic Art of W. H. Auden* [Princeton: Princeton University Press, 1965], 148). Spears also speaks of "Canzone" in terms of "virtuoso style" but, like Blair, does not venture an interpretation of the poem (Monroe Spears, *The Disenchanted Island: The Poetry of W. H. Auden* [Oxford: Oxford University Press, 1963], 199). Fuller notes that Auden's poem is modeled on Dante's poem and indicates that "such formalism . . . was always a natural interest of Auden's"; he proceeds to give a one-sentence reading of the poem: "The canzone seems to be trying to come to terms with the violence of his feelings about Kallman and Kallman's unfaithfulness, and to relate such feelings to the state of the world at large" (John Fuller, *W. H. Auden: A Commentary*, [Princeton: Princeton University Press, 1998], 401). Most recently, Mendelson's wide-ranging study describes the poem as a "grand show of technical bravura" (Edward Mendelson, *Later Auden* [New York: Farrar, Straus and Giroux, 1999], 215). While placing "Canzone" in the context of Auden's contemporaneous poetry, Mendelson faults it for being "histrionic" (217).

15. For a discussion of the dating of Dante's poem, see Robert M. Durling and Ronald L. Martinez, *Time and the Crystal: Studies in Dante's "Rime Petrose"* (Berkeley: University of California Press, 1990), 2; throughout this essay I draw on their text and translation of the poem (282–87) and have profited from their careful and impressive analysis of its formal features (138–64).

16. Much Dante scholarship wrongly refers to "Amor, tu vedi ben" as a double sestina—a designation that fails to recognize the novelty of this poem's unique form; see Durling and Martinez (144–45 and accompanying footnotes). In addition to noting the novel form of "Amor, tu vedi ben," the authors argue that the *rime petrose* as a whole represent a new departure for Dante and mark the major turning point in his development after "Donne ch'avete intelleto d'amore" from his early work, the *Vita nuova*; see their discussion of Dante's innovations in the *petrose* (3–4).

17. See Humphrey Carpenter, *W. H. Auden: A Biography* (Boston: Houghton Mifflin, 1982), 303–17.

18. See John Fuller, *W. H. Auden: A Commentary*, 401.

19. The rhyme scheme of "Canzone" can be diagrammed as follows:

Stanza		Envoi
I.	a b a a c a a d d a e e	a
II.	e a e e b e e c c e d d	e
III.	d e d d a d d b b d c c	d
IV.	c d c c e c c a a c b b	c
V.	b c b b d b b e e b a a	b

20. Plato, *Timaeus*, in *The Collected Dialogues*, ed. Edith Hamilton and Huntington Cairns (Princeton: Princeton University Press, 1985), 1167; 37d.

21. See the authoritative study of Raymond Klibansky, Erwin Panofsky, and

Fritz Saxl *Saturn and Melancholy: Studies in the History of Natural Philosophy, Religion, and Art* (London: Nelson, 1964), esp. 9–10. It may not be completely fanciful to hear in *Autumn* an echo of Auden's own name, which he liked to believe was derived from the Norse name Auðun (see Carpenter, *W. H. Auden: A Biography*, 7–8).

22. Arendt discusses "the strange ambivalence of the English language, in which 'will' as an auxiliary designates the future whereas the verb 'to will' indicates volitions" (Hannah Arendt, *The Life of the Mind*, ed. Mary McCarthy [New York: Harcourt Brace Jovanovich, 1978], 2: 13). Auden plays with this ambiguity in his dedicatory poem to Chester Kallman in *Another Time*, which begins: "Every eye must weep alone / Till I Will be overthrown" (rpt. in W. H. Auden, *The English Auden: Poems, Essays and Dramatic Writings 1927–1939*, ed. E. Mendelson [London: Faber and Faber, 1986], 456).

23. For a contemporaneous and closely connected poetic reflection on willing, see the section of *For the Time Being* entitled "The Four Faculties." Auden presents these faculties as individuals, more exactly, as individual words—Feeling, Intuition, Thought, and Sensation—who relate the story of their origin as distinct agencies or "powers." (Critics have noted that these four faculties seem to correspond to the four principal characters in *The Age of Anxiety*; see note 11 in Chapter 2). This origin lies in the fall into time or, more accurately, the fall into the understanding of time according to which it makes sense to speak of something existing "for the time being." The four faculties speak in preparation for the Annunciation (of the Word), which is to say, the announcement of a promise of forgiveness. Under no (human) condition does this word correspond to experience. The sole experience that escapes all four faculties as long as they remain distinct from one another is what Auden calls "awakening." At the end of "The Four Faculties," Feeling does not so much speak *of* this experience as point toward its paradoxical temporality: "The garden is unchanged, the silence is unbroken / . . . None may awake there but One who shall be woken" (CP, 358–59). To enter into the garden is to enter into a place of responsibility: a place where it is *possible* to respond to a word (or the Word) and not merely to intuit, think, sense, and feel. Auden presents the terms of responsibility in Mary's responses to Gabriel's pronouncements. True responsibility does not consist in speaking back: when Mary speaks, she does not answer Gabriel, and the silence in the garden remains "unbroken." Rather, true responsibility has something to do with the "will." Auden introduces this surprising term in Gabriel's final speech—surprising because it is one of the traditional "faculties" over which philosophers have argued but is not among those delineated in "The Four Faculties." The will is absent from the list of faculties because it cannot be itself as long as the faculties are distinguished from one another; under this (human-all-too-human) condition the will can only

be a capacity to order the world according to an image of itself. Gabriel asks Mary to accept the promise of a willed or willing helplessness:

GABRIEL

Since Adam, being free to choose,
Chose to imagine he was free
To choose his own necessity,
Lost in his freedom, Man pursues
The shadow of his images:
To-day the Unknown seeks the known;
What I am willed to ask, your own
Will has to answer; child, it lies
Within your power of choosing to
Conceive the Child who chooses you. (CP, 361)

In the context of the garden, as the space of true responsibility, the term *will* does not designate an independent faculty of choice through which one demonstrates one's independence and autonomy; on the contrary, it functions as the name for the ability to answer the appeal to be something other than a sovereign subject who structures the world in accordance with its own conceptions.

24. Auden may describe melancholia as "bald" because, according to Kretschmer, the "pyknic" (bald and rotund) physiological type generally develops a "cycloid" (manic-depressive) character; see Ernst Kretschmer, *Physique and Character: An Investigation into the Nature of Constitution and of the Theory of Temperaments*, trans. W. J. H. Sprott, 2nd ed. (New York: Harcourt, Brace & Company, 1925), esp. 122–45. Auden studied Kretschmer's rather loopy theories and, much to the consternation of his colleagues, lectured on "Schizophrenic and Cycloid Poetry" at the University of Michigan in 1942 (see Nicholas Jenkins, "Some Letters from Auden to the Sterns," in W. H. Auden, *"In Solitude for Company": W. H. Auden after 1940*, ed. Katherine Bucknell and Nicholas Jenkins, *Auden Studies*, Vol. 3 [Oxford: Clarendon Press, 1994], 73); see also the notes for a play to be based on Kretschmer's two types of personality (W. H. Auden, *Plays: and Other Dramatic Writings 1928–1938* [with Christopher Isherwood], in *Collected Works*, ed. E. Mendelson [Princeton: Princeton University Press, 1989], 462).

25. W. H. Auden, *The Enchafèd Flood: or the Romantic Iconography of the Sea*, (Charlottesville: University Press of Virginia, 1979), 36; hereafter, EF.

26. See Nietzsche's Postscript to *The Case of Wagner*: "Well, then, you old-seducer, the cynic warns you—*cave canem* [beware of the dog]" (Friedrich Nietzsche, *Der Fall Wagner*, reprinted in *Sämtliche Werke*, ed. Giorgio Colli and Mazzino Montinari [Berlin: de Gruyter, 1967–1977], 6: 44; *The Case of Wagner*, trans. Walter Kaufmann [New York: Vintage, 1974], 184).

27. In *A Certain World* Auden quotes Nietzsche's description of Dante "or the

hyena *poetizing* among the tombs" (Auden, *A Certain World*, 372; the quotation comes from *Götzen-Dämmerung*, reprinted in *Sämtliche Werke*, 6: 111).

28. Arendt, *The Life of the Mind*, 2: 3; hereafter LM.

29. Arendt discusses Auden's poetry and poetological reflections throughout *The Life of the Mind*. She opens the first volume's opening chapter, "Appearance," with one of Auden's late experiments in pure syllabic form derived from the Japanese *haiku*: "Does God ever judge / us by appearances? I / suspect that he does" (LM, 1: 17). Arendt also refers to "Talking to Myself" (LM, 1: 60–61), "As I Walked Out One Evening" (LM, 1: 212–13), "Precious Five" (LM, 2: 92 and 187), and *The Dyer's Hand and Other Essays* (LM, 1: 213).

30. See Arendt's discussion of *otium* and *nec otium* in *The Human Condition*, 14–15 and *The Life of the Mind*, 2: 215. Arendt transposes the problem of action into that of willing. The relation of willing to thinking is coordinated but not identical to the relation of action to contemplation. For an analysis of the transposition of Arendt's schema in *The Human Condition* to her late reflections in *The Life of the Mind*, see Jacques Taminiaux, *La Fille de Thrace et le penseur professionel: Arendt et Heidegger* (Paris: Éditions Payot, 1992).

31. All three chapters of *The Life of the Mind*, including the chapter on willing discussed here, were written near the end of Arendt's life, never completed, and not put into book form at the time of her death.

32. This formulation is derived from three separate but closely related statements Arendt makes in her notes on Willing: "Let us start with Contingency as the price to be paid for freedom" (LM, 2: 134); "[The willing ego] knows very well how to heal itself of the consequences of the priceless and yet highly questionable gift of human freedom, questionable because the fact that the will is free, undetermined and unlimited by either an exterior or an internally given object, does not signify that man qua man enjoys unlimited freedom" (LM, 2: 141); "Of all the philosophers and theologians we have consulted, only Duns Scotus, we found, was ready to pay the price of contingency for the gift of freedom—the mental endowment we have for beginning something new, of which we know that it could just as well not be" (LM, 2: 195).

33. See *Der Liebesbegriff bei Augustin* (Berlin: Springer, 1929); *Love and Saint Augustine*, trans. J. V. Scott and J. C. Stark (Chicago: University of Chicago Press, 1996). As early as 1925 Heidegger writes to Arendt: "Amo heißt volo, ut sis, sagt einmal Augustinus: ich liebe Dich—ich will, daß Du seiest, was Du bist [Amo means volo, ut sis, Augustine once said: I love you—I want that you be what you are]" (Hannah Arendt and Martin Heidegger, *Briefe 1925–1975*, ed. Ursula Ludz [Frankfurt am Main: Klostermann, 1998], 31). Although the *Origins* is an unlikely place to find the same quotation, Arendt nevertheless repeats Augustine's account of love toward the end of her section on imperialism: "This mere existence, that is, all that which is mysteriously given us by birth and which

includes the shape of our bodies and the talents of our minds, can be adequately dealt with only by the unpredictable hazards of friendship and sympathy, or by the great and incalculable grace of love, which says with Augustine, '*volo ut sis* (I want you to be),' without being able to give any particular reason for such supreme and unsurpassable affirmation" (Arendt, *Origins*, 301).

34. Arendt quotes from Nietzsche, *Die fröhliche Wissenschaft*, book 4, § 341; see *Sämtliche Werke*, 3: 570. For a remarkable analysis of Nietzsche's concept of the will, which shows that the will, for Nietzsche, must release itself from willing, see Werner Hamacher, "'Disgregation of the Will': Nietzsche on the Individual and Individuality," in *Premises: Essays on Philosophy and Literature from Kant to Celan*, trans. Peter Fenves (Cambridge, Mass.: Harvard University Press, 1996), 143–80.

35. Nietzsche, *Die fröhliche Wissenschaft*, book 4, § 310: see *Sämtliche Werke*, 3: 546.

36. Elaborating Auden's complex relationship to the iconography of the city would be an enormous project, but would include at the very least an exposition of the idea of Rome, including the city of God, particularly as it is developed by Charles Norris Cochrane (the planned city); Paris as it appears to Baudelaire (the city dynamic); and the "Unreal City" of Eliot's "Wasteland," which resembles nothing so much as the ruins about which Auden writes disapprovingly in his essay "The Fall of Rome" (see W. H. Auden, "The Fall of Rome," "*In Solitude for Company*," 120–37). In *The Enchafèd Flood*, Auden is primarily concerned with two opposing interpretations of the city, both of which Romanticism rejects: the city is both a place of finite repetitions (which connects it through the land to the natural rhythms of the seasons) and a place of infinite possibility (which is tantamount to meaningless freedom and sheer contingency of choice). The sea as counterpart to each of these interpretations is both "infinite novelty" and "stern necessity" (EF, 68–71).

37. This context makes comprehensible not only Auden's decision to include Nietzsche among the figures of Romanticism but also his uneasy allusions to both Nietzsche and Riefenstahl in "Canzone." The first section of *Zur Genealogie der Moral* is an exposition of the conflict between the will-to-will figured in "the blond beast" and the will-not-to-will whose great exemplar is the "semitic priest" (Nietzsche, *Sämtliche Werke*, 5: 266–77). In 1942, the year "Canzone" is written, it is impossible to understand this struggle as merely an ontological one between two opposing "standpoints."

38. See Dorothy Farnan, *Auden in Love*, (New York: Meridian, 1984), 56–57; see also Richard Davenport-Hines, *Auden* (New York: Pantheon, 1996), 214.

39. W. H. Auden, Untitled chapter, *Modern Canterbury Pilgrims*, ed. James Pike (New York: Morehouse-Gorham, 1956), 41. I have altered what I consider to be a typographical error in this quotation: "I was forced to know in person

what it is to feel oneself the prey of demonic powers." It makes little sense to say that I was forced to know a feeling "in person." And as Auden writes in his foreword to the Bloomfield bibliography of his work: "What I need more than a bibliographer is a good textual critic to make the proper emendations, for I am, probably, the worst proofreader in the world" (W. H. Auden, "Foreword," *W. H. Auden: A Bibliography. The Early Years Through 1955*, ed. B. C. Bloomfield [Charlottesville: The University Press of Virginia, 1964], viii). Auden frequently repeated phrases from his poetry in his prose and from his letters in his poetry, and therefore it makes much more sense to read this line by inserting "my own."

40. In *The Life of the Mind*, Arendt identifies the separability or inseparability of love from desire as one locus of the scholastic debates concerning the primacy of will. Arendt describes the transformation of the will into a love emptied of desire as the "highest manifestation" of the willing ego, as she returns, once again, to Augustine's doctrine of love: "'*Amo: Volo ut sis*,' 'I love you; I want you to be'—and not 'I want to have you' or 'I want to rule you'—shows itself capable of the same love with which supposedly God loves men, whom he created only because He willed them to exist and whom He *loves without desiring them*" (LM, 2: 136, emphasis in original). Arendt finds that it is because love without desire is "unthinkable" for Thomas that he maintains the primacy of intellect over will. She continues her reflections: "It is noteworthy to see Dante in full agreement [with Thomas]: 'Hence may be seen how the celestial bliss / Is founded on the act that seeth God, / Not that which loves, which comes after this'" (LM, 2: 122).

41. Auden seems to delight in playing with the various connotative possibilities that accrue to a word, and *noise* is a case in point. In *A Certain World*, Auden recounts the following tale: "The story goes that during World War I a Guards Officer was on leave. 'Do tell us,' said his clubmates, 'what is war like?' 'Awful!' he replied. 'The noise! And the *people*!'" (Auden, *A Certain World*, 383). For other appearances of the word *noise*, see, among many other examples, the poems "In Memory of Sigmund Freud": "little noises we dared not laugh at" (CP, 273); "In Sickness and in Health": "Dear, all benevolence of fingering lips / That does not ask forgiveness is a noise" (CP, 317); "Their Lonely Betters": "We, too, make noises when we laugh or weep: / Words are for those with promises to keep" (CP, 583); and "Homage to Clio": "forgive our noises" (CP, 613).

42. "Canzone" was written one month after he began his closet drama, *The Sea and the Mirror*: according to Auden's annotation, *The Sea and the Mirror* was begun in August 1942 (CP, 445); "Canzone" was written in September 1942 (CP, 331).

43. This last characterization, "hot rampageous horses of my will," clearly alludes to Socrates' palinode in *The Phaedrus* (in Plato, *The Collected Dialogues*, ed. Edith Hamilton and Huntington Cairns [Princeton: Princeton University Press, 1985], esp. 499–500; 253b–254b); for an account of "the dark horse" Socrates

describes, see Herman Sinaiko, *Love, Knowledge and Discourse in Plato: Dialogue and Dialectic in "Phaedrus," "Republic," "Parmenides"* (Chicago: University of Chicago Press, 1965), 83–96. Auden, in contrast to Socrates, speaks of at least *two* unruly horses. For Auden, the phenomenology of love that Plato develops with reference to the image of the two-horse chariot does not hold, and this stanza of "Canzone" gives an indication why: Socrates is concerned only with the experiences of the lover and with those of the beloved in turn, not with the "lively traffic" between them; once this traffic is taken into consideration, Plato's image must make room for the multiplication of unruly horses, each of which is generated by a particular circumstance in the lovers' relationship to each other and none of which can be integrated into a project whose end is known—or knowledge pure and simple.

44. Auden's innovation goes unremarked by any of Auden's readers, including Hollander, who attributes the form—with Auden's alteration—to Dante (John Hollander, *Rhyme's Reason: A Guide to English Verse* [New Haven: Yale University Press, 1989], 59–61). Ashbery's "Canzone" and Merrill's "Samos" also follow Auden's lead. See, respectively, John Ashbery, *The Mooring of Starting Out* (Hopewell, N.J.: Ecco Press, 1997), 31–33; and James Merrill, *Scripts for the Pageant* (New York: Atheneum, 1980), 87–88.

Conclusion

1. W. H. Auden, "Thinking What We Are Doing," *Encounter* 12 (June, 1959): 72.

2. Auden, "Thinking What We Are Doing," 72.

3. Hannah Arendt, *The Human Condition* (Chicago: University of Chicago Press, 1958), 240.

4. W. H. Auden, *The Age of Anxiety*, reprinted in *Collected Poems*, ed. Edward Mendelson (New York: Vintage, 1991), 530; hereafter cited in parentheses in the text.

5. Wendy Doniger, *Other People's Myths* (Chicago: University of Chicago Press, 1995), 52; emphasis in original.

6. Hannah Arendt, *The Origins of Totalitarianism*, rev. ed. (New York: Harcourt Brace Jovanovich, 1979), 438.

7. Arendt, *Origins*, 434.

8. Arendt, *Origins*, 434–35.

9. Walter Benjamin, *Gesammelte Schriften*, ed. R. Tiedemann and H. Schweppenhäuser (Frankfurt am Main: Suhrkamp, 1977–1985), 1: 695: "Nur *dem* Geschichtsschreiber wohnt die Gabe bei, im Vergangenen den Funken der Hoffnung anzufachen, der davon durchdrungen ist: auch die Toten werden vor dem Feind, wenn er siegt, nicht sicher sein. Und dieser Feind hat zu siegen nicht

aufgehört"; *Illuminations*, intro. Hannah Arendt, trans. Harry Zohn (New York: Schocken, 1985), 255; emphasis in the English translation published under Arendt's approval.

10. Arendt, *The Human Condition*, 220.

11. "Totalitarian solutions may well survive the fall of totalitarian regimes in the form of strong temptations which will come up whenever it seems impossible to alleviate political, social, or economic misery in a manner worthy of man" (Arendt, *Origins*, 459).

12. See Immanuel Kant, *Critique of Practical Reason*, reprinted in *Gesammelte Schriften*, ed. Königlich Preußischen [later, deutschen] Akademie der Wissenschaften (Berlin: Reimer; later, De Gruyter; 1900–), 5: 86: "*Duty!* You sublime great name that embraces nothing charming or insinuating but requires submission and yet seeks not to move the will by threatening aught that would arouse natural aversion or terror, but only holds forth a law which of itself finds entrance into the mind and yet gains reverence against my will (though not always obedience) before whom all inclinations are silenced."

13. Hannah Arendt, *The Life of the Mind*, ed. Mary McCarthy (New York: Harcourt Brace Jovanovich, 1978), 2: 92. The poem from which Arendt quotes is "Precious Five," in *Collected Poems*, 591 (Arendt preserves Auden's emphasis).

14. Arendt, "Remembering Wystan H. Auden," 186. In *The Life of the Poet: Beginning and Ending Poetic Careers* (Chicago: The University of Chicago Press, 1981), Lawrence Lipking also discusses Auden's great elegy in terms of praise: "The way to freedom is praising: to perceive the tragedies of an era or the frailties of a man with a clarity that conceals nothing yet indomitably sings" (160).

15. Auden, *The Dyer's Hand and Other Essays* (New York: Vintage, 1968), 60. In a letter to Stephen Spender Auden identifies another "object" of praise: "Whatever else it may or may not be, I want every poem I write to be a hymn in praise of the English language" (Humphrey Carpenter, *W. H. Auden: A Biography* [Boston: Houghton Mifflin, 1981], 419).

16. W. H. Auden, *Litany and Anthem for S. Matthew's Day*, written for the Church of S. Matthew, Northampton, for the Dedication and Patronal Festival, 21 September 1946, last unnumbered page.

17. W. H. Auden, *Epistle to a Godson and Other Poems* (New York: Random House, 1969), 62. See note 103 in Chapter 2 for a discussion of the different variants of this poem.

18. Auden, *Epistle to a Godson*, 62.

19. See Desiderius Erasmus, *The Praise of Folly*, trans. Clarence Miller (New Haven: Yale University Press, 1979). Scholars have broadly examined the poetry of praise—encomium, panegyric, and epideictic—from antiquity to the enlightenment era: for an examination of the function of praise poetry in eighteenth-century England, see J. T. Rowland, *Faint Praise and Civil Leer: The "Decline" of*

Eighteenth-Century Panegyric (Newark, Del.: University of Delaware Press, 1994; for a lucid exposition of praise and blame poetry in antiquity, see W. R. Johnson, *The Idea of Lyric* (Berkeley: University of California Press, 1982), 24–77. Johnson's analysis of Simonides is especially illuminating in the context of Auden's praise poetry: "Neither angels nor beasts, we have this ordinary human life, in all its bafflements, confusions, weaknesses; and it is enough. . . . It is a message of guarded hope" (*The Idea of the Lyric*, 57). To my knowledge there is no large-scale study of the praise poetry of literary modernity. As noted above, Arendt aligns Auden with Mandelstam and especially with Rilke, who understood the task of poetry entirely in terms of praise; see especially the ninth Duineser Elegie, in *Sämtliche Werke*, ed. Ruth Sieber-Rilke et al. (Frankfurt am Main: Insel, 1987), 1: 717–20: "Preise dem Engel die Welt [Praise the world to the angel]" (719). The absence of a significant body of scholarship on praise in modern poetry and indeed the general absence of praise poetry in modernity (Robert Hass's volume *Praise* [New York: Ecco Press, 1979] is a notable exception) may indicate something about modernity itself—that its poets have not yet learned what Auden hopes the poetic voice can accomplish: "In the prison of his days / Teach the free man how to praise."

20. Orlan Fox attests that Auden's favorite from among his own poems was "In Praise of Limestone" (see Orlan Fox, "Friday Nights" in *W. H. Auden: A Tribute*, ed. Stephen Spender [New York: Macmillan, 1975], 174).

21. Many critics have written thoughtful and illuminating essays on "In Praise of Limestone." Certainly among the best of these studies is the short essay by Lawrence Lipking, "Faults," which appears as part of a "Symposium" on the poem in *"In Solitude for Company": W. H. Auden After 1940*, ed. Katherine Bucknell and Nicholas Jenkins, *Auden Studies*, Vol. 3 (Oxford: Clarendon Press, 1994) 263–71. See also Anthony Hecht's appreciative and lengthy studies in *The Hidden Law: The Poetry of W. H. Auden* (Cambridge, Mass.: Harvard University Press, 1993), 304–10 and *Obbligati: Essays in Criticism* (New York: Atheneum, 1986), 27–50; Lucy McDiarmid, *Auden's Apologies for Poetry* (Princeton: Princeton University Press, 1990), 134–37; and Edward Mendelson, *Later Auden* (New York: Farrar, Straus and Giroux, 1999), 290–97.

22. "It was still the same spirit and the same game which made Goebbels, long before the eventual defeat of Nazi Germany, announce with obvious delight that the Nazis, in case of defeat, would know how to slam the door behind them and not be forgotten for centuries" (Arendt, *Origins*, 332).

23. At the very end of *The Concept of Anxiety*, in the penultimate footnote, Kierkegaard indicates the relation of anxiety to homesickness by way of the following quotation from Johann Georg Hamann: "Diese Angst in der Welt ist aber der einzige Beweis unserer Heterogeneität. Denn fehlte uns nicht, so würden wir es nicht besser machen als die Heiden und Transcendental-Philosophen,

die von Gott nichts wissen und in die liebe Natur sich wie die Narren vergaffen; kein Heimweh würde uns anwandeln [However, this anxiety in the world is the only proof of our heterogeneity. If we lacked nothing, we would do no better than the pagans and the transcendental philosophers, who know nothing of God and like fools fall in love with lovely nature, and no homesickness would come over us]" (quoted from J. G. Hamann, *Schriften*, ed. Friedrich Roth [Berlin: Reimer, 1821–1843], 6: 194; *The Concept of Anxiety*, ed. and trans. Reidar Thomte [Princeton: Princeton University Press, 1980], 162).

24. Auden, "In Praise of Limestone," in *Selected Poems* (New York: Vintage, 1979), 185; for the version in *Collected Poems*, Auden changed this line to: "the flirtatious male who lounges / Against a rock in the sunlight" (540).

25. Arendt, *The Human Condition*, 183.

26. For a beautiful study of the frailty and faults in which freedom is born and their relation to poetic creation, see W. R. Johnson, *Horace and the Dialectic of Freedom: Readings in Epistles 1* (Ithaca, N.Y.: Cornell University Press, 1993). As Lipking notes, Auden acknowledges Horace as his tutor in both "The Horatians," and "A Thanksgiving" (see Lipking, "Faults," in *"In Solitude for Company": W. H. Auden after 1940*, ed. Katherine Bucknell and Nicholas Jenkins, 266).

27. As Arendt writes in her preface to the first edition of the *Origins*: "This book has been written against a background of both reckless optimism and reckless despair. It holds that Progress and Doom are two sides of the same medal; that both are articles of superstition, not of faith" (Arendt, *Origins*, vii).

Bibliography

Works by Arendt

Between Friends: The Correspondence of Hannah Arendt and Mary McCarthy: 1949–1975, ed. and intro. C. Brightman. New York: Harcourt Brace & Company, 1995.

Between Past and Future: Eight Exercises in Political Thought, enlarged ed. New York: Penguin, 1977.

Eichmann in Jerusalem: A Report on the Banality of Evil, rev. ed. New York: Penguin, 1977.

Essays in Understanding: 1930–1954, ed. Jerome Kohn. New York: Harcourt Brace & Company, 1994.

Hannah Arendt and Kurt Blumenfeld, *". . . In keinem Besitz verwurzelt": Die Korrespondenz*, ed. Ingeborg Nordmann and Iris Pilling. Hamburg: Rotbuch, 1995.

Hannah Arendt and Martin Heidegger: Briefe 1925–1975, ed. Ursula Ludz. Frankfurt am Main: Klostermann, 1998.

Hannah Arendt, Karl Jaspers: Briefwechsel 1926–1969, hrsg. L. Kohler and H. Saner. Munich: Piper, 1985.

Hannah Arendt, Karl Jaspers: Correspondence 1926–1969, ed. Lotte Kohler and Hans Saner, trans. Robert and Rita Kimber. New York: Harcourt Brace Jovanovich, 1992.

The Human Condition. Chicago: University of Chicago Press, 1958.

The Jew as Pariah: Jewish Identity and Politics in the Modern Age, ed. and intro. R. Feldman. New York: Grove Press, 1978.

"Kultur und Politik," *Merkur* 12, 12 (1958): 1122–45.

Lectures on Kant's Political Philosophy, ed. R. Beiner. Chicago: University of Chicago Press, 1982.

Letter to Auden (14 February 1960; #004864 and #004865); General Correspondence, 1938–1976, n.d.—Auden, W. H.—1960–1975. Hannah Arendt Papers,

Manuscript Division, Library of Congress, Washington, D.C. A digitized version of this letter can be found at http://memory.loc.gov/ammem/arendthtml/arendthome.html.

Letter to Auden (15 June 1971; #004888); General Correspondence, 1938–1976, n.d.—Auden, W. H.—1960–1975 (see above).

Der Liebesbegriff bei Augustin. Berlin: Springer, 1929.

The Life of the Mind, ed. M. McCarthy. New York: Harcourt Brace Jovanovich, 1978.

Love and Saint Augustine, trans. J. V. Scott and J. C. Stark. Chicago: University of Chicago Press, 1996.

Men in Dark Times. New York: Harcourt, Brace & World, 1968.

On Revolution. New York: Penguin, 1963.

The Origins of Totalitarianism, rev. ed. New York: Harcourt Brace Jovanovich, 1979.

Rahel Varnhagen: Lebensgeschichte einer deutschen Jüdin aus der Romantik. Frankfurt am Main: Ullstein, 1975.

Rahel Varnhagen: The Life of a Jewess, ed. L. Weissberg, trans. R. and C. Winston. Baltimore: The Johns Hopkins University Press, 1997.

"Remembering Wystan H. Auden," in *W. H. Auden: A Tribute*, ed. Stephen Spender (see below), 181–87.

"Thinking and Moral Considerations: A Lecture." *Social Research* 38, 3 (Fall, 1971), 417–46; reprinted in *For W. H. Auden: February 21, 1972*, eds. Peter H. Salus and Paul B. Taylor (see below), 3–32.

Von der Menschlichkeit in finsteren Zeiten: Rede über Lessing. Munich: Piper, 1960.

Works by Auden

A Certain World: A Commonplace Book. London: Faber and Faber, 1982.

Collected Poems, ed. E. Mendelson. New York: Vintage, 1991.

The Double Man. New York: Random House, 1941.

The Dyer's Hand and Other Essays. New York: Vintage, 1968.

The Enchaféd Flood: or the Romantic Iconography of the Sea. Charlottesville, Va.: University Press of Virginia, 1979.

The English Auden: Poems, Essays and Dramatic Writings 1927–1939, ed. E. Mendelson. London: Faber and Faber, 1986.

Epistle to a Godson and Other Poems. New York: Random House, 1969.

"The Fall of Rome," in *"In Solitude for Company": W. H. Auden after 1940*, ed. K. Bucknell and N. Jenkins (see below), 120–37.

"The Fallen City," *Encounter* 13, 5 (November, 1959), 21–31.

"Foreword." *W. H. Auden: A Bibliography*, ed. B. C. Bloomfield (see below), vii–ix.

Forewords and Afterwords. New York: Vintage, 1989.

Journey to a War (with Christopher Isherwood). New York: Paragon House, 1990.

"K's Quest," in *The Kafka Problem*, ed. A. Flores (see below), 55–60.

"Lament for a Lawgiver," *Horizon* 17, 99 (March, 1948): 161–63.

Lectures on Shakespeare, ed. Arthur Kirsch. Princeton: Princeton University Press, 2000.

Letter to Arendt (5 July 1973; #004858); General Correspondence, 1938–1976, n.d. Auden, W. H.—1960–1975. Hannah Arendt Papers, Manuscript Division, Library of Congress, Washington D.C. A digitized version of this letter can be found at http://memory.loc.gov/ammem/arendthtml/arendthome.html.

Letters from Iceland (with Louis MacNeice). New York: Paragon House, 1990.

Litany and Anthem for S. Matthew's Day, written for the Church of S. Matthew, Northampton, for the Dedication and Patronal Festival, 21 September 1946. Northampton: Stanton and Son, 1946.

"Nature, History and Poetry," *Thought* 15, 98 (September, 1950): 412–22.

The Platonic Blow. New York: Fuck You Press, 1965.

Plays: and Other Dramatic Writings by W. H. Auden 1928–1938 (with Christopher Isherwood). A volume of *Collected Works*, ed. E. Mendelson. Princeton: Princeton University Press, 1989.

Prose: and Travel Books in Prose and Verse, Vol. 1. A volume of *Collected Works*, ed. E. Mendelson. Princeton: Princeton University Press, 1996.

Secondary Worlds. London: Faber and Faber, 1968.

Selected Poems, ed. E. Mendelson. New York: Vintage, 1979.

"Thinking What We are Doing," *Encounter* 12 (June, 1959): 72–76.

Untitled chapter, *Modern Canterbury Pilgrims*, ed. James Pike. New York: Morehouse-Gorham, 1956, 32–43.

Das Zeitalter der Angst, trans. Kurt Heinrich Hansen, intro. Gottfried Benn. Wiesbaden: Bechtold & Co., 1954.

Bloomfield, B. C. *W. H. Auden: A Bibliography. The Early Years through 1955*. Charlottesville, Va.: The University Press of Virginia, 1964.

Bloomfield, B. C., and Edward Mendelson. *W. H. Auden: A Bibliography 1924–1969*. Charlottesville, Va.: The University Press of Virginia, 1972.

General References

Adorno, Theodor W. *Prismen: Kulturkritik und Gesellschaft*. Frankfurt am Main: Suhrkamp, 1955.

———. *Prisms*, trans. Samuel and Shierry Weber. Cambridge, Mass.: MIT Press, 1986.

Agamben, Giorgio. *Homo Sacer: Sovereign Power and Bare Life*, trans. Daniel Heller-Roazen. Stanford: Stanford University Press, 1998.

The Anatomy of God, trans. Roy Rosenberg. New York: Ktav Publishing House, 1973.

Anders, Günter. *Mensch ohne Welt: Schriften zur Kunst und Literatur*. Munich: Beck, 1993.

Aristotle. *Politics*, trans. Ernest Barker. Oxford: Clarendon Press, 1950.

——. *The Nichomachean Ethics*, trans. David Ross. Oxford: Oxford University Press, 1980.

Aschheim, Steven E. *Scholem, Arendt, Klemperer: Intimate Chronicles in Turbulent Times*. Bloomington: Indiana University Press, 2001.

Ashbery, John. *The Mooring of Starting Out*. Hopewell, N.J.: Ecco Press, 1997.

Auerbach, Erich. *Scenes from the Drama of European Literature*, 1959, reprint. Minneapolis: University of Minnesota Press, 1984.

Bahlke, George. *The Later Auden: From "New Year Letter" to "About the House."* New Brunswick, N.J.: Rutgers University Press, 1970.

Bahti, Timothy. *Allegories of History: Literary Historiography after Hegel*. Baltimore: Johns Hopkins University Press, 1992.

Barrett, William. *What Is Existentialism?* New York: Partisan Review, 1947.

Beach, Joseph Warren. *The Making of the Auden Canon*. Minneapolis: University of Minnesota Press, 1957.

Bell, Kathleen. "Introduction to 'A Change of Heart: Six Letters from Auden to Professor and Mrs. E. R. Dodds Written at the Beginning of World War II,'" in *W. H. Auden: "The Map of All My Youth": Early Works, Friends and Influences*," ed. Katherine Bucknell and Nicholas Jenkins (see below), 97–98.

Benhabib, Seyla. *The Reluctant Modernism of Hannah Arendt*. Thousand Oaks, Calif.: Sage Publications, 1996.

Benjamin, Andrew, and Peter Osborne (eds.). *Walter Benjamin's Philosophy*. London: Routledge, 1994.

Benjamin, Walter. *Gesammelte Schriften*, ed. R. Tiedemann and H. Schweppenhäuser. Frankfurt am Main: Suhrkamp, 1977–1985.

——. *Illuminations*, ed. and intro. Hannah Arendt, trans. Harry Zohn. New York: Schocken, 1985.

——. *Selected Writings*, ed. M. Bullock and M. Jennings. Cambridge, Mass.: Harvard University Press, 1996.

Berger, Gaston. *Existentialism and Literature in Action*. Buffalo: University of Buffalo, 1948.

Bernstein, Richard. *Hannah Arendt and the Jewish Question*. Cambridge, Mass.: MIT Press, 1996.

Biale, David. *Gershom Scholem: Kabbalah and Counter-History*. Cambridge, Mass.: Harvard University Press, 1979.

Blair, John G. *The Poetic Art of W. H. Auden*. Princeton: Princeton University Press, 1965.

Bloch, Ernst. *Thomas Münzer als Theologe der Revolution*. Munich: Wolff, 1921.

Bold, Alan (ed.). *W. H. Auden: The Far Interior*. London: Vision Press, 1985.

Boly, John. "Auden and the Romantic Tradition in *The Age of Anxiety*," *Daedalus* 111, 3 (summer, 1982): 149–71.

Bowen, Christopher L. Letter to Auden (28 March 1964; #004853); General Correspondence, 1938–1976, n.d.—Auden, W. H.—1960–1975. Hannah Arendt Papers, Manuscript Division, Library of Congress, Washington, D.C. A digitized version of this letter can be found at http://memory.loc.gov/ammem/arendthtml/arendthome.html.

Brooke-Rose, Christine. "Notes on the Metre of Auden's 'Age of Anxiety,'" *Essays in Criticism* 13, 3 (July, 1963): 253–64.

Brooks, Cleanth. *The Well Wrought Urn: Studies in the Structure of Poetry*. New York: Harcourt, Brace & World, 1947.

———. *Modern Poetry and the Tradition*. Chapel Hill, N.C.: University of North Carolina Press, 1939.

Buber, Martin. *On the Bible: Eighteen Studies*, ed. Nahum Glatzer. New York: Schocken, 1982.

———. *Two Types of Faith*, trans. Norman Goldhawk. New York: Collier, 1951.

Buchdahl, Gerd. "Comments on 'Newton's Achievement in Dynamics,'" in *The Annus Mirabilis of Sir Isaac Newton*, ed. Robert Palter (see below), 136–42.

Bucknell, Katherine and Nicholas Jenkins (eds.). *"In Solitude for Company": W. H. Auden after 1940*, Vol. 3. *Auden Studies*. Oxford: Clarendon Press, 1994.

———. (eds.). *W. H. Auden: "The Language of Learning and the Language of Love": Uncollected Writing, New Interpretations*, Vol. 2. *Auden Studies*. Oxford: Clarendon Press, 1994.

———. (eds.). *W. H. Auden: "The Map of All My Youth": Early Works, Friends and Influences*, Vol. 1. *Auden Studies*. Oxford: Clarendon Press, 1990.

Burke, Edmund. *A Philosophical Enquiry into the Origin of Our Ideas of the Sublime and the Beautiful*, ed. James Boulton. Notre Dame and London: University of Notre Dame Press, 1968.

Butler, E. M. *The Tyranny of Greece over Germany: A Study of the Influence Exercised by Greek Art and Poetry over the Great German Writers of the Eighteenth, Nineteenth and Twentieth Centuries*. Boston: Beacon Press, 1958.

Calhoun, Craig, and John McGowan (eds.). *Hannah Arendt and the Meaning of Politics*. Minneapolis: University of Minnesota Press, 1997.

Callan, Edward. "Allegory in Auden's *The Age of Anxiety*," *Twentieth Century Literature* 10, 4 (January, 1965): 155–65.

———. *Auden: A Carnival of Intellect*. Oxford: Oxford University Press, 1983.

Canovan, Margaret. *Hannah Arendt: A Reinterpretation of Her Political Thought.* Cambridge: Cambridge University Press, 1992.

Carpenter, Humphrey. *W. H. Auden: A Biography.* Boston: Houghton Mifflin, 1981.

Cohen, Arthur, and Paul Mendes-Flohr (eds.). *Contemporary Jewish Religious Thought.* New York: Free Press, 1987.

Cohen, Hermann. *Jüdische Schriften,* ed. Bruno Strauß. Berlin: Schwetschke, 1924.

———. *Die Religion der Vernunft aus den Quellen des Judentums.* Leipzig: Fock, 1919.

———. *Religion of Reason from the Sources of Judaism,* trans. Simon Kaplan. Atlanta, Ga.: Scholars Press, 1995.

Dan, Joseph. "Gershom Scholem and Jewish Messianism," in *Gershom Scholem: The Man and His Work,* ed. Paul Mendes-Flohr (see below), 73–86.

Dante Alighieri, *The Divine Comedy,* ed. and trans. Robert M. Durling. Vol 1. *Inferno.* New York and Oxford: Oxford University Press, 1996.

Dante. *Divina Commedia,* trans. Charles Singleton. Princeton: Princeton University Press, 1970–1975.

———. *Monarchy,* trans. and ed. Prue Shaw. Cambridge: Cambridge University Press, 1996.

Davenport-Hines, Richard. *Auden.* New York: Pantheon, 1996.

Deleuze, Gilles. *Proust et les signes.* Paris: Presses Universitaires de France, 1964.

d'Entrèves, Maurizio Passerin. *The Political Philosophy of Hannah Arendt.* London: Routledge, 1994.

Derrida, Jacques. *Specters of Marx: The State of the Debt, the Work of Mourning, and the New International,* trans. Peggy Kamuf. London: Routledge, 1994.

De Ruggiero, Guido. *Existentialism: Disintegration of Man's Soul.* New York: Social Science Publishers, 1948.

Diels, Hermann. *Die Fragmente der Vorsokratiker,* 4th ed. Berlin: Weidmann, 1922.

Disch, Lisa. *Hannah Arendt and the Limits of Philosophy.* Ithaca, N.Y.: Cornell University Press, 1994.

Doniger, Wendy. *Dreams, Illusions and Other Realities.* Chicago: University of Chicago Press, 1984.

———. *Other People's Myths.* Chicago: University of Chicago Press, 1995.

Durling, Robert, and Ronald Martinez. *Time and the Crystal: Studies in Dante's "Rime Petrose."* Berkeley: University of California Press, 1990.

Eliot, T. S. *The Complete Poems and Plays.* London: Faber and Faber, 1969.

Empson, William. *Some Versions of Pastoral.* New York: New Directions, 1974.

Erasmus, Desiderius. *The Praise of Folly,* trans. Clarence Miller. New Haven: Yale University Press, 1979.

Ettinger, Elzbieta. *Hannah Arendt—Martin Heidegger.* New Haven: Yale University Press, 1995.

Farnan, Dorothy. *Auden in Love.* New York: Meridian, 1984.

Fenves, Peter. *"Chatter": Language and History in Kierkegaard.* Stanford: Stanford University Press, 1993.

———. "Hölderlin," in *Encyclopedia of Aesthetics,* ed. Michael Kelly, 2: 415–22. New York: Oxford University Press, 1998.

———. *A Peculiar Fate: Metaphysics and World-History in Kant.* Ithaca, N.Y.: Cornell University Press, 1991.

———. "Politics of Friendship—Once Again," *Eighteenth Century Studies* 32, 2 (winter, 1998–1999): 133–55.

Fioretos, Aris. *Word Traces: The Poetry of Paul Celan.* Baltimore: Johns Hopkins University Press, 1994.

Flores, Angel (ed.). *The Kafka Problem.* New York: Gordian Press, 1975.

Fox, Orlan. "Friday Nights," in *W. H. Auden: A Tribute,* ed. Stephen Spender (see below), 173–81.

Fremantle, Anne. "Reality and Religion," in *W. H. Auden: A Tribute,* ed. Stephen Spender (see below), 79–92.

Fuller, John. *W. H. Auden: A Commentary.* Princeton: Princeton University Press, 1998.

Gadamer, Hans-Georg. *Truth and Method,* trans. Joel Weinsheimer and Donald Marshall. New York: Continuum, 1993.

Geiger, Abraham. *Urschrift und Übersetzung der Bibel in ihrer Abhängigkeit von inneren Entwicklung des Judentums.* Breslau: Hainauer, 1857.

Gesenius, William. *A Hebrew and English Lexicon of the Old Testament with an Appendix Containing the Biblical Aramaic,* trans. Edward Robinson, rev. ed. Francis Brown, S. R. Driver, and Charles Briggs. Oxford: Clarendon, 1951.

Gilman, Sander, and Jack Zipes (eds.). *The Yale Companion to Jewish Writing and Thought in German Culture, 1096–1996.* New Haven: Yale University Press, 1997.

Glatzer, Nahum. "Remnant of Israel," in *Contemporary Jewish Religious Thought,* ed. Arthur Cohen and Paul Mendes-Flohr (see above), 779–83.

Goethe, Johann Wolfgang von. *Goethes Werke* (Weimarer Ausgabe), 50 vols., ed. Hermann Böhlau et al. Weimar: Böhlau, 1887–1919.

Gordon, E. V. *An Introduction to Old Norse.* Oxford: Clarendon Press, 1927.

Gottlieb, Susannah Young-ah. "'Reflection on the Right to Will': Auden's 'Canzone' and Arendt's Notes on Willing," *Comparative Literature* 53, 2 (spring, 2001), 131–50.

Greenberg, Herbert. *Quest for the Necessary.* Cambridge, Mass.: Harvard University Press, 1968.

Grene, Marjorie. *Dreadful Freedom, a Critique of Existentialism.* Chicago: University of Chicago Press, 1948.

Griffin, Howard. *Conversations with Auden*, ed. Donald Allen. San Francisco: Grey Fox Press, 1981.

Gunew, Sneja. *Framing Marginality: Multicultural Literary Studies*. Carlton, Vic.: Melbourne University Press, 1994.

Haar, Michel. *Nietzsche et la métaphysique*. Paris: Gallimard, 1993.

Habermas, Jürgen. "Hannah Arendt's Communications Concept of Power," in *Hannah Arendt: Critical Essays*, ed. Lewis P. Hinchman and Sandra K. Hinchman (see below), 211–29.

———. *The Theory of Communicative Action*, trans. Thomas McCarthy. Boston: Beacon Press, 1984–1987.

Haffenden, John (ed.). *W. H. Auden, The Critical Heritage*. London: Routledge & Kegan Paul, 1983.

Hamacher, Werner. "Afformative, Strike," trans. Dana Hollander, in *Walter Benjamin's Philosophy*, ed. Andrew Benjamin and Peter Osborne (see above), 110–38.

———. "The Gesture in the Name," in *Premises: Essays on Philosophy and Literature from Kant to Celan*, trans. Peter Fenves (see below), 294–336.

———. "Lingua Amissa: The Messianism of Commodity-Language and Derrida's *Specters of Marx*," trans. Kelly Barry, in *Ghostly Demarcations: A Symposium on Jacques Derrida's "Specters of Marx,"* ed. Michael Sprinker (see below), 168–212.

———. *Premises: Essays on Philosophy and Literature from Kant to Celan*, trans. Peter Fenves. Cambridge, Mass.: Harvard University Press, 1996.

Hamann, J. G. *Schriften*, 9 vols., ed. Friedrich Roth. Berlin: Reimer, 1821–1843.

Hansen, Philip. *Hannah Arendt: Politics, History and Citizenship*. Stanford: Stanford University Press, 1993.

Hass, Robert. *Praise*, New York: Ecco Press, 1979.

Hayes, Carlton. *A Generation of Materialism: 1871–1900*. New York: Harper & Brothers, 1941.

Hecht, Anthony. *The Hidden Law: The Poetry of W. H. Auden*. Cambridge, Mass.: Harvard University Press, 1993.

———. *Obbligati: Essays in Criticism*. New York: Atheneum, 1986.

Heidegger, Martin. *Nietzsche*. Pfullingen: Neske, 1961.

———. *Sein und Zeit*. Tübingen: Niemeyer, 1979.

———. *Phänomenologische Interpretationen zu Aristoteles: Einführung in die phänomenologische Forschung*, ed. Walter Bröcker and Käte Bröcker-Oltmann, Vol. 61. *Gesamtausgabe*. Frankfurt am Main: Klostermann, 1985.

———. *Kant und das Problem der Metaphysik*. Frankfurt am Main: Klostermann, 1973.

Henrich, Dieter. *Hegel im Kontext*. Frankfurt am Main: Suhrkamp, 1981.

Herbert, George. *The Complete English Poems*, ed. John Tobin. Harmondsworth: Penguin, 1991.

Heschel, Susannah. *Abraham Geiger and the Jewish Jesus*. Chicago: University of Chicago Press, 1998.

———. "1857: Abraham Geiger's Epoch-Making Book *Urschrift und Überset-zung der Bibel in ihrer Abhängigkeit von inneren Entwicklung des Judentums* Disseminates the Jewish Version of the Origins of Christianity," in *The Yale Companion to Jewish Writing and Thought in German Culture, 1096–1996*, ed. Sander Gilman and Jack Zipes (see above), 193–98.

Hilferding, Rudolf. *Das Finanzkapital: Eine Studie über die jüngst Entwicklung des Kapitalismus*. Vienna: Ignaz Brand & Co., 1910.

Hill, Melvin (ed.). *Hannah Arendt: The Recovery of the Public World*. New York: St. Martin's Press, 1979.

Hinchman, Lewis, and Sandra Hinchman (eds.). *Hannah Arendt: Critical Essays*. Albany, N.Y.: SUNY Press, 1994.

Hobson, John A. *Imperialism: A Study*. London: Archibald Constable, 1905.

Hoggart, Richard. *Auden: An Introductory Essay*. New Haven: Yale University Press, 1951.

Hölderlin, Friedrich. *Sämtliche Werke: Stuttgarter Ausgabe*, 8 vols., ed. Friedrich Beißner. Stuttgart, 1943–1985.

———. *Theoretische Schriften*, ed. Johann Kreuzer. Hamburg: Meiner, 1998.

Hollander, John. *Rhyme's Reason: A Guide to English Verse*. New Haven: Yale University Press, 1989.

Honig, Bonnie (ed.). *Feminist Interpretations of Hannah Arendt*. University Park, Pa.: Pennsylvania State University Press, 1995.

———. *Political Theory and the Displacement of Politics*. Ithaca, N.Y.: Cornell University Press, 1993.

Isherwood, Christopher. *Christopher and His Kind: 1929–1939*. New York: Farrar, Straus and Giroux, 1976.

Jacobs, Carol. *In the Language of Walter Benjamin*. Baltimore: Johns Hopkins University Press, 1999.

Jarrell, Randall. *The Third Book of Criticism*. New York: Farrar, Straus and Giroux, 1941.

———. *Kipling, Auden & Co.: Essays and Reviews, 1935–1964*. New York: Farrar, Straus and Giroux, 1980.

Jenkins, Nicholas. "Some Letters from Auden to James and Tania Stern," in W. H. Auden, *"In Solitude for Company": W. H. Auden after 1940*, ed. Katherine Bucknell and Nicholas Jenkins (see above), 31–109.

Johnson, W. R. *Darkness Visible: A Study of Vergil's "Aeneid."* Berkeley: University of California Press, 1976.

————. *Horace and the Dialectic of Freedom: Readings in Epistles 1*. Ithaca, N.Y.: Cornell University Press, 1993.

————. *The Idea of Lyric*. Berkeley: University of California Press, 1982.

————. *Momentary Monsters: Lucan and His Heroes*. Ithaca, N.Y.: Cornell University Press, 1987.

Jonas, Hans. *The Gnostic Religion*, 2nd. ed. Boston: Beacon Press, 1963.

Joyce, James. *Finnegans Wake*. Harmondsworth: Penguin, 1978.

Kafka, Franz. *Gesammelte Schriften in zwölf Bänden*, 12 vols., ed. Hans-Gert Koch. Frankfurt am Main: Fischer, 1994.

Kant, Immanuel. *Gesammelte Schriften*, 29 vols., ed. Königlich Preußischen [later, deutschen] Akademie der Wissenschaften. Berlin: Reimer; later, De Gruyter; 1900–.

————. *Critique of Pure Reason*, trans. Norman Kemp Smith. New York: St. Martin's, 1965.

Kaplan, Morris. "Refiguring the Jewish Question: Arendt, Proust, and the Politics of Sexuality," in *Feminist Interpretations of Hannah Arendt*, ed. Bonnie Honig (see above), 105–33.

Kateb, George. *Hannah Arendt: Politics, Conscience, Evil*. Oxford: Martin Robertson, 1984.

Kierkegaard, Søren. *The Concept of Anxiety*, ed. and trans. Reidar Thomte and Albert Anderson. Princeton: Princeton University Press, 1980.

————. *The Concept of Dread*, trans. Walter Lowrie. Princeton: Princeton University Press, 1944.

————. *Fear and Trembling—Repetition*, ed. and trans. Howard Hong and Edna Hong. Princeton: Princeton University Press, 1983.

————. *The Sickness unto Death*, trans. Howard Hong and Edna Hong. Princeton: Princeton University Press, 1980.

Kisiel, Theodore. *The Genesis of Heidegger's "Being and Time."* Berkeley: University of California Press, 1993.

Kissinger, Henry. *Diplomacy*. New York: Simon & Schuster, 1994.

Klausner, Joseph. *The Messianic Idea in Israel, from its Beginning to the Completion of the Mishnah*. London: Allen and Unwin, 1956.

Klibansky, Raymond, Erwin Panofsky, and Fritz Saxl. *Saturn and Melancholy: Studies in the History of Natural Philosophy, Religion, and Art*. London: Nelson, 1964.

Kretschmer, Ernst. *Physique and Character: An Investigation into the Nature of Constitution and of the Theory of Temperaments*, trans. W. J. H. Sprott, 2nd ed. New York: Harcourt, Brace & Company, 1925.

Lacan, Jacques. *The Four Fundamental Concepts of Psychoanalysis*, trans. Alan Sheridan, Vol. 11, *The Seminars of Jacques Lacan*, ed. Jacques-Alain Miller. New York: Norton, 1998.

Lacoue-Labarthe, Philippe. "Catastrophe," in *Word Traces: The Poetry of Paul Celan*, ed. Aris Fioretos (see above), 130–56.

Lamm, Norman. *The Shema: Spirituality and Law in Judaism as Exemplified in the Shema, the Most Important Passage in the Torah*. Philadephia and Jerusalem: The Jewish Publication Society, 5758 (= 1998 C.E.).

Larkin, Philip. "What's Become of Wystan?" *Spectator* 205 (15 July 1960), 105; reprinted in *W. H. Auden, The Critical Heritage*, ed. John Haffenden (see above), 414–19.

Lenin, Vladimir Ilyich. *Imperialism, the Highest Stage of Capitalism*, trans. anon. Moscow: Progress Publishers, 1966.

Lessing, Gotthold Ephraim. *Werke*, 8 vols., ed. Karl Eibl and Herbert Georg Göpfert. Munich: Hanser, 1970–1979.

Liddell, Henry George, and Robert Scott. *Greek-English Lexicon*, rev. ed. Henry Stuart Jones and Robert McKenzie. Oxford: Clarendon Press, 1968.

Lipking, Lawrence. "Faults," in *"In Solitude for Company": W. H. Auden after 1940*, ed. Katherine Bucknell and Nicholas Jenkins (see above), 263–71.

———. *The Life of the Poet*. Chicago: The University of Chicago Press, 1981.

Litt, Toby. "From 'Acedia' to 'Zeitgeist': Auden in the 2nd Edition of the OED," in *The W. H. Auden Society Newsletter* 4 (October 1989).

Logan, William. "Auden's Images," in *W. H. Auden: The Far Interior*, ed. Alan Bold (see above), 23–46.

Löwith, Karl. *From Hegel to Nietzsche*, trans. David E. Green. Garden City, N.Y.: Anchor, 1967.

Luban, David. "Explaining Dark Times: Hannah Arendt's Theory of Theory," in *Hannah Arendt: Critical Essays*, ed. Lewis and Sandra Hinchman (see above), 79–109.

Luxemburg, Rosa. *Die Akkumulation des Kapitals: Ein Beitrag zur ökonomischen Erklärung des Imperialismus*. Berlin: Vereinigung internationaler Verlags-Anstalten, 1923.

Lyotard, Jean-François. *Toward the Postmodern*, ed. and trans. Robert Harvey and Mark Roberts. Atlantic Highlands, N.J.: Humanities Press, 1995.

Macpherson, Crawford Brough. *The Political Theory of Possessive Individualism: Hobbes to Locke*. Oxford, Clarendon Press, 1962.

Maritain, Jacques. *Existence and the Existent*, trans. Lewis Galantiere. New York: Pantheon, 1948.

Marx, Karl. *Capital: Critique of Political Economy*, trans. Ben Fowkes. New York: Vintage, 1977.

———. *A Contribution to the Critique of Political Economy*, trans. S. W. Ryazan-skaya. New York: International Publishers, 1976.

———. *Das Kapital: Kritik der politischen Ökonomie*. Berlin: Dietz, 1981.

Mathers, S. L. MacGregor (trans.). *The Kabbalah Unveiled [Kabbalah denudata]*,

Containing the Following Books of the "Zohar": the Book of Concealed Mystery, the Greater Holy Assembly, the Lesser Holy Assembly. London: Redway, 1887 (partial translation of Knorr von Rosenroth's *Kabbalah denudata*).

McDiarmid, Lucy. *Auden's Apologies for Poetry*. Princeton: Princeton University Press, 1990.

McGowan, John. "Must Politics Be Violent? Arendt's Utopian Vision," in *Hannah Arendt and the Meaning of Politics*, ed. Craig Calhoun and John McGowan (see above), 263–96.

McLane, Maureen N. *Romanticism and the Human Sciences: Poetry, Population, and the Discourse of the Species*. Cambridge: Cambridge University Press, 2000.

Meltzer, Françoise. *Hot Property: The Stakes and Claims of Literary Originality*. Chicago: University of Chicago Press, 1994.

Mendelson, Edward. *Later Auden*. New York: Farrar, Straus and Giroux, 1999.

Mendes-Flohr, Paul (ed.). *Gershom Scholem: The Man and His Work*. Albany, N.Y.: SUNY Press, 1994.

Merrill, James. *Scripts for the Pageant*. New York: Atheneum, 1980.

Meyer, Michael, and Michael Brenner (eds.). *German-Jewish History in Modern Times*. New York : Columbia University Press, 1996–1999.

Miller, Charles. *Auden: An American Friendship*. New York: Paragon House, 1989.

Milton, John. *Complete Poems and Major Prose*, ed. Merritt Y. Hughes. Indianapolis: The Odyssey Press, 1957.

Monk, Ray. *Ludwig Wittgenstein: The Duty of Genius*. New York: The Free Press, 1990.

Mounier, Emmanuel. *Existentialist Philosophies: An Introduction*. London: Rockliff, 1948.

Müller, Ernst (ed. and trans.) *Der Sohar: Das heilige Buch der Kabbala nach dem Urtext*. Wien: Eugen Diedrichs Verlag, 1989.

Musulin, Stella. "Auden in Kirchstetten," *"In Solitude for Company": W. H. Auden after 1940*, ed. K. Bucknell and N. Jenkins (see above), 207–30.

Nabokov, Nicolas. "Excerpts from Memories," in *W. H. Auden: A Tribute*, ed. Stephen Spender (see below), 133–48.

Nelson, Gerald. *Changes of Heart: A Study of the Poetry of W. H. Auden*. Berkeley: University of California Press, 1969.

Neusner, Jacob. *Messiah in Context: Israel's History and Destiny in Formative Judaism*. Philadelphia: Fortress, 1984.

Newton, Isaac. *Mathematical Principles*, trans. Andrew Motte, rev. Florian Cajori. Berkeley: University of California Press, 1934.

Niebuhr, Ursula. "Memories of the 1940s," in *W. H. Auden: A Tribute*, ed. Stephen Spender (see below), 104–18.

Nietzsche, Friedrich. *Sämtliche Werke: Studien Ausgabe*, 15 vols., ed. Giorgio Colli and Mazzino Montinari. Berlin: de Gruyter, 1967–1977.

———. *The Case of Wagner*, trans. Walter Kaufmann. New York: Vintage, 1974.

Norris, Andrew. "Arendt, Kant, and the Politics of Common Sense," *Polity* 29 (winter, 1996): 165–91.

Novalis. *Studienausgabe*, ed. Gerhard Schulz. Munich: Beck, 1987.

Osborne, Charles. "Auden as Christian Poet," in *W. H. Auden: The Far Interior*, ed. Alan Bold (see above), 23–46.

———. *W. H. Auden: The Life of a Poet*. New York: Harcourt Brace Jovanovich, 1979.

Overbeck, Franz. *Christentum und Kultur: Gedanken und Anmerkungen zur modernen Theologie*, ed. Carl Albrecht Bernoulli. Basel: Benno Schwabe, 1919.

Palter, Robert (ed.). *The Annus Mirabilis of Sir Isaac Newton*. Cambridge, Mass.: MIT Press, 1970.

Pinkard, Terry. *Hegel: A Biography*. Cambridge: Cambridge University Press, 2000.

Plato. *The Collected Dialogues*, ed. Edith Hamilton and Huntington Cairns. Princeton: Princeton University Press, 1985.

Proust, Marcel. *Le côté de Guermantes*. Paris: Gallimard, 1954.

———. *Sodome et Gomorrhe*. Paris: Flammarion, 1987.

———. *Remembrance of Things Past*, trans. C. K. Scott Moncrieff and Terence Kilmartin. New York: Vintage, 1982.

Ramazani, Jahan. *Poetry of Mourning: The Modern Elegy from Hardy to Heaney*. Chicago: The University of Chicago Press, 1994.

Replogle, Justin. *Auden's Poetry*. Seattle: University of Washington Press, 1969.

Rilke, Rainer Maria. *Sämtliche Werke*, 6 vols., ed. Ruth Sieber-Rilke et al. Frankfurt am Main: Insel, 1987.

Ring, Jennifer. *The Political Consequences of Thinking: Gender and Judaism in the Work of Hannah Arendt*. Albany, N.Y.: SUNY Press, 1997.

Romilly, Giles. "The Age of Despair," reprinted in *W. H. Auden: The Critical Heritage*, ed. John Haffenden (see above), 371–74.

Rosenthal, M. L. "Speaking Greatly in an Age of Confusion," reprinted in *W. H. Auden: The Critical Heritage*, ed. John Haffenden, (see above), 363–64.

Rosenzweig, Franz. *Der Stern der Erlösung*. rpt. Frankfurt am Main: Suhrkamp, 1988.

Rowland, J. T. *Faint Praise and Civil Leer: The "Decline" of Eighteenth-Century Panegyric*. Newark, Del.: University of Delaware Press, 1994.

Sacks, Peter. *The English Elegy*. Baltimore: Johns Hopkins University Press, 1985.

Said, Edward W. *Culture and Imperialism*. New York: Vintage, 1994.

Sallust. *The Jugurthine War*, trans. S. A Handforth. Harmondsworth: Penguin, 1963.

Salus, Peter H., and Paul B. Taylor (eds.). *For W. H. Auden: February 21, 1972.* New York: Random House, 1972.

Sartre, Jean-Paul. *Existentialism and Humanism*, trans. Philip Mairet. New York: Philosophical Library, 1947.

Schelling, Friedrich. *Werke*, 6 vols., ed. M. Schröter. Munich: Beck, 1927–1954.

Schmitt, Carl. *Politische Romantik*, 2nd ed. Munich: Duncker & Humblot, 1925.

———. *Politische Theologie: Vier Kapitel zur Lehre von der Souveränität* Berlin: Duncker & Humblot, 1990.

Scholem, Gershom. *Briefe*, ed. Itta Shedletzky and Thomas Sparr. Munich: Beck, 1994–1999.

———. *The Kabbalah.* New York: Meridian, 1974.

———. *Major Trends in Jewish Mysticism.* New York: Schocken, 1941.

———. *The Messianic Idea in Judaism and Other Essays on Jewish Spirituality,* trans. Michael A. Meyer and Hillel Halkin. New York: Schocken, 1971.

———. *On Jews and Judaism in Crisis: Selected Essays*, ed. Werner J. Danhauser. New York: Schocken, 1976.

———. *On the Kabbalah and Its Symbolism*, trans. Ralph Manheim. New York: Schocken, 1969.

———. *On the Mystical Shape of the Godhead*, trans. Joachim Neugroschel. New York: Schocken, 1991.

———. *Walter Benjamin: The Story of a Friendship*, trans. Harry Zohn. New York: Schocken, 1981.

Schopenhauer, Arthur. *Werke in fünf Bänden*, 5 vols., ed. Ludger Lütkehaus. Zürich: Haffmans, 1994.

Schumpeter, Joseph. *A History of Economic Analysis.* New York: Oxford University Press, 1954.

Schwartz, Delmore. "Delmore Schwartz on Auden's 'Most Self-Indulgent Book,'" reprinted in *W. H. Auden: The Critical Heritage*, ed. John Haffenden (see above), 368–71.

Schwarz-Bart, André. *Le Dernier des justes.* Paris: Éditions du Seuil, 1959.

———. *The Last of the Just*, trans. Stephen Becker. New York: Atheneum Publishers, 1960.

Scott, Nathan A. "The Poetry of Auden," *Chicago Review* 13 (winter, 1959): 48–63.

Sedgwick, Eve Kosofsky. *Epistemology of the Closet.* Berkeley: University of California Press, 1990.

———. *Between Men: English Literature and Male Homosocial Desire.* New York: Columbia University Press, 1985.

Shakespeare, William. *The Complete Works*, ed. Alfred Harbage. New York: Viking, 1969.

Siebers, Tobin. "Kant and the Origins of Totalitarianism," *Philosophy and Literature* 15 (April 1991): 19–39.

Sinaiko, Herman. *Love, Knowledge, and Discourse in Plato: Dialogue and Dialectic in "Phaedrus," "Republic," "Parmenides."* Chicago: University of Chicago Press, 1965.

Skinner, Quentin. *The Foundations of Modern Political Thought.* Cambridge: University of Cambridge Press, 1978.

Smith, Stan. *W. H. Auden.* New York: Blackwell, 1985.

Spears, Monroe (ed.). *Auden: A Collection of Essays.* Englewood Cliffs, N.J.: Prentice-Hall, 1964.

————. *The Disenchanted Island: The Poetry of W. H. Auden.* Oxford: Oxford University Press, 1963.

Spender, Stephen. "W. H. Auden and His Poetry," reprinted in *Auden: A Collection of Essays*, ed. Monroe Spears (see above), 26–38.

————. (ed.). *W. H. Auden: A Tribute.* New York: Macmillan, 1975.

Sprinker, Michael (ed.). *Ghostly Demarcations: A Symposium on Jacques Derrida's "Specters of Marx."* London: Verso, 1999.

Stern, James. "The Indispensable Presence," *W. H. Auden: A Tribute*, ed. Stephen Spender (see above), 123–27.

Sumida, Stephen. "Centers without Margins: Responses to Centrism in Asian American Literature," *American Literature* 66 (December, 1994): 803–15.

Swift, Jonathan. *The Writings of Jonathan Swift*, ed. Robert Greenberg and William Piper. New York: Norton, 1973.

Tacitus. *Histories IV–V, Annals I–III*, trans. Clifford H. Moore and John Jackson. Cambridge, Mass.: Harvard University Press, 1992.

Taminiaux, Jacques. *La Fille de Thrace et le penseur professionel: Arendt et Heidegger.* Paris: Éditions Payot, 1992.

————. "Athens and Rome," in *The Cambridge Companion to Hannah Arendt*, ed. Dana Villa. Cambridge: Cambridge University Press, 2000, 165–77.

Tanakh: A New Translation of the Holy Scriptures According to the Traditional Hebrew Text. Philadelphia and Jerusalem: Jewish Publications Society, 5746–1985.

Thucydides. *The Peloponnesian War*, trans. Rex Warner. Harmondsworth: Penguin, 1983.

Tillich, Paul. "Existential Philosophy," *Journal of the History of Ideas* 5, 1 (January, 1944): 44–70.

Villa, Dana. *Arendt and Heidegger: The Fate of the Political.* Princeton: Princeton University Press, 1996.

Von Molnár, Géza. *Novalis' "Fichte Studies": The Foundations of His Aesthetics.* The Hague: Mouton, 1970.

Weinfeld, Moshe. *Deuteronomy I–XI: A New Translation with Introduction and Commentary.* New York: Doubleday, 1991.

Werblowsky, R. J. Zwi. "Messianism," in *Contemporary Jewish Religious Thought*, ed. Arthur Cohen and Paul Mendes-Flohr (see above), 597–602.

Weston, Jessie. *From Ritual to Romance*. Gloucester, Mass.: Peter Smith, 1983.

Williams, Patrick, and Laura Chrisman (eds.). *Colonial Discourse and Post-Colonial Theory: A Reader*. New York: Columbia University Press, 1994.

Wilson, Edmund. *Letters on Literature and Politics, 1912–1972*, ed. Elena Wilson. New York: Farrar, Straus and Giroux, 1977.

———. "W. H. Auden in America," reprinted in *W. H. Auden, The Critical Heritage*, ed. John Haffenden (see above), 405–11.

Wittgenstein, Ludwig. *Notebooks: 1914–1916*, ed. G. H. von Wright and G.E.M. Anscombe, trans. G.E.M. Anscombe. Chicago: University of Chicago Press, 1979.

Wölfflin, Heinrich. *Principles of Art History: The Problem of the Development of Style in Later Art*, trans. M. D. Hottinger. New York: Dover, 1950.

Wordsworth, William. *Selected Poems and Prefaces*, ed. Jack Stillinger. Boston: Houghton Mifflin, 1965.

Yanowsky, V. S. "W. H. Auden," *Antaeus* 19 (autumn 1975): 107–35.

Young-Bruehl, Elisabeth. *Hannah Arendt: For Love of the World*. New Haven: Yale University Press, 1982.

Zohar, trans. Harry Sperling and Maurice Simon. London: Soncino Press, 1931–1934.

Index

Abraham, 152–53, 237n88, 240n105

absence: in *For the Time Being*, 27, 208n104; of perspective, 16; in *Rahel Varnhagen*, 26; of thinking, 205n71; in Wittgenstein, 27

abyss, 22, 64, 89, 92–93, 156; "abyss of the 'possible'," 20, 66, 185, 189–90, 192, 196

action, 22, 141, 185–86; abyssal structure, 186; contrasted with "bundles of reaction," 24, 67, 185, 186; and disclosure, 161–62; and forgiveness, 22, 153–56; and freedom, 148; "frustration of action," 150, 189; and helplessness, 186; and history, 146; and irreversibility, 150–51; compared to making, 149–50; as "miracle," 24, 136, 148; as novelty, 136; promises and, 151; redemption and, 156; totalitarianism and, 24, 67, 185, 186; and unpredictability, 150–51; and vanity, 147; and willing, 261n30. *See also* Arendt, *The Human Condition*; labor; miracle; natality; work

Adam Kadmon, 105–6, 235n72; 235n75; and gender, 235n74. *See also Zohar*

advertising. *See* propaganda

Adorno, Theodor W.: Arendt's low regard for, 207n81; culture and barbarism, 18–19; *Prisms*, 18, 248–49n15

Agamben, Giorgio, 211n13

alien, 36, 42, 44

alliteration, 21, 71; interlinguistic, 132; and repetition, 90; and speechlessness, 128; and stress, 84–85

America: and Nazism, 228n24. *See also* Auden, biography; Arendt, biography

analogy, 84

"ancient quarrel" between philosophy and poetry, 12–15

Anders (Stern), Günter, 220n50

animals, 35; *animal laborans* (*see* labor); "human animal," 62

Ansen, Alan, 240n103

anti-Semitism, 38–45, 59, 132, 218n45

anxiety: 64–67, 77–79; and "abyss of the 'possible'," 65–66; and explanation, 67; and hope, 122, 133–34; of individuation, 86, 107; and Jews, 122; overcoming of, 195; and promising, 153; and responsibility, 160; and speechlessness, 103, 192–93; and totalitarianism, 21, 64–67; and war, 68–70

Crossing Aesthetics

Ernst Bloch, *The Spirit of Utopia*

Giorgio Agamben, *Potentialities: Collected Essays in Philosophy*

Ellen S. Burt, *Poetry's Appeal: French Nineteenth-Century Lyric and the Political Space*

Jacques Derrida, *Adieu to Emmanuel Levinas*

Werner Hamacher, *Premises: Essays on Philosophy and Literature from Kant to Celan*

Aris Fioretos, *The Gray Book*

Deborah Esch, *In the Event: Reading Journalism, Reading Theory*

Winfried Menninghaus, *In Praise of Nonsense: Kant and Bluebeard*

Giorgio Agamben, *The Man Without Content*

Giorgio Agamben, *The End of the Poem: Studies in Poetics*

Theodor W. Adorno, *Sound Figures*

Louis Marin, *Sublime Poussin*

Philippe Lacoue-Labarthe, *Poetry as Experience*

Ernst Bloch, *Literary Essays*

Jacques Derrida, *Resistances of Psychoanalysis*

Marc Froment-Meurice, *That Is to Say: Heidegger's Poetics*

Francis Ponge, *Soap*

Philippe Lacoue-Labarthe, *Typography: Mimesis, Philosophy, Politics*

Giorgio Agamben, *Homo Sacer: Sovereign Power and Bare Life*

Emmanuel Levinas, *Of God Who Comes To Mind*

Bernard Stiegler, *Technics and Time, 1: The Fault of Epimetheus*

Werner Hamacher, *pleroma—Reading in Hegel*

Serge Leclaire, *Psychoanalyzing: On the Order of the Unconscious and the Practice of the Letter*

The authorized representative in the EU for product safety and compliance is:
Mare Nostrum Group
B.V Doelen 72
4831 GR Breda
The Netherlands

www.ingramcontent.com/pod-product-compliance
Lightning Source LLC
Chambersburg PA
CBHW030641270326
41929CB00007B/156